Families, History,
and Social Change

Families, History, and Social Change

Life-Course and
Cross-Cultural Perspectives

Tamara K. Hareven

University of Delaware

Westview
PRESS
A Member of the Perseus Books Group

Cover photo: Three generations of the Reagan family. Photo taken in Syracuse, New York, in April 1945, to mark the 50th wedding anniversary of Burnett and Cora Fyler Reagan. Courtesy of James Reagan.

Published in 2000 in the United States of America by Westview Press, 5500 Central Avenue, Boulder, Colorado 80301-2877, and in the United Kingdom by Westview Press, 12 Hid's Copse Road, Cumnor Hill, Oxford OX2 9JJ

Find us on the World Wide Web at www.westviewpress.com

Library of Congress Cataloging-in-Publication Data
Hareven, Tamara K.
  Families, history, and social change : life-course and cross-
cultural perspectives / Tamara K. Hareven.
      p. cm.
  Includes bibliographical references and index.
  ISBN 0-8133-9087-7 (hc.) — ISBN 0-8133-9079-6 (pbk.)
  1. Family—History.   2. Family Cross-cultural studies.   3. Social
change.   I. Title.
HQ515.H37   1999
306.85'09—dc21   99-38532
                                                                                    CIP

The paper used in this publication meets the requirements of the American National Standard for Permanence of Paper for Printed Library Materials Z39.48-1984.

10   9   8   7   6   5

In memory of my parents, Mirjam and Saul Kern
Heroes of their own lives

Contents

vii

Part 3
Comparative Perspectives

Part 4
Broader Perspectives

Tables and Figures

Preface

Over the past thirty years, I have had the opportunity and privilege to participate in the development of a new field—social history and its related subdiscipline, the history of the family. The 1960s and 1970s witnessed the unfolding and the development of the "new social history," which was also closely related to the "new urban history," labor history, ethnic history, and the history of the family (see Chapter 14, "What Difference Does It Make?").

Underlying these new historical pursuits was a commitment on the part of scholars to come as close as possible to retrieving the experiences of ordinary people in the past, to reconstruct the social context of various groups and classes, sometimes entire communities, and to tell the story from the perception of the participants rather than from the vantage point of the upper classes, employers, and custodians. The history of the family and the new social history have now become established fields in their own right. But those of us involved in the initial discoveries and deliberations still feel the excitement of those early days.

Within this very broad tapestry of scholarly enterprise, characterized by the exciting search for new methods and previously unexplored sources, I focused on the history of the family. From 1967 on, I made the historical study of the family my main objective, and I devoted my energies to my own scholarship as well as to the development of this new field. The reason I became so interested in this area is because I viewed the family as the "missing link" between individual lives and the larger processes of social change. The family is the arena in which many of these interactions with the larger processes take place. Hence, my own research focused on the family's relationship to the process of industrialization. My overall commitment has been to study the family and individuals *in time and place* rather than focusing on the family in isolation, as was often done in earlier sociological research (see Chapter 1, "The History of the Family and the Complexity of Social Change").

The route by which I arrived at the history of the family was, however, a circuitous one. Similarly to other historians from my generation who "discovered" the family, I came from a different direction, but one that placed me in a fortuitous position to address the historical study of the family. I arrived in the United States in 1961 after graduating from the Hebrew University in Jerusalem, where I majored in European history. In my first year in the United States, I completed my master's degree at the University of Cincinnati in Byzantine history. I decided, however, that for my Ph.D. I would concentrate on U.S. history, in order to have a better understanding of American society.

I wrote my doctoral thesis on the emergence of Eleanor Roosevelt as a social reformer and her impact on the New Deal's relief and reform program. The dissertation resulted in my book *Eleanor Roosevelt: An American Conscience* (1968). Research on Eleanor Roosevelt led me into the National Archives and the U.S. Children's Bureau, where I ploughed through the enormous collections of correspondence between Eleanor Roosevelt and her "pet" agencies. Among those, the National Youth Administration (NYA) and the Children's Bureau were central. It was the records of these agencies that brought me into firsthand contact with the problems of children and youth in American society, particularly during the Great Depression. The voluminous correspondence that Eleanor Roosevelt received from individuals and the field reports by journalist Lorena Hickock brought me close to the problems of families coping with adversity during the Great Depression. Following the granting of my Ph.D., I took my first faculty position at Dalhousie University in Nova Scotia. Two years later, I was invited by Robert Bremner to coedit with him and other historians a documentary history of children and youth in American society. I joined this project as associate editor in 1967. Research on this project became a major turning point in my career, because it brought me face-to-face with the emergence of the historical study of the family in its early stages. At the Charles Warren Center for Studies in American History at Harvard University, where the project was based, I met John Demos, who was engaged in writing his pioneer work on the history of the family, resulting in *A Little Commonwealth* (Demos, 1970). Stephan Thernstrom was there at the same time, developing his groundbreaking work in the "new" urban history (Thernstrom and Knights, 1971).

Research for the documentary history, which resulted in the multivolume *Children and Youth in America* (Bremner et al., 1970–1974), led me to a multiplicity of archival collections on children and youth all over the United States. The documentary history was initiated by the U.S. Children's Bureau and was, therefore, intended to be a public history of children and youth. However, my delving into primary sources, including family documents, led me to the exploration of the relationship between childhood and the family. My research on child labor led me most significantly to the study of the interaction between the family and the process of social change. Philippe Ariès's book, *Centuries of Childhood* (1962), had appeared in English translation prior to my arrival at the Warren Center. This book had a profound impact on me, as it had on other scholars at that time, and could be considered one of the major sources of inspiration for the emergence of this new field (see Chapter 1).

While at Harvard University, I also participated in the last faculty seminar that Erik Erikson led on biography and history. Erikson's approach dramatized for me the importance of studying lives over time and of focusing on the interaction between life history and history. Whereas Erikson concentrated on the individual life cycle, I began to search for ways to understand the interaction between individuals and the family as a collective unit, under changing historical conditions. This prepared my way for later developing the life-course approach (see Chapter 6, "Synchronizing Individual Time, Family Time, and Historical Time").

After the completion of my research and writing *Children and Youth in America* in 1969, I joined the faculty at Clark University in Worcester, Massachusetts. This placed me in the web of New England industrial communities, particularly the ones that had been centers of textile production. My first years at Clark University were devoted, therefore, to the development of the field of family history, as well as to my own research on the family and industrial work—most notably in focusing on Manchester, New Hampshire, as a case study.

Activities in the development of the field of family history involved organizing two national conferences, one on the history of childhood (1970), followed by one on the history of the family (1971), and the launching and editing in 1973 of an international newsletter, *The Family in Historical Perspective*, which was supported by the Rockefeller Foundation and published by the Newberry Library. Support from the Rockefeller Foundation and the National Endowment for the Humanities' Education Division enabled me to organize research and training activities in the history of the family, nationally, on all levels: for undergraduate students, graduate students, and faculty. By 1975, the profusion of scholarly activities in this new field justified the need for a scholarly journal on the history of the family. That very year the National Council on Family Relations accepted my proposal for publishing the *Journal of Family History: Studies in Family, Demography and Kinship*, of which I was editor for twenty years. The success of that journal rested on the high quality of scholarship in the field and on the associate editors—Robert Wheaton during the first decade, and Andrejs Plakans during the second decade. After completing my second decade as editor of the *Journal of Family History* in 1995, Andrejs Plakans and I founded a new journal that reflects recent developments in the field: *The History of the Family: An International Quarterly* started publication in 1996.

Seeking new approaches and methodologies in order to capture family change over the lifetime of its members and under different historical conditions emerged as a key issue in my own research on family and work in the textile industry, as well as in my efforts and those of my collaborators to further develop the field. To that end, in collaboration with Maris Vinovskis, I organized a special workshop for historians of the family with the support of the National Science Foundation. The 1976 workshop, which resulted in the publication of *Family and Population in Nineteenth Century America* (Hareven and Vinovskis, 1978), led us to search an alternative to the family-cycle approach as a way to examine family development under different historical contexts. As we continued to search for a more comprehensive and dynamic approach that captures the interaction between individual and family development, we arrived at the life course. I first encountered the life-course approach in 1975, in Glen H. Elder Jr.'s book, *Children of the Great Depression* (1974). In 1977, I invited Glen Elder to join the second workshop of historians of the family. Again, with the help of Maris Vinovskis and the National Science Foundation, we convened historians to analyze together a common data set—a sample from the U.S. Federal 1880 Census for eight select communities in Massachusetts. Following a life-course perspective, each author analyzed a different life transition on the *same* data set. This way, we were able to demonstrate the difference between static stages of the family cycle and dynamic life transitions. The book *Transitions: The Family and the Life Course in Historical Perspective* (Hareven, 1978), which emerged from this workshop, interprets these patterns. The book also includes articles by Glen Elder, laying out the life-course approach; by Peter Uhlenberg, providing a demographic perspective on the life course; by Stanley Eugerman, contributing an economic perspective; and by Robert LeVine, offering a cross-cultural perspective.

The remarkable outcome of these early collaborations and of subsequent ones through numerous specialized conferences and special sessions at national and international meetings has been the continuity of our network, to the extent that several of us are still part of each others' scholarly lives. My collaboration with Glen Elder in integrating the life course into a historical perspective and in linking it with the history of the family is exemplified in Chapter 8, "Rising Above Life's Disadvantage: From the Great Depression to War," with Glen Elder.

A major aspect of my own research, from 1971 on, has focused on the relationship between family and work in the textile industry. After joining Clark University, I discovered the Amoskeag Mills and the city of Manchester, New Hampshire, which was developed around them. From my survey of the historical holdings in archives and collections in New England industrial towns, Manchester emerged as the community that was richest in its surviving documentary sources and original architecture for my study of the family's interaction with the process of industrialization. The surviving 100,000 individual employee files that were kept by the

Amoskeag Manufacturing Company, as well as a treasury of company records and the vital records in the city archives, enabled me to reconstruct work and family histories of several thousand former employees over the twentieth century. Tracing employee files to birth, marriage, and death records made it possible to reconstruct the workers' kinship networks for an American industrial community in an unprecedented way and to examine the interaction of kin with the factory system, as evidenced in Chapter 2, "The Dynamics of Kin in an Industrial Community." Research on the laborers of the Amoskeag Company became a ten-year-long enterprise.

The most remarkable aspect of this research for me as a historian and a human being was my interaction with the Amoskeag Company's former workers in oral-history interviews. The two- to three-hour long interviews with several hundred former workers exposed me to the ways in which these men and women interpreted their own lives. This experience transformed me as a historian. The book *Amoskeag: Life and Work in an American Factory City* (Hareven and Langenbach, 1978) presents selections of the narratives of former workers and managers in their own words. *Family Time and Industrial Time: The Relationship Between the Family and Work in a New England Industrial Community* (1982) integrates the quantitative analysis of work histories and family patterns with the qualitative analysis of individual narratives. My conclusion that rather than breaking down, the family interacted with the process of industrialization—while following its own strategies and pursuing its own timing—became central to my subsequent work (see Chapter 2 and Chapter 3, "A Complex Relationship: Family Strategies and the Processes of Economic and Social Change").

Data analysis on this large-scale project enabled me to examine life-course transitions of the former Amoskeag workers in detail because of the longitudinal character of the data set that I constructed. It led me to a desire to explore the life transitions of the next generation as well—the children of the Amoskeag's former workers—and their relations with the parent generation. With support from the National Institute on Aging, in 1981 I launched the second phase of my research in Manchester, New Hampshire. The project "Aging and Generational Relations: A Cohort Comparison" pursued the key questions of the life-course approach into the lives of the Amoskeag workers' children (see Chapter 5, "Aging and Generational Relations: A Historical and Life-Course Perspective"). Anthropologist Kathleen Adams directed the field research of this project, and we interviewed as many of the pertinent population (children of the former Amoskeag workers, their spouses, siblings of the spouses, and their parents) whom we could trace in Manchester, New Hampshire, and who were willing to be interviewed. These interviews became the basis of the chapters in this volume that examine generational supports in the later years of life and the impact of historical events on the life course. (See Chapter 7, "The Generation in the Middle: Cohort Comparisons in Assistance to Aging Parents in an American Community," with Kathleen Adams; Chapter 8, with Glen Elder; and Chapter 6, all in this volume.)

The sequel volume to *Family Time and Industrial Time*, which will be entitled *Generations in Historical Time*, is based on the narrative of the children's interviews linked with those of the parents. The children were in their sixties and seventies when we interviewed them. Following a life-course approach, this project represents a marriage between "cohort"[1] and "generation." It enabled us to examine the impact of historical events on the life course and to identify the location of cohorts in the historical times in which they made their major life transitions. It thus becomes possible to compare the impact of the Great Depression and World War II on the life course of respective cohorts, to examine their members' interaction with historical events and their perceptions of these interactions. Rather than following a deterministic approach, my research on these cohorts, along with Glen Elder's findings on the California cohorts, also documents the ways in which individuals counteracted the negative impact of historical events on their life course (see Chapter 8).

My work on the history of the family and the life course is driven by issues of timing in individuals' lives and family action in various contexts. It is concerned with how the timing of individual life transitions is synchronized with the family's transitions over its life course and with the larger processes of social change. From this perspective, one examines individuals in the context of families and families in the context of individuals rather than studying individuals in isolation. Issues of coordinating the timing of individual life events with those of the family as a collective unit also impinge on family conflicts, particularly in areas where individual preferences clash with the needs of the family unit and the larger kinship group (see Chapters 5 and 6).

Emphasis on timing and on a life-course perspective has also affected my research on aging and the relations between the generations. A life-course perspective has enabled me to address the complexities of men's and women's adaptation to old age by examining the ways in which support networks for elderly people were formed and re-formed over life and the ways in which people carried their historical and cultural "baggage" into old age. Examination of the cohorts in Manchester, New Hampshire, has brought home this point dramatically, since the cohort comparison has shown consistency in differences in terms of their attitudes and practices of support for elderly parents, as well as perceptions of turning points and continuities and discontinuities in their own lives (see Chapter 7). My contacts with Matilda Riley over the years have made me sensitive to the ways in which the "structural lag" affects adaptation in the later years of life—namely, the lag between pressing social changes impinging on the family and the life course, and the time it takes public policy to respond with appropriate measures to the needs arising from these changes (Riley and Riley, 1994; Hareven, 1994b).

The effort to capture the complexity of social change is central to my historical research on the family and the life course. My findings cast serious doubt on linear interpretations of social change. Particularly, the patterns of interaction between family and work, exemplified in *Family Time and Industrial Time*, have led to the rejection of simplistic models of modernization theory: My data have shown that workers from nonindustrial backgrounds did not simply conform to the "modern" factory system. Rather, they adapted it to meet their needs and cultural traditions. Nor did the family "modernize" at the same pace as the world of work. The family was both an agent of change and a custodian of tradition. The family followed its own strategies in its decisions as to when to innovate and when to carry on its traditions (see Chapter 2).

Findings in my research in the United States drove me into a quest for a comparative perspective. The opportunity for cross-cultural comparisons arose when the Social Science Research Council asked me in 1981 to coordinate the plans for a binational comparative project on the family and the life course in Japan. My first trip to Japan in 1981–1982 and my introduction to a team of Japanese sociologists led by Professor Kiyomi Morioka in Tokyo exposed me to cultural and social differences governing the life course and the family in a dramatic way. Collaboration with the members of the Japanese team, particularly with Kanji Masaoka, led to our comparison of perceptions of turning points and transitions in the lives of the Manchester cohorts and the Japanese cohorts, who were comparable in age. These findings, which are presented in Chapter 6, exemplify the differences in the cultural and social construction of the life course. At the same time, the comparison demonstrates the differences in the phasing of social change in the two societies (see Hareven and Masaoka, 1988).

My first visit to Japan led me to Nishijin—the traditional silk-weaving district of Kyoto. With the help of an interpreter, I talked to the highly skilled traditional weavers working there. One of the older weavers said sadly, "We are the last generation to weave here." I was shocked by this statement, having already experienced through the interviews the impact on people's lives of the shutdown of the Amoskeag Mills. I wanted to find out why the older skilled artisans in Japan made this statement. That was the beginning of an eleven-year engagement with Japan. While continuing my research and writing in American society, I embarked on interviews of active and former silk weavers and manufacturers and their relatives in Kyoto. Over the ensuing eleven-year period, I went back to Japan for three months each year during the university summer recess and during my sabbatical year, 1986–1987. Chapter 10, "Between Craft and Industry: The Subjective Reconstruction of the Life Course of Kyoto's Traditional Weavers," which examines the relationship between family and work in this traditional industry, as well as Chapter 11, "The Festival's Work as Leisure: The Traditional Craftsmen of the Gion Festival," are products of this research and anticipate the forthcoming book *The Silk Weavers of Kyoto: Family and Work in a Changing Traditional Industry*. My close contact with the Japanese people I interviewed and with the colleagues with whom I collaborated opened a new world for me: According to Alexis de Tocqueville, studying another culture is like turning the mirror onto ourselves. The research in Japan provided me with a comparative perspective on how people negotiate change and how family patterns and the gendered division of labor differ in various cultural settings. At the same time, this comparative research revealed the similarities in craftspeople's behavior, in their self-perception, and in their family patterns, traits that are inherent in the textile industry in many cultures (see Chapter 10).

My opportunity for further cross-cultural comparisons with Asia was extended when the National Academy of Science sent me as a "Distinguished Visiting Scholar" to the People's Republic of China in 1984. During my two-month lecture tour in universities and local academies of social science in China, hosted by the Chinese Academy for Social Science, I greatly expanded my comparative repertory through various discussions with Chinese colleagues about their own research on family change and through firsthand interviewing and participant observation in Shanghai and in rural communities. These interviews and the interactions with ordinary people in China opened new windows for me. Interviews of peasants and urban craftspeople, who were experiencing rapid economic change under the new economic "individual" and "family responsibility" system, enabled me to see how people revised their strategies in response to new economic opportunities (Chapter 3). At the same time, my participant observation and interviews around two divorce cases in Shanghai family courts provided important insights into the experience of people who were caught between liberalized legislation and community control over their family decisions (see Chapter 12, "Divorce, Chinese Style").

Following the completion of my research in Japan in 1993, I decided to pursue my comparison of family and work in traditional textile industries in Lyon, France. Lyon was the silk capital of Europe in the seventeenth and eighteenth centuries. The Jacquard mechanism, which was invented in Lyon in the early nineteenth century, revolutionized the gendered division of labor in Japan after it was brought to Kyoto in the late nineteenth century. In both societies, the production of luxury fabrics was household-based in a putting-out system. This similarity stimulated further need for systematic comparison, because phenomena that are similar on the surface are not necessarily the same. My research in Lyon has now continued over a four-year period, and my interviews are capturing the experiences of former weavers and manufacturers as well as those of the very last people still engaged in this traditional process. The remarkable discovery in this comparative research is the extent to which the commonality in the experience of textile work transcends cultural and national boundaries.

Tamara K. Hareven

Acknowledgments

Over my career I have incurred many debts to various individuals and organizations who supported my work in generous ways. I have expressed specific acknowledgments of gratitude in the respective chapters in this collection. In addition, I would like to express my profound thanks to those whose sustaining support over time has greatly facilitated and enriched my scholarly work. My collaboration with Kathleen Adams, Howard Chudacoff, Glen Elder, Kanji Masaoka, John Modell, Kiyomi Morioka, Peter Uhlenberg, and Maris Vinovskis has been crucial to the development of the themes and methodologies as they emerged in my work. Kathleen Adams, Glen Elder, and Maris Vinovskis, in particular, have enriched my work through continuous interaction and support, as have Bengt and Gretta Ankarloo, Irene and Richard Brown, Antoinette Fauve-Chamoux, Akira Hayami, and Ronald Walters. Olivier and Martine Zeller have greatly facilitated the launching and sustaining of my research in Lyon. Robert Wheaton and later Andrejs Plakans have had crucial roles in the launching and editing of the *Journal of Family History* and subsequently the *History of the Family: An International Quarterly*, which Andrejs Plakans currently coedits. All the colleagues mentioned above have also been warm friends, as have Rolande Bonaine, George and Susan Cicala, Sam and Shelly Gaertner, Perry and Sheila Goldlust, Joanne Nigg, and Judy Wilson. I am grateful to them all for their support and friendship.

I am indebted to many foundations and associations for their generous support of my work: The National Endowment for the Humanities, the Ford Foundation, the Rockefeller Foundation, the Japan Foundation, the Social Science Research Council, and the International Council for the Exchange of Scholars. The support of the National Institute on Aging has been crucial in enabling me to orient my scholarship toward the study of aging. A five-year "career" grant from the National Institute on Aging enabled me to acquire conceptual and methodological approaches to the study of aging, and two research grants from the National Institute on Aging enabled me to carry out the research on the life course, aging, and generational relations reported in several chapters in this book.

I am grateful to Clark University and to the University of Delaware for their support for my various research projects, to my research assistants for all their meticulous help, to my students in these universities for asking valuable questions, and to Doshisha University in Kyoto and Keyo University in Tokyo for their generous support of my research in Japan. My deep gratitude also goes to the Center for Population Studies and Public Health at Harvard University, which housed my research projects and supported me in numerous ways over a decade.

Finally, I would like to express my gratitude to Brooke Bollinger and Gina Simon for their meticulous editorial help in putting this manuscript together and in preparing it for publication, to Anton Badinger for his great help with the copyedited manuscript, and to the editorial team of Westview Press for their efficient management, editing, and support: Cathy Murphy, Leo Wiegman, Andrew Day, David McBride, Kristin Milavec, Michele Wynn, and Kay Mariea.

T.K.H.

Part One

Family and Kinship

Continuity and Change

1

The History of the Family and the Complexity of Social Change

Recent historical research on the family has revised some widely held myths about family life in the past as well as generalizations about the impact of the grand processes of social change on the family and society. Family history has complex roots in both the historical demography of the early 1960s and the "new social history" of the same period. Particularly in the United States, it has shared with the latter a commitment to reconstructing the life patterns of ordinary people, to viewing them as actors as well as subjects in the process of change. Out of such concerns has come research that explores previously neglected dimensions of human experience such as growing up, courting, getting married, bearing and rearing children, living in families, becoming old, and dying, from the perspective of those involved. Contemporary historians of the family have sought to reintroduce human experience into historical research and to emphasize the complexity of historical change (see Hareven, 1971, 1987a; Stone, 1981; Tilly and Cohen, 1982; Tilly, 1987; Plakans, 1986).

The challenge for such scholars is the reconstruction of a multitiered reality—the lives of individual families and their interactions with major social, economic, and political forces. This enterprise is complicated by our increasing appreciation of the changing and diverse nature of "the family," rendered fluid by shifts in internal age and gender configurations across regions and over time. The formidable goal is to understand the family in various contexts of change, while allowing the levels of complexity to play themselves out at different points in historical time. In

---

*This chapter first appeared as "The History of the Family and the Complexity of Social Change," *American Historical Review* 96 (February, 1991):95–124.

short, it represents an effort to understand the interrelationship between "individual time," "family time," and "historical time" (Hareven, 1977b; Elder, 1978, 1981).

Before systematic historical study of the family began, various social-science disciplines had generated their own myths and grand theories about continuities and changes in family behavior in the past. Sociologists in particular argued that in preindustrial societies, the dominant household form contained an extended family, often involving three coresident generations, and that the "modern" family, characterized by a nuclear household structure, family limitation, the spacing of children, and population mobility, was the product of industrialization. Also associated with these generalizations was the popular myth that industrialization destroyed familial harmony and community life. But historical research on the family has provided a perspective on change over time as well as on family behavior within specific social and cultural contexts in discrete time periods. It has led to the rejection of these assumptions and to the resulting questioning of the role of industrialization as a major watershed for American and European history (Wrigley, 1972, 1977; Laslett, 1972, 1977a; Goode, 1963; Smelser, 1959; Anderson, 1979).

Over the three decades of its existence, family history has moved from a limited view of the family as a static unit at one point in time to an examination of the family as a process over the entire lives of its members; from a study of discrete domestic structures to the investigation of the nuclear family's relations with the wider kinship group; and from a study of the family as a separate domestic unit to an examination of the family's interaction with the worlds of religion, work, education, correctional and welfare institutions and with processes such as migration, industrialization, and urbanization (Hareven, 1977b, 1987a; Stone, 1981; Vinovskis, 1977).[1]

As research in this field developed, efforts to explore decisionmaking processes within the family have led to an investigation of strategies and choices that individuals and family groups make. The life-course approach added an important developmental dimension to the history of the family by focusing on age and cohort comparisons in ways that link individual and family development to historical events. As historical research on the family developed further, new findings and approaches led to the revision of the pioneers' findings. Research also expanded chronologically to ancient Greece and Rome and geographically from Western Europe, North America, and Japan to Northern and Eastern Europe, to Southern Italy and the Mediterranean, and to China. The cumulative impact of studies in the history of the family has been to revise simplistic views of both social change and family behavior. These revisions have generated a host of new questions that have been answered only in part. Given the richness and diversity of research in family history, it would be impossible to cover here all the aspects of this large volume of scholarly endeavor. I will try to follow the main strands of research and will illustrate them with select examples (Hareven and Plakans, 1987; see also Soliday et al., 1980; Cox, 1988; Hunter, 1989; Cantarella, 1987; Hallett, 1984; Rawson, 1986; Dixon, 1988; Rheubottom, 1988; Peristiany, 1976; Duben, 1985; Wolf and Huang, 1980; Pasternak, 1983; Hanley and Wolf, 1985; Ebrey, 1981, 1986; P. C. Smith, 1980; Hareven, 1987b).

The emergence of the history of the family as a special area of inquiry received its major impetus from the publication of Philippe Ariès's *Centuries of Childhood* (1960 in French and 1962 in an English translation). Ariès argued that childhood as we know it emerged only in the early modern period and that its discovery was closely linked to the emergence of the "modern" or conjugal family, in which parents' private relationships with their children were more important "than the honor of a line, the integrity of an inheritance, or the age and permanence of a name." Looking back to premodern France and England, when the family was actively involved with the community and the household was open to nonrelatives engaged in familial activities, Ariès idealized the family's sociability in the "big house." "The big house fulfilled a public function. . . . It was the only place where friends, clients, relatives and protégés could meet and talk." In the big house, "people lived on top of one another, masters and servants, children and adults, in houses open at all hours to the indiscretions of the callers. The density of society left no room for the family. Not that the family did not exist as a concept," but its main focus was sociability rather than privacy. The "modern" family, he argued, emerged as sociability retreated. In thus lamenting the loss of earlier sociability in the family, Ariès laid the foundation for a debate as to which family type best prepares children to function in a complex, modern society: the family of the past, which exposed children from a young age to a diversity of role models, or the contemporary, private, intimate family (Ariès, 1962, p. 393, pp. 405-406; Sennett, 1970).

By linking the "discovery" of childhood to transformations in family and social structures as well as economic and demographic changes, Ariès inspired a whole new generation of scholars (Ariès, 1962; Demos, 1970; Stone, 1977; Shorter, 1976; Wheaton, 1987). His emphasis on sentiment and privacy as the defining characteristics of the "modern family" was emulated by John Demos, Edward Shorter, and Lawrence Stone, among others. Equally influential was Ariès's integration of diverse, previously neglected sources with demographic data, especially his use of iconography and art. In recent years, however, historians have challenged Ariès's thesis that West European society before the eighteenth century was characterized by indifference to children (Pollock, 1983). Shortly before his death, Ariès himself acknowledged that if he had looked at medieval sources, he might have modified his conclusions about the emergence of sentiment in the early modern period (Ariès, 1980). Ariès's focus on attitudes toward children and the concept of childhood remains nevertheless the major reference point for studies of the historical transition to the "modern family," especially for historians who employ cultural rather than socioeconomic and demographic approaches. *Centuries of Childhood* has served as a catalyst for family history in the same way Henri Pirenne's *Medieval Cities* affected medieval and early modern European history (Pirenne, 1946).

Although historians often point to Ariès's book as the first major work in family history, historical research on the family was rooted in several disciplines, such as psychology, anthropology, sociology, economics, and most notably historical demography, which preceded it (Wrigley, 1966a; see also Wheaton, 1987; Goubert, 1954, 1960; Henry, 1953, 1956, 1968; Imhof, 1976, 1977; Mitterauer and Sieder, 1979; Ägrent, 1973; Kälvemark, 1977; Andorka and Balazs-Kovács, 1986; Kahk, Palli, and Uibu, 1982; Hayami, 1973; Hayami and Uchida, 1972; Cornell and Hayami, 1986; T. Smith, 1977; Demos, 1965, 1970; Greven, 1970; Henrepin, 1954; Landry and Légaré, 1987; Charbonneau, 1975; Charbonneau et al., 1987).[2] In the early 1960s, historical demographers in France provided family historians with a powerful "new weapon" for the analysis of vital processes related to life and death in the past. Louis Henry and Pierre Goubert had developed a family-reconstitution technique in the 1950s that, in E. A. Wrigley's words, enabled historians "to assemble all the information about the vital events in a given family which can be gleaned from the register of a parish or a group of parishes" (Wrigley, 1966b, p. 82). The Institute National des Études Démographiques took the lead in the development of this new methodology. Using first genealogies and then marriage, baptismal, and death records from parish registers, demographers reconstructed aggregate patterns of fertility, nuptiality, and mortality for vast numbers of people and, in some instances, over several generations (Flandrin, 1976; Burguière, 1978, 1987; LeRoy Ladurie, 1976; Segalen, 1980, 1983; Wheaton, 1980).

In France, historical demography and family history developed into two parallel but interrelated streams from the 1960s on. One stream continued to concentrate on demographic analysis, along the lines of Henry and Goubert; the other, influenced by Ariès, anthropology, and the French social history tradition, integrated demographic analyses with patterns of family and sexuality, linking community and social and cultural variables with *mentalité*, as exemplified in the work of Emmanuel LeRoy Ladurie, André Burguière, and Jean-Louis Flandrin, among others. Family reconstitution subsequently became a powerful tool in the hands of the Cambridge Group for the History of Population and Social Structure. Established in 1964, the Cambridge Group adapted the family reconstitution method to English parish registers, while also pursuing analysis of a seventeenth-century nominal household register for Clayworth, which Peter Laslett had discovered. In an analysis of Colyton from 1538 to 1837, Wrigley found—in the decline in seventeenth-century fertility and the eighteenth-century recovery—evidence that rural births and marriages responded to changing economic conditions. As Wrigley explained, the demographic transition did not involve a change from uncontrolled fertility to its reduction by the "exercise of prudential restraint" but "from a system of control through social institution and custom to one in which the private choice of individual couples played a major part in governing the fertility rate." This family reconstitution for Colyton in East Devon and the analysis of the Clayworth household register became the base for Laslett's book *The World We Have Lost* (1965) (Laslett, 1977a; Wrigley, 1966b, 1968, 1974, 1977; Wrigley and Schofield, 1981).

Such demographic analyses for France and England revealed that in the preindustrial period, age at marriage was later than had been generally assumed, couples practiced some form of family limitation and child spacing as early as the seventeenth century, households were predominantly nuclear rather than extended, and preindustrial populations experienced considerable geographic mobility (Wrigley, 1977; Laslett, 1965; Goubert, 1977). From today's perspective, it is difficult to recover the excitement of being able to re-create such patterns from the past. The evidence about the practice of family limitation in particular demonstrated the control that couples exercised over their own lives and the implicit choices (what Wrigley called "unconscious rationality") that they followed in relation to changing social and economic conditions.

Similarly, the discovery of late age at marriage helped explain the timing of household and family formation. Late marriage served as a method of family limitation. It was also closely related to the expectation that a newlywed couple would establish a separate household. Hence, marriage was contingent on a couple's ability to accumulate resources that would enable them to live independently, as well as contribute to their families of orientation. Linking late age at marriage to the nuclearity of the household, John Hajnal developed his thesis of the "West European Marriage Pattern," which served as the basic model for the analysis of West European families until recently (Hajnal, 1965, 1983).[3]

Using nominal census records, Laslett found evidence of continuity in nuclear household structure in England, at least since the sixteenth century. In 1969, he convened a demographic conference on family and household structure, concentrating on Europe and North America but also including papers on Japan, China, and Africa. The conference essays were published in *Household and Family in Past Time* (Laslett and Wall, 1972), with an extensive introduction from Laslett that provided a classification scheme of household types. The essays from Western Europe and North America affirmed Laslett's findings for England that there has been little variation in mean household size and a continuity in the predominance of the small nuclear family since the sixteenth century. Akira Hayami and Robert Smith also found evidence for the existence of nuclear household structures in certain regions of Tokugawa Japan. The volume's conclusions, combined with those deriving from subsequent analyses of nominal censuses for urban communities in the United States and Canada, dispelled the previously held assumption that industrialization brought about a nuclear family form. The myth of what William Goode termed "the great family of Western nostalgia," namely, the coresidence of three generations in a single household, was laid to rest. Subsequent studies showed that coresidence with extended kin tended to increase, not decrease, after the "industrial revolution," because of the need of newly arrived migrants to industrial cities to share housing space (Laslett and Wall, 1972; Goode, 1963; R. J. Smith, 1972; see also Sennett, 1970; Griffen and Griffen, 1978; Hareven, 1977b; Hayami and Uchida, 1972; Anderson, 1971).

Subsequently, David Herlihy traced a nuclear household structure in medieval Tuscany back to the twelfth century, and Richard Smith, using poll tax lists for the village of Suffolk from 1377 to 1381, concluded, "There seems to be good reason to suppose that the general shape and membership of the familial group differed very little from that of early modern England." This conclusion was reinforced by Smith's analysis of manorial contracts for the same period: Three-fourths of the contracts contained proof of separate residence of the two generations (Herlihy, 1985; Herlihy and Klapisch-Zuber, 1978; Macfarlane, 1978; R. Smith, 1979a, quoted in Macfarlane, 1978, p. 31). In an imaginative reconstruction of family and community life of the medieval village of Montaillou in Southern France, LeRoy Ladurie found a variety of forms of family structures in the *domus* (household), ranging from ordinary nuclear families to families including an aged widowed mother or father to some groups of brothers sometimes coresiding with an elderly mother or with both parents. "The purely nuclear family was perhaps the most common, but it did not have a local monopoly." Most important, family structure varied over the life cycle of its members. The Vidal family, for example, was nuclear at first; then, with the death of the father, "we have a truncated nucleus, which soon becomes a phratry, the position of the brothers gaining in importance" as the mother withdraws and lives in a semiseparate room by herself and one of her sons succeeds to the position of headship. The family becomes more or less "extended" again when one of the brothers—Bernard—marries and the new couple lives with the mother and the other brothers. After the mother's death, all the brothers leave the parental house and set up separate households or join other households, except for Bernard, who now heads a nuclear family (LeRoy Ladurie, 1978, pp. 47–48).

Scholars' emphasis in the 1960s on the continuity of nuclear households and the subsequent wave of studies inspired by them had several limitations that left their mark on the new field for at least a decade. Although Laslett's early work implied that the nuclear "family" persisted over historical time, the major unit discussed was the household, not the family. A nuclear household was not identical with a nuclear family, since the domestic group may have included nonrelatives as well. Nor was a "family" restricted to the household, since extended family ties transcended the household unit (Goody, 1972; Hareven, 1974).

Early generalizations also led to the formation of new stereotypes: By combining the findings about the nuclearity of the household with the Hajnal thesis on the Western marriage pattern, Laslett developed the "Western family" type, which he characterized as having a nuclear family form or simple household; a relatively late childbearing age; a relatively narrow age gap between husband and wife, with a relatively high proportion of wives older than their husbands; and the presence in the household of "life-cycle servants," unrelated to the family with which they were residing. By contrast, he characterized the South European and Mediterranean family type as having a complex household structure and early marriage, in which nuclear households are formed by the breakup of extended ones rather than through marriage. Recently, however, these generalizations about regional family forms have come under criticism (Laslett, 1977a, 1983). For example, on the basis of research in Italy, David Kertzer refuted the thesis that links early female marriage to joint household organization as a characteristic of the "South European" family pattern and claimed that household complexity was not universal; rather, it depended on variations in landholding and sharecropping. Similarly, Haim Gerber, on the basis of his analysis of households in the seventeenth-century Turkish city of Bursa, concluded that "certain widespread notions about the traditional Middle Eastern family do not have a solid base" (Kertzer, 1984; Kertzer and Brettell, 1987; Kertzer and Hogan, 1989; Gerber, 1989, p. 419).

Scholars have also questioned the initial preoccupation with household structure and size and have seen the need to investigate internal family dynamics. Lutz Berkner has emphasized the fact that coresidence under the same roof was not the crucial variable. Of greater significance was whether family members cooked together and ate together and the nature of their social and economic relations. Similarly, Hans Medick warned about the dangers of using structural criteria of household classification in isolation from the sociohistorical conditions:

[T]he danger arises of computing the incomputable. It is true that the industrial proletarian grandmother may have lived in an "extended family" as did
the peasant grandmother, but this apparent uniformity by no means indicates an identity of household structures. The "extended family" of the pro-
letariat primarily functioned as a private institution to redistribute the
poverty of the nuclear family by way of the kinship system. The extended
family of the peasant, on the other hand, served as an instrument for the conservation of property and the caring of the older members of the family.
(Berkner, 1975; Medick, 1976, p. 295; Wheaton, 1975)

When interpreted in the context of economic and social institutions (such
as landholding, inheritance, religion, community structure, and religious
attitudes), demographic patterns served as the backbone of rich family and
community analyses. For example, in his 1970 analysis of the demographic
patterns and household and family structure in Andover, Massachusetts,
from 1650 to 1800, Philip Greven reconstructed multilayered family patterns. By relating age at marriage and household structure to landholding
and inheritance, he revealed the power relations between fathers and sons
and the limits of the sons' autonomy within a complicated web of kinship
networks (Greven, 1970). The term "modified extended family," which
Greven borrowed from sociologist Eugene Litwak, best described the realities of family life in Andover, where households were primarily restricted
to members of the nuclear family and nonrelatives, but where a "complex
web" of family connections reinforced by proximity of residence, often on
the same land, permeated the community. The strength of Greven's book
also lies in his comparison of the generations. By the third generation, Andover society had stabilized considerably. The major change occurred in
the fourth, when a land shortage led to the dispersal of sons and to out-mi-
gration, which in turn weakened patriarchal ties by the end of the nineteenth century (Greven, 1970; Litwak, 1960).

Demos's study of colonial Plymouth, Massachusetts, also published in
1970, uses family reconstitution, the analysis of nominal census records,
and a great variety of other sources, such as wills and court records, archi-
tectural evidence, and sources of material culture, to reconstruct family
and community patterns. It reminds us that even though households
were nuclear, they differed considerably from those of contemporary society. Families were larger then and included nonrelatives, such as servants, apprentices, and boarders and lodgers in the households. Families
lived in smaller household dwellings, with little chance to "differentiate
between various forms of living space . . . individuals were more constantly together and their activities meshed and overlapped at many
points"(p.181). Age configurations were also considerably different. In
some families, the oldest child in the household would be an adult while

the youngest was still at the breast. Even though some disagreed with Demos's application of Eriksonian notions of developmental stages to the Puritans, his reconstruction of the stages of the life cycle is masterly in its own right. It provides a dynamic picture of individuals within families and households as they move from childhood to old age in relation to the prescriptions of their society (Demos, 1970, 1971; see also Walsh, 1979; Menard, 1981; D. B. Smith, 1980, 1982; Wells, 1982; Schlissel, 1989).

Although the emphasis on the continuity of the nuclear household structure challenged the overly simplistic categories of modernization theory, it also sometimes obscured important historical differences between past and present family patterns. Nuclear households in the preindustrial period were considerably different in their membership and age configurations from contemporary ones. Within medieval nuclear households, for example, family behavior differed from that of the seventeenth and eighteenth-century families. Preindustrial households were larger and also contained different age configurations because of later marriage, later childbearing, higher fertility, and lower life expectancy (Laudrie, 1978; Demos, 1970).

A major critique of early studies of household structure was their reliance on "snapshots" in the census household schedules. On the basis of his reconstruction of peasant households in the villages of Heidenreichstein in Northern Austria in 1763, Berkner provided evidence that household structure changed several times over the course of the family lives. For example, stem family patterns (involving a household composed of a married couple living with their retired parents) recurred several times, as the family moved through its cycle in relation to the household; after a man's marriage and his father's retirement, the man lived in a stem family; after his father's death, he lived in a nuclear family; but later in life, he found himself again in a stem family, when he coresided with his married son following his own retirement. Such phases of the family cycle were often of short duration because they were terminated by the death of the head of the family.

In contrast to Laslett's emphasis on uniformity, articles by anthropologists Eugene Hammel and Jack Goody in *Household and Family in Past Time* (1972) emphasized the fluidity in the structure of domestic groups as "processes" in relation to agricultural production, migration, and the family cycle. After analyzing the Zadruga—the large coresident kinship groups in Serbia—Hammel warned that "the Zadruga is not a thing but a process." The Zadruga formed and reconstituted itself under the impact of demographic processes and external constraints, dictated by agriculture. Similarly, Goody pointed to the confusion in Western scholarship between a "family" and a "dwelling group." He proposed instead the concept of the "domestic group" as the economic unit (meaning production and consumption). By documenting the changing configurations of domestic groups of the La Dagaba and the Lo Wiili in Ghana, he demonstrated the ways in which domestic groups change in their composition over their cycle and in relation to migration and agricultural production (Berkner, 1972, 1975; see also Goody, 1971, 1972; Hammel, 1972; Mitterauer and Sieder, 1979; R. J. Smith, 1978; Hareven, 1974).

Even though Laslett may have contributed inadvertently to a static view of the household, he nevertheless focused attention on the massive movement of individuals from one household to the next at certain points in their lives. In his analysis of Clayworth, Laslett found the presence of "life-cycle" servants—young men and women in their teens—who lived and served in other people's households in the transitional period between leaving home and marrying. Servants did not always come from a lower class; in many cases, they were members of the same class, engaged in exchanges between households for educational purposes. Demos found a similar pattern in colonial Plymouth, where, significantly, the exchanges of young people as servants followed kinship lines (Laslett and Harrison, 1963).

The case of the life-cycle servants, as well as the presence of other unrelated individuals in the household, proves the remarkable flexibility of households in the past. Nuclear family members engaged in exchange relations with nonrelatives, servants, apprentices, boarders and lodgers, and, at times, with extended kin. Households expanded and contracted in accordance with the family's needs. In American urban households, John Modell and I found a high proportion of boarders and lodgers, whose presence and functions within the household paralleled those of the life-cycle servants in an earlier period. Throughout the nineteenth century and the early part of this century, approximately one-half to one-third of all households had boarders and lodgers at some point; about the same percentage of individuals had lived as boarders and lodgers in other people's households in the transitional period between leaving home and getting married. Boarding and lodging provided young migrants to the city with surrogate family arrangements and the middle-aged or old couples who took them in with supplemental income and sociability. In younger families, the income from boarders contributed to the payment of a mortgage and, in some cases, enabled the wife to stay out of the labor force. Boarding and lodging represented an exchange across families by which young people who had left their own parent's households temporarily replaced their counterparts in other households (Modell and Hareven, 1973; see also Glasco, 1977; Katz, 1975; Hareven, 1982).

The discovery of boarders and lodgers in nineteenth-century households and of the overall fluidity of household structure led us to search for a framework that would allow us to capture the movement of individuals through various household forms over their lives and the changes in the composition of the family and the household in relation to these movements, under various historical conditions. Initially, the family-cycle approach proved satisfactory, for it helped explain changes in the composition of the family over its development. When applying the family-cycle approach, historians discovered that household patterns that appeared constant at one point actually varied significantly over the life of the family unit. Individuals living in nuclear households at one time in their lives were likely to live in households containing extended kin or nonrelatives at other times. The family cycle proved especially valuable for identifying those stages in the family's development when it was economically vulnerable and prone to poverty (see Berkner, 1972; Segalen, 1977; Mitterauer and Sieder, 1979; Rowntree, 1901; Hareven, 1974; Duval, 1957; Hill 1964, 1970; Hill and Rodgers, 1964). Quickly, however, the shortcomings of the family-cycle approach became apparent. The stages of the family cycle were derived from contemporary American middle-class families, and they were not always appropriate for the study of families in the past. The a priori stages were based on the progression of the couple from marriage through parenthood, the launching of children, widowhood, and family dissolution. As sociologist Glen Elder explained, the family cycle identifies stages of parenthood rather than the more dynamic aspects of individual transitions into and out of various family roles (see Hareven, 1978a; Elder, 1978).

Dissatisfaction with the family-cycle approach led me in 1976 to invite Elder, who had developed the life-course approach, to collaborate with a group of historians on its application to historical analysis. For this purpose, we selected the Federal Census Manuscript schedules for Essex County, Massachusetts. (We deliberately used a census, rather than a longitudinal data set, in order to examine the potential of life-course analysis for data restricted to one point in time.) In a series of intensive seminars during 1976 and 1977, project members analyzed the timing of individual household members' life-course transitions into and out of various household situations and in and out of various familial and work roles. Our analysis of the timing of life-course transitions from the census manuscript schedules included marriage, schooling, women's labor force participation, and later life transitions, all in relation to the family configurations of the individuals undergoing these transitions. We found a significant difference between the pacing of early life transitions and the later ones. Transitions into adult roles were more rapidly timed, whereas the later life transitions, such as launching children and retirement, were much more gradual and, in many cases, did not occur until the end of life. All transitions, even the ones related to labor force and schooling, were strongly integrated with the family, and collective family requirements and strategies governed their timing (Hareven, 1978e). The timing of leaving home and of marriage brought forth a recurring dilemma in generational relations in past time: How did individuals and couples cope with conflicting goals and allegiances to their families of orientation and families of procreation? How did they make their transitions from one family to the other in a regime of economic insecurity, without jeopardizing the independence and self-sufficiency of one or the other? Historical research on the timing of life transitions and on generational relations since the 1970s has begun to address these questions and has raised new ones (see Chudacoff and Hareven, 1978a, 1979; Hareven, 1981b; D. S. Smith, 1979; Arcury, 1986; Plakans, 1989; Vinovskis, 1989b; Hayami, 1983; Cornell, 1983).[4]

The life-course approach has introduced a dynamic dimension into the historical study of the family, and it has moved analysis and interpretation from a simplistic examination of stages of the family cycle to an analysis of individuals' and families' timing of life transitions in relation to historical time (Hareven, 1978e; Elder, 1974, 1978b; see also Riley, 1978; Riley, Johnson, and Foner, 1972; Ryder, 1965; Hareven, 1977b; Hareven and Masaoka, 1988). The pace and definition of timing patterns are determined by their social and cultural context. On the familial level, timing involves the synchronization of individual life transitions with collective family ones. Because individual lives in the past were more integrated with familial goals, many decisions today considered "individual," such as starting work, leaving home, and getting married, were part of collective family timing strategies (Elder, 1978; Hareven, 1977b; Modell and Hareven, 1978).

Life-course research also illuminates the links between behavior and perception. Although the actual timing of life transitions can be reconstructed from demographic records, its meaning to the individual and family members undergoing these transitions hinges on the examination of qualitative, subjective sources (see Neugarten and Hagestad, 1976; LeVine, 1978; Hareven and Masaoka, 1988; Chudacoff, 1980). In his provocative book *Into One's Own* (1989), Modell examined twentieth-century changes in the timing of transitions to adulthood and found that these transitions have become increasingly well defined, more precisely timed, and more compressed in the time period it takes an age cohort to accomplish them. Using both demographic evidence and prescriptive literature, Modell found a major historical change from the erratic timing of life transitions governed by collective family needs to more individualized timing in conformity with age norms (Modell, 1989; Modell, Furstenberg, and Hershberg, 1976). He concluded that over this century, the life course has become "individualized" (especially since World War

II) to the point that a young person's decision to marry is contingent on finding a suitable partner at a suitable age rather than on the requirements and constraints imposed by the family of orientation. Such individualization of the timing of life transitions first occurred in the native-born middle class; the process and pace by which various ethnic groups adopted similar attitudes still requires investigation (Hareven, 1977b; Modell, 1989).

A life-course perspective has made an important contribution to the study of kinship by directing attention to the changing configurations of kin with whom individuals travel together over their lives. Such configurations are formed and reformed; they change in their composition, their relationship to the individual and the nuclear family, and to each other over the life course.

During the second decade of the development of the field of family history, kinship ties outside the household received increasing attention. Studies now show that nuclear households, rather than being isolated, were embedded in kinship ties outside their confines. Members of the nuclear family were engaged in various forms of mutual assistance, collaboration, and rituals with extended kin. Even though aging parents did not reside in the same household with their married adult children, they lived in the vicinity, often on the same land (Greven, 1970; Berkner, 1972; R. Smith, 1979b).

By applying network theory, Richard Smith effectively reconstructed kinship networks in a thirteenth-century Suffolk community. In his comparison of individuals' interaction with kin and neighbors, Smith found a strong embeddedness of nuclear households with nonresident kin. The intense interaction with kin led him to conclude that on Redgrave Manor, "the bulk of the rural population . . . had a social structure that was for the most part familistically organized." The contacts he identified, however, were not among groups of kin but between individuals (Macfarlane, 1978, p. 139; R. Smith, 1979a, pp. 219–256). Suffolk may have had a higher concentration of kin because of partible inheritance. English villages in which impartible inheritance was practiced showed a lower concentration of kin, because the noninheriting sons tended to migrate out. On the basis of these findings, Alan Macfarlane concluded that kinship ties in medieval English villages did not resemble the characteristic "clans" and lineages of peasant societies. He used this as proof of his much-disputed claim for the uniqueness of "English individualism." LeRoy Ladurie, however, found similar patterns of kin interaction in Montaillou. He found very little evidence subordinating the *domus* to a formal lineage. What was more important were the linkages between the *domus* and other kin, as well as non-kin. "The *domus* was thus the center of a whole network of links of varying importance: They included alliance through marriage, family relationship, and friendship" (Macfarlane, 1978; LeRoy Ladurie, 1978, pp. 48–50).

When trying to understand the kinship patterns in the villages discussed above, as well as in other communities in which kinship networks were not codified in clans and lineages, it is important to remember the fluidity of kinship networks over the life course and under the impact of migration. For example, a brother residing in a nuclear family becomes an extended kin member when he moves out. As Greven showed for Andover, it took more than two generations to form significant kin networks in the community, which then were disrupted again through migration in the fourth generation (Greven, 1970; also see Plakans, 1977, 1982, 1984; Gunda, 1982; Netting, 1981; Segalen, 1985; Segalen and Richard, 1986; Dupaquier, 1981; Wheaton, 1982; Wheaton and Hareven, 1980).[5]

For nineteenth and twentieth-century urban populations, Anderson and I, respectively, have documented the central role of family members and more distant kin in organizing migration from rural areas to industrial cities, in facilitating settlement in urban communities, and in helping migrants adapt to new working and living conditions. Most of the migration to industrial centers was carried out under the auspices of kin. Kinship networks in communities of origin were reinforced by the back-and-forth migration of individual members and the transfer of resources. Following "chain-migration" routes, villagers who went to work in urban factories spearheaded migration for other relatives by locating housing and jobs. Those who remained in the communities of origin often took care of aging parents and other relatives who stayed behind (Anderson, 1971; Hareven, 1978b; see also Hareven, 1982; Tilly and Brown, 1974; Schwarzweller, Brown, and Mangalam, 1971).[6]

In my study of late nineteenth and early twentieth-century textile workers in Manchester, New Hampshire, I found that workers' kinship networks cushioned the adaptation of immigrant workers to new industrial working conditions. As will be seen below in greater detail, kin acted as brokers between the workers and their industrial employers: They recruited new workers, placed them in workrooms where they could cluster together, initiated the young and the new immigrants into industrial discipline and the work process, taught them how to manipulate machinery, and provided protection inside the factory. At the same time, they socialized new workers to collective working-class behavior, teaching them how to resist speedups in production through the setting of quotas on piecework and through the slowdown of machinery (see Chapter 2). These findings about the role of kin refuted those who argued that migration to industrial centers eroded kinship networks. As discussed below in detail, rather than disrupting kinship ties, migration often strengthened them and led to the development of new functions for kin in response to changing economic conditions and pressures in the workplace (Hareven, 1982, pp. 85–106; Garigue, 1956).

Kinship networks within the industrial community were most effective in mediating interactions with local institutions and in responding to immediate crises such as strikes and depressions. Their strength was in their accessibility and stability. But kin also retained ties of mutual assistance with relatives in the community of origin. The long-distance networks provided, in one direction, care to family members who remained behind and, in the other, backup assistance from the communities of settlement, especially during crises. Thus, kin networks in industrial communities retained both traditional functions as mediators between individual members of the nuclear family and public institutions and added new ones in response to the requirements of the industrial system (Hareven, 1982).

Research on kinship awaits further development in several directions. First, one needs to examine systematically the interaction between the nuclear family and kin outside the household. To explore this question, Andrejs Plakans applied Meyer Fortes's model of "structural domains," which is based on the assumption that an individual participates in several domains simultaneously and fulfills a different role in each. Sometimes these roles are complementary; at other times, they are in conflict. An individual can be engaged simultaneously in obligations to coresident family members and to nonresident kin. How these roles have been negotiated and played out in various settings during different periods remains an important topic of research (Plakans, 1984; Fortes, 1969). Second, the question of why families in the West drew their household boundary at coresidence with kin but included unrelated individuals in the household has not been answered.

Pursuing these questions requires careful attention to the term "kinship." We need to distinguish between perceptual categories and definitions of kinship developed within a given society and the analytical categories used by social scientists (Wheaton, 1987, pp. 285–302). Reconstruction of kinship categories from within is extremely difficult, given the limitations of traditional historical sources, but essential. As Robin Fox put it:

> No Australian Aborigine sat down and worked out a blueprint for the complicated systems of kinship and marriage for which he is justly famous; but his ability to conceptualize and classify was as much a factor in this successful development as the claws of the tiger or the neck of the giraffe were in the survival and success of these species. (Fox, 1967, p. 31)

Ideally, historians should juxtapose the actors' categories and definitions of kin with externally defined notions.

As in other areas of research in the history of the family, we need to find a comfortable equilibrium between quantitative analysis and "thick description." Too often, quantitative and qualitative methodologies have been presented as mutually exclusive. Analysis of kinship will be served best by merging the two. For example, quantitative analysis identifies the composition or extensiveness of a kinship network, but qualitative analysis reveals patterns of assistance or areas of conflict among kin (Wheaton, 1987; Hareven, 1982, pp. 371–382; see also Geertz, 1973; Davis, 1977; Segalen, 1986). Finally, we need to understand how kin relations changed over time in relation to the "grand processes" of change.

An examination of the family's interaction with the process of social and economic change enables us to understand more precisely not only what occurred internally within the family but how such changes were accomplished on a societal level as well. This provides new insights into the process of industrialization and urbanization, into how labor markets functioned, and how industrial work processes and labor relations were organized. These are only several of many areas in which the role of the family is critical for an understanding of social change and, conversely, for our understanding of societal influences on the family. Recent historical research on the family has led to the rejection of simplistic models of social change. How the family both initiates and adapts to change and how it translates the impact of larger structural changes into its own sphere are issues governing the richest area of intersection between the family and the process of social change. Much of this interaction still awaits thorough examination (Hareven, 1977b).

The important principle underlying these questions is a view of the family as an active agent. The family planned, initiated, or resisted change; it did not just respond blindly. Historical research over the past two decades has provided ample evidence to reject stereotypes about the family's passivity. We have therefore revised questions such as "What was the impact of industrialization on the family?" to ask instead "What was the family's impact on the industrial system?" (Hareven, 1982; Goode, 1963, pp. 1–18).[7] Some of the studies that reversed the stereotype of the family as a "passive" agent have, in turn, generated new stereotypes that exaggerate the family's ability to influence and modify its environment. Since historical realities are better expressed in a process of interaction than in the reversal of unilateral processes, I have recast the question into a more complex form: Under what circumstances was the family more able to control its destiny and to affect the larger social processes, and under what circumstances did the family succumb to declining markets, changing modes of production, business cycles, and other external forces? How did families interact with these processes, and how did they react to opportunities or constraints? For example, how did they respond to technological developments and to new industries that were attracting a labor force? How did they save themselves from the decaying industries that had recruited them during their prime but had left them stranded when they were no longer needed? (Hareven, 1982).

The family's interaction with the industrial system has received attention from two types of historical studies: a study of family production systems in artisanal and proto-industrial settings and the study of family and work in the context of large industrial enterprises. Proto-industrialization was a household-based form of production that preceded the "industrial revolution" in the countryside and in some urban areas in England, France, Belgium, Switzerland, and Austria, from the seventeenth to the early nineteenth centuries. It was characterized by the production of goods in local cottages for a capitalist employer who controlled the means of production and sold the products in external markets. When Rudolf Braun first "discovered" this process for Zurich, he emphasized its centrality as a household-based enterprise, which drew heavily on the labor of women and children and engaged the entire household unit. Braun and the historians who identified these patterns in other regions, especially Franklin Mendels, Hans Medick, and David Levine, developed a model of demographic behavior they claimed was typical of proto-industrial families—an earlier age at marriage, higher fertility, and delays in children's departure from the home, all of which were conducive to maximizing a family labor force (Braun, 1960, 1974; Mendels, 1972; Medick, 1976; Levine, 1977, 1985).[8] Marriage formed the key to the spread of the cottage industry, because it led to the formation of a new nuclear family unit, which was also a "unit of labor." As Medick explained it, "Marriage and family formation slipped beyond the grasp of patriarchal domination; they were no longer 'tangibly' determined by property relationships, but they did not lose their 'material foundation' in the process of production." The prevalent pattern became that of "beggars'" marriages between partners without any considerable dowry or inheritance, between "people who can join together two spinning wheels but not beds" (Medick, 1976, p. 303).

Recently, the demographic model of proto-industrialization has come under criticism. On the one hand, scholars have questioned whether the demographic changes had been sufficiently widespread to warrant generalizations. For example, in their comparison of two proto-industrial regions in Eastern Belgium, Myron Gutmann and René Leboutte concluded that high ages at marriage were sustained in some regions but not in others. Demographic behavior in response to new economic conditions "differed according to the environment (i.e., land ownership, social structure and inheritance) and the exact nature of the economic change which took place." Shifting the analysis from demographic behavior to the internal division of labor in proto-industrial households, Ulrich Pfister found considerable differences in the division of labor between men and women in relation to the type of manufacturing families engaged in various proto-industrial settings in Switzerland. Again, regional variation, interaction with the local agricultural structure, as well as the type of cottage industry (whether weaving or spinning), made a difference (Gutmann and Leboutte, 1984, p. 589; Mitterauer, 1986; Pfister, 1989; Ehmer, 1980; see also Saito, 1983).[9]

On the other hand, despite these critiques, the concept of proto-industrialization has helped focus attention on the diversity of types of family-based production, some of which preceded the "industrial revolution" and some of which coexisted with the factory system. As a transition, proto-industrial production prepared a family labor force for industrial work: In certain regions, women and children were first cast into the roles of "industrial" laborers at the cottage-production phase. Members of proto-industrial households who eventually entered factories brought their skills with them and may therefore have faced an easier adaptation to industrial work. The family had a central role in charting the transitions to various modes of industrial production by following diverse routes: from a rural economy to a proto-industrial or industrial one or from a rural economy directly to an industrial one. Families of traditional craftsmen or artisans, in their struggle to survive in a changing economy, sent some of their members to work in new industries, while maintaining a crafts production system in their own households. Rural families released members through migration to work in urban factories or took in machinery and transformed their own households into proto-industrial domestic factories. Proto-industrial families as well as those of factory workers provided housing, employment, and training for new migrants in their households. In all these cases, while following its own priorities, the family facilitated the advance of industrialization by releasing the labor force needed for the newly developing factories and by organizing migration to industrial centers (Smelser, 1959; Tilly and Scott, 1978; Rose, 1988; Scott and Tilly, 1975; Quataert, 1985; Struminger, 1977; see also Hareven, 1990b).

Like research on the family in the proto-industrial system, the study of the family in the factory system has provided considerable evidence documenting the family's role as an active agent in its interaction with the process of industrialization. Such research effectively undermined the theory of "social breakdown" that had haunted sociology and social history. According to this notion, throughout the history of industrial development, migration from rural to urban centers had led to the uprooting of people from their traditional kinship networks. The pressures of industrial work and urban life caused a disintegration of the family unit, and adaptation to industrial life stripped migrants of their traditional culture (Thompson, 1963; Parsons, 1955, ch. 1; Ogburn, 1955; Wirth, 1938; Thomas and Znaniecki, 1918–1920; Handlin, 1951).

Historians and sociologists alike have challenged the assumption that families and kin groups broke down under the impact of migration to urban industrial centers and under the pressures of industrial work. Neil Smelser, in his pioneer study of the family in the early stages of industrialization in Britain, documented the recruitment of entire family groups as work units in the early textile factories. Fathers contracted for their children, collected their wages, and at times, disciplined them in the factory. Entire families depended on the factory as their employer; the factories, in turn, depended on the recruitment of family groups to maintain a continuous labor supply. Beginning in the 1820s, however, as a result of factory legislation and technological change, recruitment and training functions were gradually removed from the workers' families. Child workers were separated from the supervision of their parents. Smelser connected the increasing labor unrest, expressed in numerous strikes from 1820 on, to the workers' loss of control over their family members' work in the factory, which led to the break of the "link between parent and child on the factory premises." He viewed this process as the culmination of the differentiation of the working-class family, a process "involving a clearer split between home and factory, a split between the economic and other aspects of the parent-child relationship" (Smelser, 1959, 1968, p. 34).

Michael Anderson disagreed with Smelser in his analysis of family work patterns in nineteenth-century Lancashire. He documented a continuity of recruitment in family units in the textile industry, at least through the middle of the nineteenth century. Most important, Anderson stressed the survival of kinship ties and the continuity of the vital role of kin in migration and in adaptation to industrial life. Thus, the practice of family members working together in the factory, which Smelser identified for the early phase of industrialization, survived in different forms in Lancashire throughout the nineteenth century. It was carried over into the United States as the factory system developed there and was still present among immigrant workers in the twentieth century. Rural as well as urban families functioned as crucial intermediaries in recruiting workers from the countryside in the early phases of industrialization. The very success of the early industrial system depended on a continuous flow of labor from the countryside to the newly industrializing centers, which usually followed kinship lines (Anderson, 1971; Hareven, 1982, pp. 3–4, 85–100).

As mentioned above, my study of family and work in the Amoskeag Mills in Manchester, New Hampshire, has documented the role of the family as an active agent in relation to the industrial corporation. My findings show that the family type most "fit" to interact with the factory system was not an "isolated" nuclear family but rather one embedded in extended kinship ties. In cushioning adaptation to industrial work without excessively restricting the mobility of individual workers, kin were instrumental in serving the industrial employer and, at the same time, in advancing the interest of their own members and providing them with protection (Hareven and Langenbach, 1978; Hareven, 1978b, 1982, ch. 5). The active stance that the family took in relation to the factory system does not imply that the family was in full control of its destiny, nor does it mean that workers and their families were successful in changing the structure of industrial capitalism. Workers' ability to influence their work environments greatly depended on fluctuations within the factory system, on business cycles, and on production policies. In Manchester, control of kin over the factory weakened after World War I, as the corporation shifted to a regime of labor surplus. As Neil Smelser and Sydney Halpern observed, it has not been the steady or continued growth of industrial capitalism so much as its crises that have put strains on modern kinship networks (Smelser and Halpern, 1978).

The functions that kin fulfilled in their interaction with the factory system were not merely an archaic carryover from rural society but a selective use of premigration kin assistance patterns in response to the needs dictated by industrial conditions. Among working-class and ethnic families, some preindustrial family characteristics persisted, though in modified form. Even after the workplace had been separated from the household, the family continued to perceive itself as a work unit. Family members experienced a continuity between work outside the home and household production, especially where women were involved. Similarly, the survival of important functions of kin in the workplace suggests that the historical separation of family and work had not occurred throughout the society.

The encounter of immigrant workers with the modern factory system led neither to the abandonment of nor the rigid adherence to premigration family traditions. Rather, the workers adapted their customs and social organization to the new conditions they confronted. In doing so, they addressed the factory system on its own terms. Selectivity was the key principle in their adaptation. The family selected those aspects of traditional culture that were most useful in coping with new conditions and adapted them to new needs (Hareven, 1982; see Chapter 2; see also Scott and Tilly, 1975, pp. 319–323; Yans-McLaughlin, 1974).

The patterns of selectivity in the transmission of premigration and family culture to the industrial system described here call into question the linear view of social change advanced by modernization theory. As the detailed documentation in Chapter 2 suggests, modernization at the workplace did not automatically lead to the "modernization" of family behavior. Although the family underwent significant changes in its adaptation to new work roles and urban living, family behavior did not modernize at the same pace as workers' conduct in the factory. The family was both a custodian of tradition and an agent of change. As a guardian of traditional culture, the family provided its members with a sense of continuity, which served as a resource to draw on when confronting industrial conditions. Familial and industrial adaptation processes were not merely parallel but were interrelated as a part of a personal and historical continuum (Hareven, 1982; see also Inkeles and Smith, 1974).

To better understand the family's role in these processes, it is necessary to examine how families charted their strategies in relation to external opportunities and constraints. Family strategies involved not only the decisions individuals or families made but also the actual timing of such decisions in response to opportunities or need: when to send a son or daughter to another community, for example; when to join other kin; and when to change residence. Strategies involved, at times, calculated trade-offs in order to find employment, achieve solvency, buy a house, facilitate children's education or their occupational advancement, control or facilitate a child's marriage, save for the future, and provide for times of illness, old age, and death. Strategies were part of a larger life plan. As people encountered new circumstances, they modified and reshaped their plans and strategies in the context of their own culture and traditions. A complete discussion of family strategies appears in Chapter 3.

The multidimensional research effort in family history has produced impressive results and identified new lines of investigation. At a 1986 conference convened to assess the state of research in family history, two interrelated future directions emerged: One is to pursue established topics that have not received sufficient attention, including the family's relationship to social space, and to engage in a more systematic study of the family in relation to religion, the state, and the legal system. Further expansion is also needed in the study of kinship, particularly as it relates to friendship, family transitions over the life course, generational relations, especially in the later years of life, and family strategies, especially where the family's interaction with other institutions is concerned. Today, we can expand the list by adding the need for more systematic studies of the "edges" of family life, such as solitary individuals, orphans and foundlings, and the process of family breakdown through divorce or death. Further research is needed on the relationship of the family to foodways as well. A second direction is the forging of more systematic linkages between interrelated family patterns and processes: These include a closer linkage of demographic patterns with household structure and internal family dynamics; a closer integration of the study of the household with nonresident kin; and a more careful linkage of kinship and household patterns with various processes such as work and migration. Another significant area to pursue is the relationship between demographic and structural family patterns with cultural dimensions and rituals (see Hareven, 1987a).

In addition to this specific agenda, the larger questions of historical changes in the family over time still need to be explored systematically in several directions. First, if industrialization did not bring about the emergence of "modern" family behavior in Western Europe and the United States, what did cause it? One plausible explanation that has been advanced is the commercial revolution of the sixteenth and seventeenth centuries. This does not explain, however, the existence of nuclear household patterns in the Middle Ages.

Second, what were the most significant changes in the family over time? The most ambitious and comprehensive interpretation of change in the family was advanced and documented by Lawrence Stone in *Sex and Marriage in England, 1500–1800* (1977). Stone developed a typology of change in the English family over this 300-year period. He identified the major historical transition as one from an "open lineage" family in the seventeenth century to a companionate nuclear family in the eighteenth century. By a "nuclear" family, he meant not merely a unit of cohabitation but a social and psychological unit based on emotional bonding and affective relations. According to Stone, the emergence of the "nuclear" family was related to the transfer of loyalty from extended kin to the private family and the nation-state. Advancing a multicausal explanation, Stone cited three concurrent and interrelated changes: the decline of kinship as the main organizing principle in society and the rise of the modern state, with its takeover of some of the economic and social functions previously carried out by the family or the kin group; the subordination of kin loyalties to the higher obligations of patriotism and obedience to the sovereign; and the missionary success of Protestantism. Stone's explanation is limited, however, by his heavy reliance on source materials describing upper-class families and by the linearity of the process he sketched (Stone, 1975, p. 13; 1977).

Whereas Stone, like Ariès, has dated the emergence of the modern family in the late seventeenth and early eighteenth centuries, Shorter placed it in the late eighteenth and early nineteenth century. Carl Degler dated the emergence of the American modern family in the late eighteenth or early nineteenth centuries as well. Following in Ariès's footsteps, Stone, Shorter, and Degler have focused on the rise of affective individualism as the major criterion of "modern" family life. They generally agreed that the modern family is privatized, nuclear, domestic, and based on the emotional bonding between husband and wife and between parents and children. The correlates of its emergence were the weakening influence of extended kin, friends, and neighbors on family ties and an isolation of the family from interaction with the community. Although there has been general agreement among these scholars on these characteristics, there is some disagreement and, at times, lack of clarity about which class initiated these changes. Ariès, Stone, and, more implicitly, Degler viewed the bourgeoisie and the gentry as the vanguard, whereas Shorter has assigned a crucial role to peasants and workers. Degler placed the origins of the "modern" family in the middle class, although he generalized from the experience of that class to the entire society. Not only is there a lack of consensus over the relative importance of ideological or socioeconomic causes in long-term changes in the family but there is also a greater need to know how the changes took place and what the nature of interaction among these different factors was. The "grand" explanations of change are vulnerable, particularly in some of these studies' claims for linear change over time (Stone, 1977; Shorter, 1976; Degler, 1980).

Related to the emergence of the family as a private, intimate entity is the widely accepted interpretation that this transformation was based on the family's surrender of earlier functions. As Demos put it, "broadly speaking, the history of the family has been a history of contraction and withdrawal; its central theme is the gradual surrender to other institutions of functions that once lay very much within the realm of family responsibility" (Demos, 1970, p. 103).

It is still an open question whether the loss of various functions had an impact on the quality of family relationships. The family's surrender of its functions of production, welfare, education, and social control to other institutions and its withdrawal into privacy has become one of the standard clichés of family history and sociology. But the meaning of this generalization has not been fully explored. Did the functions left to the modern family retain the character they had exhibited in the past? To answer this question, we need to understand the process by which these functions were transferred to other institutions. This process has not been documented, however. A systematic exploration of the family's relationship to public agencies and institutions will help historians escape the trap of viewing the family as an isolated institution, completely divested of its earlier public functions. It will reveal areas where even middle-class families ensconced in domesticity retained some of their previous functions and added some new ones. Child rearing is a case in point. The family was already responsible for child rearing prior to its becoming a specialized domestic unit. Following the transfer of its various functions to other agencies, the family's patterns of child rearing changed. The family became child centered, and motherhood emerged as a full-time career (Welter, 1966; Ryan, 1981; Cott, 1977). Another such example is the family's role in health care. Even though hospitals assumed the major health-care functions once held by the family, the family continued to care for its own members during illnesses that did not justify hospitalization or when such services were not available.

We also need to examine the family's relationship to the institutions of education, welfare, and social control after the family's functions were transferred to these institutions. Historical studies of the family have generated several models governing this interaction. The first model, articulated by Demos, emphasizes the family's integration with the community. In preindustrial society, the family interacted closely with the community and authorities in the areas of education and welfare. The family served the community by maintaining social order, and conversely, the community regulated family comportment. The family provided simultaneously for its members and the community in a variety of ways: It was a workplace, an educational institution, a house of correction, a welfare institution, and a church (Demos, 1970, pp. 181–183).

The second model, by Jacques Donzelot, plots the emergence of the private, domestic family that specializes in child rearing after the functions of welfare and social control have been transferred to other institutions. According to this model, middle-class families enjoyed considerable privacy from public institutions, but working-class families, particularly families of the poor, were subject to control and "policing" by the state and various agencies of social control. Eventually, middle-class families became an instrument of the state for controlling and manipulating lower-class families (Katz, 1968, 1986; Donzelot, 1979).

The third model, advanced by Christopher Lasch, expands the concept of social control of the family to all classes but uses evidence primarily from the middle-class family. After the family had transferred all its functions to external agencies, it became a "haven in a heartless world." Rather than being left alone in its retreat, the family was subjected to interference and control by government, social workers, efficiency experts, and even social scientists:

> Most of the writing on the modern family takes for granted the "isolation" of the nuclear family. . . . It assumes that this isolation makes the family impervious to outside influences. In reality, the modern world intrudes at every point and obliterates its privacy. The sanctity of the home is a sham in a world dominated by giant corporations and by the apparatus of mass promotion. (Lasch, 1977, p. xvii)

The models of "policing" the family proposed by Donzelot and Lasch share a view of the family as a passive entity vis-à-vis public agencies and the state. But as historians of the 1990s return to an interest in the state and in public policy as subjects of inquiry, it would be fruitful to reexamine the family's relationship to public agencies and bureaucracies as a dynamic process of interaction. There are many other examples of the family's interaction with powerful institutions: David Herlihy documented the "emergence of the couple" in the Middle Ages as a result of a "fit" between the strategies of the Catholic Church and those of families: In order to consolidate property and maintain it within the family, families cooperated with the church and accepted laws of monogamy and prohibitions of incest (Herlihy, 1987).

Maris Vinovskis examined the family's uneasy relationship with the school during the transfer of educational functions to the state in nineteenth-century American society. Although "parents during the nineteenth century increasingly turned their children over to the schools . . . [and therefore] sometimes . . . had to accept educational and disciplinary practices which they did not favor," they were able to exercise influences over the school "since schoolteachers and administrators in most communities still were not sufficiently powerful simply to ignore the demands of parents" (Vinovskis, 1987, pp. 19–38).

Even if the family could not be an equal partner, it was by no means a "passive" agent. For example, Linda Gordon found that even under the worst cases of powerlessness, victims of child abuse and family violence struggled against their caretaking agencies and their abusers to retain control:

> Even in the worst times, there were many family violence victims attempting to become the heroes of their own lives. . . . Using the powers of the weak . . . attempting to replace with creativity and stubbornness what they lack in resources, they manipulated every device at their disposal to free themselves from abuse. (Gordon, 1988, p. 290)

A dramatic example of the family's resilience and resistance is its interaction with the most oppressive of all institutions—slavery. In this area, the lasting contribution of Herbert Gutman's work has been to document the vitality of family and kinship ties among slaves and their survival despite the breakup of families by the masters (Gutman, 1976a).

Most recent historical studies have emphasized an integrated view of the family both as a private entity and as an object of the state. *The History of Private Life*, a multivolume series under the general editorship of Philippe Ariès and Georges Duby, deserves particular comment. The fourth volume, *From the Fires of Revolution to the Great War*, edited by Michelle Perrot, presents the experiential history of the family in its diverse forms. The authors view the family's private life, its domestic life and sexuality, as inseparable from the state: "The history of private life is more than anecdotal," wrote Perrot in her introduction, "It is the political history of everyday life." Establishing an equilibrium between public and private was a delicate matter: "The nineteenth century made a desperate effort to stabilize the boundary between public and private by mooring it to the family, with the father as sovereign: But just when things seemed firmly in place, they began to slip and slide" (Perrot, 1990, p. 669).

A natural extension of the earlier explorations by French scholars, Perrot's volume does not merely use *mentalité* as an explanatory variable but treats it as a subject of investigation in its own right. The study goes beyond the earlier works on roles and attitudes within the family's domestic abode and reaches not only into the family's private life and activities but also into the realm of emotions. Inspired by the "new cultural history" and anthropology, this exploration of the internal dynamics of family life exploits an imaginative array of sources, including art, in its efforts to reconstruct family rituals and relationships. What makes this ambitious approach particularly valuable is the authors' linking of patterns derived from cultural and literary sources and personal documents with demographic patterns.

It is important to note that privacy in the nineteenth century as documented in this volume does not connote individual privacy. Rather, the authors emphasize the privacy of the family as a collective entity. Ariès's original message runs through the entire script: The family enshrined itself in the privacy of the home and supported its domestic existence with various material props, myths, and rituals. The negative consequences of this process were predictable: The private family isolated its individual members from sociability and diversity of role models and exercised excessive control over them. This powerful control by the family over the individual led eventually to the "cries and whispers"—to rebellion and suffering, as expressed in emotional dysfunction, breakdown, impotence, neurasthenia, and psychosomatic diseases in individuals who felt trapped by the family and confused about their social identity. The next historical step was the emancipation of the individual from the oppression of the conformity-seeking private family (Perrot, 1990, pp. 615–649).

The emphasis of Perrot and her contributors on the family as the creator of its own lifestyle, history, and identity, even of its own documents (letters, for example), emerges as a significant theme in this study—one that historians have not sufficiently addressed. Perrot's characterization of the family contributes to a research agenda: "The family describes itself, thinks of itself and represents itself as a unified entity maintained by a constant flow of blood, money, sentiments, secrets, and memories" (Perrot, 1990, p. 131). The family as the creator of its own documents and memories is also emphasized by Christiane Klapish-Zuber. Through her analysis of the *Ricordanze* (individual autobiographies and memoirs) in Renaissance Florence, she discussed the creation of family histories and genealogies as part of the family's effort to reaffirm its lineage for its descendants and to establish its "name." Both Klapish-Zuber and Perrot focused on the significance of property, real and symbolic, as a source of the family's power identity and future legacy as well as a source of conflict and competition among family members (Klapish-Zuber, 1990).

It is important to link the new dimensions of the family's private and inner life that emanate form the "new cultural history" with the demographic patterns of household structure and kinship and economic activity reconstructed over the past two and one-half decades. One would then be able to interpret the family's inner life in the past in a rich social-structural context.

As further research continues to emerge, it becomes necessary to develop a comprehensive model of change in family behavior that does justice to its complexity. The main dissatisfaction with the studies of change over time that emerged in the 1970s has been their linearity and their generalizations for the entire society based on the experience of one class, usually the middle class. The most important dimension still absent from studies of long-term changes in the family involves more systematic distinctions in family patterns and processes of change among different social classes. We need a more detailed understanding of the historical process by which other classes adopted middle-class family behavior, if, indeed, that was the case, and of what class differences have survived such a process. How did patterns of family behavior that first emerged in the middle class transfer to other classes in society and by what processes? If one rejects simplistic models of a "trickle-down" theory, how did other social classes make their transition from a collective family economy enmeshed in a multiplicity of functions in the household to a domestic, child-centered, private family?

Equally important, at the end of that process, had rural and working-class families really adopted middle-class family forms, or did differences persist underneath apparent similarities? The intense focus on family history in Western Europe and in the United States has left similar questions about Eastern Europe and other parts of the world unanswered. A cursory comparison of changes in the family in the United States and Japan, for instance, suggests how profoundly different internal family relations are in the two societies, even though on the surface the Japanese family seems to be heading in the direction of the American family (see Morioka, 1987; Hareven and Masaoka, 1988; Kumagai, 1983; R. J. Smith, 1983; Hogan and Mochizuki, 1988).

The question about when and how change takes place needs to be asked again. Various strands of change in family history still need to be

traced individually, to the point of their culmination as visible transformations. The process is rendered more difficult by the fact that not all the
strands undergo change at the same pace. Since the family is not a mono-
lith, different members within it may initiate change or accept change at
different points. For example, women were agents of change in certain aspects of family life, such as the introduction of family limitations, while
men were innovators in others. Even children were innovators in certain
areas (Hareven, 1976b). They may have brought literacy into the family,
new perceptions of behavior they learned in school, or new work habits
and new technologies. Thus, when we examine the family's role in the
process of social change, we need to differentiate among the respective
roles of members within the family in interacting with these processes.
This is an important task for future decades.

When the historical study of the family first emerged, it drew its vitality and motivation from the need to link discrete family patterns to the
community and to the larger processes of social change. That original impetus was shared by the pioneer generation of family historians, and it
endowed the historical study of the family with its initial depth and energy. Doing justice to this goal and achieving the proper equilibrium between the reconstruction of time-specific family patterns and their linkage to larger social processes continues to be a major challenge.

2

The Dynamics of Kin in an Industrial Community

Introduction

This chapter examines the role of kinship in the process of migration and the adjustment of immigrant workers to industrial conditions. It focuses on three interrelated areas of kin activities: first, the recruitment of immigrant workers to the textile industry under the auspices of kin—a process that joins migratory origin and destination into one social system; second, the role of kin within the factory, particularly in hiring, job placement, and the control of work processes; and third, overlapping both processes, the general function of kin assistance in critical life situations, most notably during periods of unemployment and insecurity. The last section examines these patterns in the larger context of the significance of kin assistance and of historical changes in the functions of kin. I explore these areas empirically in a case study of French-Canadian immigrants in an American industrial community, Manchester, New Hampshire, from 1880

*The larger project of which this chapter is part was supported by grants from the National Endowment for the Humanities, the New Hampshire Council for the Humanities, the Merrimack Valley Textile Museum, and the New Hampshire Charitable Funds and Affiliated Trusts. I am grateful to the above foundations and to all the research assistants who worked on this ten-year-long project, all of whom are acknowledged in *Family Time and Industrial Time* (Hareven, 1982), and to the Manchester Historic Association, where the Amoskeag Company's individual employee files are housed and where a major part of this research was conducted.

This chapter combines parts from the article "The Dynamics of Kin in an Industrial Community," which originally appeared in the *American Journal of Sociology*, 84 Supplement, 1978, with the chapter "The Dynamics of Kin," in Tamara K. Hareven, *Family Time and Industrial Time: The Relationship Between the Family and Work in a New England Industrial Community* (New York: Cambridge University Press, 1982; reprint Lanham, MD: University Press of America, 1993). Reprinted with the permission of the University of Chicago Press. © 1978 by the University of Chicago. All rights reserved.

to 1930, a period encompassing both the peak of Manchester's industrial development and its subsequent decline. The chapter interprets these empirical findings in the context of sociological theories of kinship. In doing so, it points to those areas of research where sociological theories have influenced historical analyses of kinship; and conversely, it suggests the extent to which historical findings can reorient current thinking about the role of kin and modify historical and sociological generalizations about family change.

Until recently, historians have paid little attention to changing functions of kin in relation to industrialization and to the role of kin in adaptation to industrial life. Only since the 1970s have historians begun to address the role of kin as an important aspect of family behavior in the past. Prior to that, the literature on the history of the family focused primarily on household structure rather than on the organization and functions of kin. This concentration on the household has led to a definition restricting the "family" to the household, thereby overlooking the role of extended kin members who did not reside with the nuclear family. This was partly a product of historians' efforts to document the persistence of nuclear household structures in Western society over the past three centuries. This emphasis, however, has reinforced the confusion of household with family and, except for preindustrial society, has confined most analyses of family structure to the household unit. Historical scholarship has thus contributed inadvertently to the myth of the "isolated nuclear family" in modern urban society, which was prevalent in sociological theories (Parsons, 1943, pp. 22–23).

By contrast, sociological studies in the 1960s by Eugene Litwak, Marvin Sussman, and others have challenged the notion of the "isolated nuclear family" by documenting the pervasiveness of informal kin relationships outside the confines of nuclear households in contemporary American society. Sussman focused on patterns of mutual assistance among aging parents and married children, and Litwak viewed extended kin structures as "a series of interconnected nuclear families." The focus of most of these studies was limited, however, to the relationships between extended kin members and the nuclear family. Kin interaction with larger social institutions, especially their role as intermediaries between individuals and nuclear families and the industrial system, has received less attention (Sussman, 1959; Sussman and Burchinal, 1962; Litwak, 1960).

Most sociological research on the family and industrialization was misguided by the theory of social breakdown, arguing that industrialization led to the disruption of traditional family patterns. The theory of social breakdown pointed to the erosion of primary group relationships under the stress of the urban, industrial life. This argument, made frequently by the Chicago School of Sociology and some of its followers, maintained that through the history of industrial development, migration from rural to urban centers uprooted people from their traditional kinship networks; that adaptation to industrial life thereby stripped migrants of their traditional culture; and that the pressures of industrial work and urban life caused a disintegration of the family unit (Thomas and Znaniecki, 1918–1920; Wirth, 1938; Linton, 1959).

At the same time, modernization theory emphasized the "fit" between the isolated nuclear family and the modern industrial system (Parsons, 1943, pp. 22–23). Even sociologists such as William Goode who disagree with the notion of social breakdown have claimed that there was a "fit" between the nuclear family and the requirements of the industrial system. Goode insisted that because the occupational system is based on achievement rather than ascription, individuals' detachment from rigid rules of extended kin rendered them more mobile and therefore more adaptable to the labor demands of modern industry. It should be noted, however, that Goode views the conjugal family's integration with the industrial system as one that serves industry but at the same time places workers at the mercy of the factory system. "The lower-class family pattern is indeed most 'integrated' with the industrial system," Goode wrote, "but mainly in the sense that the individual is forced to enter its labor market with far less family support—his family *does not prevent industry from using him for its goals*. He may move where the system needs him, hopefully where his best opportunity lies, since no extended kin network will interest itself greatly in his fate" (italics in original; Goode, 1963, pp. 12–13). As will be shown here, however, entire families depended on the factory as their employer; the factories, in turn, depended on the recruitment of family groups to maintain a continuous labor supply.

The challenge to the theory of social breakdown followed several stages. Neil Smelser's (1959) contribution was significant. First, his discovery that in the early phases of industrialization in England, entire families were recruited as work units in the early factory system has challenged prevailing theories of family breakdown under the impact of industrialization. Subsequently, Michael Anderson's (1972) study of family structure and the functions of kin in nineteenth-century Lancashire has documented the survival of vital kin functions among industrial workers in Preston, especially the continuation of family involvement with textile factories in the period 1830–1850. Anderson also provides significant documentation for the vital role of kin in the process of migration and in adaptation to industrial conditions. However, his analysis is limited primarily to the role of kin assistance in critical life situations rather than to their continuing active involvement in the workplace. No comparable historical analysis of kinship in industrial communities has been attempted so far for the United States.

As this study will show, kin fulfilled a major role in workers' adaptations to the industrial system. The significance of their function is clear, particularly in what is generally considered an impersonal industrial system where each worker presumably represents only one link in the production system and where the factory environment is considered alienating and threatening. In reality, the workers created their own world within the factory, a world in which kinship ties and family status were used to manipulate the system.

The Historical Context: Manchester, New Hampshire

This study examines the role of kin among French-Canadian immigrant textile laborers who worked in the Amoskeag Manufacturing Company in Manchester, New Hampshire, during the period 1880–1936. French Canadians composed at least one-third of the labor force in the Amoskeag Mills at the peak of the corporation's industrial development during the first two decades of the twentieth century and during its subsequent decline. Manchester, a city of 55,000 inhabitants at the beginning of the twentieth century, was the site of the world's largest textile mill, the Amoskeag Manufacturing Company, which employed an average of 14,000 workers each year. The Amoskeag Company provides an important setting for this study. It enables us to document the interaction between the family and industrial work in the context of corporate paternalism at the turn of the century.

Originally developed by the Amoskeag Company as a planned textile community, Manchester, unlike the sister communities of Lawrence and Lowell, Massachusetts, on which it was modeled, continued to be dominated by the corporation that originally founded it in the 1830s. Following the example of the textile manufacturing towns on which Manchester was patterned, the Amoskeag Company recruited its early labor force from among rural New Englanders. From the 1850s on, immigrants from England, Scotland, and Ireland began to replace native American workers. In the 1870s, following the textile industry's discovery of French Canadians as a most "industrious" and "docile" labor force, the corporation embarked on the systematic recruitment of laborers from Quebec. By 1900, French Canadians constituted about 40 percent of the labor force in the mill and more than one-third of the city's population. Although French-Canadian migration continued through the first two decades of the twentieth century, the corporation also absorbed small numbers of Germans and Swedes, followed by increasing numbers of Polish and Greek immigrants in the second decade of the twentieth century.

As a planned industrial town, Manchester did not experience the classic problems of social disorganization generally attributed to urban living. The carefully designed and maintained corporation space, encompassing the mill yard and housing for a large segment of the workforce, enclosed the workers in a total environment. The industrial environment was augmented by cohesive neighborhoods organized along kinship and ethnic lines that, from the late nineteenth century on, developed in a fan shape, radiating east, south, and west of the mill yard.

As will be detailed later, the social environment of the city, and particularly the changing history of the Amoskeag Company, significantly affected roles and relationships of kin. The period 1890–1919 represented the peak in the corporation's development. With the exception of a temporary slump during the recession of 1907, the Amoskeag Company reached its peak of production in 1911. During World War I, the corporation made its largest profits. Following the war, however, a curtailment of production set in, and from that point on, the corporation went into a gradual decline resulting from its inability to confront Southern competition because of antiquated machinery, inefficiency, and relatively higher wages.

During the pre–World War I period, the Amoskeag Company introduced a series of efficiency measures and launched a new company welfare program that was grafted onto the continuing tradition of nineteenth-century paternalism. Following the war, the corporation was forced to curtail different aspects of production and gradually to taper its labor force. During this period, the workers began to experience an increasing breakdown in job security and a general deterioration in working conditions. The strike of 1922, the first major one in the company's history, lasted for nine months and marked a point of no return in the corporation's history. It virtually paralyzed the city. Following the strike, which failed completely from the perspective of both management and workers, the corporation never recovered full production. The labor force gradually dwindled, and most of the welfare programs were abandoned. Manchester began to experience serious unemployment from about 1926 on, and by 1933, the Amoskeag's labor force had begun its final decline, dropping to a mere 400 in 1936, the year of its shutdown (Creamer and Coulter, 1939).

The role of kin in relation to the corporation is best understood in the context of industrial paternalism. Initially, there was a close fit between the corporation's policy and the function of kin as intermediaries. Paternalism in the factory system matches closely the hierarchical organization of the workers' families. As long as the corporation followed a policy of family employment, the balance between corporation policy and kin-group interest continued. After World War I, when a conflict of interest emerged, the balance was gradually shaken, and workers pitted their own interests against those of the corporation (Hareven, 1975, pp. 365–389).

These historical changes in the corporation are particularly significant for our understanding of its interaction with the workers' families. The first half of the period studied here was marked by labor shortages, whereas the later half was marked by labor surplus and resulting unemployment, and therefore a weakening of the influence of kin on the corporation system. Preceded by a prolonged decade of decline, the sudden shutdown of the mills in 1936, which left two-thirds of the city's working population unemployed, placed a heavy burden on kin. This chapter examines, therefore, the role of kin in periods of relative stability as well as in times of crisis.

The dynamics of kin, particularly modes of adaptability, emerge more clearly when viewed over time than when examined at one point in time. Within the relatively short time period between 1880 and 1936, it is possible to explore successive changes in the functions and effectiveness of kin in relation to the changing organization of production and labor policies within the corporation. In this study, I utilize longitudinal data files that I have reconstructed from individual employee files in the Amoskeag's corporation records and that I subsequently linked with vital records and insurance records. It is thus possible to reconstruct, to some extent, the life and work histories of a sample of workers employed by the Amoskeag Company between 1910 and 1936. The individual employee files kept by the Amoskeag were particularly valuable for this study because they recorded all fluctuations in each worker's career within the mill, including stated reasons for leaving or dismissal. Beyond the reconstruction of individual careers, the project reconstructed family and kinship clusters of individual workers by linking the employee files with the city directory, vital records, and fraternal insurance records (see Appendix).

In addition to these quantitative data, the study utilized corporation records and oral-history interviews. Whereas the quantitative analysis provides structural evidence for organization and behavior of kin, the oral-history interviews offer insight into the quality of relationships and into their significance to the participants. The empirical analysis reported here—while attempting to weld both types of evidence—actually presents two different levels of historical reality, each derived from a distinct type of data. Although these two different types of evidence are mutually reinforcing, they also often reflect divergent experiences. For example, both the quantitative and the qualitative data provide documentation for the effectiveness of kin in initiating workers into the factory system, but only the qualitative data provide insight into the internal conflicts between siblings or between children and parents resulting from the pressures of joint work situations.

Recruitment and Migration

From approximately the beginning of the century through World War I, workers fulfilled the corporation's expectations that they would bring their relatives to the factory, assist in their placement, and socialize them into industrial work. In their interaction with the corporation, kin served as an informal recruitment and hiring agency. As the Amoskeag Company began to recruit French Canadians systematically, management again relied primarily on the workers' efforts to bring their relatives to Manchester and to introduce them to work in their departments. The corporation thus utilized the workers' own informal networks by encouraging those already living in Manchester to attract their French Canadian kin and to provide the necessary support for newly arriving relatives. The corporation could thus restrict its own efforts to organizing transportation and did not need to concern itself with assistance to new workers.

French-Canadian migration to Manchester was part of the general process of recruitment of Quebec immigrants to New England textile towns, which had begun shortly after the Civil War. By 1882, there were approximately 9,000 French Canadians in Manchester; according to the 1890 census, they constituted 28 percent of the city's population; and by 1910, they composed one-third of the labor force in the Amoskeag Company. Informal recruitment through kin continued throughout the first two decades of the twentieth century. Workers who went to visit Canada on their vacation or to dispose of farmland back in their village encouraged others to migrate and often brought relatives back with them. The Amoskeag Company embarked on a formal recruitment campaign in Quebec, by placing announcements in *Le Canado-Americain*, the newspaper published by the Association Canado-Americaine in Manchester: "More than 15,000 persons work in these mills. . . . It is true that the large company to which they sell their labor treats them as its own children" (*Le Canado-Americain*, November 10, 1913, p. 19). Kin recruitment and assistance in migration and placement meant, in effect, that the trainloads of workers from Quebec were not crowds of helpless people, moving in a disorganized fashion into completely unknown territory. They had already received some firsthand descriptions of the place to which they were going and most likely had someone awaiting them upon arrival. They also had many relatives who were still left behind in Canada. If things failed in Manchester, there was still a place to which they could return.

Chain migration formed the basic pattern. First came the young un-married sons and daughters of working age or young married couples without their children. After they found work and housing, they sent for other relatives. Workers without relatives in Manchester joined former neighbors who were already living there.

As Antonia Bergeron summarized the process in her own family:

> So when my neighbors went to the U.S., I decided to go with them. It cost [my parents] a little to let me go (not money cost, but feeling cost) but they knew the people well and they had faith in me. . . . I didn't know anyone when we arrived. . . . Then I met a woman who had taught me school in Canada when I was small. She worked in the mills here. She helped me, found me a job in the mills. . . . My mother came up later with my little brother and my little sister. . . . As time went on, we'd have another person come up, and another, and finally the whole family was here. (Hareven and Langenbach, 1978 [hereafter cited as *Amoskeag*], p. 60)

The Simoneau family provides a classic example of chain migration: Eugene and his wife first migrated to Lisbon Springs, Maine, in the 1880s and worked in the textile mills there. Their first three children were born in Maine, and the family subsequently returned to Canada, where the re-maining four children were born. After his mother's death, the oldest son migrated to Manchester in 1908 and started working as a weaver; he then brought his father and all his younger brothers. The father entered the same weaving room that the son was working in; subsequently, each child entered the mills upon reaching age fourteen or sixteen.

In families where most of the children had passed school age, first the oldest son went to Manchester, then the other children followed in age se-quence. Once they were established, they encouraged their children and other relatives in Quebec to come to work in Manchester. Chain migra-tion was not limited to Manchester. Although the major migration route led from Quebec to Manchester, a good deal of circular and back-and-forth migration also occurred. One former worker articulated the migra-tory character of kin most strikingly and succinctly: "Our family was five minutes in Canada, and five minutes here. . . . One child was born here, one in Canada" (interview with Jean Dione). French Canadians followed their kin into New Hampshire and Maine towns as well.

In addition to facilitating the migration of workers to New England towns, chain migration maintained continuity between families in Man-chester and Quebec as part of one social system. Kin assistance continu-ously flowed back and forth between Manchester and the community of origin. Those who went to the United States spearheaded the migration for those left behind and prepared the housing and jobs, while those who remained in Quebec took care of the property and family responsibilities. In order to migrate, individuals needed not only assistance upon arrival but also psychological and economic support in preparation for departure. A backup system in the community of origin was especially important, because French-Canadian immigrants to New England industrial towns during the early part of the century did not consider their migration final. Ties with the relatives remaining behind had to be maintained to ensure that elderly parents would be taken care of and that the property or the farm (often still functioning) would be tended to while the owners migrated on a provisional basis. The knowledge that relatives remaining behind would assume those responsibilities provided the immigrants with a needed sense of security.

Hiring, Placement, and Job Control

Kin fulfilled a major role in labor recruitment and in the placement of workers in Manchester. Routine functions in this area started with simple assistance in finding employment for newly arrived immigrants or young relatives starting to work and later developed into the more complex service of specifically placing relatives in preferred jobs and departments. As Mary B.'s letter suggests, the practice of kin recruitment was common even locally in New England:

Dear Birt,

Before you come up go and get your permit to go to work. You will work with me all day and a boss over you. I hope you can come up before Sat. I know you will like it. Millie send her love to Kit and Rufie. I hope they will come up soon. Nell hates to go home. Love from all. Come up soon.

Mary B.

Workers at the mill often exploited their good relations with the overseers to place their kin. As the following letters suggest, this practice was not limited to French Canadians:

June 22, 1904

Please mister if possible you get job to give it to that man because he is my cousin and he is family man for family holder.

no signature

Sept. 16, 1904

Dear Sir (Mr. Foreman)

*I am sure that you know that my Brother is working here quite long,
while now all most six months since, and I hope you be kinde if you Please,
and give him another one which with little more Pay to satisfying his own
Poor self and he will be very much obliged to you.*

Very truely yours,
E. Piter

Workers utilized the good offices of their relatives who were already
working in the mill and were able to exploit their good relations with the
overseers to place their kin, especially the young ones, in rooms where
the "bosses" were known to be safe and paternal and where parents did
not fear their daughters' exposure to bad habits. As will be detailed later,
these informal patterns of placement eventually influenced the composition of workrooms and the work process within them.

Even after the introduction of a formal employment office by the
Amoskeag Company in 1911, workers continued to influence these informal patterns of placement for their relatives, through the overseers. After
the centralized personnel system was created, an overseer retained the
privilege of requesting a specific worker through the employment office.
Workers in a desirable room interceded with the overseers to request their
relative from the employment office for the same room. If the overseer did
not immediately find an appropriate place, the new worker took an interim
position, while relatives continued to watch. When an opening appeared in
a suitable workroom, the overseer arranged for a transfer. The gigantic size
of the corporation, with its many departments and the existence of several
workrooms for each operation, made such transfers possible.

The pervasiveness of family influence over hiring and placement is expressed by the clerk who ran the employment office from its establishment in 1911 until 1929. Joseph Debski, having been appointed to introduce a centralized and depersonalized hiring system in 1911, proceeded
to hire his own relatives, one after another. His description of that process
contradicts his raison d'être: "I was the first in my family in the mills.
Then I got my brother in, my other brother, my sister, and my wife
[laughs]. . . . But they don't make jobs. But if there's one job and three
people looking, naturally you can give it to your own" (*Amoskeag*, pp.
135–136).

Overseers supported recruitment through kin because they were thus
assured of having a position filled by someone they trusted. They could

TABLE 2.1   Percentage of French-Canadian Workers with Relatives Working in the Mill at Any Time

Relatives Ever in the Mill	Percentage (N = 717)
None	24.4
1	29.9
2	17.5
3	9.9
4	5.9
5	3.5
6	3.1
7	2.1
8	1.8
9 or more	1.9
Mean N relatives ever working in the mill	2.0

NOTE: Includes people who worked before 1912 as well.

SOURCE: Reconstructed from Amoskeag Manufacturing Company individual employee files.

also rely on workers to teach their jobs to newly arrived relatives and to hold some responsibility for the new workers. This practice was commonly followed by most workers, regardless of level of skill. As a result of this informal recruitment process, clustering along kinship and ethnic lines in the mills became common practice.

Analysis of the kinship networks of the French-Canadian workers in the different workrooms reveals patterns of kin clustering: Out of 717 French-Canadian workers in the original sample of the individual employee file, 75.6 percent had relatives working in the mill at any time, without necessarily overlapping (Table 2.1). These findings are conservative, since the reconstruction of kinship work clusters is limited to those retrieved through the linkage of employee files with vital records (see Appendix) and thus does not include all kin working in the mill, only those whom we were able to identify. Even so, 75.6 percent of the entire sample of French-Canadians had one or more relatives working in the mill at a given time. These figures reveal the tendency of members of the same family to work in the Amoskeag Mills. Of 121 clusters within which kin relationships were established, 20.7 percent included both husband and wife working in the mill, 23.1 percent had couples and their parents working in the mills, and 24.1 percent had extended kin as well as members of the nuclear family working in the mills (Table 2.2).

The most frequent correlation, which involved two members of the same kin group working in the same department, was repeated 93 times and constituted 61.6 percent of all coincidences of kin (Table 2.3). These figures represent kin working in the same department, but not necessarily

TABLE 2.2   Kinship Clusters Working in the Mill

Cluster	N	Adjusted percentage [a] (N = 121)
Original informant only	31	25.6
Husband and wife only	25	20.7
Husband and/or wife and their parents	34	28.1
Husband and wife and their children	2	1.6[b]
Nuclear and other members	29	24.0

[a]Total number of kinship clusters working in the mill for which exact relationships of all members are known. The reconstruction of the kinship clusters is explained in the appendix to Chapter 2.

[b]The small percentage of children working with their own parents is a result of the linkage and trace process. Because marriage and employment records were used predominantly for the trace, it was impossible to retrieve larger numbers of sons and daughters who were still unmarried and living at home.

SOURCE: Reconstructed from Amoskeag Manufacturing Company individual employee files.

at the same time. They demonstrate, however, the tendency of members of the same family to hold certain occupations in the same department. Once a family member was established in a particular department, it was only natural for other relatives to follow, even if the original family member was not working there anymore.

Even more significant for socialization and mutual assistance was the tendency of relatives to coincide in the mills at the same time: Of 103 instances of overlap of kin, there were 65 instances (63.1 percent) involving two or more members at the *same* time and 21 instances (20.4 percent) involving three members (Table 2.4). Of the 105 clusters working in the mill, 59 percent had two or more members working at the same time (Table 2.5). Members of two generations in the same kin group coincided or overlapped frequently: Of the kinship clusters with known relationships,

TABLE 2.3   Percentage of Times Members of Kinship Clusters Worked in the Same Department at Any Time

Kin in a Department	Times This Occurred	Percentage of Times This Occurred (N = 151)
2	93	61.6
3	23	15.2
4	18	11.9
5 or more	17	11.3

SOURCE: Reconstructed from Amoskeag Manufacturing Company individual employee files.

TABLE 2.4   Percentage of Times Members of Kinship Clusters Worked in the Same Department at the Same Time

Kin in a Department	Times This Occurred	Percentage of Times This Occurred (N = 103)
2	65	63.1
3	21	20.4
4	7	6.8
5 or more	10	9.7

SOURCE: Reconstructed from Amoskeag Manufacturing Company individual employee files.

TABLE 2.5   Percentage of Relatives Coinciding in Kinship Clusters with Members Working in the Same Department at the Same Time

Members Coinciding	Clusters	Percentage (N = 105)
1	43	41.0
2	31	29.5
3	17	16.2
4	14	13.3

SOURCE: Reconstructed from Amoskeag Manufacturing Company individual employee files.

TABLE 2.6   Generations in Each Cluster Working in the Mill at the Same Time

Generations Working in the Mill at the Same Time	Clusters	Percentage (N = 105)
None	6	5.7
1	29	27.6
2	69	65.7
3	1	1.0

SOURCE: Reconstructed from Amoskeag Manufacturing Company individual employee files.

65.7 percent had two generations of the same family working in the mills at the same time (Table 2.6).

The frequency of these overlaps in different workrooms is also significant. Out of 151 instances of departmental overlap, the highest incidence occurred in the weave room and the spinning room. Thirty-one percent of all overlaps occurred in the weave departments and 34 percent in the spinning departments. This high frequency reflects the character of these two departments: They had the highest concentration of semiskilled workers, were the two most populated departments, and attracted French

Canadians in large numbers. These were also the departments to which sons and daughters were typically sent for their apprenticeship. The dress room, the card room, and the spool room also accounted for 7.6 percent, 5.3 percent, and 8 percent, respectively, of all instances of overlap. Kin also overlapped in the boiler room (6 percent), in the yard (2.6 percent), and in the bleach room (6 percent). The tendency of relatives to drift to certain workrooms was common to most of the family clusters analyzed.

In assessing the significance of these patterns, it is important to note that the large number of French Canadians in the mills is in itself merely the outcome of the dependence of a major part of the working population on the Amoskeag Mills. Although a high proportion of French Canadians in the workforce could account for the overall presence of larger kinship clusters in the mills, the high degree of clustering that occurred in the same workrooms suggests that clustering was deliberate. There were, in fact, some family-specific workrooms, rooms to which members of the same family tended to return again and again. And this was not limited to French Canadians. The Scottish dye house was a case in point. Certain departments and workrooms tended to attract members of specific ethnic groups and were known, in fact, for the ethnic group most commonly within them. Thus, kin and ethnic clustering often overlapped and were mutually reinforcing. Virginia Erskine recalled the presence of this pattern in the dye house:

> My uncle Johnnie Carlin was superintendent in the dye house. . . . My aunt also worked as a clerk in the dye house office, and practically all of my mother's family worked there. Their father had come over to work in the dye house and when their children grew up they went to work there. My father was Swedish, but he went to work there after he married my mother by virtue of her [Scottish] family connections. (*Amoskeag*, p. 222)

In the Anger family, for example (Figure 2.1), eight siblings and their spouses overlapped in various configurations over their work careers in several departments. In one of the twisting departments, ten incidents of overlap of different durations occurred, involving different pairs of Anger siblings at various points in time, followed by in-laws and brothers and sisters of in-laws. At one point, Florida (Anger) Gelly, her brother Henry, and the aunt of Henry's wife worked in the same room (Figure 2.2). At another point, Florida Gelly, her husband, George, and George's sister and brother-in-law worked there. The next case of overlap occurred when two of George's sisters and one of Florida's sisters joined the room. At another time, one of Florida's sisters and her sister-in-law overlapped; and on another occasion, one of Florida's sisters and the brother-in-law of another sister overlapped. The Anger siblings and their extended kin offer numerous other examples of configurations as well. In addition, the configurations repeated themselves in different forms in other workrooms. For example, in one of the spinning rooms, Ora (Anger) Pelletier overlapped with her sister Robella and Robella's husband, George Gentes. At another point, George Gentes overlapped in that room with his wife's brother Henry Anger. During a period of almost forty years, the members of the Anger family, their in-laws, and their in-laws' relatives moved through the various workrooms in different configurations.

Ora Pelletier's account sheds some light on those movements: Initially, all the siblings old enough to work started work together: "My brothers and sisters and I would go down to the mill together. We'd work together all day and come back home together." Ora was initiated to work by her sister Robella. "Bella had got me a job working with her at the Langdon Mill [part of the Amoskeag] spinning, and Henry [her brother] was working there, too, in the room upstairs." Ora then moved to the warp room, where she got her sister Irene a job as a tie-over girl. "We sisters were always working with one another. We used to exchange our lunches" (*Amoskeag*, pp. 242, 186, and 189).

A new worker with relatives in the mill did not walk into a social vacuum on his or her first day. Relatives were there to assist, teach, and prod. Kin were particularly important in the beginning of one's career, when their presence in the same workroom not only might have made the difference between finding or not finding a job but also offered the guidance and support needed on first entry into the factory by their young relatives. The presence of kin helped initiate the new worker into the techniques and social regulations involved in the job. But the development of a successful career in the mill depended on more than the mere presence of kin. It was related to how well connected these kin were, to their reputation, and to their status in the mill.

Given the nature of textile work and the size and structure of the mill, kin assistance cushioned the first encounter of young men and women with their job. Officially, young men and women started their first job at age fourteen or sixteen. In reality, many entered at age twelve or thirteen. Typically, a relative accompanied them on their first venture to the employment office or to a workroom. The young new workers learned their first jobs from their own relatives in a specific workroom. This saved time for the corporation and made special training and apprenticeship programs superfluous. Workers were able to continue their own work while teaching their relatives, at least in the period preceding speedups and the intensification of the piece-rate system. Parents, older brothers and sisters, aunts, uncles, and cousins invested in the training of their progeny or other young kin, because the work was essential to the family's economy and because they wanted their relatives to succeed in the factory

46

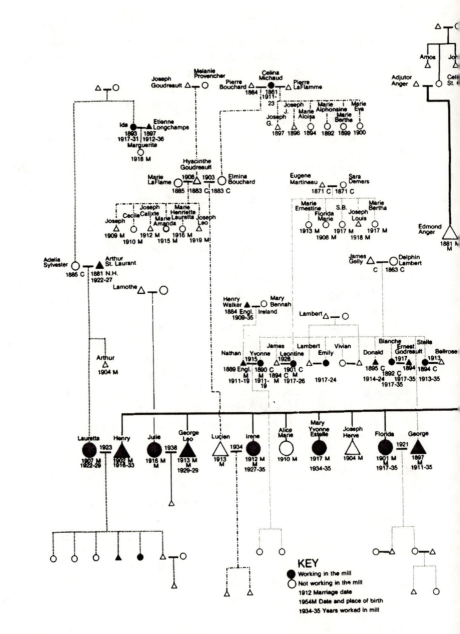

FIGURE 2.1   Kinship Chart of the Anger Family

SOURCE: Reconstructed from Amoskeag Manufacturing Company individual employee files, vital records, and interviews.

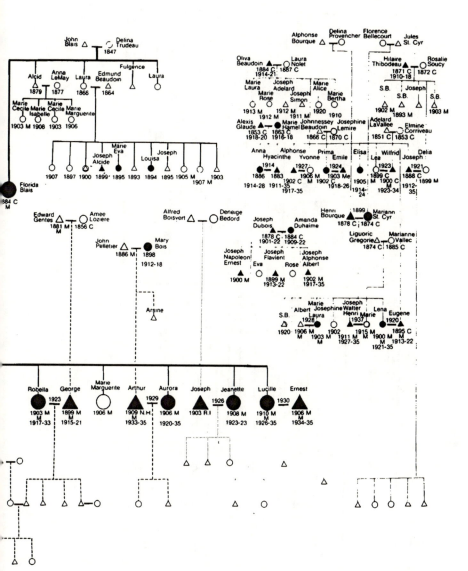

48

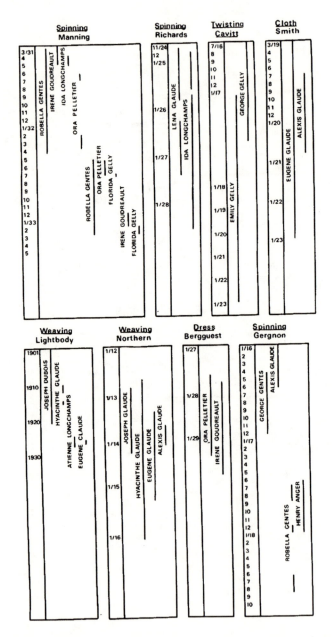

FIGURE 2.2 Work configurations of Anger family members and extended kin in the Amoskeag Mills over time

NOTE: Name at top of each column is of overseer in charge.

SOURCE: Reconstructed from Amoskeag Manufacturing Company individual employee files, vital records, and interviews.

49

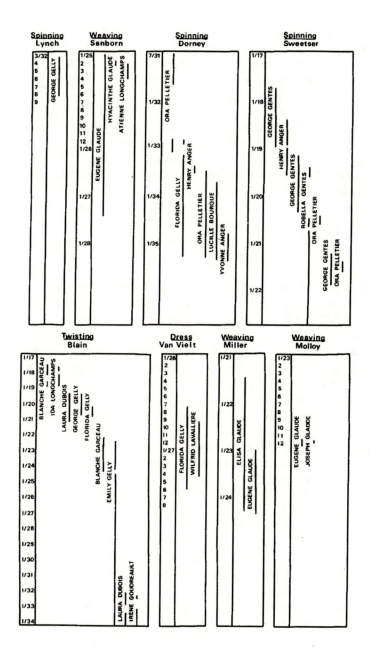

without violating cherished family attitudes toward work or compromising the reputation that other family workers had achieved.

Beyond the immediate assistance extended by kin present, kinship ties provided an identification and a reference for new workers. Workers entering the factory bore the label of their kin. An individual was identified and often judged by the family to which he or she belonged or by association with other known relatives in a department. Incoming workers partly inherited the status of relatives already present in the mill. They were labeled immediately as Joe DuBois's daughter or Anna Gagnon's niece. The status of relatives present in the mill sometimes descended on the shoulders of a new worker, even though the sins of the fathers were not necessarily being visited upon the sons and workers were uniformly treated as independent agents. Nonetheless, the reception accorded a worker depended largely on the standing and interpersonal relations of his or her relatives. In this respect, kinship ties bestowed advantages as well as disadvantages.

Some workers preferred, therefore, to enter as free agents rather than to carry the assets or bear the stigma of their kinship ties. Also, workers whose relatives had supervisory status did not want to be accused of receiving special privileges. Several young men cited unwillingness to work with their father as a reason for leaving their jobs. Particularly, children or close relatives of overseers preferred not to be in the same workroom as their overseer father in order to allay any suspicion that they were being treated more favorably than the other workers—a suspicion that might provoke a conflict situation or cause them to be discriminated against.

The continuity between family ties and work relationships in the factory was pervasive even though the workplace was separated from the home. In contrast to contemporary society, where taking a job generally involves an individual's separation from the family of orientation and the assumption of at least a partially independent career, young Amoskeag workers carried their family affiliations into the factory system. Family ties in the workplace, along with continued residence of unmarried daughters and sons at home and their contribution of most of their wages to the family, show how little individual autonomy was actually achieved with the commencement of a first job.

Training by relatives and carrying out the first few weeks of work under their supervision had the tremendous advantage of obtaining tips on shortcuts and "tricks" along with established work procedures. By imitating the techniques of other workers or by adapting them to one's own tempo, a worker had some control over the pace of work and was even able to secure some leisure time while tending to machinery. Older relatives in the mill also provided comfort, reassurance, and a sense of belonging. The unspoken but clearly conveyed code of behavior in the workrooms and the presence of more experienced workers from one's family group made new workers—particularly young women—less vulnerable to the work hazards, fatigue, and pressure from bosses. Parents took this into consideration when trying to decide to which workroom to send their children.

Relatives were also instrumental in setting limits on work loads or improving conditions that could not be achieved through regular channels. Marie Landry, for example, wanted to be assigned a set of window looms because she had problems with her eyesight. The "boss" told her that she would have to wait her turn till such a set became available. One day she asked permission to switch with her son, who had window looms, and the next morning the son gave notice. The overseer saw through the timing of the switch and eventually ordered Marie to return to her original looms. He then turned the window looms over to a woman who had been waiting for a chance to work near the windows because she wanted to be near her husband.

Kin present in the same workroom provided some protection from accusations by second hands or from misunderstandings and conflicts, particularly where filing a formal grievance was involved, because kin were able to support each other and corroborate each other's statements. For example, Susan Gagne was dismissed by the "boss" because she had missed one day without notifying him that she was sick. When she reported for work the next day, the second hand asked her to leave. She was ready to leave when her sister, who spoke English, interceded on her behalf and filed a grievance with the Adjustment Board. As a result, Susan was reinstated (Grievance Files, Amoskeag Company 1920, 1922). When workers lost their tempers with one another or with the "bosses," relatives frequently interceded on their behalf to smooth things out, to apologize, or to bring about a compromise. The presence of relatives or close friends was particularly important when the work processes were structurally interconnected and where the speed of one worker depended on that of fellow workers.

Relatives alternated running machinery and taking breaks, substituted for each other during illnesses, childbirth, or trips to Canada, and often helped slower kin to complete their piecework quotas. Out of consideration for each other, they rarely exceeded what they had informally agreed upon. This type of family work pattern was particularly important insofar as older workers were concerned. Those in speedier and more exacting jobs traded their know-how for assistance from younger relatives. When family groups worked together, as in the case of the Scottish dyehouse workers, older workers could stay on the job as long as younger relatives were willing to perform the more physically taxing tasks. Relatives thus provided mutual support in facing supervisors and in handling the work pace. The presence of kin in the same workroom, especially those who were well respected or in supervisory positions, sheltered workers from fines, layoffs, and, in certain circumstances, mistreatment by management or conflict with other workers.

It is not surprising, therefore, that workers with kin present in the workrooms or with strong kin connections were more likely than others to advance up the ladder of skill. Workers whose parents or other relatives had developed stable careers in the Amoskeag were more likely to have alternative job options available in the mill, which often aided their advancement, slight as it was.

Family manipulation of the work process could provide a partial explanation for the absence of unions from the Amoskeag until World War I. As long as the corporation's paternalism was harmonized with the workers' familistic orientation and as long as the flexibility in the system enabled the workers to exercise controls informally, workers showed little enthusiasm for union membership. Perhaps it is no coincidence that the union was successful in recruiting larger numbers of workers and in calling a strike during a period when kinship groups were beginning to lose their influence over the work process.

Kin Assistance in
Critical Life Situations

The interdependence of kin in the factory was part of a larger role that kin fulfilled as the very source of security and assistance in all aspects of life. Within the family, relatives provided major support over the entire life course, both on a routine basis and in times of stress. Kin assistance was essential both in coping with the insecurities dictated by the industrial system, such as unemployment and strikes, and in coping with personal and family crises, especially death.

The basic axis of kin assistance, both in families living in nuclear households and in extended ones, was that of siblings with each other and parents with their children. Most mutual assistance among kin was carried out between brothers and sisters and between adult children and aging parents, even after they had left their common household. Older brothers and sisters were expected to care for their younger siblings as a matter of course, even to act as surrogate parents in the event of the death of a parent. Given the wide age spread of children within the family, it was not unusual for the oldest child to be about the age at which he or she could have been a parent of the youngest child.

Grandmothers and aging aunts cared for grandchildren and for nieces and nephews, without necessarily living in the same household. They also cooked meals, cleaned house, and mended clothes when a mother was working. Older female relatives assisted young women in childbirth and took care of the other children in the family while the mother was recovering. Relatives cared for each other during illness (at a time when people rarely stayed in hospitals). Relatives reared orphans, along with their own children, and also took in invalids and retarded family members. Male relatives helped each other in the repair and maintenance of their apartments or homes; when they owned farmland outside the city, they cooperated in planting and harvesting. They shared tools and implements, traded services and transportation.

As siblings left home and established their own households, modes of assistance in the nuclear family were broadened to include extended kin. In addition to this basic interaction of the core siblings and parents, nuclear families were enmeshed in larger kinship networks that often spanned two or three generations and were expanded through marriage. The distance of the relationship affected, of course, the intensity of the interactions. Instead of close involvement with child rearing, health care, and the collective work and maintenance of the household, assistance was of a more casual nature. The level of obligation varied depending on how closely kin were related. In times of crisis or in the absence of other sources of support, however, more distant kin often took on major responsibilities as well.

Even though nuclear families resided in separate households, they extended their reach beyond the household by sharing and exchanging resources and labor with their kin. Autonomous nuclear households drew their strength and support from extended kin. Living in proximity to one's kin was essential for survival, particularly in periods when transportation was difficult or when a shortage in housing occurred. Despite the predominance of the nuclear household, relatives opened up their homes to each other during periods of transition or need. Some newlywed couples initially lived either with their parents, usually the wife's parents, or with an older brother and sister. Couples often shared housing temporarily with relatives after their arrival in Manchester or during periods of scarcity. Generally, however, they adhered to the custom of separate residence of the nuclear family from extended kin. They lived near each other, often in the same building, separate but available in time of need.

The social space of the Simoneau family in Manchester illustrates the conscious effort of kin to reside near each other and the flexibility kin exercised in extending to each other temporary help with housing. When the oldest son first arrived to settle in Manchester in 1908, he lived in a boardinghouse. When his widowed father and younger siblings joined him two years later, the family lived in a tenement close to the mills. Shortly thereafter, they moved to the West Side of Manchester to be near other relatives. His father married a woman from his hometown who lived nearby in Manchester. She brought her niece, who had been living with her, into the household. The niece later married the oldest Simoneau son.[1]

As each of the Simoneau sons and daughters married, they set up separate residences within several blocks of their father's house. When only two unmarried teenage children remained, the father moved to the nearby village of Goffstown. Because commuting to work in the mill was difficult for the young daughter still living at home, she moved in with her married sister in Manchester. The father lived in Goffstown until his death, at which point the youngest son moved to Boston. The other siblings continued to live in proximity to each other. Two brothers and their wives shared housing temporarily, first during the 1922 strike, when a brother lost his home because of unemployment, and again after the shutdown of the Amoskeag, when another brother sold his home and moved to Nashua to seek work. Upon his return, he and his family moved in with the oldest brother for a limited period while looking for their own place to live.

The experience of people who had no relatives to assist them demonstrates the bitter price paid for isolation from kin. Lottie Sargent's father, for example, had no relatives in the city. After his wife died in childbirth, he took Lottie as a baby to bars and clubs, where the "ladies of the night" kept an eye on her. Eventually, he placed her in the orphanage until he remarried; then he took her into his newly established household. Another example of the consequences of isolation from kin is provided by Cora Pellerin, who had no relatives in Manchester to take care of her two daughters. When both she and her husband were working in the mill, she had a housekeeper. But during her husband's prolonged illness, she had to place the children in the Villa Augustina, a Catholic boarding school. To both Cora and her daughters, it was a heartrending experience:

> I had never been to a school with the nuns. It was hard for me to put them in there. It is a big, big building, and it seemed that it was just like a jail. That's the way I felt inside. I used to go and see them every Wednesday night, and they'd come home every Saturday. They'd have supper with me and leave every Sunday afternoon at four o'clock. If they didn't come, it was because they'd been bad and were being punished. I used to cry on my way home. I wiped my eyes before seeing my husband because if he'd notice it, he'd take the girls out. (*Amoskeag*, p. 211)

Even though a systematic measure for the consistency of kin assistance is not available, it is clear from the interviews that assistance from distantly related kin was frequent. The people interviewed were conscious of kinship ties that often included extended kin to whom one might be related through in-laws or cousins. Thus, in addition to the actual communication with kin, the mental kinship map, which was often reinforced by an elaborate genealogy, encompassed distantly related kin as well.

The fluidity and informality in the functions and roles of kin in Manchester was characteristic of the overall kinship structure in American society. Normatively defined in American culture, rather than legislated, the obligations among extended kin have always been flexible and voluntary (Parsons, 1943, pp. 22–28). The boundaries for extended kin were loosely defined, centering on the nuclear family as a focus. Goode characterizes kin in contemporary American society as "ascriptive friends." Kin are involved in mutual reciprocity as friends, but "they may not intrude merely because they are relatives" (Goode 1963, p. 76):

> There is no great extension of the kin network. . . . Thus the couple cannot count on a large number of kinfolk for help. Just as these kin cannot call upon the couple for services. . . . Neither couple nor kinfolk have many *rights* with respect to the other, and so the reciprocal *obligations* are few. . . . the couple has few moral controls over their extended kin, and these have few controls over the couple. (italics in original; Goode, 1963, p. 8)

As opposed to more generationally defined kinship systems in traditional agrarian societies, where the place of each member was more clearly determined within the kinship system and where obligations among kin were more rigidly legislated and defined, the extended kinship system in Manchester (and in the United States generally) was loosely defined. Kin relations and obligations revolved around individuals or the nuclear family.

In Quebec, children's opportunities and obligations were ranked in relation to inheritance practices,[2] whereas French Canadians in Manchester adopted a more flexible and voluntary system. However, they followed several basic implicit rules governing kin assistance, which also specified that nuclear family members (and later parents and their adult children) were first in priority for assistance. Customarily, couples also drew a line between in-laws and their family of orientation. The closest kin connections followed a mother-daughter dyad—adult women were usually engaged in closer exchanges with their own mothers than with their mothers-in-law and drew explicit boundaries with their husbands' families.

This sequence of priorities usually led to a multilayered pattern of kin interaction over the life course. As younger children grew up, older siblings helped them find jobs. They aided younger sisters, especially in preparing for marriage and in setting up households. In addition, they cared for aging parents and often continued to assist their siblings later in life. Older children thus were sometimes caught in a squeeze between helping younger siblings and caring for aging parents simultaneously. Marie Anne Senechal, for example, had no sooner finished rearing her younger siblings than she encountered the responsibility of caring for her aging father and continuing to aid her siblings in their adult years.

Within each family or kin group, one member, usually a woman, emerged as the "kin keeper." Larger networks had several kin keepers, but within a nuclear family, the task usually fell upon one member. Most commonly, the oldest daughter or one of the older daughters was cast in the role of kin keeper when a crisis arose, such as the death of the mother. Ora Pelletier viewed herself as a kin keeper (even though she was not the oldest daughter):

> But if they need me, if they have any trouble or you know they're in trouble or they're worried about something or if they need a recipe or something they always call me like if I was the mother . . . No matter what happens you know they will call me and ask me. Ask me for advice, or, "Do you remember how Mom used to do this or that?" (interview with Ora Pelletier)

Kin keepers usually retained their role throughout their lives. Although needs and responsibilities changed, their centrality to the kin group as helpers, arbiters, and pacifiers continued over life and became even more pivotal with age. Kin keepers were at times designated by parents in advance or were thrust into that position by circumstances and by their skills and personalities. Given the wide age spread of children within the family, designating the oldest or middle children as kin keepers was an important strategy for large families.

Some kin keepers remained single because the responsibility of care extended and escalated as they grew older. They commanded greater authority among their siblings, nieces, and nephews and were in the center of family communication. Kin keepers kept track of different family members who immigrated or who married and left town; they scheduled family reunions and celebrations of birthdays and anniversaries. When adult siblings were in conflict with each other, kin keepers tried to resolve the feud by acting as intermediaries.

Kin keeping thus carried with it prestige and respect, in addition to the many tasks and services. For a woman, in particular, this position also bestowed a power and influence she rarely held within her nuclear family, where the father was the source of authority and the final arbiter. But kin keeping was also confining and bestowed many obligations on the person so designated.

Marie Anne Senechal explained how she became a kin keeper. The oldest daughter, she was left at age twenty with eleven children, including two infants, when her mother died. She opposed her father's plan to place the nonworking children in an orphanage, and along with her work in the mill, she took charge of them. Committed to rearing her siblings, Marie Anne allowed her sister, two years her junior, to get married, knowing that this decision sealed her own fate—the entire care of the home would be on her shoulders forever. "It's my fault that my sister got married. I should have told her not to. She was eighteen, and she was the one who was taking care of the house. She asked for my advice, and I said, 'Well, an old maid doesn't have a very good name.' . . . I pushed my sister to get married." But the sister's departure was not free of guilt. "When she left with him [her husband], all of us were at the window; all the little kids. She never forgot our faces in the window. As long as she lived, she always said, 'Marie Anne, why did I get married and leave you all by yourself?'" (*Amoskeag*, pp. 280–281).

Florida Anger, the oldest daughter, helped with the rearing of her younger siblings even though both parents were alive. She and her sisters and brothers worked together in the mill, and her parents assigned her the task of making sure her siblings actually went to work and stayed with their jobs. She also helped at home with child rearing and housework. After they married, her younger sisters turned to her for assistance, especially during the illness and death of a child of one of her sisters. Throughout their adult lives, her brothers and sisters sought her help. She mediated the quarrels over the use of their father's insurance money and his car after his death and subsequently tried to reconcile her feuding siblings when petty conflicts arose.

How were the multiple patterns of kin assistance that extended over the entire life course and flowed back and forth across a wide geographic region enforced? Why did kin assist each other over long time periods? What prepared them to pay the high personal cost of self-sacrifice that often led to the postponement or denial of marriage for women?

The most eloquent explanation advanced for kin assistance has been the theory of exchange relations, which Michael Anderson employs in his study of nineteenth-century textile workers in Lancashire (1971). His emphasis on instrumental relationships is particularly relevant to this study. Using economic exchange theory, Anderson argues that the basis for kin assistance was exchange in services and in supports during critical life situations. The motives that led kin to help each other, he argues, were "calculative": Parents aided their children with the expectation of receiving assistance in old age; and more distant kin helped each other in the hope of receiving returns when they were in need. These calculative relationships were reinforced by strong societal norms dictating mutual obligations among relatives. Anderson thus sees kin assistance as a series of exchanges revolving around self-interest and reinforced by social norms.³ Although the time period is different, the Manchester workers share several characteristics with Lancashire's laborers. In both communities, kin provided the almost exclusive source of assistance for a low-resource population with a high proportion of migrants. However, the interviews of former Manchester workers, which provide crucial information on their own perceptions of instrumental relationships, make it clear that certain aspects of kin assistance cannot be entirely explained by economic exchange theory.

In the context of Manchester, instrumental relationships fell into two categories: short-term routine exchanges in services and assistance in critical life situations and long-term investments in exchanges along the life course. In addition to those forms of assistance previously discussed, kin provided money on a short-term basis and traded skills, goods, and services. For example, mill workers supplied their relatives with cheap cloth and received farm products in exchange. Plumbers and masons traded services with each other, and storekeepers exchanged merchandise for medical or legal assistance from relatives.

Long-term investments were more demanding and less certain in their future returns, and the most pervasive exchange along the life course was that between parents and children—old-age support in return for child rearing. Under conditions of frequent migration, exchanges across the life course also occurred among aunts and uncles and their nieces and nephews, with the former frequently acting as surrogate parents for their newly arrived young relatives in Manchester. Such exchanges were horizontal as well as vertical. Horizontally, aunts and uncles were fulfilling obligations to or reciprocating the favors of brothers or sisters by taking care of their children; vertically, they were entering into exchange relationships with their nieces and nephews, who might assist them later in life. Godparents also represented long-term exchanges. Because godparents assumed obligations of future assistance to their godchildren, the people selecting them preferred relatives or nonrelatives with resources.

Although the benefits of short-term exchanges are easily understandable, it is difficult to accept calculative motives as the exclusive base of long-term kin assistance, especially when the rewards were not easily visible. For example, those women who substantially delayed or even sacrificed an opportunity for marriage to fulfill their obligation to care for younger siblings or aging parents did so for no apparent reward. Men and women supported members of their nuclear families even when a more distant relative might have been a better long-term contributor to an exchange bargain. These forms of kin behavior exceed benefits that could be measured by economic exchange.

Young family members who subordinated their own careers to family needs did so out of a sense of responsibility, affection, and familial obligation rather than with the expectation of eventual gain. Within this context, kin assistance was not strictly calculative. Rather, it expressed an overall principle of reciprocity over the life course. Reciprocity, as Julian Pitt-Rivers (1973) defines it,

> is undifferentiated in that it requires that a member of the group shall sacrifice himself for another, that kinsmen shall respect preferential rules of conduct towards one another regardless of their individual interests. Such reciprocity as there is comes from the fact that other kinsmen do likewise. Parents are expected to sacrifice themselves for their children but they also expect that their children will do the same for theirs. The reciprocity alternates down the chain of generations, assuming that the grand parental generation will be repaid in the persons of the grandchildren. (p. 101)

The sense of duty to family was a manifestation of family culture—a set of values that entailed not only a commitment to the well-being and self-reliance or survival of the family but one that took priority over individual needs and personal happiness. The preservation of family autonomy was valued as a more important goal than individual fulfillment. Family autonomy, essential for self-respect and good standing in the neighborhood and the community, was one of the most deeply ingrained values: It dictated that assistance be sought among kin. Few of the people interviewed turned for help to the church, ethnic mutual-aid associations, public welfare, or charity. (It must be remembered that given the stigma attached to receiving charity, many may not have admitted they were aided in this manner.) The first significant acceptance of public welfare occurred in the 1930s when workers turned to the federal Emergency Relief Administration and the Works Progress Administration after enduring weeks of unemployment and the subsequent shutdown of the mills.

In a regime of insecurity, where kin assistance was the only continuing source of support, family culture by necessity dictated that family considerations, needs, and ties guide or control most individual decisions. Collective family needs were not always congruent with individual preferences. Migrating to Manchester, locating jobs and housing, and conversely leaving the mills and returning to Canada were all embedded in family strategies rather than in individual preferences.

At times, such family decisions ignored individual feelings to a degree that would seem callous from the vantage point of our times; Mary Dancause, for example, was at age four sent back by her parents to live with relatives in Quebec when she had an eye disease. When she reached age twelve, her parents uprooted her from a loving environment in Quebec to bring her back to Manchester to take care of younger siblings. She recalled her bitterness and loneliness: "I was so lonesome, I cried so much, you won't believe it. My mother would be working in the kitchen and I would be talking to myself: 'I want to go back, I want to go back'" (interview with Mary Dancause).

Her older brother, who had also been left behind but who was not summoned back, decided to strike out on his own for Manchester. When he knocked on his parents' door, his father did not recognize him. "There was a knock at the back door. 'We don't want anything,' Father said, and he banged the door. So my brother went around to the front. He rang the bell, and my father said, 'It's you again.' Brother said, 'Wait a minute, can I talk to you?' He told him, 'I'm your son'" (*Amoskeag*, p. 51).

Both career choices and economic decisions were made within the family matrix. Families might be described as being composed of units that were switched around as the need arose. Each unit was relied upon and used when appropriate. Following such strategies, families timed the movement of members in response to both individual schedules and external conditions. Family strategies revolved around a variety of decisions: when to migrate, when to return, when those who were left behind should rejoin the family in Manchester, who should be sent to explore other working opportunities, who should be encouraged to marry, and who should be pressured to stay at home.

The subordination of individual needs to family decisions did not always take place without conflict. Many interviewees who had made personal sacrifices expressed long-repressed anger and pain during the interview. Anna Fregau Douville, for example, as the last child of working age who could support her parents, left school and started working at age fourteen and postponed her own marriage. When Anna finally announced she was going to get married, her sisters pressured her to cancel her engagement, claiming that her fiancé was a drunkard. Actually, "they were scheming to get me to support my folks until they died. . . . But my mother told me, 'Anna, don't wait too long. What if I die or your father dies? Then you'd insist on staying with me, and you'll lose your boyfriend.'" She got married and lived two houses away from her parents. Although Anna was determined to live her life independently of her family, she was never quite free of guilt. Having grown up in a large family where she experienced firsthand the pressures imposed by kin, Anna subsequently set strict boundaries with her husband's family immediately following her marriage: She refused to pay her mother-in-law's debts and made it clear to her husband and her in-laws that they could not rely on her to compensate for their extravagances:

I put my foot down the first year that I got married. . . . When his parents used to come and visit me and ask to borrow money . . . I said, "Listen, I don't go down to your house to bother you. I'm happy with my husband

and get the hell out. Don't ever come here and try to borrow anything from him or from me." . . . My husband agreed with me. He said, "I'm glad that you can open up with them. I couldn't talk that way to my own family." (*Amoskeag*, p. 291)

Interestingly, despite her resentment of extended family obligations and her own bitterness toward her siblings, Anna Douville kept the most complete family albums and follows the traditional Quebec custom of maintaining a family genealogy. Her personal resentment of the intrusions of kin into her own privacy was divorced from her ideological commitment to keeping a complete family record for posterity.

Anna's refusal to provide assistance to her husband's family represented a common pattern among women who had been deeply enmeshed in responsibilities with their own kin. Once they married, they refused involvement with their husbands' relatives to avoid taking on new obligations, having just emerged from their own families' burdens. Cora Pellerin, for example, postponed her marriage until the death of her fiancé's ailing mother rather than join his household and take on the responsibility of caring for her. When she married, Cora closed her home to her husband's older sister. She allowed her housekeeper to give her husband's sister an occasional meal, but she did not admit her as a regular member of the household even though her sister-in-law could have acted as a babysitter and a housekeeper. Eventually, her sister-in-law moved to a convent (interview with Cora Pellerin).

Marie Anne Senechal, who spent most of her life rearing her own siblings and finally married when she was in her sixties, drew a firm line with her husband's sister. Even though she allowed her own siblings to live in her house, she would not tolerate her sister-in-law. Marie Anne drove her out of the house, finally, after provoking a quarrel. Ora Pelletier, whose six older sisters worked in the mills, was ostracized by her siblings ever since she cashed in their father's insurance policy after his death and used the money for her own needs. She felt entitled to the money because she was the last remaining daughter at home and had taken care of her father until his death. Alice Olivier still resented being sent to work in the mill at age fourteen while her two brothers were sent to the seminary at Trois-Rivières in Canada. At age sixty, she returned to high school to fulfill her old dream of an education. The interview took place just at the point when she was about to graduate from high school. After all these years she finally confronted her mother, asking her why she had sent her to work instead of letting her stay in school (*Amoskeag*, pp. 268–269).

And Marie Anne Senechal, who defended her lifelong sacrifices for her family without any aura of martyrdom, finally wiped away a tear at the end of the interview and said: "I thought I'd never marry. I was sixty-seven years old when I got married. . . . It was too much of a wait, when I think of it now, because I would have been happier if I'd got married. . . . I knew I wasn't living my own life, but I couldn't make up my mind" (*Amoskeag*, pp. 281–282).

Limitations of Kin Assistance

Paradoxically, the very source of strength of kin in the factory and in family relations was also its source of weakness. The integration of kin with the factory was a potential source of conflict and problems in both the workplace and the family. In a setting where relatives were considered responsible for each other's performance and where new workers were hired on a relative's recommendation, workers often had to deal with a relative who did not conform to factory discipline or who violated some of the basic rules of work behavior. How far should loyalty to kin go? Although workers were not held responsible for the misconduct of a relative, their access to the boss was diminished when relatives hired on their recommendation proved unsuitable. Their own standing was affected as well by a relative's conflict with bosses or with other workers. Competition with one's own kin presented another dilemma. Did one hide the fact of being a better worker? Did one slow down and sacrifice a bonus to protect a slower relative or give up one's lunch break to fix the warps for a young relative?

Some workers chose to enter the mill as free agents to avoid the stigma of kinship ties. Several young men quit because they did not want to work with their fathers. To allay any suspicion of receiving more favorable treatment, children and close relatives of overseers preferred working in different rooms. Marie Proulx, for example, first worked in the room where her husband was second hand. But she decided to transfer after a while: "I was afraid there would be conflict. They'd say that I get sugar and the others get dirt. . . . I'd rather leave instead" (*Amoskeag*, p. 70).

The piecework system and the speedup of production imposed additional strains on kin. Because time was no longer available to teach younger relatives, it had to be guarded jealously. Anna Douville's sisters, for example, did not want to be saddled teaching her spinning. She started work, therefore, in another room. After she had learned how to spin, she asked to be transferred to work with her sisters (*Amoskeag*, p. 286). The anxieties expressed by Anna's sisters are consistent with many grievance cases that were instigated by workers who objected to teaching other workers

Identification with a kinship group whose reputation was less than ideal made work relations more difficult. Once the labor union entered the Amoskeag, family loyalties and the use of kinship ties for advancement conflicted with the principles advocated by the union. The use of kin to get a job, to escape layoffs, to be rehired, and to advance in the mill clashed with the principle of seniority, which the union struggled to introduce as the basis for rehiring and promotions. Workers accustomed to using kinship ties were reluctant to surrender their access to patronage for an objective system of seniority. Even though management itself had tried to replace the informal family patronage system with a rational personnel policy, it, too, opposed the union's demands for seniority, claiming the principle would undermine the traditional practice of rehiring and promotion on the basis of merit.

Ironically, in some situations the union was inconsistent on the principle of seniority, suggesting that workers' relatives have priority in hiring. But management refused to be committed to any specific hiring policy. When the wool sorters' local, for example, insisted in 1920 that families of wool sorters should have priority in the hiring of apprentices, Agent Herman Straw unequivocally rejected the proposal. Although he agreed that giving preference to families of wool sorters was a nice idea when feasible, he would not accept a ruling that only a son or brother of a wool sorter could be hired.[4]

The ability of kin to influence the factory system fluctuated with changes in the fortunes and policy of the factory itself. Kinship ties were most effective when labor was in short supply and prior to World War I, when hiring was more loosely organized. During periods of labor surplus, which became increasingly common in the 1920s, kinship ties continued to be useful in finding a job, particularly as the lines at the employment office became endless. The strike of 1922, the subsequent decline of the mill, and particularly its final shutdown in 1936 revealed the insecurities inherent in a one-company-dominated town.

When most family members worked for a single employer, the family unit was vulnerable to the vicissitudes of the company. Because of the dependence of a major portion of a family group on one employer, relatives were unable to assist each other when layoffs occurred, especially during the strikes and the final shutdown. Unable to save on their subsistence budgets, they had few or no reserves left to share during the strike and shutdown. The strike itself set relatives at odds with each other. Whether or not to strike divided some families and caused conflicts that took years to overcome. Some relatives, in fact, have not spoken to each other since their split over the strike in 1922.

During periods of unemployment, the effectiveness of kin as migration agents continued, though the route of migration was reversed. Kin outside Manchester enabled unemployed Amoskeag workers to find temporary or more permanent work elsewhere in New England or to migrate

back to Canada. As the economic crises in the city and the resulting unemployment rendered local kin assistance ineffectual, workers in Lowell,
Lawrence, and, to a lesser extent, Rhode Island found jobs for unemployed Manchester relatives and shared housing with them. Some workers commuted to jobs in other New England industrial towns. With a
mother or aunt nearby to care for her children, a woman was able to work
outside Manchester. In many instances, an older female relative cared for
the children for the entire week while the parents shared housing with
kin and worked in Lawrence or in other industrial towns. Young women
who returned to Quebec during the strike worked on the family farm or
as waitresses or maids in restaurants and hotels while residing with their
relatives. The existence of relatives in these communities and in Quebec
thus provided access to employment and housing when local kin were
unable to extend such help.

Migration and the Continuity of the Kinship System

Although historians and sociologists have long recognized the importance of kin in communities of destination in facilitating migration and
settlement, less attention has been paid to the role of relatives remaining
in the communities of origin. Kin who remained in Quebec fulfilled a crucial function in providing backup assistance and security for the migrating family. Availability of continued support in the community of origin
was therefore an essential consideration in the decision to migrate.

The networks of relatives, besides serving as important backups, also
enabled workers to experiment with different employment opportunities, to send their sons to scout for better jobs, and to marry off their
daughters. "Long-distance" kin, like those nearby, were sources of security and assurance in times of crisis and often served as a refuge. Some
people who worked until their later years of life retired to their villages
of origin. Some unmarried pregnant women, for whom life in Manchester was unbearable because of shame and social pressure, went to live in
convents in Quebec until their children were born and then either remained there or returned to work in Manchester. Some parents left
young children with relatives in Quebec until they found jobs and housing in Manchester. Others sent sick children back to Quebec to recuper-
ate with relatives.

This interaction between immigrants in Manchester and their kin in
Quebec leads to a revision of existing models of the territoriality of kin.
Most recent historical studies of kinship in the industrial environment
have focused on geographic proximity as the chief measure of kin interac-

tion. Elizabeth Bott's (1957) model of urban networks emphasizes residence in the same neighborhood as the most salient feature of kin interaction.[5] Although the Manchester data offer important examples of the interconnectedness of kin with neighborhood, which is central to Bott's model, they also reflect kin as mobile units transcending the specific boundaries of one neighborhood or community.

Manchester's French-Canadian textile workers had many of the same characteristics listed by Bott as generally conducive to the formation of strong kinship networks: neighborhood proximity; similarity in work (particularly where one industry dominates the local employment market), occupational status, and migration patterns; and lack of opportunity for social mobility. Despite their common characteristics, the Amoskeag's French-Canadian workers differed considerably from London's East Enders in their interaction with kin. The Manchester study reveals that strong ties over several generations can still be maintained under conditions of kin dispersion.

In Manchester, as in mid-nineteenth century and twentieth-century East London or Preston, kinship networks were embedded in the city's neighborhoods. But the social space of French-Canadian kin extended from Quebec to Manchester and spread over New England's industrial map. French-Canadian kinship behavior in Manchester thus demonstrates the importance of intensive kin networks in one's immediate neighborhood and workplace, as well as persistence of distant kinship ties laced through a larger geographic region.[6] Geographic distance did not disrupt basic modes of kin cooperation but led, rather, to a revision of priorities and forms of assistance. Under certain conditions, migration strengthened kinship ties and led to new kin functions, which evolved as changing conditions dictated.

The historic pattern of long-distance kinship ties found in Manchester has many contemporary parallels, most notably among Appalachian migrants to Ohio. In their study of Beech Creek, Ohio, Harry K. Schwarzweller, James S. Brown, and J. J. Mangalam (1971) concluded that the kinship structure provided a highly pervasive line of communication between kinfolk in the home and in the urban communities. Their study channels information about available job opportunities and living standards directly and therefore tends to orient migrants to those areas where kin groups are already established. In this context, their definition of a "migration system" is particularly pertinent to this study: "Two subsystems together form the interactional system in which we wish to consider the adjustment of a given group of migrants, individually and collectively. We have then one migration system to consider, namely, the Beech Creek–Ohio migration" (pp. 94–95).[7]

Continuities and Discontinuities
in the Functions of Kin

To understand fully the role of kin in twentieth-century Manchester, one must place it in historical perspective. Ideally, the kinship patterns of French Canadians in Manchester should be compared to those of their communities of origin in rural Quebec. Unfortunately, only two studies of kinship in Quebec are available for comparison: an ethnographic study of the village of St. Denis by Horace Miner (1939) and a more recent study of urban kinship ties in Montreal by Philippe Garigue (1967).[8]

Were the kinship patterns characteristic of St. Denis transported to Manchester? In the absence of a full-fledged comparison of family structure, demographic behavior, women's labor-force participation, and family economy for Manchester and the Quebec parishes of origin, it would be impossible to answer this question conclusively. This discussion is limited, therefore, to a comparison with the kinship patterns found in Quebec by Miner and Garigue, respectively. In rural St. Denis, kin were at the base of the organizational structure. They controlled the channels of land transmission and all major aspects of assistance and discipline. Symbols of kin permeated religious life, and reverence for ancestors constituted an important component of socialization. Even marriage partners were chosen within the kinship network. Kin directed and dominated most important career decisions. In outlining the stages of the family cycle in rural Quebec, Miner stressed the farmer's perception of the interrelatedness of generations: "Life is like a turning wheel. The old turn over the work to the young and die, and these in turn get old and then turn the work to their children. Yes, life is like a wheel turning" (Miner, 1939, p. 85). Particularly important for comparative purposes is Miner's emphasis on the interchangeability of sons for inheritance rather than on primogeniture. The father decided which son would inherit the farm and launched the other sons into the outside world by providing them with assistance to migrate to the towns to find jobs or by helping with their education. After the father's death, the other brothers customarily left the household, because it was considered a disgrace to live in a brother's home. Also important, for comparative purposes, was the prevalence of mutual assistance and shared effort, especially among brothers who farmed in the same village or in nearby villages.

Migration to Manchester shifted the economic base of the family from landholding to industrial work. It therefore disrupted the basic territorial continuity and the interlocking of generations within the family cycle. The move to an industrial economy obviously exposed the French-Canadian immigrants to different occupational careers and economic organization. Accordingly, it necessitated a reorganization of family roles and a redefinition of kinship rules. The stem family structure found by Miner in St. Denis was not present in Manchester. As indicated earlier, sons and daughters in Manchester tended to set up their own households after marriage even though they did not move far away from their parents. At most, some spent the first two years of marriage in their parents' household. Once removed from the land, fathers in Manchester lost the bargaining power and control they had held by virtue of their land ownership. Thus, the move to industrial cities may have weakened the patriarchal authority of traditional rural families.

However, despite this major change, migration to Manchester did not result in a breakdown of kinship ties. Traditional family structures were not disrupted through the migration of sons and daughters. Migration was an essential component of the family cycle in Quebec. Noninheriting sons left home to work in cities, often in textile towns such as Trois-Rivières. Daughters usually entered domestic service or textile work. Migration to Manchester was, therefore, part of the larger historic pattern of rural-urban migration of Quebec sons and daughters at specific stages of the family cycle.

The factory system in some ways reinforced family ties. Industrial work allowed adult sons and daughters to remain in the parental household until marriage and to establish their own households nearby after marriage. In this respect, life in an industrial town (provided the entire nuclear family had migrated) offered greater opportunities for cohesion and contact among relatives throughout their lives. The dispersal of children by inheritance practices did not affect families in Manchester. As long as employment in the mills was available, children and parents continued to work in the same place, thus allowing continued interaction with parents as well as siblings.

Life in the industrial town added new functions to an already long repertory of kin interaction. The legacy of rural Quebec to industrial Manchester—the principle and practice of kin solidarity—was extremely significant in the adaptation of rural workers to industrial conditions. Once villagers left the land, their kin ceased to be the exclusive organizational base of social life and lost many of their sanctions. However, a corporate view of family life and an orientation to a collective family economy was maintained in Manchester, at least in the first generation. The principle of resource exchanges across the life course took new forms, such as the provision of housing, child care, the teaching of skills, and brokerage within the factory.

A comparison of the organization and behavior of kin in Manchester with that of kin in urban Quebec communities is also illuminating. Garigue (1956) found large kinship networks in Montreal, which were vitally linked with relatives in their rural community of origin, as well as in a number of other French-Canadian communities. These networks did not contain scattered nuclear families but instead exhibited concentrations in each location of kin clusters that, as part of a larger network, maintained contact with each other in several different communities. Individuals and nuclear families generally migrated to join a specific cluster. Migrants often moved to a certain urban community because other relatives lived there. The pattern outlined by Garigue places kinship ties in Manchester into a larger world of French-Canadian networks, a cell in a larger series of clusters—many located in Quebec.

This examination of the kinship patterns in Manchester and its comparison with Quebec raises crucial historical questions: What changes in kinship patterns resulted from migration and settlement in new communities? What behaviors were transferred with modifications and which remained intact? Answers hinge on an overall understanding of the transmission of premigration organizations and traditions to new settings. A systematic distinction between complete transfers of traditional patterns or their modification and new adaptation will considerably advance our understanding of the role of kin in adaptation to modern, industrial life.

The French-Canadian case in Manchester suggests that what has been considered a survival of premodern patterns may also represent modern responses to new industrial conditions. French-Canadian immigrants initially transported kinship ties and traditional practices of kin assistance to Manchester. They subsequently adapted their kin organization to the industrial system by developing new modes of interaction and new functions.

Although the basic kinship ties had been imported from rural Quebec, their functions, responsive to the demands of industrial production, were different from those customarily performed by kin in rural society. Functioning in an industrial environment required a familiarity with bureaucratic structures and organizations, adherence to modern work schedules, planning in relation to the rhythms of industrial employment, specialization in tasks, and technological skills. The roles assumed by kin—hiring young relatives and manipulating the pace of production—required a mastery of "modern" processes, a high level of expertise and sophistication. The role of kin in these areas, as well as in the more personal areas, such as housing, required a comprehension of the complexity and diversity inherent in an urban industrial system. The selective use of kinship ties by the workers of Manchester represented, therefore, both earlier practices and their modification.

The selectivity used by immigrants in adapting their traditional ties and resources to industrial conditions is most significant in this process. Modernization theory has frequently viewed integration with kin as an obstacle to geographic mobility and adaptation to modern ways (Moore, 1965; Inkeles and Smith, 1974). The Manchester case suggests, rather, that kin not only facilitated migration to industrial communities but also served as agents of adaptation and modernization by providing role models and by offering direct assistance. Under the insecurities of the factory system, the selective use of kinship was part of survival strategies and under certain circumstances also facilitated mobility.

Conclusion

This study obviously represents only the first stage of a more comprehensive analysis of kinship patterns in industrial communities. It still leaves a series of questions for further exploration: How did degrees of intensity in kin interaction correlate with different degrees of affinity? What was the difference, for example, between interaction with kin on the mother's side and kin on the father's side? What were the relative roles of men and women in developing and maintaining kinship networks and in shaping different modes of interaction? To what extent did kinship ties hinder or advance social and occupational mobility outside the mill? The extent to which kin also facilitated the movement of individuals into urban white-collar or mercantile occupations also remains an open question.

Another major area that is still subject to exploration is the relative role of several overlapping but not completely identical networks. Most of the individuals studied here were involved in kinship networks, workroom networks, ethnic networks, and neighborhood networks, all of which were enmeshed with each other. Further analysis will have to differentiate among these networks and identify the functional boundaries and sources of potential conflict between them.

Questions must also be raised about the degree of typicality of this study. The textile industry has been particularly alluring to students of the family because of its practice of family employment. This study shares, therefore, the limitations of Smelser's and Anderson's studies, namely, in that it lacks comparability with other industries involving a role segregation between men and women, such as mining or metal industries. It is hoped that future historical research will examine such communities as well.

Despite these limitations, these findings, although incomplete, begin to suggest some direction for a reconsideration of theories of kin and family behavior. First, the Manchester study documents the survival premigration kinship networks in an urban, industrial setting. Second, and more important, it shows that the function of kin in modern industrial communities represented not merely an archaic carryover from rural society but

rather the development of new responses to needs dictated by modern industrial conditions. Third, this study suggests some direction for a re-
assessment of the territoriality of kin. The Manchester study offers a dual
model of kin organization: One views kinship ties as embedded within
the territorial boundaries of the community and is most effective in
studying interaction with local institutions; the other views kinship networks strung over several communities or an entire region. The strength
of the former lies in its stability; the latter's utility is drawn from its fluidity and continuous reorganization. Under certain historical or life-course
conditions, neighborhood networks are more salient. Under other conditions, intercommunity kinship networks are more instrumental. Kinship
is a process; kinship ties can be latent at one point in time and can be revived at some other point, depending on circumstances. Fourth, the functions of kin can be examined more effectively by looking from the nuclear
family outward—not only as it relates to extended kin but also in its relationship to larger social institutions. The brokerage model of kin interaction examined in this study can be extended from the factory to other bureaucratic institutions.

Finally, this study raises some questions about the relationship between
social change and family behavior. Recent scholarship has generally accepted a model of change over time that sees the history of the family as
one of retreat from interaction with the community into an isolated nuclear family. The Manchester data point to the value of examining those
areas in which the family has taken on new functions in response to the
complexity of modern society.

The patterns of selectivity in the transmission of ethnic and family culture to the industrial system described here call into question the linear
view of social change advanced by modernization theory. In their study,
Inkeles and Smith (1974) view the factory as a modernizing agent and
claim that modernity in the factory led to modernity at home, a generalization based on the assumption that modernization in one part of life affects all others. Historically, however, modernization at the workplace did
not automatically "modernize" family behavior. Although the family underwent significant changes in its adaptation to new work roles and urban living and although workers adapted to "modern" work processes
within the factory, family behavior did not modernize at the same pace as
workers' conduct in the factory. Workers adapted to industrial schedules
and work processes more rapidly, whereas changes in family life occurred
more gradually. But in both cases, traditional ways of life were neither
preserved in their entirety nor obliterated.

The observation of Robert E. Park and Herbert Mill concerning the
transplantation of Old World traits to American society also holds true for
family and work, namely, that the mutual-aid associations of immigrants

"are not, in fact, pure heritages, but the products of the immigrants' efforts to adapt their heritages to American conditions" (1921, p. 120). During the transitional stage in their adaptation to industrial life, the Amoskeag's immigrant workers modified their attitudes and behavior patterns in relation to mainstream American culture and created a new synthesis between the old and the new.

In this process, the family was both a custodian of tradition and an agent of change. As a guardian of traditional culture, the family provided its members with continuity, a resource to draw upon in confronting industrial conditions. Familial and industrial adaptation was not merely parallel but interrelated as a part of a personal and historical continuum.

Appendix: The Data Base

Most of the analysis of family patterns in the late nineteenth and early twentieth centuries is based on cross-sectional data, utilizing census manuscript schedules at *one* point in time or at *several* points in time. This study was based on longitudinal data that have been reconstructed from employee files in corporation records and that have subsequently been linked with vital records and insurance records. First, it reconstructed individual work histories of textile workers between 1880 and 1936. Next, it linked individuals to family groups, reconstituting kinship clusters. The data utilized here differ from census data, not only in their longitudinal character but also in the detailed information they provide on both work patterns (in contrast to the simple occupational listings in the census) and kinship linkages (as opposed to mere snapshots of household structure).

Sampling

The original sample of individual work histories, from which the kinship clusters have been constructed, consists of 2.5 percent of individual employee files that were kept by the Amoskeag Manufacturing Company for each worker for the period 1910–1936 (when the mill shut down). The 1,816 original individual files represent every fortieth file out of a total of 73,640 in the corporation's employee files. These files listed each hiring and termination of a worker on an individual slip. In addition to the type of job department and name of overseer at each hiring, the files also recorded age, marital status, number of dependent children, and number of dependents at each termination. Particularly important were the corporation's listing of the reason for and nature of each termination (voluntary, dismissal, or transfer), information on ethnic background, and address at each termination.

The first stage of the project involved the reconstruction of work histories for each individual in the original sample and the coding of each for the computer. The second stage was a directory trace. Each individual from the employee sample was traced in the Manchester city directory, starting from the year in which the individual was first found in the employee file. The trace followed the individual every two years, moving backward to the earliest listing and forward to the last listing found in the directory during or after employment. This trace enabled us to reconstruct the careers of those individuals who worked in other occupations prior to or subsequent to their employment by the Amoskeag or after the shutdown of the mill in 1936. The trace also revealed the workers' occupations in the city during gaps in their work history at the Amoskeag Company or whenever they were working simultaneously in the mill and outside it. The directory listed all males older than eighteen, and after 1916, it also included women, married as well as single. Prior to 1916, it listed only widows. In addition to occupational career, the directory also provided information on home ownership, boarding, or renting and address changes during the period when the individual was not working in the mills.

Reconstruction of Kinship Networks

The kinship networks were reconstructed only for the French Canadians in the sample. These constituted 39.7 percent of the employees sampled whose ethnicity was known (ethnicity was unknown for only nine individuals in the file). The individual work histories reconstructed from the employee file and the directory were used as the basis for the construction of kinship networks.

Step 1: Identification. After locating the individual from the original sample in the city directory, we culled all those with the same last name as the original individual who were listed in the city directory at the same address. We then traced those individuals listed in the directory to the vital records at City Hall. We utilized the alphabetical index file, and whenever we identified individuals from the original employee file and those from the city directory in marriage and birth records, we added them to the kinship file. On the basis of age, birth date, name of parents, and address, we were able to verify kin relationships. Those whose relationships were confirmed were then traced back to the employee files, and if found there, their life and work histories were reconstructed in a similar way.

Step 2: Parish Records. All doubtful kin relationships were cross-checked in the parish records of St. Marie Parish in Manchester to check inaccuracies and omissions in the city records or misspelling and anglicizing of French-Canadian names. The parish records also revealed additional members of the kin cluster who were tracked back to the original employee file.

Step 3: Insurance Records. The Association Canado-Americaine was a French-Canadian fraternal insurance organization for practicing Catholics of French, French-Canadian, or Franco-American descent. Every employee form was checked in the master file and traced to the insurance record, if the individual held insurance. The listing of beneficiaries in the insurance record provided an additional check on kin relations and also revealed relatives not retrieved in the previous search.

Step 4: Finding New Relatives. The last accessible census for the analysis of manuscript household schedules is that for 1900. Accordingly, we traced all individuals in the sample who were alive in 1900 or later to the census through the Soundex system. Whenever an individual was found in the census (linkage only through males), we added the particular household data for that individual in 1900 to the file.

From the 717 French Canadians in the original sample, we were able to identify 136 kinship clusters. Of these 136 clusters, fifteen had kin whose exact relationship to the original individual was uncertain, and they were therefore eliminated. This left us with a total of 121 kinship clusters. For thirty-one of them, or 22.8 percent, we had only the name of the original individual working in the mill, for whom the information was complete, but we could not be sure that we had retrieved every member of that group actually working in the mill at that time. Two major obstacles limited us in reconstructing more extensive networks. The first was the fact that female kin in the employee files were obscured through maiden names. This problem was only partially overcome through linkage with marriage records. Second, since the employee files did not start until 1910, we lacked the sources for the identification of kin whose work career in the mill had terminated before then.

Oral Histories

The quantitative data linkage provided the major base for this reconstitution. Whenever possible, however, we also verified the linkages through oral histories of surviving members of the original sample or their relatives in Manchester. Whenever there was a conflict between our findings from the records and the oral information, we checked the records and made the necessary adjustments. Figures 2.1 and 2.2 are examples of these reconstructions.

Limitations

The process of retrieval of relatives and the reconstruction of kinship networks was *conservative*. We included only those for whom relationships were confirmed through two or more sources. We excluded all cases where there was a potential ambiguity in names. Since the employee files and the vital records were the major sources for the identification of relatives, the resulting clusters are weighted toward nuclear units, parents and children, or adult siblings with their families. The reconstruction of more extended kinship ties, such as are depicted in the chart of the Simoneau family (Figure 2.3), were less prevalent in the majority of the sample.[9]

75

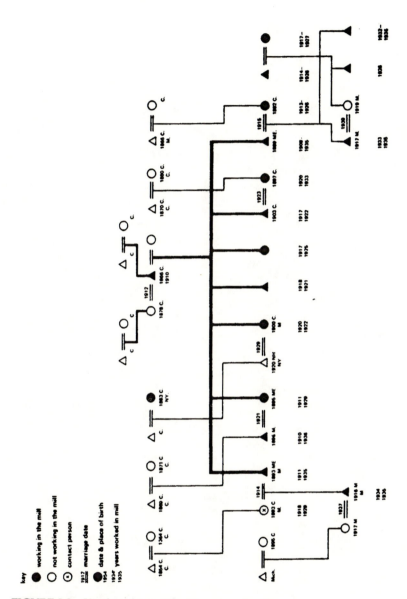

FIGURE 2.3   Kinship chart of the Simoneau family

SOURCE: Reconstructed from Amoskeag Manufacturing Company individual employee files, vital records, and interviews.

3

A Complex Relationship

Family Strategies and the Processes
of Economic and Social Change

Introduction

The historical study of the family has provided important linkages between individual lives and larger social and economic processes such as industrialization, technological change, urbanization, and business cycles. An examination of the family's interaction with the grand processes of economic and social change enables us to understand more precisely how such change was accomplished: how industrial production processes evolved, how labor markets functioned, and how consumption patterns changed. The nature of the family's response to these processes—namely, how it both initiates change and adjusts to change and how it translates the impact of larger structural changes and demands to its own sphere—is best unraveled through the study of family strategies.

As we already know, historical studies of the family have reversed the economists' and sociologists' views of the family as a passive unit to that of an active agent. The key questions that emerged were: How did families plan their lives under conditions of adversity and rapid social change? What kinds of strategies did they follow in their adaptation to changing economic conditions? How did family members juggle multiple roles and obligations as husbands and wives, parents, and children and as members of a kinship network over their life course and in relation to changing external economic conditions? And how were individual ca-

*I am indebted to Kathleen Adams and Nancy Wilson for their valuable comments and editorial assistance and to Claudia Goldin for her constructive critique.

This chapter first appeared as "A Complex Relationship: Family Strategies and Processes of Economic and Social Change," in Roger Friedland and A. F. Robertson, eds., *Beyond the Marketplace* (New York: Aldine de Gruyter, 1990).

reers synchronized with collective family goals (Hareven, 1982)? Current historical research has redirected attention to the ways in which families took charge of their lives, allocated their resources, and charted their strategies in reaction to institutions and larger processes of social and economic change. Such strategies can best be described as a set of interrelated family decisions and plans governing the family or household membership, migration, demographic behavior, labor-force participation, and consumption patterns.

Family strategies involve explicit or implicit choices families make for the present, for the immediate future, or for long-term needs (Goldin, 1981). Formed in response to opportunities and constraints, strategies are also aimed at generating new opportunities. They cover various aspects of family life, ranging from inheritance to the decision to migrate and the organization of one's relatives' migration, from decisions on the membership of one's household to family limitation and child rearing, and from labor-force participation to family income and expenditure patterns.

Family strategies involved not only the decisions individuals or families made but also the actual timing of such decisions in response to opportunities or needs; for example: when to send a son or daughter to another community, when to join other kin, and when to change residence. Strategies involved, at times, calculated trade-offs in order to find employment, achieve solvency, buy a house, help with children's education or their occupational advancement, control or facilitate a child's marriage, save for the future, and provide for times of illness, old age, and death. Strategies were part of a larger life plan. As people encountered new circumstances, they modified and reshaped their plans and strategies in the context of their own culture and traditions.

By examining family strategies, we can reconstruct the ways in which family decisions were made in response to external economic opportunities and constraints and the ways in which the family's internal values, which guided these choices, interacted with external, societal values. As W. I. Thomas put it, "A family's behavior is influenced by what it brings to new situations, the demands and options or constraints of the situation, and situational interpretations. . . . The family is both the product and the producer of its career" (quoted in Elder, 1981, p. 500).

Central to this perspective is an emphasis on family action as a dynamic process, which involves a constantly changing interaction of personalities within it, rather than as a monolithic organization or institution. This approach is strongly linked to a life-course perspective because it assumes changes in strategies and their redefinition over the life course as well as in relation to external historical conditions (Elder, 1981). The stage at which a family finds itself at different points in its life course affects its interactions with economic processes and elements within the marketplace (such as marriage markets, job markets, and housing markets). This interaction also influences family members' timing of life transitions, as their roles, needs, and obligations change over their life course.

A crucial contribution of historical research on the family has been to shift attention from viewing the interaction of individuals with changing economic conditions as being a strictly *individual process* to its being tied to a *collective* family process (Anderson, 1971; Tilly and Scott, 1978; Hareven, 1982). Individuals did not enter the market as completely free agents, considering only their own utilities. They operated, instead, within a system in which family responses played a significant role. In the past, the family often made decisions as a collective, corporate unit rather than as the sum of its individual members. Using family strategy, individuals and families weigh benefits of acting "now" rather than later, by comparing the value of the present state to the value of the future state, discounting for the uncertainties of attaining the desired state in the future. For example, a young person may undertake an additional year of school when either the school itself or its consequences are desirable or at a time when leaving school immediately would not lead one into a new job, a new family status, or some other utility. Or a young person would leave school, however beneficial further schooling might be, if waiting would involve a serious chance of losing the job or the intended spouse.

Thus, the timing of present transitions depends on the intended timing of subsequent (or simultaneous) ones and on the certainty with which subsequent conditions can be predicted. But it also depends on the needs and priorities of the family of orientation. A synchronization of individual members' careers and priorities with family ones is at the base of most family strategies. The collective familial character of decisions pertaining to individuals' interactions with the economy (not only that of families) distinguishes many historical patterns from contemporary ones.

This chapter examines the role of family strategies in relation to external economic and social forces in a historical context and in relation to the process of industrialization, the role of kinship, and internal family strategies on labor-force participation, household membership, allocation of resources, and consumption patterns. It focuses primarily on American society but draws comparisons from European cases as well.

Since the family is a dynamic, complex organization, economists may have exaggerated the degree to which families plot strategies rationally and calculate the respective economic values of their members' services to one another (Becker, 1960). By contrast, historians are much more inclined to examine the interrelationship between economic and cultural variables in the strategies that families use. As Stanley Engerman has observed in his commentary on late nineteenth-century family strategies in American urban communities:

Family decision-making has peculiar aspects of jointness, since it affects and is meant to affect, the entire family group. The family is in essence a group of individuals of varying ages with rather unequal decision-making power, and with a bond of "love" and "altruism" not generally thought to be found in other groups in our society. The family unit operates as a primary income redistribution unit, pooling the income (those funds actually received being only a part of its potential income since some of the potential is forgone for current or future family good) of one or more of its members, and allocating it among its members whether or not they earned it. Moreover, the "altruism" felt for offspring, and their futures, by parents requires considering the integrational impact of certain key decisions. This involves determining the magnitude of intergenerational transfers and their specific form, such as the choice between physical assets and educational expenditures that increase the value of human capital. (Engerman, 1978, p. 275)

Without necessarily assuming rational calculation as the major mode of action in family decisionmaking, historians have, nevertheless, identified purposeful planning and the weighing of options as the basis of the family's interaction with the economy. Strategies that were often implicit in people's actions in the past were not always consciously defined.

The discovery of family strategies in relation to the abandonment of infants has led to a revision of prevailing interpretations. Whereas earlier scholars viewed this practice in Italy primarily as a form of family limitation, recent work has interpreted it as part of a family strategy. Studies by Volker Hunecke and David Kertzer, respectively, have brought to light new evidence supporting the claim that the parents (usually mothers) who abandoned their children to foundling homes followed a family strategy for temporarily relieving economic pressure on the family. Mothers attached identification marks to the infant (such as half a coin), hoping to retrieve these children and bring them back into the parental home. Even though those hopes were rarely fulfilled, the intent is revealing in itself (Hunecke, 1988; see also Corsini, 1976, 1977; Ransel, 1988; Kertzer and Brettell, 1987).

Since very few ordinary people left behind diaries and correspondence, it has often been necessary to detect implicit strategies in demographic or other types of family behavior. For example, Daniel Scott Smith (1974) has inferred women's strategies of family limitation in early nineteenth-century New England from the gender of the last-born child and strategies of parental control over the timing of marriage through an analysis of marriage records and wills in the same period. Similarly, many of the strategies of children's and women's labor-force participation that will be discussed here are inferred from the census manuscript household schedules in the late nineteenth century.

The strategies most frequently uncovered by historians have been those underlying inheritance contracts in rural society, where sons agreed to support aging parents in exchange for inheriting the family farm or other property (Demos, 1970; Berkner, 1972; Gaunt, 1987; Segalen, 1987; Plakans, 1987) or in the planning of marriages intended to preserve or consolidate family estates or lineages. Other common strategies include the selection of relatives or godparents to act as custodians of children in times of crisis (Stone, 1977), family work strategies and the division of labor along gender lines, and family expenditure and consumption patterns (Tilly and Scott, 1978; Mason, Vinovskis, and Hareven, 1978; Hareven, 1982).

The use of oral history and ethnographic methods has enabled historians to reconstruct conscious strategies for the late nineteenth and twentieth centuries in areas such as family work strategies, kin assistance, intergenerational supports, and prudential planning for the future, some examples being education, savings, and insurance (Hareven, 1982; Tilly, 1979). The use of these methods has enabled us to reconstruct the actors' own perceptions of the strategies they charted, the ways in which they and their family members tried to implement these strategies, and the ways in which they revised them in response to changing economic and social circumstances.

Strategies were part of a larger life plan, or what W. I. Thomas called "life organization," defined as "the individual's conception of his aims and the codes and rules by which the individual seeks to maintain this conception and this project in a changing world." Life organization constantly changes over the life course in relation to other family members and in response to new challenges and crises arising from personal circumstances or historical conditions. People adapt their life plans in response to the "continually increasing sphere of social reality." As people encounter new circumstances, they modify and reshape their life plans and strategies in the context of their own culture and traditions (Volkhart, 1951, p.157).

The use of the term "strategies" presupposes that individuals and families make choices and exercise priorities when responding to external constraints or opportunities, at times generating new opportunities. The most important contribution of historical research has been to emphasize that these choices were not guided exclusively by economic needs but rather by the interaction of economic and cultural factors. Individuals and families in the past did not always respond to economic conditions strictly in economic terms. In issues such as children's or wives' labor or expenditure patterns, even economically marginal families did not always make the most "prudent" choices from a strictly economic point of view, if such choice was inconsistent with their family history and their own cultural value (Modell and Hareven, 1978; Hareven and Modell, 1980).

Labor-force participation by married women and children, for example, posed a critical dilemma for working-class families. The participation of women and children in a collective family effort was sanctioned by the cultural values that immigrant workers brought with them to the United States from the premigration communities. Even under conditions of economic marginality, the strategies of immigrant families were guided by their cultural values, which were sometimes in conflict with middle-class values in the dominant culture (Hareven and Modell, 1980; Yans-McLaughlin, 1974; Scott and Tilly, 1975, pp. 319–323).

The Family in the Process of Industrialization

The family's relationship to the process of industrialization provides grand examples of the interaction between internal family strategies and external economic processes. It also reveals the extent to which the family not only responded to the process of industrialization but actually facilitated its advancement.

As shown above, over the past two decades some of the most important contributions of historical studies of the family have revised the stereotypical assumptions that the family was passive in the process of industrialization. This significant reversal of a long-standing stereotype in sociological and economic theory was initially proposed by Goode (1963) on the basis of the experience of industrialization in the Third World. Indeed, historical research provided support for Goode's hypothesis. However, historians have gone beyond Goode to reconstruct a more complex pattern of interaction between the family and the process of industrialization in the past.

Instead of simply reversing the stereotype of the family from a "passive" agent to an "active" agent, historians have addressed the questions: Under what historical conditions and at what points in its own development was the family able to control its environment? And conversely, under what circumstances did the family's control diminish? How did the family reorder its priorities to respond to new conditions, and how did this reordering affect internal family relations?

A view of the family as an "active agent" does not imply that the family was in full control of its destiny; nor does it mean that factory workers and their families were successful in changing the structure of industrial capitalism. It suggests that families were actively responding to the new opportunities presented by industrial capitalism and were organizing their members' migration and employment patterns to take advantage of these opportunities. Conversely, when the system "let them down" by imposing insecurities through unemployment, the shutdown of factories, or depressions, families charted alternative strategies rather than passively succumbing to adversity.

Families did not merely formulate their strategies in response to the structures, constraints, and opportunities that were dictated by external processes. Family strategies encompassed both the family's interaction with the industrial system externally and the marshaling of its members' labor force and resources internally. When following its own priorities, the family also facilitated the advance of industrialization by releasing the labor force needed for the newly developing factories and by organizing its migration to industrial centers.

The case of proto-industrialization provides an especially poignant example of this point: The development of spinning and weaving, knitting, lace making, hatmaking, and other such crafts in the countryside enabled families under this system to introduce new modes of production and new sources of income into their households while supplementing their agricultural production. In England, for example, the opportunities presented by the introduction into rural households of machinery and new production systems for outside markets enabled farmers to maximize their family income by engaging their entire household in proto-industrial production. In Leicestershire, the families of frame knitters employed one or both of the following strategies to increase production and income: (1) hire additional workers from the outside, and (2) establish independent households earlier (Levine, 1983). The frame knitters married earlier, had more children, and concentrated childbearing in the years immediately following their marriage. Thus, the economic opportunities presented by the proto-industrial system led families to revise their strategies and to increase family size at a time when the overall population in these countries had begun to experience a fertility decline (Wrigley, 1977).

Family involvement in proto-industrial production in Europe set the stage for the subsequent recruitment of entire family groups into factories as a new system gradually began to replace the cottage industry from the early nineteenth century on. Once proto-industrial production began to decline, rural families that had invested in cottage industries became vulnerable to unemployment. Recruitment to the factories provided them with a viable alternative, since workers who had already gained experience in proto-industrial production were more attractive to the manufacturers. With the introduction of the factory system, families revised their labor-force strategies and either entered factory work as family units or sent individual members to work. Since the family was the main labor recruiter of its own members, rural as well as urban working-class families participated actively in the initial stage of the industrial revolution.

Even after families ceased to work as units in the factory, they continued to function as collective units in the family wage economy. The continuation of the practice of recruitment of workers along kinship lines led to the clustering of several members of a kin group in the same factory. Working together with one's kin in the same workroom emerged as a high priority. The nuclear family and the larger kin group functioned as important intermediaries between individual members and the factory system in recruiting workers from rural areas, not only during the initial phases of industrialization but throughout the nineteenth and twentieth centuries (Hareven, 1982).

The very success of the industrial system depended on a continuous flow of labor from the countryside to the newly emerging factories. Most of the migration of workers to factory towns was carried out under the auspices of kin. Families that were prepared to leave their rural communities and enter industrial employment or to send some members (usually daughters) to the factory were indispensable to the early development of industry. The strategies of industrial employers coincided, therefore, with those of rural families. The declining fortunes of rural families led them to the release of the necessary labor force required for industry. The conscious use of kinship ties for labor recruitment and migration to industrial centers became a widespread practice as the factory system emerged as a major force in New England in the early nineteenth century. This pattern can be seen in both styles of recruitment of rural laborers for the emerging textile mills in New England—the "family system" and the "mill-girl" system.

The family employment model, which was imported from England in the late eighteenth century, was most prevalent at first in small, company-owned industrial villages in Rhode Island and southern Massachusetts. Since factory wages were low and survival often depended on the employment of all family members, laboring families retained some choice and control over their economic endeavors by maintaining subsistence farming as a backup if factory work failed. Even when entire families moved to industrial centers, they did not completely abandon their rural bases. Much to the frustration of industrial employers, some rural families worked in factories for a time, then returned to their villages and at a later point returned to the factory, often following the rhythms of the agricultural and hunting and fishing seasons.

The second system employed "mill girls"—young women from rural New England, the dominant labor base of the planned, large-scale textile towns such as Lowell, Massachusetts, and its sister communities, including Manchester, New Hampshire. This system depended heavily on the strategies of rural families. Most of these young women viewed factory work as a transitional phase—usually one or two years—between work in their parents' farm homes and marriage. The "mill girls" sent part of their earnings from their factory labor back to their families on the farm and also saved some for their dowries (Dublin, 1979). In the United States as well as in Europe, this work by single women was part of a family labor-force strategy governing who should be sent to work where. It was the common expectation that these single women workers would send their wages back home (Tilly and Scott, 1978).

The back-and-forth migration of rural laborers, according to their strategies, linked the countryside and the factory into an interdependent system. The need for young women's labor in the new factory system corresponded with the strategies of rural families, which had declining income and were trying to find a source of income for their daughters. The factory provided more attractive temporary employment for girls in the transitional stage prior to marriage than the earlier outlet of domestic service.

From the middle of the nineteenth century on, however, as New England "mill girls" gradually left factory work because they refused to accept lower wages, they were replaced by a cheaper immigrant labor force. Family employment emerged once again as the dominant pattern—but with a difference. New immigrant workers, first Irish, and later French, Canadian, Portuguese, Italian, Greek, and East European, were recruited in family units, replicating, in some respects, the experience of the earlier family employment systems. Unlike the New England and French-Canadian factory workers, however, European immigrants could not maintain their access to a rural hinterland in their home communities while working in American factories (Hareven, 1982).

Strategies of Kin Assistance

As Chapter 2 suggests, among transatlantic immigrants, despite the long-distance migration, kin in the communities of settlement continued to function as part of the same social system. Relatives on both sides of the Atlantic and over the American continent continued to engage in various exchanges, and kin assistance flowed back and forth. The assurance that the property and kin would be taken care of in the community of origin provided migrants and immigrants with a much-needed sense of security. Relying on one's kin to find a job was an important strategy among immigrants to industrial communities. As seen in Chapter 2, finding employment for newly arrived immigrants or young relatives later developed into more complex patterns of assistance, such as placing relatives in preferred jobs or departments.

Chain migration—the organizing principle in this movement of workers to factory cities—was itself the product of carefully calculated family strategies. Even when people migrated as individuals, they represented a family strategy. Living in proximity to one's kin in the community of settlement was a critical housing strategy. Despite the pervasiveness of residence in nuclear households, working-class populations in industrial cities lived near each other—whenever possible, in the same neighborhood, often on the same street, and at times even in the same building. The main goal was to be available in times of need, even if they lived in separate households.

Strategies in the use of kin also extended beyond the immediate community to encompass long-distance functions. Assuring the availability of kin over one's life course and during critical life situations necessitated dual strategies: From a demographic perspective, it was necessary to secure an available pool of kin, especially during periods of high infant mortality and risk; from a geographic perspective, it was necessary to assure the presence and proximity of kin in the communities of settlement.

The role of kin was central in the lives of immigrants and urban working classes because kin were the main, if not the only, source of assistance and survival. In the absence of public welfare agencies and social security, kin were the exclusive source of social insurance. Kin assistance was crucial in handling personal and family crises (such as childbearing, illness, and death) and in coping with the insecurities imposed by the industrial system (such as unemployment, accidents, and strikes). In an environment of insecurity, where kin assistance was the only continuing source of support, collective family considerations and needs guided or controlled most individual decisions.

Having kin engaged in mutual assistance required careful planning and negotiation of exchange with kin at different points in the life course and the socialization of the young to subordinate personal preferences to obligations toward kin. Strategies for kin assistance required both short-term and long-term investments over the life course. As detailed in Chapter 2, short-term investments entailed assistance in the workplace, in housing, in loaning money or tools, and trading skills, goods, or services. Long-term investments were more demanding and less certain in their future returns. Among the long-term investments, the most pervasive exchange was that between parents and children—old-age support in return for child rearing (Anderson, 1971; Hareven, 1982; D. S. Smith, 1979). Under conditions of frequent migration, exchanges along the life course also occurred between aunts and uncles and nieces and nephews, with the older relatives frequently acting as surrogate parents for their young immigrant relatives. As shown above, the opportunities and pressures presented by the industrial system led immigrant laborers to revise their original strategies for kin. Traditional functions of kin in rural society were modified to fit the needs and requirements of urban, industrial life. Immigrants from rural backgrounds transferred to the industrial city the principles of kin solidarity and the practice of exchanging resources and assistance along the life course. These principles in the use of kin were, however, put to new uses and developed new functions in response to new industrial conditions: Functioning in an industrial environment, kin developed familiarity with bureaucratic structures and organizations, manipulated work schedules, taught each other new skills, and helped each other interact with the rhythms of industrial production.

Family Labor-Force Strategies and the Household Economy

The various aspects of the family's interaction with external economic processes necessitated a careful marshaling of the family's internal resources, the management of the family members' labor-force participation, consumption patterns, and household resources. This section examines the family's internal strategies in these areas.

Women's and Children's Work

The gainful employment of children and married women outside the home posed a critical dilemma for working-class families. Economic constraints and aspirations for mobility necessitated contributions from women's and children's labor. The participation of women and children in a collective family effort was sanctioned by the cultural values that immigrant workers brought with them from their rural preimmigration communities. Nevertheless, mothers' gainful employment outside the home was not always consistent with premigration values governing married women's work and was in conflict with middle-class norms in American society.

In these areas, family strategies had to accommodate economic constraints and ethnic or class traditions, as well as the values of the dominant culture. The dilemma inherent in juggling wives' work outside the home vis-à-vis economic need in the family and the attraction of employment opportunities frequently recurred among urban working-class and immigrant families. The conflict between family needs and the values of the American native-born middle class, which censored the employment of married women and mothers, necessitated major adjustments by immigrant and working-class families.

The nineteenth-century American ideal that the fathers' incomes were to support their entire families was at odds with the realities of life for working and peasant classes in the communities of origin. It was uncharacteristic of immigrants who came from a setting in which both agricultural tasks and some household manufacturing were carried out collectively, with a division of labor among family members. Working-class families in Europe, too, had learned that multiple incomes were required to meet the high cost of urban living. Consequently, immigrant families frequently brought to the United States a view of the family as a collective work unit. The American middle-class ideal that men were to work, women to tend the home, and children to attend school was new to them.

This discrepancy in values did not pose great problems of adjustment until the late nineteenth century, when the American ideal was fully developed and in the area of child labor mandated by law. At that point, compulsory school-attendance laws and legal limitations on child labor challenged the complex family economy that had been characteristic of both European and American industrial settings. These restraints were particularly disturbing to newcomers because of the insecurity caused by frequent fluctuations of the economy and by the absence of social insurance.

The ethnic culture in which families developed guided their strategies in managing their children's transitions into the labor force, their marriage patterns, and their wives' and daughters' labor-force strategies. Even under conditions of economic marginality, the strategies of immigrant families were guided by their cultural values: Foremost was their commitment to survival, and that usually meant autonomy—maintaining their own family unit, heading their own household, and raising their children at home. Despite pressures of poverty and insecurity, most immigrant husbands, like their native U.S. counterparts, tried to keep their wives out of the labor force, especially if they had children. The degree of immigrant workers' commitment to this goal varied in accordance with the families' economic needs and employment opportunities for women in various communities (Hareven and Modell, 1980; Goldin, 1986).

Throughout the nineteenth and early twentieth centuries, women's labor-force participation followed a life-course pattern. Working-class women commenced work in their teens and dropped out after marriage or the birth of their first child. Unlike what occurred in the 1950s and 1960s, they rarely returned to the labor force after the completion of child rearing. Mothers who engaged in outside employment did so intermittently throughout their childbearing years. Even if married immigrant women did not work regularly on a full-time basis outside the home, many spent at least some portion of their time working for pay, often by taking in laundry and sewing or by housing a boarder (Byington, 1910). Whenever possible, immigrant women followed their traditional premigration strategies—trying to select those occupations that were least in conflict with traditional practices and viewing necessary outside work as inseparable from their duties at home.

Although working-class families viewed children's work as a basic source of income, they considered wives' work outside the home merely as a supplement to the family budget. However, despite the reluctance to send wives to work, women's labor-force participation in certain urban areas was much more widespread than would be believed from a "snapshot" gleaned from the census. The underenumeration of women's labor-force participation in the census has been a recurring problem in the historical analysis of women's work patterns (Mason, Vinovskis, and Hareven, 1978). Even when married women pursued regular and continuous careers, they considered their work outside the home as an extension of their domestic roles and as ancillary to their husband's role as the main breadwinner rather than as a primary occupation (Hareven, 1982; Scott and Tilly, 1975).

Women tended to move in and out of the labor force in accordance with childbearing, familial needs, and the availability of employment (Hareven, 1982; Mason, Vinovskis, and Hareven, 1978). Thus, the occupational structure of cities, in terms of the availability of jobs for women, also had an impact on families' labor-force strategies. The tendency of married women to work in industries such as textiles and food processing reflects both the greater availability of opportunities for women in such female-intensive occupations and a cultural preference for sending wives and daughters to jobs related to what had been traditional "home" production (Yans-McLaughlin, 1977). When employment alternatives were available, wives and daughters tended to prefer work in industries in which several other members of their family were employed. This provided a continuity between the family and the workplace, as well as an opportunity for the supervision and protection of young workers, especially females, by their older relatives.

The recurring pattern in the family's response to economic conditions in the nineteenth and early twentieth centuries was shaped by the dictates of their family's culture. In this pattern, family strategies were to rely first on the labor of their children to supplement the income of the head of the household or to substitute for a missing, unemployed, or sick father. The widespread preference was first to send the children to work and next to take boarders into the household and for the wife to do other paid work at home or a combination of these strategies. Sending the wife to work was the last resort. But families on the margin of subsistence followed all three routes: They sent children and wives into the labor force and took boarders into the household.

Although taking in a boarder or lodger eased economic pressures somewhat, most immigrant families depended on the wages of their children either simply to survive or to lay aside savings to buy a house. As Thernstrom (1964) has shown for nineteenth-century Newburyport, Massachusetts, Irish immigrant families chose to defer or forgo entirely children's education to buy a house. Reformers concerned with the child-labor issue viewed immigrant families' dependence on the labor of their children as a form of exploitation by employers and parents and as a product of indifference or even hostility to formal education. On the one hand, child labor in their view was not a solution to poverty but rather a cause of future poverty. From the perspective of immigrant parents' strategies, on the other hand, child labor was a means of family survival and an investment in future security. The definition of "future security" initially also had a different meaning for native-born families than for immigrants. For native-born families, it meant education and occupational mobility for their children; for immigrants, it meant property ownership first (Modell, 1978).

The economic contribution to the family's income from children's work, especially from that of older children, was the steadiest crucial supplement or substitute for the family head's earnings. Child labor was a common recourse in cases of need, which varied greatly according to time, place, and stage in the life course. Employment opportunities for children varied according to the occupational structures of the communities. Manufacturing, especially low-capitalization, low-wage, large-shop industry, offered fewer economic rewards to skilled operatives but extensive work opportunities for young children. The availability of employment opportunities for children was thus a major incentive for families with numerous children to migrate to certain areas (Goldin, 1981; Hareven 1978b, 1982; Mason, Vinovskis, and Hareven, 1978; Modell, 1978).

Despite its critical importance to the family's economy, child labor in itself was not a uniform practice. Family strategies caused differentials within child-labor patterns among various groups in the population and in accordance with family need. Whether a child worked depended on the family's income, the child's gender and age, the labor-force participation of other siblings, the presence of a father in the household, and, of course, the family's ethnic background. The stage in the life course in which the family found itself was one of the most crucial determinants of the labor-force participation of children. The older the head of the household, the greater the family's reliance on the children's work (Haines, 1981a). As Benjamin Seebohm Rowntree and subsequent generations of analysts of poverty pointed out, children's contribution to the family economy was crucial in the parents' later years of life, as the head of the household's earning power was declining. Child labor was typically the only source of support for widowed mothers, since widows rarely reentered the labor force. In Philadelphia in the late nineteenth century, a younger child's labor-force participation often depended on whether older siblings worked. Daughters were less likely to work if they had older brothers working—a clear expression of cultural preferences (Goldin, 1981). Among the textile workers in Manchester, New Hampshire, however, parents sent sons and daughters to work in the factory from a young age. It was their strategy to keep sons in high school longer, whereas the daughters would have to keep the family solvent through their labor (Hareven, 1982).

At the peak of immigration to the United States, the extent to which families were dependent on the work of several members is apparent from Modell's reconstruction of labor-force participation rates of children ten to fifteen years of age in 1900. In a great majority of cases, such children were living at home and contributing to a complex family income. Wage and occupational structures encouraged child labor more in some cities than in others. In all cities, foreign-born children formed a larger percentage of the child-labor force than did the native born or blacks. This tendency was less pronounced but still visible in immigrant families whose children had been born in the United States. Black children were not as likely to work as immigrant children; however, black married women had a very high employment rate, including those who had husbands present (Hareven and Modell, 1980).

The differences in employment patterns of white and black women and children confirm the interactions of cultural values with economic constraints in guiding family strategies. The fact that both married and widowed black women were more likely than white women to be gainfully employed could be interpreted as a result of the greater poverty of black families. But the lower tendency for black than white children to be employed may reflect a trade-off within black families—a strategy of keeping children in school longer as well as a greater acceptance of married women's work among blacks. Or it might reflect the absence of employment opportunities for black children, which increased the family's dependence on the work of wives (Goldin, 1981).

Household consumption patterns, another area governed by family work strategies, again reflect the centrality of children's work to the family's economic strategies. The allocation of family resources to realms such as necessities, luxuries, leisure, and investments in the mobility of the next generation depended on active planning within the constraints of the family's income. Similar to labor-force strategies, family consumption patterns thus reflect strategies based on the interaction between the family's cultural values and economic opportunities.

An examination of family consumption and expenditure patterns over the late nineteenth century reflects changes in family strategies. By comparing the family budgets of Irish and native-born workers collected by the Massachusetts Bureau of Labor Statistics, Modell (1978) found that by the end of the nineteenth century, Irish workers' consumption patterns were moving in the same direction as those of American native-born workers. Changing values among Irish immigrants led them increasingly to approximate American values on child labor as well as "tastes" in expenditure priorities. By 1889, the Irish had developed essentially the same consumption patterns as Yankee working-class families had, although the income of Irish working fathers still constituted only 85 percent of the income of native-born working fathers.

To approximate the expenditure patterns of the American native-born, Irish families had to rely on the labor of at least one child to supplement the father's lower income. "The Irish, kept in a tight position by the lower earning capacity of fathers, found children's earnings essential to consume in an American Way" (Modell, 1978, p. 221). Thus, although the Irish had become "Americanized" in their tastes, they had not yet become Americanized in their values concerning child labor. By the late nineteenth century, however, Irish families gradually further approximated the Yankees: They replaced child labor by taking in boarders.

Both Irish and American-born families were discriminating in their expenditure patterns: Neither spent money earned by children on labor union dues or on vacations and amusements. On the whole, even Irish families avoided using income from children as a source of expenditure when alternatives (other than the wife's gainful employment) were available. Modell concluded, therefore, that "for working-class people in the American Northeast in 1889, it was father's income more than any other income category that determined the style of life to which a family would direct its expenditures. All dollars were not equal" (Modell, 1978, p. 225). Even though the Irish relied more heavily on child labor than native-born families, they did not use that income indiscriminately. Modell summarized that in their family strategies, the Irish were "embryonic Yankees." By 1889–1901, Irish family incomes from fathers' jobs were converging with those of Yankees, and their labor-force strategies were converging accordingly; eventually Irish fertility patterns also converged with those of the native born.

Use of the Household as a Resource

Strategies concerning membership and composition of the household were closely related to labor-force strategies and consumption patterns. Among immigrant and working-class families in the past, the determination of who, besides nuclear family members, resided in the household was guided by the family's internal economic strategies and depended on migration patterns and housing markets. Unlike today, when the household—the "home"—serves primarily as a private retreat for the family and is, therefore, predominantly a locus of consumption, in the past the household was an important resource for exchanges over the life course. Families could share housing space with boarders and lodgers in exchange for services or rent or share it with children who had already left home and married but who, during periods of economic crisis or housing shortages, returned with their spouses to reside with their parents in exchange for services or support.

The flexible responsiveness of the household to changing economic needs was negotiated and achieved within a fairly rigid framework of an overall commitment to nuclear residence that was practiced by ethnics and native-born Americans alike. Despite the continuity in the predominance of a nuclear household structure in Western Europe and the United States at least since the seventeenth century, households did expand to include kin in times of need or at the later years of the head's life (Laslett and Wall, 1972; Hareven, 1977c). Households expanded and contracted like accordions, as family members moved over their life course, either by choice or under the pressure of external social or economic conditions. This flexibility, rarely seen today, due to a strong commitment to privacy, provided households and families in the past with their special resilience.

Since the household was considered, to a large extent, an economic resource, household arrangements changed in relation to the family's changing economic needs over the life course or in response to new opportunities. Households were like a revolving stage on which different family members appeared, disappeared, and reappeared at their own initiative or under the impact of external conditions such as migration, labor markets, or housing markets. Households engaged in direct exchanges across neighborhoods and wide geographic regions. As some members went out into the world, newcomers moved in. Individuals whose families were disrupted by migration or death were often absorbed into other people's households. Young people could move to new communities, confident that they would board or lodge with relatives or strangers. Similarly, working mothers were able to place young children in the homes of relatives or strangers, and dependent elders, at times, moved into their children's or other people's households. Such exchanges among relatives, neighbors, or complete strangers were laced through the entire society.

The most widespread reliance on the household as a family strategy was the taking in of boarders and lodgers. Throughout the nineteenth century and the early part of the twentieth century, between one-half and one-third of all households had boarders or lodgers at some point over their life course. In the later years of the life course, boarding and lodging represented "the social equalization of the family," a strategy by which young men or women who left their own home communities moved into the households of people whose own children had left home (Modell and Hareven, 1973). Boarding and lodging provided young migrants to the city with surrogate family arrangements, middle-aged or older couples with supplemental income, and families with young children with alternative sources of income and child care. The income from boarders and lodgers enabled new home owners to pay mortgages and allowed wives to stay out of the labor force. The taking in of boarders and lodgers thus made it easier for families to adhere to their traditional values without slipping below the margin of poverty.

In a regime in which nuclear family residence predominated, taking boarders into the household was a more widespread family strategy than admitting extended kin. Why families preferred to take in unrelated individuals rather than kin is still an open question. Possibly, heads of households could negotiate arrangements with boarders on a more strictly economic basis and more rationally than with kin; they could also set time limits for residence and firmer boundaries within the households.

Despite these preferences, sharing one's household space with kin was an important migration and life-course strategy. Families also took kin into the household, though usually for limited time periods and at specific stages in the life course. (Only about 12 to 18 percent of all urban households in the late nineteenth and early twentieth centuries took in extended kin [Hareven, 1977c].) The proportion of households with kin increased to 25 percent over the twentieth century and declined to seven percent by 1950 (Ruggles, 1988). In industrial communities, which attracted large numbers of migrants from the countryside or immigrants from abroad, there was a visible increase in household extension over the nineteenth century. Newly arrived migrants usually stayed with their relatives, albeit for a limited time period—until they found jobs and housing (Glasco, 1978; Hareven, 1982).

Sharing household space with kin was a most effective strategy in the later years of life, when aging parents traded much-coveted household space with their newlywed children, who delayed establishment of an independent household because of housing shortages. Holding on to the space and headship of their household in exchange for assistance in old age was a prudential life-course strategy for urban elders—one reminiscent of the contracts between inheriting sons and rural elders in preindustrial Europe and Colonial New England. Under these circumstances, it was usually the older people's preference to continue heading their own households.

The least-common, though nonetheless important, use of the household was when children took in aging parents, especially widowed mothers, when they had become too poor or too infirm to live alone. In these cases, the child taking in the parent headed the household, whereas in the case of the newlywed couples discussed above, the parents retained the headship of their own household (Chudacoff, 1978; Chudacoff and Hareven, 1978a, 1979). Continuing to head one's own household was an almost sacred goal in American society among natives as well as the foreign born. It was a guiding principle in family strategies. Older people avoided at all cost moving into their children's households. They usually expected the youngest daughter to postpone her marriage and stay with them; if that was not possible, they took in boarders and lodgers. Only when all these failed did they move in with a child or another relative.

Wives and children's labor-force participation, family consumption patterns, and the sharing of the household with boarders or kin were all interrelated strategies and were used as needs arose at different stages in the life course and in response to external conditions.

Whose Strategies Were Family Strategies?

The emphasis on the family as charting its own strategies and making its own choices raises the questions: Whose strategies within the family were "family" strategies, and how were these strategies charted? To what extent and in what ways did various family members participate in the collective decisions impinging on their lives? Feminist scholars in particular have directed attention to the fact that an emphasis on collective family strategies might lead to obscuring the respective roles of individual members in the decisionmaking process. The limited availability of historical sources containing conscious articulations of strategies has made it difficult to differentiate attributes within the family and to identify the respective roles and positions of various members in the charting of collective strategies. It has been impossible to reconstruct perceptions and priorities from census and family budget schedules and demographic data, except by inference from behavioral patterns.

The use of oral history, however, has enabled us to reconstruct some of the internal dynamics of the family's collective decisionmaking process. Family collectivity did not necessarily imply mutual deliberation or "democratic" participation in the process. It is possible that major decisions were imposed by the male head of the family on the other members, although there is significant evidence that consultation and bargaining took place between husbands and wives and occasionally between parents and children (Hareven, 1982; Tilly and Scott, 1978; Tilly and Cohen, 1982).

Within "patriarchal" family systems, where husbands officially had the dominant role in charting strategies pertaining to migration and to their own as well as their family members' work careers, wives made major decisions in areas more directly related to their responsibilities. For example, strategies of family limitation were commonly left to the initiative of women, especially at a time when such matters were not discussed openly (D. S. Smith, 1974). This is particularly true in nineteenth-century society, where roles of husbands and wives were separated within their respective spheres. As evidenced in the case of proto-industrial families, wives gained a greater role in family decisionmaking because of their central place in household production (Medick, 1976). Wives also had a major role in deciding whether and when their children, especially their daughters, should go to work.

When walking the tightrope between keeping the family solvent and violating some of the traditional sanctions about women's roles, wives often attempted compromises such as working outside the home but at the same time reassured their husbands and other kin that this work was only "temporary." Women were also resourceful in finding supplemental sources of income by bringing various jobs into the household, taking in boarders, and producing various goods for informal sale (sandwiches or candy, for example). Maria Lacasse, the wife of a textile worker in the Amoskeag Mills, worked in the mills intermittently during the 1920s while raising nine children and carrying out a variety of other household jobs: "My husband never stopped me going to work when we needed the money. I had to make all the clothes, even the pants for the little boys. I used to sell sandwiches to the girls in the mill if they didn't bring their lunch" (Hareven, 1982, p. 205).

Maria's daughter remembered, however, the domestic conflict provoked by her mother's attempt to work outside the home:

> My father didn't really want her to work. That was a big issue because she always wanted to go in and earn a little money. But the minute she said she wanted to work, there would be a big fight. He'd say, "No, you're not going to work. You're going to stay home." And that's why she did other things. She'd make clothes for him, take in boarders, rent rooms. . . . Sometimes she'd also work little stretches at night in the mills, from six to nine because we lived right in front of the mills. When there were big orders, the mills were always looking for people to work. But my father didn't want to keep the children. That was women's work; his work was outside. (Alice Olivier, in Hareven, 1982, p. 205)

Although men were considered to be the main breadwinners and were, therefore, expected to make the major economic decisions for the family, women were much closer to the routine management of household resources. Women made the daily decisions regarding the family budget, the allocation of household space, and family consumption. Since the responsibility of feeding and clothing family members was primarily theirs, women were more sensitive to shortages in food and supplies and pursued independent strategies to fulfill these basic tasks.

Wives also took the leadership in family decisionmaking in times of depressions, unemployment, or strikes. They were more inclined to make compromises to secure food for the family, a tactic that men, due to their pride and standing among peers, would have considered demeaning. For example, in the Amoskeag Mills, wives went in to work while their husbands (forced by peer pressure more than by conscience) were striking. Maria Lacasse describes her decision to cross the picket line during the 1919 strike at the Amoskeag Mills:

> It was the men who didn't want to go back during the strike, because there were pickets. They were afraid they were going to get killed. There was another woman on the block who said, "How about us women going to work? If we go to work, they're not going to attack us because we're women." So I decided I was going to go back because fall was coming, and we didn't have any money. We didn't know how we were going to live. That's what the strike was all about: They didn't give the workers enough money. But I knew they were not going to win; so when that woman asked me, I had the children kept, and I went in to work. I told my husband to stay home; I was afraid he would be hurt by the pickets. (Hareven and Langenbach, 1978, pp. 260–261)

Similarly, during the Great Depression it was the women who surreptitiously went to welfare agencies to receive food staples for the family, while their husbands pretended that the family continued to be self-sufficient.

Strategies governing the care of relatives during critical life situations—childbirth, illness, infirmity, or death—were also primarily in the domain of women. Because women usually had nurturing responsibilities in all these areas, they had the main initiative in managing exchanges with kin. In this way, women became the "kin keepers," maintaining ties with kin over the life course and holding kinship networks together across geographic distances (Hareven and Langenbach, 1978, pp. 253–274; Hareven, 1982, pp. 105–107).

The extent to which children had an active role in family decisionmaking has yet to be explored. The decision to send a child into the labor force was primarily, but not entirely, a parental one. Collective family values dictated that children follow their parents' decisions; however, the very dependency of the family on the earnings of children gave the latter considerable maneuverability in implementing these decisions. Under certain circumstances, children working and living at home had less latitude or bargaining power with their parents than children who left home to work in other communities. John Gillis found, for example, that in England, mothers in proto-industrial households pressured their children to postpone marriage in order to retain them as workers in the family's collective enterprise. Louise Tilly and Joan Scott, countering Edward Shorter's claim that young women workers in urban areas became "liberated" from obligations to their families of origin, emphasized the strong continuity of familial obligations for daughters, even for those who had left their rural homes to work in urban areas. Anderson has pointed out, however, that in nineteenth-century Lancashire, to continue to maintain control over faraway children and keep them more closely tied to the collective family economy, parents had to exercise greater flexibility in bargaining and tolerating these children's preferences, to the extent that they differed with their own (Gillis, 1989; Tilly and Scott, 1978; Shorter, 1971; Anderson, 1971).

Within the dictates of "collective" family strategies, individual members did not always succumb blindly to family demands. Interviews used to supplement quantitative behavioral data have suggested areas of tension surrounding the trade-offs and sacrifices that individuals were expected to make for the collective good of their families. Whenever possible, individuals tried to resist having to pay the high price expected of them for maintaining family solidarity. Strain and conflict revolved around such issues as when to leave home, when to marry, how to allocate responsibilities among siblings for parental support, and how to divide resources and inheritance.

Under certain situations, individuals pursued their own strategies to protect themselves from excessive family control over their own opportunities to live individual lives. This was particularly true for young daughters, who tried to avoid the predicament of being the last child at home and having to carry the burden of support for aging parents. Anna Douville, whose case is described in part in Chapter 2, delayed marriage and then set her own strict household rules to prevent further incursions on her life. But her regrets about her behavior plagued her later on:

> They [her parents] were on the city welfare. . . . even with the hard times I had during my life, I never stopped for sympathy for myself, because I knew about my mother's life. . . . A lot of things go through your head when your folks are gone. . . . You don't realize it when they are living. You want to live your own life; but when folks are gone and you think of all the good things that you have today, you wish they could share them. (Hareven, 1982, p. 110)

Collective family strategies, although uniform on the surface, were never simple and streamlined in reality. Most individuals and families living under conditions of economic insecurity found themselves in a double bind: On the one hand, the family's collective requirements imposed enormous pressures and burdens on individuals; on the other, individuals were dependent on family collectivity for assistance in time of need. Thus, a rebellion against familial requirements, however onerous, would deprive individual members of access to the only source of support under conditions of insecurity.

Conclusion: Long-Term Historical Changes

This excursion into nineteenth-century and early twentieth-century family, migration, work, and household economic strategies has highlighted the continuous interaction between the family and the process of economic change. It has provided various examples of the family's role as an active agent, where, whenever possible, the family followed its own strategies and priorities. It has shown that under certain historical and economic conditions, the family had greater latitude to exercise its own initiatives, whereas under other conditions, it had to respond to the adversities imposed by business cycles and depressions.

In interacting with the larger processes of social change and with the institutions of industrial capitalism, the family exercised a considerable degree of flexibility in organizing migration, placing its members in various labor-force configurations, allocating resources, and using land or the household as trade-offs during periods of need. The family modified its strategies in response to its changing needs over the life course as well as to external conditions. At times when the family had less control over the economic system, it exercised adaptive strategies to cushion its members from the adverse impact of these conditions and to devise alternative means of survival.

The family developed these flexible strategies within the constraints imposed by markets and historical circumstances, within the context of the cultural prescriptions guiding its behavior. Such prescriptions were especially powerful in the context of a collective family economy where the choices and preferences of individual members were subordinate to the dictates of the family unit. As shown above, individual choices were not always uniformly streamlined within the family collectivity. Families experienced internal tensions and, at times, conflict when individual members pulled in various independent directions. But the collective goals usually won out.

Historical changes since the early part of the twentieth century, especially since the 1920s, have gradually modified the models of the family's interaction with the economy discussed above. Changing values have led to an increasing separation of individual careers from collective family ones. The erosion of values of interdependence among kin has frequently led individuals to place priority on their own careers, independently of the dictates of the family. Consequently, the timing of life transitions has become more individualized and subject to personal choice rather than to collective family needs.

This type of individualization has weakened the family's impact on the economy as a labor recruiter and as an active agent in the workplace. Family needs, such as child care for working mothers, have continued to influence the workplace and have an impact on mothers' labor-force participation. But the family as a unit does not interact with the workplace in the same manner as it did in the past, nor does it influence styles of production or work schedules.

As part of an ongoing historical process, the family's economic behavior came to focus predominately, if not exclusively, on consumption. The household ceased to be the main unit of production following industrialization in the nineteenth century. Urban working-class families, however, continued to behave as collective work units in the wage economy, even when their members were individually employed in separate establishments. Family members working as individuals, often living away from home, still viewed their wage labor as an integral part of a collective family economy and continued to send remittances home.

Institutional and legislative changes have further fragmented the family's functioning as a collective work unit, primarily since the 1920s. The implementation of child-labor laws and compulsory school attendance laws, especially since the 1930s, has led to the exclusion of children from the family's collective work process. The regulation of child labor was finally achieved because technological changes rendered industrial child labor obsolete from the employer's point of view. Parents also changed their attitudes toward child labor, when new values and aspirations among second-generation immigrants led to an increasing acceptance of the middle-class white native-born standard that children stay out of the labor force (Bremner et al., 1971). The increase in married women's labor-force participation since the 1950s, especially in married women entering into continuous careers rather than returning after the completion of child rearing, has rendered the typical contemporary family a dual-earner family (or single-earner family where only one parent is present). This pattern is significantly different from that of the multiple-income family of the past that rested so heavily on the labor of children.

Since the middle of the nineteenth century, the family itself has undergone dramatic changes that have impinged on the family's economic role and on its interaction with economy and society. Following the processes of urbanization and industrialization, functions previously concentrated within the family were gradually transferred to other institutions

(Smelser, 1959). The preindustrial family embraced a variety of functions: It was a workshop, church, reformatory, school, and asylum (Demos 1970). Over the past century and a half, these various familial functions have become the responsibility of other institutions. The surrender of these functions also reversed the family's relationship to the market and to the state. The market now provides the goods families once produced; it also provides insurance, vocational training, and many financial transactions once carried out mainly within families. Similarly, the state now provides education, social insurance, and health care in old age. The family has become a specialized, private consumption unit.

The role of the household has changed from being an economic resource to being...mainly a unit of consumption.... An increasing commitment to privacy has led to the segregation of the family from the larger community. Rather than producing goods and generating income, the household has become...mainly a unit of consumption.... The family as a unit has withdrawn from the world of work, insisting on the privacy of the home and its separation from the outside world. The workplace has generally become impersonal and bureaucratic. Once considered an asset, familial involvement in the workplace is now denigrated as nepotism. The home is viewed increasingly as a retreat from the outside world. The family has turned inward and has assumed domesticity, intimacy, and privacy as its major characteristics. As a consequence, the family has lost some of its earlier flexibility in relying on the household as an economic resource.

This historical transition of the family from a collective production unit to primarily a consumption unit, in which members follow individual careers, has not occurred uniformly across American society. Although these patterns predominate overall, they are more typical of the urban middle classes. Among working-class and new ethnic families, however, some of the historical characteristics of family behavior have persisted, although in modified form. Similarly, the survival of viable functions of kin in relation to economic change suggests that the privatization and individualization of family life has not been consummated across the entire society.

The family's interaction with the economy has followed a complex, uneven pattern. The family has been both a custodian of tradition and an agent of change. As a guardian of traditional culture, the family provided its members with a sense of continuity and with resources on which to draw when confronting change. As an innovator, the family charted new strategies in response to social and economic change. An understanding of how the process of economic change takes place can be enhanced, therefore, through an understanding of the complexity of family behavior.

Part Two

Studying Lives in
Time and Place

4

Historical Changes in Children's Networks in the Family and Community

Introduction

Children have interacted with those who nurtured them, played with them, educated them, disciplined them, and employed them. Such activities have taken place in networks that include family members, other kin, friends, peers, caretakers, and employers, within the family and in educational, correctional, and welfare institutions.

This chapter examines historical changes in children's social networks in American society. Its main argument is that children's networks have changed over time from complex and age-diverse patterns to simpler and age-standardized ones; that, on the one hand, age and functions have become streamlined and homogenized within the family; and, on the other hand, institutions and peer groups have come to play an important role in children's networks, often at the expense of familial ties. These two developments have occurred along parallel tracks since about the middle of the nineteenth century. This chapter examines these changes and their impact on children's lives and raises some questions about their implications for child development.

Over the past two centuries, the processes of urbanization and industrialization, combined with demographic change and cultural factors, have affected the status of children in the family and in the larger society. These changes have shaped children's interactions with various family members and with the larger community. They have had a significant impact on the

*This chapter first appeared as "Historical Changes in Children's Networks in the Family and Community," in Deborah Belle, ed., *Children's Social Networks and Social Supports* (New York: John Wiley & Sons, 1988). Reprinted with permission of John Wiley & Sons, Inc. © 1988 by John Wiley & Sons, Inc.

changing configurations and functions of networks accessible to children. Urbanization has also led to the emergence of institutions of education, welfare, and social control specifically aimed at children and youth. Children have, therefore, been placed in larger peer groups. Urbanization has led to a higher concentration of people in cities and therefore to a greater exposure of children to larger numbers of age peers outside the family. Demographic factors have affected both the number of surviving relations available to children and the length of their temporal overlap.

Industrialization rendered children (initially even young children) desirable as workers and established them as an important commodity in the labor market as well as in their family's economy. Local migration and immigration from abroad have frequently brought children into new social environments, thus providing them with new networks outside the family and challenging them to form new networks.

Demographic Changes Affecting the Position of Children in the Family

Over the past century and a half, the configurations of family members with whom children travel through life have changed considerably, as a result of the decline in mortality and fertility rates and changes in the age of marriage. These changes have affected both the composition of the networks available to children and the character of their interaction.

Life and Death

Declining mortality and fertility rates since the late nineteenth century, combined with changes in the timing of the transition to parenthood, have affected the age configurations and the position of children in the family. The decline in mortality in American society over the nineteenth century, most prominently since the 1870s, has increased the chances for children's survival to adulthood, after surviving the hazards of infancy. The decline in mortality has also enabled children to grow up with their siblings and to overlap with them over an extended period (Uhlenberg, 1978). Before the late nineteenth century, the birth rate had not declined sufficiently to deprive children of large numbers of siblings. Moreover, the decline in fertility among the native born was counteracted by the higher fertility of immigrants (Vinovskis, 1972, 1981). Even though mortality began to decline in the 1850s, the most dramatic decline has occurred since the 1870s. Peter Uhlenberg calculated that in 1870, only about 70 percent of children survived to age ten: "Nevertheless, a child born in 1870 to a mother who gave birth to seven children (the mean number of siblings for a person in this cohort was over six) would be expected to have at least four siblings survive past age fifteen" (1978, p. 177).

Changing Age Configurations of Children in the Family

The decline in mortality since the 1870s along with the decline in fertility has also affected the size and the configurations of membership in the family. One of the major historical changes in this respect has been a transition from a large family size to a smaller one and from a broad age spectrum of children within the family to the compressed, closely spaced 2.3-child family in contemporary American society. Prior to the 1870s, a larger number of children in the family meant not only the presence of a larger number of siblings but also a diversity in their age configurations.

Children were exposed to a greater age spread within their own families. Thus, for example, in families where children were spaced two or three years apart and where the family had five children, the oldest child would be fifteen and the youngest child five, meaning generally that in families with five or six children, the oldest child would be ready to leave home or get married when the youngest child was still in primary school. As Uhlenberg put it:

Consider, for example, children in a family in which eight children are born, compared with those in a two-child family. In the larger family, the firstborn enters a family with three members, but as he ages it keeps expanding up to a maximum of ten. The youngest child in the family enters a very large unit, which then contracts in size as he ages until finally he or she is the only remaining child. Furthermore, the ages of parents and ages and numbers of siblings present at different childhood stages will vary considerably for the various children in the large family, depending upon their birth order. In the small family, in contrast, the two siblings may be born a few years apart, and throughout their childhood no additional changes occur (1978, p. 77).

Such varied age configurations among siblings had significant implications for their relationships to one another, especially for their interaction over their life course. Children growing up in families with age diversity were exposed to a variety of roles and responsibilities among their own siblings. Teenagers or young adults often acted as surrogate parents—they took care of their younger siblings, played with them, tutored them, and at times, disciplined them. Child care by older siblings was especially needed when mothers worked in factories. In working-class families, eight- or ten-year-olds took care of children two to five years old (Hareven,

1978c, 1982). This type of interaction among siblings of various age groups was disrupted, however, in immigrant families, where the older children migrated first in order to prepare the way for the rest of the family. Although the parents and the younger children eventually followed, there were many cases where young siblings met up with older ones only in adulthood or were never reunited.

In families with a wider age spread among children, the youngest children had greater contact with the older siblings than with their own parents. Given the later age at marriage, parents would already have been in middle age when their youngest child was growing up. Under such circumstances, older siblings (especially sisters) often functioned as caregivers for their younger siblings. When one or both parents were dead, older siblings acted as surrogate parents (Hareven, 1978c, 1982).

In working-class families, older brothers or sisters initiated younger siblings into jobs and provided them with role models. Children of mill workers' families, for example, envied their siblings for starting to work in the factory and earning money. Many former textile workers reminisced about their desire to follow their siblings. After seeing their brothers or sisters go to work, they could barely wait to start work themselves. The example of their older siblings stimulated many children's aspirations to embark on factory work, even when their parents were not pushing them out of school and into the workplace. As just noted, older siblings also provided younger siblings with access to jobs and with skills and training if they worked in the same place (Hareven, 1982).

Another significant demographic change since the 1870s has been the increasing survival of parents beyond the child-rearing stage and their opportunity to see their children reach adulthood. Uhlenberg has calculated that of 1,000 infants born around 1870, only 515 survived to age fifteen and had both parents still alive, whereas of those born in 1950, 925 had this experience. Thus, there has been an 80 percent decline in the number of children who die in childhood and an 85 percent decline in orphanhood among those who do survive. Uhlenberg concluded that "the necessity of coping with the economic, social, and psychological problems associated with orphanhood moved from a fairly common childhood experience to a rare one" (1978, p. 178).

Before the turn of the twentieth century, in the demographic regime of late marriage, high fertility, and lower life expectancy, the overlap in age between children and their parents also differed significantly. The oldest child in a family was the one most likely to overlap with his or her father in adulthood; the youngest child was the least likely to do so. The oldest child was most likely to embark on an independent career before the parents reached old-age dependency; the youngest child was most likely to be left with the responsibilities for parental support and to overlap in adulthood with a widowed mother. The oldest child had the greatest chance of knowing his or her grandparents, at least in childhood; the youngest child had the least. Late-marrying children were most likely to be responsible for the support of a widowed mother, whereas early marrying children depended on their parents' household space after marriage.

Thus, in the larger families of the past, age differences among siblings and birth order were much more powerful factors affecting children's lives than they are today. Since 1870, however, the continuous decline in fertility (except for the "baby boom" cohort) has led to a shrinking of the family of orientation to three or fewer children. This has resulted in much greater age uniformity within the family.

Configurations of Other Family Members in the Household

As shown above, contrary to the prevailing myths, it is now a commonly accepted historical reality that children did not grow up in extended households with kin other than their parents and siblings. Even in the colonial period, the basic household unit was that of a nuclear family, consisting of parents and children. Grandparents, aunts, uncles, and cousins rarely shared the same household (Demos, 1970; Greven 1970). (There were, however, unrelated individuals living in the household. Their role will be discussed in the next section.)

Despite this similarity in the nuclear family, historical households differed from contemporary ones in the composition of their membership and in the relations with extended kin. In the seventeenth and eighteenth centuries, grandparents and other relatives resided in greater proximity to the nuclear family than in later time periods, even though they did not share the same household. Therefore, young children may have experienced greater contact with their grandparents on a daily basis and may have had greater opportunities to interact with aunts, uncles, and cousins than they do in contemporary society. This situation varied considerably, of course, among ethnic groups and also depended on the family's migration status. Among immigrant families, grandparents often remained behind in the old country.

Proximity to extended kin was also counteracted by a briefer temporal overlap between children and their grandparents. Before the end of the nineteenth century, the average grandfather lived to see only his first grandchild. Grandparents rarely survived to see their grandchildren into adulthood. By contrast, grandparents today generally overlap with all of their grandchildren into adulthood, and they also experience great-grandparenthood as a new demographic luxury of our times (Cherlin and Furstenberg, 1990).

Ironically, in recent decades, the opportunities for the temporal over-lap of grandparents with their grandchildren as a result of the longer life span have been counteracted by increasing geographical dispersion. Ero-sion of values of interdependence of extended kin, especially in the mid-dle class among second-, third-, and fourth-generation ethnics, has fur-ther weakened the chances for grandchildren's interaction with their grandparents on a regular basis. Consequently, even though there is the opportunity for grandchildren to overlap with grandparents over a longer period of their lives, grandparents' communication with their grandchildren is often limited only to family reunions because of geo-graphical distance or lack of familial involvement (Cherlin and Fursten-berg, 1990).

Throughout the twentieth century, demographic factors affecting the life course have also led to a greater age uniformity within the family. Earlier marriage, earlier childbearing, and the bearing of fewer children have brought parents and children closer together in age. Most children now know their parents as young people, whereas in the past, only the oldest child knew the parents as young people, and the youngest child knew his or her parents in middle age only. (There now seems to be a partial return to this historical pattern, because many professional cou-ples now have children when they are in their thirties and early forties.) Contemporary families have been characterized by an increasing age uniformity.

Nonrelatives in the Household

The presence of nonrelatives in the household has been another area of change affecting the networks available to children. In contrast to the private, isolated family today, the family in past centuries customarily admitted various unrelated individuals into its abode. In the colonial period, households typically included apprentices, servants, and depen-dent members of the community, placed with the family by the local au-thorities (Demos, 1970). The presence of such nonrelatives reflected the household's important functions as the main place of production, as an institution of welfare and social control, and as a refuge designated by the local authorities for members of disrupted families.

The live-in presence during the colonial period of orphans, depen-dent elderly or sick people, delinquents, servants, and apprentices meant that children growing up in the cramped quarters of such house-holds were exposed to a variety of nonrelatives, many of whom were in their teens. Servants or boarders often took care of children, along with performing other tasks. In the colonial period especially, servants were "life-cycle" servants—young people who had been sent out by their own parents to live and serve in other people's homes. The exchange of children across households was customary, since parents (especially Puritans) did not trust themselves to discipline their own children (Demos, 1972).

By the nineteenth century, the custom of sending children out into other people's households had disappeared almost completely, except where children of very poor or broken families were concerned. Following the first stage of industrialization, apprenticeship almost completely disappeared as a household-based practice. The employment of servants had become more strictly a practice of middle- and upper-class families rather than a form of a life-course exchange. The social origins of servants changed as well. The majority of servants were immigrant women, especially women from Ireland. They replaced the native-born young farm women who had formerly worked as servants. Despite the decline in live-in apprenticeship and in the number of servants, children continued to be exposed to nonrelatives in the household, since all through the nineteenth century, working-class as well as middle-class families took in boarders and lodgers.

The practice of boarding and lodging was widespread in families of all classes, in urban as well as rural society, throughout the nineteenth century. As discussed above, boarders and lodgers were young adults within the age range of fourteen to twenty-one who had left their parents' households to migrate into new areas where they could find employment opportunities. They often served as surrogate children of the families with whom they boarded and replaced the head of the household's own children, who had left home (Hareven, 1982; Modell and Hareven, 1973). The economic exchange relationship between boarders or lodgers and their host families varied considerably across classes and occupational and ethnic groups. In urban working-class families where the mother held a job outside the home, boarders often fulfilled child-care functions in exchange for room and board. Whether they were involved directly with child care or whether they only attended meals and some household activities, boarders and lodgers formed an important component of children's networks in the household.

In the late nineteenth century, as the practice of boarding and lodging became widespread, especially in urban areas, social reformers began to worry about the potentially corrupting impact that the presence of strangers in the household might have on children's age peers as well as on younger children. These moralists lacked an understanding of the constructive impact of boarding and lodging in facilitating the absorption of young migrants into chaotic urban areas. In reality, boarding and lodging provided stability, cohesion, and sociability for young people during periods of frequent migration (Modell and Hareven, 1973).

The presence of boarders and lodgers in nineteenth-century households, similar to that of servants in earlier periods, provided other role models for children in addition to those coming from their own relatives and siblings. Until about the 1920s, when the practice of boarding and lodging died out due to the increasing commitment to familial privacy and the increasing availability of separate housing for young individuals, a considerable number of American urban children were growing up in households containing some unrelated individuals.

In summary, children prior to 1900 grew up in households that were considerably more diverse in membership and age than households in contemporary society. The implications that this diversity in households and kinship networks had for the development and socialization of children is an important question to which we shall return (Hareven, 1985a).

Impact of the Domestic Child-Centered Family on Children's Networks

A major development affecting children's networks was the emergence of the child-centered domestic family in the urban middle class during the early nineteenth century. The emergence of this family type, characterized by increasing specialization in child rearing, was intricately connected to the new views of childhood that became popular in that period.

The separation of the home from the workplace that followed in the wake of industrialization led to the enshrinement of the home as a domestic retreat from the outside world and to the development of a child-centered family (Demos, 1970; Welter, 1966; Wishy, 1968). The home emerged as the sphere of women and the public sphere became that of men. These developments caused a physical and temporal separation of husbands and wives and fathers and children during the workday. A clear division of labor between husbands and wives replaced the old economic cooperation in the preindustrial family. The wives' efforts concentrated on homemaking and child rearing, while men worked outside the home. Time invested in fatherhood became concentrated primarily on leisure.

The ideology of domesticity and the new view of childhood as a tender stage of life requiring nurture combined to revise expectations of parenthood. It placed children at the center of the family and redefined the role of the mother as the chief rearer of children and as the custodian of "Home, Sweet Home" (Degler, 1980; Welter, 1966). In these new roles, women were expected to concentrate on perfect homemaking and on child rearing rather than on serving as economic partners in the family. Tenderness, gentleness, affection, sweetness, and a comforting demeanor were considered the crucible of family relationships.

Philippe Ariès succinctly summarized the emergence of this domestic, child-centered family, in which sentiment emerged as the base of family relations, for West European society: "The modern family . . . cuts itself off from the world and opposes to society the isolated groups of parents and children. All the energy of the group is expended in helping the children to rise in the world, individually and without any collective ambition: the children rather than the family" (Ariès, 1962, p. 174).

Prior to the early nineteenth century, child rearing was not the exclusive domain of motherhood. In Western Europe and in Colonial America, children were reared and educated by both parents, by their siblings, by other relatives, and by the various nonrelatives living in the household, as well as by other members of the community. Except for instruction in reading, writing, and religion, actual child rearing was carried out through the participation of older children along with other members of the family or unrelated individuals in various tasks and activities. As Ariès observed:

> Generally speaking, transmission from one generation to the next was ensured by the everyday participation of children in adult life. Everyday life constantly brought together children and adults in trade and crafts. . . . In short, wherever people worked, and wherever they amused themselves, even in taverns of ill repute, children were mingled with adults. In this way, they learned the art of living from everyday contact (1962, p. 368).

Most important, however, was the diversity of activities in what Ariès referred to as the big house. Rather than being an isolated domestic abode, "The big house fulfilled a public function. . . . It was the only place where friends, clients, relatives and protégés could meet and talk." In the big house, "people lived on top of one another, masters and servants, children and adults, in houses open at all hours to the indiscretions of the callers. The density of society left no room for the family. Not that the family did not exist as a concept," but its main focus was sociability rather than privacy (Ariès, 1962, pp. 398 and 405). The "modern" family, he argued, emerged as sociability retreated. A similar pattern was common in American society from the colonial period through the early nineteenth century (Demos, 1970).

The gradual segregation of children from interaction with adult society, the specialization of child rearing, the emergence of the mother as the main rearer of children, and the establishment of schools were products of the cult of domesticity that emerged in the United States during the first half of the nineteenth century among urban middle-class families. The ideology of domesticity was closely connected to the decline in the average number of children a woman had and to the new attitudes toward childhood. The recognition of childhood as a distinct stage of life led to the treatment of children as objects of nurture rather than as contributing members to the family economy.

The emergence of child rearing as the mother's central responsibility stimulated the production of advice manuals to parents as a major enterprise of the publishing industry (Wishy, 1968). A large body of domestic advice and child-rearing literature, which started to flood the market from the early nineteenth century on, glorified the role of the mother and provided practical advice on child rearing. Urban middle-class mothers became avid readers of this literature (Sunley, 1955). The increase in mothers' consumption of child-rearing manuals represents an important shift from reliance on friends and kin for advice on child rearing to reliance on formally printed guidance.

The cult of domesticity and motherhood during the first half of the nineteenth century and the concentration on child rearing as the mother's main responsibility laid the foundation for the typical pattern of parent-child relations that has characterized American society until the 1960s and that still persists in some forms even today. Despite the resemblance of the mid-nineteenth century child-centered family patterns to those of our times, there were, however, significant differences. For example, children experienced a greater exposure to various role models, resulting as described earlier from the presence of larger numbers of siblings in the family and the presence of nonrelatives in the household.

The new domestic child-centered family was initially limited to the middle class. It took the better part of a century for this phenomenon to spread among working-class and rural families and various ethnic groups. In order to understand this phenomenon fully, it is important to remember that the specialization of child rearing in the domestic family coincided with the emergence of external agencies such as the school and the reformatory, which began to take over the family's functions of education and social control.

Emergence of Institutions and Peer Groups Outside of the Family

During the past century and a half, the family has gradually been divested of many functions—education, production, welfare, and social control—that it had originally held. New institutions emerging since the middle of the nineteenth century have taken their respective functions over from the family: Schools have become widespread, and compulsory school-attendance laws, passed first in Massachusetts and then in other states, set specific age requirements on school attendance (Kaestle and Vinovskis, 1980). Factories and other enterprises took over the household's production functions; reformatories, hospitals, and other agencies took over the functions held earlier by the family.

Most of the institutions that had sprung from the family's earlier functions modeled themselves on the family and used family metaphors to justify their new roles in society (Rothman, 1971). Despite the fact that these agencies paid lip service to the family model, they led to the regimentation of children in distinct age groups and the partial segregation of children from their families. Parents did not let the transfer of educational functions to the schools go unchallenged (Lightfoot, 1978). In the occasional "school wars" of the nineteenth century, parents tenaciously tried to retain control over their children's education because they saw in the exposure to peer groups, in the school and on the street, a potential threat to their children's character and to their own control over their children's education (Rawitch, 1974).

Whereas middle-class parents opposed the school primarily because they were concerned with retaining moral control over their children, urban working-class and rural parents were concerned with retaining control over their children's time as workers and wage earners, which was being threatened by compulsory school-attendance laws. Parents who needed their children's labor as an essential contribution to the collective family economy resisted the requirements for school attendance and the age limits imposed by child-labor legislation, which deprived them of income from their children's work (Hareven, 1982). Eventually, middle-class parents accepted the school and began to control it, but working-class parents found means to circumvent the requirements for compulsory education, often sending their children to work with falsified birth certificates (Bremner et al., 1970; Hareven, 1982).

During the nineteenth century, most of the children attending school were between the ages of eight and twelve. Only toward the end of the century did six or seven become the standardized, official school-entry age. Although reformers had little interest in lowering the school age for middle-class children, several reform movements did aim to start the schooling of the children of the poor in infancy. This concern was expressed in the infant-school movement, which, in spite of its short duration, set a precedent for kindergarten and for earlier commencement of schooling. In the 1820s, a group of civic-minded educational reformers in Boston launched the infant schools for children of the poor in order to rescue them from what the reformers considered to be damaging and corrupting environments in their families, especially during a period of such rapid urbanization.

The debates surrounding the infant schools reflect the attitudes of the times toward the age limits of childhood.

Infants, taken from the most unfavorable situations in which they are ever placed, from the abodes of poverty and vice, are capable of learning at least a hundred times as much, a hundred times as well, and of being a hundred times as happy, by the system adopted in infant schools, as by that which prevails in the common schools throughout the country. The conclusion most interesting to every friend of education is, that the infant school system can be extended through every department of the *popular education*. (italics in original; Boston Recorder and Religious Transcript, 1829, cited in Vinovskis and May, 1977)

The infant-school movement peaked by 1830, then began a slow decline in the 1840s and became extinct by the 1850s. In 1840, at least 10 percent of children under four were attending schools in Massachusetts. The percentage was even higher in many specific localities. During the 1840s, the practice of sending young children to school gradually died out in response to the formalization of the public-school system, which eventually set lower limits on the age of school admission. A resurgence of interest in infant education was expressed in the establishment of kindergarten in the 1860s and 1870s. Like the infant schools, the kindergarten was directed at poor and immigrant children (Vinovskis and May, 1977). Thus, middle-class children started their exposure to peers and teachers in the schools at around age six or seven, but working-class and immigrant children began to experience such exposure by age three or four.

The spread of the public-school system from the middle of the nineteenth century on led to the segregation of children from their families for a considerable part of the day. A slow but continuous development of age grading within the schools over the course of the nineteenth century led to the clustering of more streamlined age groups among children within the schools. The number of private and public schools rapidly increased after the American Revolution. By the mid-nineteenth century, most children in the United States received at least some schooling (Angus, Mirel, and Vinovskis, 1988).

Initially, schools accepted children of all ages and did not divide them into specific age groups. During the second half of the nineteenth century, however, the minimum school-entry age was set at seven or eight. With the establishment of public high schools during that period, the length of schooling was extended. Since students often entered high school at twelve or thirteen and most did not stay long enough to graduate, nineteenth-century children typically completed their formal education by their mid-teens. By the end of the nineteenth century, schooling had been expanded, and childhood education had become compressed to a more specific age span (between seven and thirteen). The average minimum age of leaving school increased from fourteen years and five months in 1900 to sixteen years in 1930 in the states that had enacted a compulsory schooling law.

The proportion of children's time claimed by the school also changed over the nineteenth century. The average length of the elementary and secondary public-school year has increased over the past century. School terms in urban areas have become shorter. Nearly year-round school attendance in the 1830s changed to a forty-week school year by the turn of the century, with rural terms expanding from 132 days in 1870 to 179 days in 1970 (Angus, Mirel, and Vinovskis, 1988).

Along with the increase in school attendance over the nineteenth century, more systematic age grading began to emerge within the schools. Although the typical pattern in rural schools continued to be that of the one-room schoolhouse, urban schools gradually developed a grading system over the course of the century. Initially, the grading was based on children's accomplishments in the curriculum, rather than on age per se. Age grading in the schools did not develop at a significant pace until the 1930s. The process spread unevenly across the nation and varied considerably by region. The industrial Northeast and Midwest advanced that system over the first three decades of the twentieth century, while the South and West lagged behind. The emergence of schooling thus affected children's networks in two mutually reinforcing directions. First, children became more segregated from adult society during their schooling (except from teachers), and second, children were gradually, though unevenly, segregated into age peer groups in the schools (Angus, Mirel, and Vinovskis, 1988).

The school and the peer groups within it thus became important competitors with the family for children's time and involvement. As the required age of school entry was lowered and the upper age requirements of compulsory school attendance were pushed up, children began to spend increasingly longer portions of their lives with peers outside the family. Initially, children were not rigidly separated into age groups. They were exposed to peers of a variety of ages. As the age-graded class system emerged as the norm, children began to spend most of their schooling time with their age peers and teachers. In many instances, children also became their parents' educators, bringing home new ideas and information acquired in the schools. Especially in the case of immigrants, the school functioned as an agent of acculturation for parents through their children.

School attendance in the 1800s was a privilege limited primarily to middle-class children, but the proportion of immigrant children attending school began to increase toward the end of the century. Several factors combined to increase the proportion of immigrant children attending school: Child-labor laws were more rigidly enforced; children's employment declined due to new technology, which made child labor obsolete; and attitudes toward education began to change among immigrant parents. The proportion of children attending school and the number of years spent there have increased continuously since the late nineteenth century. For recent cohorts, school attendance after the age of fifteen has become almost universal, and with few exceptions, children attend classes with other children of the same age throughout most of their childhood.

The Workplace

For working-class children, the main peer groups outside of the family were their coworkers in factories, in street trades, and in various industries such as food processing and canning. Child laborers were thus exposed to networks composed of mixed age groupings, ranging from their peers to adults and varying according to their workplace and their age. Throughout the nineteenth century, workers transferred their family networks to the workplace. Parents, older relatives, and siblings or cousins often worked in the same place, instructed the younger workers, helped them, and at times protected them. Even nonrelatives with whom younger children worked assumed the roles of surrogate parents, protecting younger children and helping them adapt to the workplace and its various routines. This surrogate familial role was especially important when children started to work at a young age (ten or eleven).

Within the mixed age groupings in the workplace, children formed peer networks among coworkers close in age. Despite the demanding pressures of the workplace, children played with their age peers during breaks (Lowell Offering, 1840–1845). Carrying some childhood mischief into the factory, they often played tricks and practical jokes on one another. The networks at the workplace were crucial for children's adaptation to difficult working conditions and taxing time schedules, as well as for diminishing the bewilderment they may have encountered upon first entering a new workplace. While older coworkers provided protection, the presence of their own-age peers meant that children could carry some of their childlike qualities into the workplace. In many cases, children were not mere recipients of adult support, however. At times, experienced child workers shared their savvy and crucial information, especially about shortcuts on the job, with new adult workers or with other children (Hareven, 1982).

The Street

One of the important networks competing with the family was the peer group on the street. In urban society, the streets had become an important arena for sociability, play, and peer activity for children aged seven and older. A more acceptable place for boys than for girls, the street became a magnet for young boys and teenagers in the middle classes as well as for the urban poor and immigrants. Moralists, educators, and clergy from the middle of the nineteenth century on denounced the corrupting dangers of the street. They viewed almost all peer-group activities as threatening, degenerate, and seductive, leading in a straight line to crime and delinquency (Bremner et al., 1971).

The mounting anxiety expressed in the moralists' and educators' writings was especially dramatic with regard to children of immigrants and the poor. One of the most striking expressions of these anxieties was in *Dangerous Classes of New York* written by Charles Loring Brace in 1854, a book that compared the "gangs" of immigrant children roaming around the alleys and wharves of New York City to the *prolétaires* of Paris, whose revolutionary activities had led to the establishment of the Paris Commune in 1848. He wrote: "There are no dangers to the value of property or the permanency of our institutions so great as those from the existence of . . . a class of vagabond, ignorant, ungoverned children." For Brace, the dangerous classes were "the outcast, vicious, reckless multitude of New York boys, swarming . . . in every foul alley and low street" (Brace, 1872, pp. 321-322).

This anxiety over the street gangs of New York and other major cities with a high concentration of immigrants led Brace to the establishment of the New York Children's Aid Society, with the major goal to rescue children from the streets and place them in the "wholesome" homes of farmers in the Midwest. Other cities followed the New York example. The most frequent solution to the problems of urban "delinquents" and dependent poor children from the 1850s on was, however, to place them in the institutions of welfare and social control that had begun to emerge in midcentury.

The Reformatory

Institutions of welfare and social control designed specifically for children and teenagers took over the family's earlier functions of welfare, education, and social control. Established in response to urbanization and to the panic caused by the influx of large numbers of poor Irish immigrants to major Eastern cities, these institutions took over some of the functions of the family. The juvenile reformatories emerging in the 1850s, first in Massachusetts and subsequently in other states, introduced the principle of segregating young offenders by age and reforming them within an institution (Rothman, 1971).

By segregating juvenile "offenders" in peer groups, these institutions unintentionally created networks of homeless and "delinquent" children and youths (Bremner et al., 1971). As the case records of some of these institutions suggest, their young inmates displayed remarkable resourcefulness within the institutions as well as back on the streets. Inmates made new friends within the reformatory. Such friendships formed the base for new networks that the young delinquents formed or joined following their release. These adolescent networks linked the streets and the reformatory, facilitating the transmission of knowledge and skills among current and former inmates. The "repeaters"—those arrested again a short time after their release—were especially instrumental in fostering and utilizing such networks.

The juvenile reformatory represented the nineteenth century's answer to a larger question: What would be a more regenerating and redeeming place for a child or an adolescent—the family or an institution? In addressing this question, educators followed a double standard: Among middle-class families, the cult of domesticity and the child-centered family extolled the virtues of the home and opposed child labor. At the same time, the advocates of this familistic ideology believed that the way to keep poor and delinquent children out of trouble and "reformed" was either to put them to work or place them in other people's homes or in institutions. Prior to the 1850s, the "binding out" of children—their contractual placement by the authorities in other people's homes as servants—was the dominant practice. Following the introduction of the reformatory, the institution triumphed over the family (Bremner, 1976).

Thus, while the middle-class family and home became the central locus for child rearing, competing forces in schools and institutions of social control made increasing demands upon the portion of children's time that came under institutional control.

The Segregation of Childhood and Children

The overall trend since the nineteenth century has therefore been one of increasing segregation of children from adult society as a distinct age group and a further segregation of children into specific age groups within the larger category of "children." This streamlining of children by age has been expressed in their increasing separation from adults in daily life, in their education, work, disciplining, and sociability, and in the introduction of age grading in the schools as well. Except for farm families and working-class families, children's activities became gradually disengaged from adult activities and from interaction with mixed age groups. The portion of time that children spend with their age peers has increased progressively since the nineteenth century.

Children are now starting to cluster with their peers in institutions outside the family at much younger ages. School entry has been lowered to age six, and kindergarten and institutional child care have become more widespread. Thus, children aged three or younger now spend a major portion of the day with peers if the mother is working outside the home.

The identification of children as distinct from adults and the recognition of childhood as a separate developmental stage with its own needs and potential underlie these developments from the early part of the nineteenth century on. In American society, childhood was "discovered" and identified as a distinct stage of life first in the private lives of middle-class urban families in the early part of the nineteenth century. The discovery itself was related to the family's retreat into domesticity discussed earlier, the separation of the workplace from the home, the redefinition of the woman's role as the custodian of the domestic sphere and as the main rearer of children, and the emergence of sentiment as the basis of familial relationships. An important consequence of these new attitudes toward children was their increasing segregation from adult society and activities. By contrast, children in the seventeenth and eighteenth centuries mingled with adult society and participated in the various tasks and "sociability" of the household. They were not sheltered as "innocent" creatures. As Nancy Cott (1976) found in eighteenth-century divorce testimonies, children even witnessed sexual activity in the household.

The new centeredness of urban domestic families in the early nineteenth century was also a response to the decline in infant and child mortality and to the conscious practice of family limitation. As detailed above, following this recognition of children as the central focus of middle-class family life, childhood became the subject of a voluminous body of the child-rearing and family-advice literature, described earlier. In addition, the moralists' and reformers' literature popularized the concept of childhood and the needs of children, prescribed the means to allow them to develop as children, and called for the regulation of child labor. Childhood became publicly recognized as a special stage through legislative and institutional efforts such as compulsory school-attendance laws, child-labor legislation, the establishment of juvenile reformatories, kindergartens, and age-graded schools. All these institutions and legislative efforts were aimed at protecting children and enabling them to realize their potential in their unique developmental stage (Hareven, 1985a; Skolnick, 1973).

Over the nineteenth century, the period of childhood gradually become prolonged, extending its boundaries into adolescence. The recognition of adolescence in the late nineteenth century and its gradual institutionalization in the twentieth century provided children with a moratorium from adult responsibilities. By the time G. Stanley Hall published his first article on adolescence (1905), "adolescent" peer groups were already easily identifiable in urban society, high-school age had been extended, and reformers were developing such organizations as the Boy Scouts and various other clubs for boys in order to keep urban teenagers out of trouble. Like kindergarten, these organizations, which were initially aimed at the children of the poor and immigrants, were eventually taken over by the middle class, which could afford leisure time for its children.

Over the course of the twentieth century, demographic and socioeconomic changes led to a further reduction in the age diversity of children within the family and their age grading in tight groups outside the family. The decline in fertility eventually resulted in a small compact family with its children closely spaced. Increasing privatization of the family led to the withdrawal of boarders and lodgers from the household. The diversity of role models previously provided by older siblings and boarders also disappeared, except among newly arrived ethnic groups and in black families.

Increase in mothers' labor-force participation since World War II, especially the dramatic increase since the 1960s, has further affected the networks of children. Whereas earlier, a mother's gainful employment had been almost exclusively a working-class phenomenon, the absence of the mother from the home for a partial or an entire working day has become widespread in the middle class as well. Day-care centers have replaced the earlier practices of child care by older siblings or by elderly relatives when the mother was employed. As a result, children of working mothers are now exposed to their peers in day-care centers even before kindergarten.

The increased participation of fathers in child rearing and in hands-on child care has been another important development since the 1960s, especially in middle-class families and among dual-career couples (Bronfenbrenner, 1969). Changing perceptions of parental roles in the wake of women's liberation and men's new consciousness, along with the increasing sentimentalization of childhood, have led to the father's more active participation in child rearing and child care. The extent to which this pattern represents a radical departure is still a question open to historical research. Ross Parke and Peter Stearns (1987) have hypothesized that fathers' involvement with their children might have been even greater during the heyday of domesticity and mother-dominated child rearing than it is today. Fathers may have invested their time and emotions to a greater extent than the mid-nineteenth century child-rearing literature may have led us to believe. Since that type of "modern" domestic family emphasized the emotional closeness among fathers and children as well as mothers and children, the authors conclude that "while systematic inquiry remains to be done, it is clear that fathers were more diverse and on balance probably more active than expert child-rearing literature allowed for" (Parke and Stearns, 1987, p. 13).

The authors consider the possibility of greater paternal involvement in shared leisure and play with their children. They date this development from the late nineteenth century and believe that this type of paternal involvement with children fulfilled the additional functions of instilling certain skills and values. If this hypothesis is borne out, we might be able to identify several significant historical transitions in fathers' involvement with child rearing: from sharing work together in the preindustrial period (and in working-class and farming families as well, following industrialization) to sharing leisure time since the late nineteenth century and to a greater sharing of child-care responsibilities over the past two decades. One could argue, therefore, that children are now more exposed to their fathers on a daily basis, and from a younger age, than they had been previously.

The more recent involvement of fathers in child rearing and child care varies considerably, of course, among various groups in the population. Data from a recent survey show that between 1975 and 1981, fathers increased their time invested in child care by 26 percent over this six-year span. Mothers were still responsible, however, for 66 percent of the child care, compared to fathers' 34 percent (Jessa, 1987, cited in Parke and Stearns, 1987). Fathers' greater involvement in child care is reflected in Dr. Spock's revision of his 1976 edition of *Baby and Child Care*: "I always assumed that the parent taking the greater share of the care of young children (and of the home) would be the mother, whether or not she wanted an outside career. . . . Now I recognize that the father's responsibility is as great as the mother's" (p. xix).

By contrast, Dr. Spock's first edition (1946) devoted only nine pages to the father's role, advising fathers to play an occasional role in child care in order to give mothers a rest. The actual extent of fathers' current involvement in child care and the ways in which it differs from earlier patterns of paternal involvement await systematic study (Weiss, 1977).

The Return of Diversity

The patterns of increasing paternal involvement in child rearing have been counteracted in recent years by the increasing numbers of American children growing up without fathers or with only occasional contact with their fathers. The increasing percentage of single-parent families (mostly headed by mothers) has led to a dramatic change in children's parental configurations. The demographic opportunities enabling fathers and mothers and their children to go through life together, which were gained over the past century through the decline of mortality, have been counteracted by divorce and single parenthood (Cherlin, 1981).

The current pattern of a great number of fatherless children and blended families is actually not an entirely new phenomenon in American society. It resembles in some ways the patterns of the seventeenth and eighteenth centuries, when high mortality disrupted families and remarriage resulted in the formation of new families.

Over the last two decades in American society, divorce has led to family disruption in a way similar to the effect of death in earlier times. Thus, there is some resemblance between the current and past one-parent families and blended families and their complicated kin networks, in terms of the complexity of networks available to children. There are also, however, several differences. When remarriage occurs after divorce (as opposed to after the death of one partner), the biological parent remains, sometimes even living in the same community. In the past, if the surviving parent began a new relationship, it usually resulted in marriage. In contemporary single-parent families, the mother or father does not always marry his or her new partner, and children are sometimes exposed to a sequence of partners of their biological parent living in the household. Thus, complexity, age diversity, and variability in family and household membership have partly replaced the streamlined age-homogenization of the family that had emerged by the 1950s.

Remarriage of the noncustodial parent often results in decreased contact between the children and that parent, and contact between the child and his or her noncustodial grandparents is often decreased as well. In their study of children's contact with their "outside" parent following divorce, Frank Furstenberg and Christine Nord (1985) found that "marital disruption effectively destroys the ongoing relationship between children and the biological parents living outside the home" (p. 900). The residential parent usually carries the major responsibilities of child rearing. Activities with outside parents are generally confined to entertainment and recreation. There is, however, a difference between children's relationships to outside mothers and to outside fathers; children tend to maintain closer contact with outside mothers and express greater satisfaction with that relationship (Furstenberg and Nord, 1985).

Blended families resulting from remarriage after divorce have brought new family and kinship ties into the lives of an increasing number of American children. These blended families are, in fact, reintroducing some of the complexity and diversity characteristic of the past. These new family arrangements bring several sets of siblings together, thus increasing the variety of age configurations in the family. They also establish contact among stepfathers or stepmothers and unrelated children, thus reintroducing nonrelatives into the household, exposing children to new extended kin. Remarriage following divorce has also led to the rearrangement of the kinship networks available to children outside the household.

Some children have three to four sets of grandparents and several new sets of aunts, uncles, and cousins. Precisely how children relate to these new and complicated networks has not been systematically studied. However, this area is one that definitely needs to be addressed.

Implications for Child Development

The twentieth century has brought a continuous stabilization and age homogenization into the networks available to children in the family and kin group (Hareven, 1985a). The decline in mortality and the younger age at marriage have provided children with the chance to survive to adulthood together with their siblings, to overlap with parents into their own adulthood, and to know their grandparents in adulthood. The decline in fertility, by contrast, has reduced the number of siblings with whom they grow up. The development of age-graded schooling and the universal requirement for school attendance have extended children's opportunities for overlap with their age peers. Increasing affluence, combined with more effective legislation and the obsolescence of child labor, has enabled children to stay in school regularly and over a longer time period and to extend their period of play and study before assuming work responsibilities. Child rearing itself has become a science, supported by various professional groups and manuals.

The question is, however, what children have actually gained from these historical developments. The answer still depends on collaborative research between historians and developmentalists. One of the key questions that links these historical developments with child psychology is the impact of diversity in age, membership, and roles in the household vis-à-vis greater uniformity. On the one hand, Talcott Parsons argued that the specialized, private, and child-focused family is much more effective in rearing adults who function effectively in a complex, bureaucratic society. Parsons claims that the ego development that enables adults to function well in a complex world is best achieved in a private family that shelters the individual. On the other hand, Ariès argued that the modern, private family serves as a retreat from the outside world and cuts children off from the rest of society. Children growing up in such families are deprived, therefore, of much of the experience of the adult world. As a result, such children are handicapped in their future adjustment to adult roles. Hence, according to Ariès, children who experience a greater diversity and variety of role models in their family of orientation and through the family's involvement with the larger society are more adaptable and able to function in a modern, complex society. Although Ariès and Parsons never debated these issues directly, Richard Sennett (1971) staged a theoretical debate between the positions of the two in order to discern the relationship between family structure and individuals' adaptability and mobility in complex, modern society.

These two connecting points of view are linked, of course, to a larger question: What price have the family and children paid for the family's retreat into privacy and the resulting loss of its earlier "sociability" (its interaction with the community)? Has the family's retreat from the community and the withdrawal of nonrelatives from the household deprived children of greater exposure to a diversity of social roles? Even though parent-child relations have become much more informal and sentimental than in the past, has the actual process of child rearing become too specialized in the family and too professionalized in the institutions outside the family?

In addressing these questions, it is important to remember that some "historical" family configurations and child-rearing patterns still survive in varying degrees and in various forms among more newly arrived ethnic groups and among black families. If the middle-class family discovers that its retreat from the community and its child centeredness have become excessive and counterproductive, some of the earlier historical models are still available for consideration of modes of adaptation.

Thus, the historical examination of these issues provides a perspective on the contemporary issues, not only because it offers an understanding of patterns of change but also because the historical experience offers models of adaptation that are still relevant in contemporary society.

5

Aging and
Generational Relations

A Historical and Life-Course Perspective

Introduction

The study of generational relations in the later years of life in American society has been present-oriented and clouded by myths about the past. An understanding of this subject in contemporary society depends on a knowledge of the larger processes of social change that have affected the timing of life-course transitions, family patterns, and reciprocal relations among kin (Bengston et al., 1985; Shanas, 1986; Bengston and Treas, 1985; Shanas and Sussman, 1981). As this chapter will suggest, both a historical perspective and a life-course paradigm are important for the exploration of these processes.

A historical perspective, in addition to providing a context of change over time, illuminates the ways in which historical events and circumstances have affected the life experience of different age groups (Hareven, 1977b; Elder, 1978). At the same time, the life-course paradigm helps focus attention on the interaction of demographic, social-structural, and cultural factors in shaping family patterns and generational relations. It illuminates the impact of historical events on the lives of various cohorts and their consequences for old age (Elder, 1974; 1993; Riley, 1978; Hareven, 1978e).

A life-course perspective provides an understanding of the ways in which earlier life experiences of older adults, as shaped by historical events and by their respective cultural heritage, have affected their adaptation to old age, their values governing family relations, their expectations of kin

---

*This chapter first appeared as "Aging and Generational Relations: A Historical and Life Course Perspective," in John Hagan, ed., *Annual Review of Sociology* (Palo Alto, CA: Annual Reviews, 1994), pp. 437–461. Reprinted with permission from the *Annual Review of Sociology*, Volume 20, © 1994, by Annual Reviews, Inc.

supports, and the nature of their interaction with welfare agencies and in-stitutions. Generational relations in old age can best be understood in the context of the entire life course and of the historical changes affecting peo-ple at various points over their lives. They are molded by individual and familial experiences and by the specific historical circumstances that have impinged on people's lives. Rather than viewing older people as a homo-geneous group, a life-course perspective considers them as age cohorts moving through historical time, each cohort with its distinct life experi-ences shaped by the circumstances encountered earlier in life (Hareven, 1978c; Elder, 1978).

Configurations of kin and unrelated individuals are formed and re-formed over the life course. Changes in these configurations affect the availability of support networks in the later years of life. Hence, life-course antecedents are crucial for the availability and nature of supports in old age. The adaptation of individuals and their families to the social and economic conditions they face in the later years of life is contingent on the pathways by which they reach old age. Relations of mutual sup-port are formed over life and are revised in response to demographic events, migration, and historical circumstances such as wars, depressions, and the decline or collapse of local economies, which people may have encountered at various points in their lives. Patterns of support and ex-pectations for receiving and providing supports in old age are part of a continuing process of interaction among parents, children, other kin, and unrelated individuals, as they move through historical time (Hareven, 1981b; Elder, 1982; Hogan, Eggebeen, and Clogg, 1993).

A life-course perspective provides a necessary dimension and an inte-grating framework for the study of aging and intergenerational relations because it is both developmental and historical. It enables us to under-stand how patterns of assistance and support networks were formed over life and were carried over into the later years, how they were shaped over life by historical circumstances and by people's cultural traditions, and what strategies individuals and families followed over their life course in order to secure future supports for their old age.

Following a historical and life-course perspective, this chapter exam-ines changes in demographic behavior, in family and household organi-zation, in the timing of life-course transitions, and in kin assistance in American society, as they have affected generational supports in the later years of life.

The Life-Course Paradigm

The life-course paradigm is developmental and historical by its very na-ture. Its essence is the synchronization of "individual time," "family time," and "historical time." Underlying this paradigm are three major dimensions: (1) The timing of life transitions over an individual life path in the context of historical change; (2) the synchronization of individual life transitions with collective familial ones; and (3) the impact of earlier life events, as shaped by historical circumstances previously encountered, on subsequent events.

The concept of timing over the life course involves the movement of individuals over their life trajectories from one state to the next rather than the segmentation of the life course into fixed stages. Such movements have been defined in life-course research as "transitions." "Timing" thus designates when a transition or an event occurs in an individual's life in relation to external events. It is a way of assessing whether a transition conforms to or diverges from societal norms of timeliness and how its timing relates to that of other people traveling with the individual through life. Thus, the variables used in the examination of timing are relative rather than absolute chronological categories. They are perceptual as well as behavioral markers for the people undergoing them. In this respect, age, although an important determinant of the timing of life transitions, is not the only significant variable. Changes in family status, in needs, and in accompanying roles are often as important as age, if not more significant. The life-course paradigm emphasizes social age rather than calendar age.

Members of different cohorts undergo transitions, which are processes of individual change within socially constructed timetables. Many of the transitions that individuals experience over their work and family lives are normative; other transitions are critical or, at times, even traumatic. Transitions are considered "normative" if a major portion of a population experiences them and if a society expects its members to undergo such transitions at certain points in their lives in conformity with established norms of timing. Under certain conditions, even normative transitions might turn into critical ones and might be perceived as turning points.

The Timing of Life Transitions

The timing of life transitions involves the balancing of individuals' entry into and exit from different work, family, and community roles over their life course, especially the sequencing of their work lives and educational and family transitions in changing historical contexts. In all these areas, the pace and definition of "timing" hinge upon the social, economic, and cultural contexts in which transitions occurred and the cultural construction of the life course in different time periods and in different societies.

The pace and definition of "timing" hinge upon the social and cultural contexts in which transitions occurred and the cultural construction of the life course in different time periods and in different societies (Neugarten and Datan, 1973; Clark and Anderson, 1976).

1. *The Timing of Life Transitions over an Individual Life Path.* In the individual life trajectory, the crucial question is how people time and organize their entry into and exit from various roles over their life course: for example, how they sequence transitions in their work life and educational life with respect to transitions in their family life, how they synchronize and sequence transitions in the context of changing historical conditions in areas such as entry into the labor force, leaving home, getting married, setting up an independent household, and becoming parents (Hareven, 1978e; Elder, 1978; 1979).

2. *Synchronization of Individual with Collective Timing.* The second dimension of the life-course approach involves the synchronization of individual life transitions with collective family transitions, such as leaving home, getting married, and entering the labor force. Individuals engage in a variety of familial configurations that change over the life course and that vary in different historical contexts. Although age is an important determinant of the timing of transitions, it is not the only significant variable. Changes in family status and in accompanying roles were often as important as age, if not more so (Hareven, 1991b; Hareven and Masaoka, 1988).

   The synchronization of individual transitions with familial ones is a crucial aspect of the life course and impinges directly on generational relations, especially when individual goals are in conflict with the needs and dictates of the family as a collective unit. In the nineteenth century, for example, the timing of young adults' life transitions often clashed with the demands and needs of aging parents. As already noted, parents discouraged the youngest daughter from leaving home and marrying so that she would continue to support them at home in their old age. Daughters succumbed to these dictates, despite their preference to leave home and start a life of their own (Hareven, 1982; Hareven and Adams, 1996). Similarly, the timing of later life transitions affected more than one generation. For example, the death of "old old" (Neugarten and Datan, 1973) parents enabled caretaking children who were themselves old to begin providing for their own old age, as well as for their adult children or grandchildren (Hogan, Eggebeen, and Snaith, 1995).

3. *Cumulative Impact of Earlier Life Events on Subsequent Ones.* The third feature of timing is the cumulative impact of earlier events on subsequent ones over the entire life course. Early or late timing of certain transitions affects the pace of subsequent ones. Events experienced

earlier in the life course can continue to influence an individual's or family's life path in different ways throughout their lives.

Historical forces thus play a crucial role in this complex cumulative pattern. Historical conditions or events that individuals encounter in their earlier life history have a direct impact on their lives; and these events in turn may have an indirect impact on the later years of life. This means that the social experiences of each cohort are shaped not only by the discrete historical conditions prevailing at the time of those experiences but also by historical processes that shaped their earlier individual and familial life trajectories (Hareven, 1982). Historical experiences have a direct impact on the life course of individuals and families at the time when they encounter them and continue to have an indirect impact over the entire life course.

A. *Generational Transmission of Timing*: The impact of historical events on the life course may continue over several generations. Each generation encounters a set of historical circumstances that shapes its subsequent life history and transmits to the next generation the ripple effects of the historical circumstances that affected its members' life history. For example, Elder and Hareven (1993) found that in the same age cohorts in two different communities, delays or irregularities in the parents' timing of their work and family transitions as a result of the Great Depression affected the subsequent timing of the children's life transitions. The children thus experienced the impact of historical events on two levels: directly, through their encounter with these events in their early adulthood, and indirectly, in the transmission of these events across the generations. A life-course perspective provides a framework for understanding both variability in the patterns of support in the later years of life and differences in the expectations of the recipients and the caregivers who are influenced by their respective social and cultural milieux (Fry and Keith, 1982; Kohli, 1986; Kiefer, 1974; Jackson, Antonucci, and Gibson, 1990).

B. *Impact of Long-Term Historical Events*: In addition to the immediate historical events that each cohort experiences, long-term historical change has a critical impact on timing over the life course in several areas: demographic behavior, the timing of marriage, fertility, and mortality patterns—all of these shape changing age configurations within the family (Uhlenberg, 1974). Similarly, external economic changes in the opportunity structure affect changes in the timing of entry into the labor force and, ultimately, retirement. Institutional and legislative changes, such as compulsory school attendance, child-labor laws, and mandatory retirement, affect the work-life transitions of different age groups and eventually influence their family life as well.

Patterns of generational assistance are shaped by values and experiences that evolve or are modified over the entire life course. In the United States, ethnic values rooted in various premigration cultures call for a more exclusive dependence on filial and kin assistance than on the more contemporary attitudes, which advocate reliance on supports available from government programs and community agencies. Such differences in values are expressed in the caregiving practices and attitudes of successive cohorts. The earlier life-course experiences of each cohort, as shaped by historical events, also have an impact on the availability of resources for their members and on their modes of assistance and coping abilities in the later years of life (Elder, 1974; Hareven and Adams, 1996; Elder, Rudkin, and Conger, 1992; Sokolovsky, 1990).

Recent research on the life course has also made an important contribution to the understanding of generational relations and social change by refining the distinction between "generation" and "cohort," two concepts that have frequently overlapped in the gerontological literature (Bengston et al., 1985; Hill, 1970). "Generation" designates a kin relationship and a genealogical lineage (for example, parents and children or grandparents and grandchildren) and often encompasses an age span as wide as thirty years or more. A "cohort" consists of a more specific age group that has shared a common historical experience. Most important, a cohort is defined by its interaction with the historical events that affect the subsequent life-course development of that group (Ryder, 1965; Riley, 1978; Riley, Johnson, and Foner, 1972). Over the past decade and a half, several scholars have warned against "confounding the genealogical and cohort meanings of 'generation.'" Building on the major problems that Elder and Vinovskis identified, Kertzer has pointed out that when a population is divided on genealogical principles into various generations, there is substantial overlapping in age among the generations. He warned that it would be "impossible to properly characterize the generations in terms of their common characteristics vis-à-vis other generations" (Kertzer, 1983, p. 130).

A generation might consist of several cohorts, each of whom has encountered different historical experiences that have affected its life course. For example, in Hareven and Kathleen Adams's comparison of patterns of assistance of two cohorts of adult children to aging parents in a New England community, members of the same generation belonged to different cohorts: In families with large numbers of children, siblings in the same family were members of two cohorts, which differed in the historical experiences they had encountered and in their attitudes toward generational supports. If one intends to examine change over time in generational relations, then, it is necessary to compare cohorts, not generations.

Myths About the Past

As pointed out above, historical research has dispelled the myths about the existence of an ideal three-generational family in the American past, according to which the elderly coresided with their adult children and were supported by the younger generations after they reached dependent old age. This is contrary to the prevailing sociological theory that industrialization destroyed the great extended households of the past and led to the emergence of a nuclear-family system and to the isolation of the elderly. In reality, in the American colonies and in preindustrial Europe, coresidence of three generations in the same household was not the modal familial arrangement. Given the high mortality rate, most grandparents could not have expected to overlap their grandchildren's lives for a significant time period (Greven, 1970; Demos, 1970; Laslett and Wall, 1972). The great extended families that have become part of the folklore of modern society rarely existed in the past (Laslett, 1977b; Goode, 1963; Hareven, 1971).

As in the present, early American households were nuclear in their structure. The older generation resided in separate households from those of their married adult children but were located nearby, often on the same land. Opportunities for contact and cooperation among the generations abounded in what was characterized as a "modified extended family system" (Greven, 1970). These voluntary, reciprocal relations were different, however, from an institutionalized stem-family system, which characterized the coresidence of generations in Central Europe (Plakans, 1987).

Nor was there a "golden age" in the family relations of older people in the European or American past. Even in the colonial period, elderly people were insecure in their familial supports, though they were revered and accorded higher social status than they are today (Fischer, 1977). Aging parents had to enter into contracts with their inheriting sons in order to secure supports in old age in exchange for land. The emphasis in such contractual arrangements on specific details suggests the potential tensions and insecurities that parents anticipated concerning their care after they became too frail to support themselves (Demos, 1978; D. S. Smith, 1973).

Similarly, in urban-industrial society in the nineteenth and twentieth centuries, older people were not guaranteed supports from their children. In American society, familial support and care for older people, as well as more general patterns of kin assistance, have been voluntary and based on reciprocal relations over the life course (Adams, 1968; Sussman, 1959). In the absence of social security and institutions of social welfare, norms dictated that kin engage in intensive reciprocal assistance. Adult children were expected to be the main caregivers for their aging parents (Demos,

1970; Hareven, 1982). Still, these patterns of care were voluntary rather than established by law. They depended, therefore, on carefully calculated strategies and on negotiated arrangements over the life course (Hareven, 1982).

Coresidence

The fact that aging parents and adult children rarely coresided in multi-generational households does not mean that the generations lived in isolation from each other. Even in urban society, throughout the nineteenth century, solitary residence—a practice that has become increasingly prevalent among older people today—was most uncommon for all age groups (Kobrin, 1976). Autonomy in old age, however, partly expressed in the opportunity for older people to head their own households, hinged on some form of support from an adult child living at home or on the presence of unrelated individuals in the household (Hareven, 1981b). The ideal was the generations' residence on the same land in rural areas or in the same building or same neighborhood in urban areas. "Intimacy from a distance," the preferred mode of generational interaction in contemporary American society, has been persistent since the early settlement and reaches back into the European past (Demos, 1970; Laslett and Wall, 1972).

Despite this overall commitment to residence in nuclear households, common to members of various ethnic groups and native-born Americans alike, nuclear households expanded to include other kin in times of need and during periods of accelerated migration or housing shortages. The most notable extension of the household occurred in the later years of life, when elderly parents and especially widowed mothers were unable to maintain themselves in separate residences. In such cases, aging parents had an adult child return to live with them or they moved into a child's household (D. S. Smith, 1979, 1981; Ruggles, 1987; Hareven, 1991a). Since household space was an important economic resource to be shared and exchanged over the life course, the configurations of household members changed over the life course in relation to the family's economic needs or in response to external opportunities (Hareven, 1990a). Older people whose children had left home shared household space with boarders and lodgers in exchange for services or rent or with their own children who returned with their spouses to the parental home because of housing shortages or their aged parents' frailty (Chudacoff and Hareven, 1979).

As already noted, in the later years of life, boarding and lodging served an important function in enabling older people to retain their autonomy. Boarders and lodgers were young men or women who left their parents' homes and moved into the households of elderly people who had no children or whose own children had left home. Trading household space with boarders and lodgers thus made it easier for elderly people to adhere to their traditional values without slipping below the margin of poverty (Modell and Hareven, 1973). For older people, particularly for widows, it provided the extra income needed to maintain their own residence and helped avert loneliness after their own children had left home. In some cases, the function was reversed, and older people who could not live alone but who had no children or relatives moved into other people's households as boarders.

Despite preferences for unrelated individuals, households expanded to include kin, though usually for limited periods during times of need or at specific points in the life course. Only about 12 to 18 percent of all urban households in the late nineteenth and early twentieth centuries contained relatives other than members of the nuclear family (Hareven, 1977b). However, the unwritten rules about separate residence of the generations in American society were modified when aging parents became chronically ill or demented and, therefore, unable to live independently. Under such circumstances, frail elderly parents usually coresided with a child or with other kin if no children were available (Hareven and Adams, 1996). In urban communities, which attracted large numbers of migrants from the countryside or immigrants from abroad, coresidence with extended kin increased greatly over the nineteenth century (Anderson, 1971; Hareven, 1982). The proportion of households taking in kin increased to 25 percent over the twentieth century but had declined to 7 percent by 1950 (Ruggles, 1987). As noted above, the presence of relatives other than members of the nuclear family in the household, though, was most common in the later years of life.

The powerful commitment to the continued autonomy of the household was clearly in conflict with the needs of people as they were aging. But aging parents and widowed mothers strove to maintain their autonomy by retaining the headship of their own households rather than moving in with their children, relatives, or strangers. In the absence of adequate public and institutional supports, older people striving to maintain independent households were caught in the double bind of living separately from their children yet having to rely on their children's assistance in order to do so (Chudacoff and Hareven, 1979). Holding on to the space and headship of their household in exchange for future assistance in old age was an important survival strategy for older people in urban society, one reminiscent of the contracts between inheriting sons and rural older people in preindustrial Europe and colonial New England. To continue living separately in their own household, parents insured that at least one adult child remain at home. In the absence of a child, frail elderly people, especially widows, had to move in with relatives or strangers

(Chudacoff and Hareven, 1978a; Hareven and Uhlenberg, 1995; D. S. Smith, 1979; Hareven, 1981b).

An examination of patterns of generational coresidence raises several questions related to household headship and the nature of the supports inside the household: When a household record in a census listed a parent as being the head of the household and an adult child as residing in the household, who in reality headed the household, and how did the resources and assistance flow? It is difficult to answer these questions from cross-sectional data, nor can this type of data provide an explanation as to what the dynamics were in these household arrangements. Did the son succeed to household headship after his father retired or became too old or frail to support himself, or did the parents move into the son's household? Under what circumstances did the older generation coreside with adult children or other kin, and under what circumstances did they reside separately and engage in various types of assistance outside the household? It would be impossible to answer these questions from cross-sectional data. They need to be addressed, however, when analyzing longitudinal and retrospective data.

Rates of coresidence recorded in cross-sectional data might reflect a life-course pattern in which elderly parents who did not coreside with their children at the time a census or survey was taken might do so later when they became more dependent. Cross-sectional data can obscure considerable variation in patterns of coresidence over the life course: In the National Survey of Families and Households, for example, only 7 percent of Americans aged fifty-five and older with a surviving parent had the parent living with them at the time the survey was taken. The retrospective questions revealed, however, that one-fourth of the persons surveyed in their late fifties had had an aging parent living with them at some point in their lives. Denis Hogan, David Eggebeen, and Sean Snaith (1995) explain this discrepancy by pointing to the short time period that a sick parent actually resides with a child. The parent stays usually less than a year, because after the parent's health deteriorates, he or she either enters a nursing home or dies.

Historical Changes in the Timing of Life Transitions

As mentioned above, demographic changes in American society since the late nineteenth century have significantly affected age configurations within the family and the timing of life-course transitions and have made possible an increasing overlap of generations into old age (Uhlenberg, 1974; Hareven, 1976a; Riley, 1984). The decline in mortality since the late nineteenth century has resulted in greater uniformity in the life course of

American families and has dramatically increased the opportunities for intact survival of the family unit over the lifetime of its members. As a result, an increasing portion of the population has lived out its life in family units. Except when disrupted by divorce, married couples have been able to live together for longer time periods, children have been growing up with their parents as well as with their siblings all still alive, grandparents have overlapped with their grandchildren into the latter's adulthood, and great-grandparenthood has emerged as a new stage of adult life (Uhlenberg, 1974, 1978). Longevity and the increasing survival to adulthood have maximized the opportunity for generational overlap and for available pools of kin, despite the decline in fertility (Townsend, 1968; Cherlin and Furstenberg, 1990).

Under the impact of demographic, economic, and cultural change, the timing of the major transitions to adulthood—particularly leaving home, entry into and exit from the labor force, marriage, parenthood, the "empty nest," and widowhood—has undergone significant changes over the past century. Underlying these changes has been an increase in age uniformity in the timing of life transitions. Over the twentieth century, transitions to adulthood have become more uniform, more orderly in sequence, and more rapidly timed. The timing of these transitions has become more regulated according to specific age norms, rather than in relation to the needs of the family. Individual life transitions have become less closely synchronized with collective familial ones, thus causing a further separation between the generations (Modell, Furstenberg, and Hershberg, 1976).

By contrast, in the nineteenth century, the transitions to adulthood were more gradual and less rigidly timed. The time range necessary for a cohort to accomplish these transitions (leaving school, starting work, getting married, and establishing a separate household) was wider, and the sequence in which transitions followed one another was not rigidly established. The nineteenth-century pattern of transitions allowed for a wider age spread within the family and for greater opportunity for interaction among parents and adult children. Later age at marriage, higher fertility, and shorter life expectancy rendered family configurations different from those in contemporary society. The increasing rapidity in the timing of the transitions to adulthood, the separation of an individual's family of origin from the family of procreation, and the introduction of publicly regulated transitions such as mandatory retirement, have converged to isolate and segregate age groups and generations in the larger society (Hogan, 1989; Modell, Furstenberg, and Hershberg, 1976; Hogan, Eggebeen, and Clogg, 1993).

Because early and later life transitions are interrelated, these changes have affected the status of older people in the family and their sources of support, generating new kinds of stresses on familial needs and obligations. In the nineteenth century, the timing of later life transitions to the empty nest, to widowhood, and out of the headship of one's own house-hold followed no ordered sequence and extended over a relatively longer time period. Older women did experience more marked transitions than men because of widowhood, although the continuing presence of at least one adult child in the household meant that widowhood did not neces-sarily represent a dramatic transition into the empty nest (Chudacoff and Hareven, 1979; D. S. Smith, 1979).

The most pronounced discontinuity in the adult life course during the twentieth century, especially since World War II, has been the empty-nest stage in a couple's middle age. The empty nest emerged as a modal pat-tern of the middle and later years of life, as a result of the decline in mor-tality and the combination of earlier marriage and the bearing of fewer children overall with closer spacing of children and the more uniform pattern of children leaving home earlier in their parents' lives. This meant that a couple experienced a more extended period of life without chil-dren, beginning in their middle years. A separation between the genera-tions thus occurred when parents were still in middle age. At the same time, women's tendency to live longer than men resulted in a protracted period of widowhood in old age (Glick, 1977).

By contrast, in the nineteenth century, the residence of children in the parental household extended over a longer time period, sometimes over the parents' entire life. Most important, the nest was rarely empty, be-cause usually one adult child was expected to remain at home while the parents were aging (D. S. Smith, 1981). Demographic factors account only in part for the empty nest. Children did not remain in their aging parents' household simply because they were too young to move out. Even when sons and daughters were in their late teens and early twenties, at least one child remained at home to care for aging parents if no other assis-tance was available (Chudacoff and Hareven, 1979; Hareven, 1982). Leav-ing home did not so uniformly precede marriage, and the launching of children did not necessarily leave the nest empty. As mentioned above, occasionally a married child returned to the parental home, or the parents took in boarders or lodgers.

Since the 1980s, more erratic and flexible patterns in the timing of life-course transitions have emerged again. These patterns depart from the earlier age-related rigidities in timing to reflect changes in family arrange-ments and new policies governing the work life. The movement of young adult children in and out of the parental home has become more erratic. Young adults stay on or return to the parental home after having left pre-viously (Goldscheider and DaVanzo, 1985). This contemporary pattern, however, differs from that of the past in a fundamental way: In the late nineteenth century, children continued to stay in the parental home or moved back and forth in order to meet the needs of their family of orientation by taking care of aging parents or, in some cases, of younger siblings. In contemporary society, young adult children reside with their parents in order to meet their own needs, because of their inability to develop an independent work career or to find affordable housing. Another contemporary variant of the filling of the nest is the return of divorced or unmarried daughters with their own young children to the parental household (McLanahan, 1988). In this instance as well, the main purpose has generally not been for the daughter to assist her aging mother but rather to receive help in housing and child care.

The timing of life transitions in the nineteenth century was erratic because it followed family needs and obligations rather than specific age norms. Familial obligations, dictated by economic insecurity and by cultural norms of kin assistance, took precedence over strict age norms. Over the twentieth century, by contrast, age norms have emerged as more important determinants of timing than familial obligations. As John Modell, Frank Furstenberg, and Theodore Hershberg (1976, p. 30) concluded: "'Timely' action to nineteenth-century families consisted of helpful response in times of trouble; in the twentieth century, timeliness connotes adherence to a socially sanctioned schedule." As greater differentiation in stages of life began to develop following the turn of the century and as social and economic functions became more closely related to age, a segregation between age groups emerged and, with it, an increasing separation among the generations. This separation occurred first in the middle class and was only later extended to the working class. The pattern still varies considerably among ethnic groups and among black families in contemporary society (Markides, Costley, and Rodriguez, 1981; Markides and Krause, 1985; Jackson et al., 1995; Taylor, Chatters, and Jackson, 1993).

Age uniformity in the family and age segregation among generations, however, may be modified as a result of remarriage following divorce. As Furstenberg pointed out, remarriage following divorce in contemporary society recreates kinship configurations that resemble those resulting through remarriage following the premature death of a partner in the eighteenth or nineteenth century. It may have a similar effect of incorporating new spouses and step siblings into a "blended family" of people who differ considerably in their ages. As age again becomes heterogeneous within the family, Furstenberg concluded, generational boundaries become less distinct in the everyday life of the family, and consequently, "the salience of generational boundaries in the larger society may decline as well" (Furstenberg, 1981, p. 136).

In contemporary American society, one is accustomed to thinking of most transitions to family roles and work careers as individual moves. This may differ among certain ethnic and cultural groups, where strong patterns of kin assistance are still extant. In the past, however, the timing of individual transitions had to be synchronized with familial ones. The family was the most critical agent in initiating and managing the timing of life transitions. Control over the timing of individual members' transitions was a crucial factor in the family's efforts to manage its resources, especially to balance different members' contributions to the family economy. The absence of a narrow, age-related timing of transitions to adult life allowed for a more intensive interaction among different age groups within family and community, thus providing a greater sense of continuity and interdependence among people and among generations at various points in the life course.

The contemporary erratic style of family transitions coincides with changing patterns of retirement. The rigid end to a work career is becoming erratic once again, but for very different reasons than those in the past. The golden handshake to encourage or force early retirement does not solve the dilemma of the structural lag in American society between social changes and institutional adaptation to accommodate them:

> Today, by contrast [with the nineteenth century], survival into old age is commonplace and many years of vigorous post retirement life are the realistic expectation. . . . Nevertheless, the major responsibilities for work and family are still crowded into what are now called the middle years of long life. . . . Despite the twentieth-century metamorphosis in human lives . . . the social structures and norms that define opportunities and expectations throughout the life course carry the vestigial marks of the nineteenth century. (Riley, Kahn, and Foner, 1994, p. 147)

In a historical context, early life transitions were bound up with later ones in a continuum of familial needs and obligations. Hence, the life transitions of the younger generation were intertwined with those of the older generation. Specifically, the timing of children leaving home, getting married, and setting up a separate household was contingent on the timing of parents' transitions into retirement, inheritance, or widowhood (Greven, 1970; Hareven, 1982). This interdependence dictated parental control over the timing of adult children's life transitions. The strategies that parents and children followed in determining exchanges and supports in relation to the timing of life transitions represent, therefore, important theoretical and empirical issues that require further exploration.

Interdependence Among Kin

As pointed out earlier, contrary to prevailing myths and sociological theories, urbanization and industrialization did not break down traditional ties and reciprocal relations among kin (Anderson, 1971; Hareven, 1978b;

Sussman, 1959). Whether extended kin resided separately or in the same household, mutual assistance with them was at the base of survival for members of the nuclear family. Kin served as the most essential resource for economic assistance and security and shouldered the major burden of welfare functions for individual family members. Earlier chapters have documented the survival of kinship ties and viable functions of kin in facilitating migration, in locating jobs and housing, in manipulating industrial production, and in providing assistance during critical life situations. Kin assistance was pervasive in urban neighborhoods and extended back to the communities of origin of immigrants and migrants through various exchanges. As pointed out above, immigrants in the United States often sent back remittances for their aging parents and other relatives in their home communities, while relatives remaining behind took care of aging parents and family farms (Anderson, 1971; Hareven, 1982).

Under the historical conditions in which familial assistance was the almost exclusive source of security, the multiplicity of obligations that individuals incurred toward kin over life was more complex than in contemporary society. In addition to the ties they retained with their family of origin, individuals carried numerous obligations toward their family of procreation and toward their spouse's family of origin. Such obligations cast men and women into various overlapping and, at times, conflicting roles over the course of their lives. The absence of institutional supports in the form of welfare agencies, unemployment compensation, and social security added to the pressures imposed on the kin group. In the regime of economic insecurity characteristic of the nineteenth century and the first part of the twentieth century, kin assistance was the only constant source of support. Family coping, by necessity, dictated that individual choices be subordinated to collective familial considerations and needs. Support from kin was crucial during critical life situations such as unemployment and illness or death, as well as for normative life transitions (Anderson, 1971; Hareven, 1982).

This strong interdependence among kin meant that individual choices had to be subordinated to collective family needs. Individuals' sense of obligation to their kin was dictated by their family culture. It expressed a commitment to the survival, well-being, and self-reliance of the family, which took priority over individual needs and preferences. Autonomy of the family, essential for self-respect and good standing in the neighborhood and community, was one of the most deeply ingrained values. Mutual assistance among kin, although involving extensive exchanges, was not strictly calculative. Rather, it expressed an overall principle of reciprocity over the life course and across generations.

Individuals who subordinated their own careers and needs to those of the family as a collective unit did so out of a sense of responsibility, affection, and familial obligation rather than with the expectation of immediate gain. Such sacrifices were not made without protest, however, and at times involved competition and conflict among siblings as to who should carry the main responsibility of support for aging parents. Close contact and mutual exchanges among parents, their adult children, and other kin persisted throughout the nineteenth century and survived into the twentieth century in various forms in the lives of working-class and ethnic families. Parents expected their grown children to support them in their old age in exchange for supports they had rendered their children earlier in life. Societal values rooted in ethnic cultures provided ideological reinforcements for these reciprocal obligations (Hareven, 1982; Eggebeen and Hogan, 1990).

Changes in the configurations of kin resulting from the increase in divorce rates and remarriage since the 1960s may have important implications for the available kinship pools in the later years of life, as well as for generational boundaries within a kinship group. As Furstenberg (1981) stressed, divorce has not necessarily led to the depletion of existing kinship ties. Especially where the older generation is involved with child rearing, ties with grandparents survive divorce. When divorce is followed by remarriage, the kinship pool expands through the addition of new relatives, without relinquishing the existing ones. This "remarriage chain," as Furstenberg has referred to it, links family and present conjugal partners and their relatives, primarily through the child. Since the older generation is likely to invest in child rearing, Furstenberg concluded that children reared within these complex configurations would maintain stronger obligations toward future supports for the older generation (Furstenberg, 1981, p. 137).

Building on the existence of such complex kinship networks in contemporary society, Jack Riley and Matilda Riley further expand the definition to include non-kin, who were members of the network as a result of cohabitation and other associations with members of the nuclear family:

> Indeed, the emerging boundaries of the kin network may be more closely influenced by gender, or even by race and ethnicity, than by age or generation. Instead, the boundaries of the kin network have been widened to encompass many diverse relationships, including several degrees of stepkin and in-laws, single parent families, adopted and other "relatives" chosen from outside the family, and many others. (Riley and Riley, 1996, p. 6)

Riley and Riley characterize these complex kinship and fictitious kinship relations as "a latent web of continually shifting linkages that provide the potential for activating and intensifying close kin relationships as they are needed" (Riley and Riley, 1996, p. 6).

The phenomenon of surrogate kinship networks is not entirely new. As shown above, in the nineteenth century and in the first part of the twentieth century, various ethnic groups and working-class families were enmeshed in similar networks consisting of surrogate kin as well as kin. Some of these networks stretched across wide geographic regions, linking migrants or immigrants in the communities of settlement with their kin in the communities of origin into one social system. Some of these ties were latent or activated in accordance with various needs as they arose (Hareven, 1982). The significance of these new networks is that they transcend the boundaries of age and generations, which may enhance their flexibility and efficacy. When comparing the contemporary networks to the historic ones, however, one needs to assess the latter's long-term effectiveness. The historic networks were also flexible and fluid, but the expectations for supports were clearly defined by long-standing norms of reciprocity. For the contemporary networks, one would need extensive research to identify the rules and principles by which they operate and would want to follow them longitudinally in order to determine their durability and effectiveness.

Generational Supports over the Life Course

Despite the strong tradition of kin assistance, spouses and children have been the main caregivers for aging parents. Both historical and contemporary studies of supports for older people have identified adult children, most commonly daughters, as the main caregivers, where spouses were not available. Even in time periods and among ethnic groups where individuals were deeply embedded in reciprocal relations with extended kin, the main responsibility of caregiving, particularly for frail, elderly parents, was that of their offspring. Kin provided sociability and occasional help, but the day-to-day involvement with caregiving fell upon the children. Regardless of how many children a couple had, one child usually emerged in the role of caregiver (D. S. Smith, 1979; Chudacoff and Hareven, 1979). As will be shown below, adult children's involvement with the care of their aging parents was closely related to their earlier life-course experiences, to their respective ethnic and cultural traditions, and to the historical context affecting their lives. Routine assistance from children to aging parents prepared the children to cope with parents' later life crises, especially widowhood and dependence in old age.

When both parents survived into old age and were able to cope on their own, the children were more likely to try to maintain them in the parental home. Children made an effort to have their parents reside nearby, preferably in the same building or the same block, but not in the same household if it could be avoided. In cases of illness or need, children visited their parents on a daily basis, arranged for medical treatment, provided bodily care, prepared meals, and ran errands. After the death of one parent, children temporarily took in the surviving parent. In some cases, several siblings contributed jointly by hiring a nurse to take daily care of a frail parent who was still living at home. Children, most commonly daughters, took a parent into their own household under circumstances of extreme duress, such as when parents were too frail to live alone or when they needed extensive help with their daily activities and regular care. There was no prescribed rule as to which child would become a "parent keeper." If the child was not already residing with the parent, the selection of a child for that role was governed by a particular child's ability and willingness to take the parent in, by the consent or support of the parent keeper's spouse, and by the readiness of the parent to accept the plan (Hareven and Adams, 1996).

As will be explained shortly, life-course antecedents were crucial determinants of whether an individual was cast in the "parent keeper's" role. Some children took on this responsibility because of a sudden family crisis, but most evolved into this role over their life course. Most commonly, the parent keeper was the child who continued to reside with a parent after the other siblings had left home. Even when both parents were alive, as noted above, the youngest daughter was expected to remain at home and postpone or give up marriage in order to ensure support for the parents in their old age. Caretaking daughters gave up marriage altogether or sometimes waited for decades until their parents died before they could marry. This pattern was pervasive among certain ethnic groups until World War II (Hareven, 1982).

Daughters fulfilled their caregiving role at a high price to themselves and to their spouses and other family members. As various gerontological studies have emphasized, caregiving disrupted a daughter's work career, led to crowding in her household, caused tension and strain in her marriage, and made her vulnerable in preparing for her own and her spouse's retirement and old age (Hareven and Adams, 1996; Brody, 1990; Cantor, 1983). More recent studies have questioned what may be an excessive emphasis on "women in the middle" as the main caregivers for aging parents. Several of these studies have explored the respective roles of women and men as caregivers and have concluded that although men performed managerial and maintenance tasks, as well as providing financial and social supports, the women predominantly performed the daily hands-on caregiving tasks (Dwyer and Coward, 1991; Kaye and Applegate, 1990; Dwyer and Seccombe, 1991; Hareven, 1993b).

Historically, it was the women who maintained the lifelong role of "kin keepers." Although needs and responsibilities changed, the kin keepers' centrality to the kin networks as helpers, arbiters, and pacifiers continued and became even more pivotal with age. It was the kin keeper who became the primary caregiver and who marshaled other relatives and negotiated their subsidiary roles in the effort to provide care for frail elderly parents (Hareven, 1982).

Cohort Differences

Historical changes in generational supports and in attitudes toward receiving and providing such supports are best reconstructed through a comparison of cohorts whose lives were located in different historical periods. As will be detailed below, in our study of two cohorts of the adult children of immigrant textile workers to the industrial community of Manchester, New Hampshire, Kathleen Adams and I found significant differences in the attitudes toward caregiving and the practices of the two cohorts in relation to their earlier historical experiences. An older cohort (born 1910–1919), which came of age during the Great Depression, and a younger cohort (born 1920–1929), which came of age during World War II, were both the children of a historic cohort that had migrated to Manchester to work in the Amoskeag Mills. (The detailed comparison of the cohort is reported in Chapter 7.)

Both cohorts were, to some degree, transitional between a milieu of deep involvement in generational assistance, reinforced by strong family and ethnic values, and the individualistic values and lifestyles that emerged in the post–World War II period. In this historical process, the lives of members of the earlier cohort conformed more closely to the script of their traditional familial and ethnic cultures, whereas members of the later cohort, as it Americanized, were being pulled in the direction of individualistic middle-class values. The transition was by no means completed. Members of the later cohort had not entirely freed themselves of their traditional upbringing. Both cohorts still expressed their parents' values, but the later cohort felt less able or inclined to implement them.

The difference between the two children's cohorts and the parents thus reflects the historical process of an increasing individualization in family relationships and a reliance on public agencies and bureaucratic institutions to shoulder the responsibilities for the care of dependent elderly. The historical process is well known, but the detailed analysis of the interviews of the cohorts' members provides firsthand testimony about how this change was perceived and experienced by the women and men who were caught up in it. The process is one of an increasing separation between the family of origin and the family of procreation over the past century, combined with a privatization of family life and the erosion of mutual assistance among kin.

These historical changes have tended to escalate insecurity and isolation as people age, most markedly in areas of need that are not met by public welfare programs. Although some of the intensive historical patterns of kin interaction have survived among first-generation immigrant, black, and working-class families, a gradual weakening of mutual assistance among kin over time has occurred (Jackson et al., 1988). Jay Sokolovsky and others have warned against a romanticization of generational interdependence among more recent immigrant groups, such as Hispanics or Koreans, and among blacks (Sokolovsky, 1990; Mutran, 1986; Burton and deVries, 1992; Taylor and Chatters, 1991; Dowd and Bengston, 1978; Burton and Dilwater-Anderson, 1991).

How consistent and continuous the support from nonresident children or other kin to aging relatives has been in the United States is still widely open to future research. Most studies in gerontology or sociology emphasizing the persistence of kin supports for older people in contemporary society have not documented the intensity, quality, and consistency of these supports in meeting the needs of older people, especially of the frail and chronically ill elderly. Most of these studies have used visiting patterns and telephone communication as evidence rather than regular caregiving and coresidence (Litwak, 1965; Shanas, 1979).

Recent studies have provided more systematic evidence of various supports from adult children to aging parents, especially for the "old old" in contemporary society. Some of these supports involve coresidence; in other cases, the caretaking child provides assistance in the parent's household (Brody et al., 1983; Brody, 1990; Dwyer and Coward, 1991). The contact that older people have with kin, as Ethel Shanas (1979) and others have found, might represent a form of behavior characteristic of specific cohorts rather than a persistent pattern. The cohorts that are currently aged, especially the "old old," have carried over the historical attitudes and traditions advocating an almost exclusive reliance on kin. Historical precedents also reveal the high price that kin had to pay in order to assist each other without the appropriate public supports (Hareven, 1978c, 1982).

Except for members of certain ethnic groups, future cohorts, as they reach old age, might not have the same strong sense of familial interdependence characteristic of earlier cohorts, nor might they have sufficiently large pools of kin on whom to rely. Alice Rossi and Peter Rossi (1990) found that in the population sample they studied in Boston, the younger respondents expressed a stronger sense of normative obligations to kin than the older ones. On this basis, they have argued that obligations to kin have not been declining over historical time. This assertion would need to be tested, however, by comparing the attitudes of the group studied in Boston with their age counterparts in the late nineteenth century.

The major changes that have confounded the problems of older people in contemporary society were rooted not so much in changes in family structure or residential arrangements of the generations, as has generally been argued, as in the transformation and redefinition of family functions and of values governing family relations and generational assistance. Over the nineteenth century, the family surrendered many of the functions previously concentrated within it to other social institutions. A retreat from public life and a growing commitment to the privacy of the family that began in the middle class have led to the drawing of sharper boundaries between family and community and have intensified the segregation of age groups within and outside the family (Demos, 1970; Rothman, 1971).

The transfer of social-welfare functions from the family to public institutions over the past century and a half has not been fully consummated, however. The family has ceased to be the sole available source of support for its dependent members and the community has ceased to rely on the family as the major agency of welfare and social control. Who actually provides supports for the elderly, and what form those supports take, has been subject to ambiguities. On the one hand, family members assume that the public sector carries the major responsibilities of care for the aged; on the other hand, the public sector assumes that the family is responsible for some of these areas. This confusion in the assignment of responsibilities often means that old people are caught between the family and the public sector without receiving proper supports from either. The expectation that family and kin carry the major responsibilities for the care of aged relatives still prevails, without the provision of the necessary supports that would enable kin to discharge such responsibilities (Litwak, 1985). The decline in instrumental relations among kin and their replacement by an individualistic orientation toward family relations, with sentimentality and intimacy as the major cohesive forces, has led to the weakening of the role of kin assistance in middle-class families in particular and to an increasing isolation of the elderly in American society (Hareven, 1977b).

Conclusion

In addition to the obvious role of providing an understanding of change over time, a historical perspective serves two additional functions: First, it enables us to compare contemporary phenomena with similar ones in the past, in order to assess how new or different from their predecessors they really are; and, second, it offers models of coping from the past that may be modified and utilized in the present.

A historical and life-course perspective has helped identify the complexity of social change itself. Even though it is possible to trace some general trends—such as the emergence of age segregation, separation among the generations, and individualization—a warning against following a linear path of change is in order. Rather than being linear, the process of social change has been uneven and multilayered. Historic forms of household extension and coresidence with relatives, which have disappeared over the twentieth century, have reappeared in different configurations. Complex kinship networks characteristic of earlier centuries, which resulted from remarriage following the death of a spouse in the past, have reappeared in different forms in "blended families" following divorce. The trend toward age uniformity and streamlined timing of life transitions has been modified or reversed by the return of an "erratic life course," which is similar to the nineteenth century one but driven by different social forces.

When examining changes over time in the family, the life course, and generational relations, one needs to pay attention to differences in class and ethnicity. The most important dimension still absent from studies of long-term changes in the family and generational relations involves an examination of systematic differences among social classes and ethnic groups. We need a more detailed understanding of the historical process by which patterns of family behavior that first emerged in the middle class were transferred to other classes, and by what process. Along these lines, it would be futile to generalize about long-term changes by comparing contemporary patterns to past ones without specifying what social class or ethnic group are being compared.

Any examination of changes in generational relations and in the family over time needs to take into consideration the diverse nature of "the family" itself, rendered fluid by shifts in internal age and gender configurations across regions and over time. Since the family is the arena in which generational relations are acted out, one needs to achieve a clearer definition of "family" and "kinship." One needs to understand the boundaries and the overlap between the two, especially as one examines the newer and complex kinship configurations that have emerged in contemporary society.

As has been noted, the historical experience can provide important models for coping in the present. Even though longevity, along with its inherent social problems, is a unique phenomenon of our times, the more general aspects of providing generational assistance and supports and coping with dependence in old age can be enriched by drawing on models of familial adaptation in the past. In doing so, one must not lose sight

of the dramatic social, economic, and institutional differences in the contemporary context. For example, it would be beneficial to adapt past
models of kin assistance and surrogate familial arrangements for the support of older people. When doing so, it would be counterproductive,
however, to idealize these patterns from the past and to expect kin to
"take care of their own."

6

Synchronizing Individual Time, Family Time, and Historical Time

Historians have been intensely aware of the importance of time as a major frame for social change, but they have discovered only recently the importance of time as a *phenomenon* or product of social change. The concept of time as a historical construct has been discussed almost exclusively by historians concerned with the transition from task and season-related work patterns and ways of life to industrial time discipline. For example, the importance of modern industrial time schedules has been a recurring theme in labor history, where it was first presented by E. P. Thompson. Thompson emphasized the introduction of the industrial time clock and discipline as a dramatic and traumatic watershed in the history of Western society (Thompson, 1963). Until recently, less attention was given to issues of time and timing as manifested over the individual life course and the family in relation to changing historical time.

Since the 1980s, however, research in the history of the family and the life course has introduced an additional dimension into the understanding of time in relation to historical change: The historical study of the family has demonstrated that in its interactions with historical change, the family of-

---

*The research for this chapter was supported by grants number 5ROIAG02468 and 5ROIAG0644I from the National Institute on Aging. The Japanese-U.S. comparisons were supported by the Social Science Research Council, the Japan Society for the Promotion of Science, and the U.S.-Japan Friendship Commission. I am grateful to Professor Kanji Masaoka for his collaboration on the U.S.-Japanese comparisons and to Professor Kiyomi Morioka for his leadership in this comparative project.

Reprinted from *Chronotypes; The Construction of Time*, edited by John Bender and David E. Wellbery, with the permission of the publishers, Stanford University Press © 1991 by the Board of Trustees of the Leland Stanford Junior University.

ten followed its own time clocks. Even though the family responded to larger forces of historical change, it formed its responses and adjustments in relation to the clock dictated by its own cultural traditions and needs, within the constraints of the larger social and economic structures. For that very reason, the periodization of family history does not fit the neat categories of established historical periodization (preindustrial, industrial, postindustrial; or premodern, early modern, modern) (Hareven, 1982).

The historical study of the life course offers an opportunity to understand the issues of synchronization of individual time, family time, and historical time. It enables one to study these interactions on the behavioral level through the timing of life transitions and on the perceptual level through individuals' own perceptions of their timing of transitions in relation to the social time clocks. By examining the various aspects of timing on the individual and familial levels in relation to changing historical conditions, the life-course approach enables us to understand the ways in which individual lives were synchronized with the larger processes of social change (Hareven, 1978e; Elder, 1979).

This chapter examines the impact of new concepts of time on the social clocks that individuals and families followed in the context of changing historical time. The type of "time" addressed here is not chronological in the strict sense. Its essence is *timing*—meaning coincidence, sequencing, coordination, and synchronization of various time clocks, those being individual, collective, and social structural. The first part of this chapter defines the concept of "timing" from a life-course and historical perspective. The second part compares the patterns and perceptions of timing of three different cohorts in the United States. The third part compares these patterns with those in Japan.

The Definition of Timing

An understanding of social change hinges to a large extent on the interaction between individual time and social-structural (historical) time. In this interaction, the family acts as an important mediator between individuals and the larger social processes. Under certain circumstances, individual timing harmonizes with family timing; under others, it is out of synchrony with family time. The tension between individual timing and the collective timing of the family, especially in transitions such as leaving home, launching a career, or getting married, has also varied considerably over historical time.

The form and content of this interaction of different time clocks has changed over historical time and has varied in different cultural settings. Timing and timeliness are defined differently in various cultures and under different historical circumstances. Even within a specific time period, a variety of definitions of timeliness may coexist; that is, whether individuals or families are "early," "late," or "on time" in the scheduling of individual or collective family transitions may vary among different ethnic groups, even within the same society during the same time period (Neugarten and Hagestadt, 1976). In order to grasp individuals' interpretations of their timing of such transitions, one needs to understand the cultural and historical contexts within which specific life transitions are timed. Definitions of timeliness derive from individuals' inner expectations and from those of their family members and their peer group. But it also depends on different societies' cultural constructions of the life course. Timeliness is shaped and defined by one's culture or subculture and by the values governing "timing" in different social and cultural contexts (Hareven, 1977a).

For example, in Japan as in the United States, the "timeliness" of transitions is a major source of cultural concern. The meaning of timeliness in Japan is somewhat different, however, from its meaning in the United States. In Japan, the term *tekirei* designates set norms of timing—the ages "fit" for accomplishing various life transitions. Individuals thus define their timing of marriage, work careers, and other roles in relation to the set norms of timing defined in *tekirei*. *Tekirei* also means the orderly sequence of life transitions. In Japan more than in the United States, the orderly and fixed sequencing of life transitions, especially in the transition to adulthood, has been considered the proper normative order for completing school, starting one's first job, and marrying. This sequence is followed by more than 90 percent of each cohort, a fact indicating a uniform tendency in timing. By contrast, the normative order is followed by only 60 percent of each cohort in the United States (Hogan and Mochizuki, 1988).

In contrast to Japan, until recently, the timing of life transitions in the United States was less related to age norms. Family needs took priority over age norms in determining the timeliness of life transitions. Hence, transitions to adulthood (leaving home, starting to work, getting married, setting up a separate household) did not always follow an orderly sequence and took a long time to accomplish, because they were timed in relation to familial needs rather than in relation to age. Only since the post–World War II period has the timing of these transitions begun to adhere more strictly to age norms (Modell, Furstenberg, and Hershberg, 1976).

The concept of timing over the life course involves the movement of individuals from one state to the next rather than viewing life as segmented into fixed stages. Such movements have been defined in life-course research as transitions. Timing thus designates when an event or a transition occurs in an individual's life in relation to external events, regardless of whether a transition conforms to or diverges from societal norms of timeliness. It also determines how a transition relates to other people traveling with the individual through life or through certain parts of life. Thus, the variables used in the examination of timing are relative rather than absolute chronological categories. They are perceptual as well as behavioral for those subject to them and for their associates.

Characteristics of Timing over the Life Course

As detailed above, three features of timing are central to the understanding of changes over the life course: first, the timing of transitions over an individual life path, particularly the balancing of individuals' entry into different family and work roles and their exit from these roles; second, the synchronization of individual transitions with collective family ones; and third, the cumulative impact of early life transitions as shaped by historical forces on subsequent ones. In all these areas, the pace and definition of "timing" hinge upon the social and cultural context in which transitions occur.

1. *Individual Timing.* In the individual life trajectory, the crucial question is how people time and organize their entry into and exit from various roles over their life course: for example, how they sequence transitions in their work life and educational life with respect to transitions in their family life; and how they synchronize and sequence transitions in the context of changing historical conditions in areas such as entry into the labor force, leaving home, getting married, setting up an independent household, and becoming parents (Elder, 1979).

2. *Synchronization of Individual with Collective Family Timing.* On the familial level, timing involves the synchronization of individual life transitions with collective family ones and the juggling of family and work roles over the life course. The familial configurations in which individuals engage change over their life course. Along with these changes, people time their transitions into and out of various roles differently. Age, although an important determinant of the timing of life transitions, is not the exclusive variable. Changes in family status and in accompanying roles are often as important as age, if not more so (Elder, 1979). Thus, the synchronization of individual transitions with collective family ones is a crucial aspect of the life course, especially where individual goals are in conflict with the needs of the family as a collective unit (Hareven, 1978e, 1982).

3. *Cumulative Impact of Earlier Life Events on Subsequent Ones.* The third feature of timing is the cumulative impact of earlier events on

subsequent ones over the entire life course. Early or late timing of certain transitions affects the pace of subsequent ones. Events experienced earlier in the life course can continue to influence an individual's or family's life path in different ways throughout their lives (Elder, 1974).

The impact of historical forces on the life course does not stop with one generation. Each generation encounters a set of historical circumstances that shape its subsequent life history and that generation transmits to the next one both the impact that historical events had on its life course and the resulting patterns of timing. In addition to the immediate historical events that each cohort experiences, long-term historical change has a critical impact on timing over the life course in several areas. In the area of demographic behavior the timing of marriage, fertility, and mortality patterns shape changing age configurations within the family (Uhlenberg, 1974). Similarly, external economic changes in the opportunity structure affect changes in the timing of entry into the labor force, and, ultimately, retirement. Institutional and legislative changes, such as compulsory school attendance, child-labor laws, and mandatory retirement, shape the work-life transitions of different age groups and eventually influence their family life as well.

Cultural norms governing the timeliness of life transitions (being "early," "late," or "on time") and norms governing familial obligations also shape individual and collective family timing. In all these areas, historical and cultural differences are critical. Particularly significant is the convergence of socioeconomic and cultural forces, which are characteristic of specific time periods and which influence directly the timing of life transitions and perceptions of the life course.

For example, "middle-age crisis" was a relatively recent invention in popular psychology in American society. It was attributed to middle-class women in particular in describing the problems connected to menopause and the "empty nest" in midadulthood. "Middle-age crises" were not widespread, however. They were a product of stereotypes and a social construction rather than of sociobiological or familial realities. Since the 1970s, a considerable volume of feminist psychological literature has placed "middle-age crisis" in its proper perspective by exposing the cultural and "scientific" stereotypes that created the concept.

Similarly, as discussed below, the definition of "adolescence" as a distinct stage of life was not a universal phenomenon. The concept of adolescence emerged in a specific historical time period. It was developed in the late nineteenth century in order to define the social and cultural characteristics accompanying stages of psychological development related to puberty. But even though all teenagers undergo a psychological transition in puberty, the cultural and social phenomena associated with it are not uniformly experienced in all societies, nor did they receive the same recognition in the past (Hall, 1904; Kett, 1977).

In summary, any examination of transitions in the life of individuals is contingent on several factors: the place of such transitions in an individual's life in relation to other transitions; the relationship of an individual's transition to those experienced by other family members; and the historical conditions affecting such transitions. For this reason, the differences among cohorts in experiencing and defining transitions is crucial for understanding the impact of social change on the life course.

Transitions and Turning Points

Transitions are processes of individual change within socially constructed timetables, which members of different cohorts undergo. Many of the transitions that individuals experience over their work and family lives are normative; others are critical or, at times, even traumatic. Transitions are considered "normative" if a major portion of a population experiences them and if a society expects its members to undergo such transitions at certain points in their lives in conformity with established norms of timing. Under certain conditions, even normative transitions might become critical ones and might be perceived as turning points.

Turning points are perceptual road marks along the life course. They represent the individuals' subjective assessments of continuities and discontinuities over their life course, especially the impact of special life events on their subsequent life course. In some cases, turning points are perceived as critical changes, but in other cases, as new beginnings (Cohler, 1982; Masaoka et al., 1985).

A central question in life-course analysis is therefore: What transitions are considered normative by the people undergoing them, and what transitions are viewed and experienced as discontinuities and "turning points"? Individuals or families may experience turning points under the impact of internal family crises, such as the premature death of a close family member, illness or physical handicap, loss or damage of property, or loss of a job. Other turning points may be externally induced by historical circumstances or events, such as depressions or wars. For example, the Great Depression and World War II caused critical turning points in the lives of the people who experienced them, both in the United States and in Japan.

This emphasis on the importance of external events in inducing turning points should not be misconstrued, however, as cohort determinism. Cohorts encountering the same historical events do not necessarily experience their impact uniformly. Even within a single cohort, one would expect the experience of turning points to vary in relation to social background, resources, earlier life history, and personality (Elder, 1979).

A normative transition may become a turning point under the following conditions:

1. When it coincides with a crisis or is followed by a crisis, for example, when the birth of a child coincides with the father's loss of a job;
2. When it is accompanied by familial conflict resulting from asynchrony between individual and collective transitions, for example, when a daughter's timing of marriage clashes with her parents' need for continued support in old age;
3. When it is "off time," for example, when a father retires early, or when a woman becomes a parent for the first time in her forties or, in a more critical case, when a man or a woman loses a spouse early;
4. When it is followed by negative consequences unforeseen at the time of the transition, for example, when a marriage ends in divorce;
5. When it requires unusual social adjustments, for example, when leaving home involves migration from a rural to an urban area.

This chapter examines the themes outlined above through the testimonies of two cohorts in a New England industrial community, whose lives span the period from the turn of the century to the present. By comparing the cohorts' experiences of timing and their perceptions of timeliness, we will gain insight into the changes that have occurred in individual and family timing over the current century. In particular, we will note differences in the patterns of timing in the transitions to adult roles and differences in people's perceptions of continuities and discontinuities in their life course.

Cohort Differences in the Timing of Transitions and Perceptions of Turning Points

The Cohorts

The cohorts from Manchester, New Hampshire, encompass two related generations: the parents' generation (Cohort 1), on which my book *Family Time and Industrial Time* (1982) is based, and the children's generation (Cohort 2; see Chapter 2). For analytical purposes, I divided the children's generation into two cohorts in relation to the historical events they encountered as they reached adulthood: Those aged sixty to seventy (Cohort 2a) came of age during the Great Depression and those aged fifty to sixty (Cohort 2b) came of age during World War II. Whereas the "historical" (parent) cohort consists primarily of immigrant workers in a textile factory, the children's cohorts consist predominantly of people born in the United States who had partly made their transition into middle-class occupations and lifestyles.

The Manchester parent cohort (Cohort 1) consists of men and women who were born before 1900. Most of the members of this group were immigrants who had come to work in what was at the beginning of the century the world's largest textile factory (the Amoskeag Mills in Manchester). They spent the early part of their work lives during periods of labor shortage in the peak of the Amoskeag Company's expansion and activity. Following World War I, they experienced frequent discontinuities in their careers. Finally, the Great Depression and the shutdown of the Amoskeag textile mills imposed traumatic discontinuities on their lives when they were middle-aged or older, just at the time when their children were about to reach independent adulthood (Hareven, 1982).

In the children's generation, the older group (Cohort 2a, born between 1910 and 1919) came of age during the Great Depression, a period of economic deprivation and unemployment, whereas the younger group (Cohort 2b, born between 1920 and 1929) came of age during World War II, a period of economic recovery and relative prosperity. The two cohorts in the children's generation thus experienced different social and economic conditions in their transition to adulthood. Since the parent cohort had large numbers of children, siblings often belonged to different cohorts.[1]

The Data Source

Data on the Manchester cohorts used in this chapter are based on a longitudinal historical data set constructed for the parents' cohort for the study resulting in *Family Time and Industrial Time* (Hareven, 1982). In order to compare the cohorts and study change over time, the research team linked this historical data with a new data set on the children's cohorts, generated from intensive interviews, demographic histories, work histories, and migration histories of the children's cohort during the period 1979 to 1983.

By tracing the children of the historical cohort, their spouses, the siblings of the spouses, and other family members in Manchester as well as in other parts of the United States, we reconstructed kinship networks as far as was possible. Following a "snowball" method, we interviewed all kin who responded: the children, their spouses, and the siblings and parents of the spouses. We interviewed each person two or three times, in two- to three-hour sessions with open-ended questions. The interviews included a broad array of questions pertaining to the life histories, work histories, and family histories of the people interviewed, their relations with their kin and the older generations, and the support networks available to them in the later years of life, as well as specific questions about timing (being "early," "late," or "on time"). Interview questions also emphasized individuals' own perceptions of continuities and discontinuities over their life course. We elicited responses about turning points in two ways: by asking directly what crisis or turning points individuals had experienced and by identifying the existence of turning points in the individuals' own references to turning points in their responses.

In addition to conducting interviews, the research team constructed a demographic history, migration history, work history, and family history for each individual. We then linked this sequential information into a "time-life line" for each individual, reconstructing the individual's life history chronologically, in relation to age and historical time. The time-life line enabled us to compare the life trajectories of the various individuals in the sample, to examine in each individual the synchronization of work-life transitions with family ones, and to relate patterns of timing to the subjective accounts of the life course in the interviews (see also Chapter 7).

The Japanese data, to which this chapter will make comparative references, are based on a study of three cohorts in the industrial town of Shizuoka conducted between 1981 and 1984, as part of a comparison of the life course in Japan and the United States. The Shizuoka cohorts consist of Cohort 1, born between 1920 and 1922; Cohort 2, born between 1926 and 1929; and Cohort 3, born between 1935 and 1937. Members of Shizuoka Cohort 1 are age contemporaries of Manchester's children's cohort (Cohort 2, especially Manchester Cohort 2b). As will be shown below, however, in the reality of its historical experience, Shizuoka's Cohort 1 more commonly shared a life experience with Manchester's historical cohort (Cohort 1). The Shizuoka sample includes only men, whereas the Manchester cohorts include men and women. Because of the absence of women from the Shizuoka sample, this chapter compares the life-course patterns of the men only (Hareven and Masaoka, 1988).

Cohort Differences in Timing and Perceptions of Turning Points

In the older cohorts, both in Japan and in the United States, the people interviewed attributed almost one-half of their turning points to their occupational careers, these turning points having been induced by external economic factors, such as business cycles, the war, and the depression. The younger cohorts, by contrast, attributed greater significance to the impact of internal events and to family conditions in causing turning points. Both the historical cohort and the children's cohorts perceived turning points as having occurred in their work life at various points over their entire life course rather than only early in life. The Manchester parent cohort (Cohort 1) generally did not identify turning points related to family life, whereas the children's cohorts, especially the younger ones, claimed to have experienced family-related turning points.

The Manchester parent cohort placed greater emphasis on migration and economic crises as causes of turning points than on personal and familial factors. Indeed, the immigrant and working-class background of this cohort led its members to emphasize economic constraints and family needs as being more critical in defining their life course in general than normatively timed transitions. Over one-half of this group considered the age at which a life transition should occur as less critical than the family's timing of migration or changes in family life dictated by external economic conditions. In Manchester, the older cohort considered interchangeable bouts of employment and unemployment or frequent job changes as the "normal" and expected life-course pattern. The older cohort did not view sporadic periods of unemployment as major turning points. However, the children's cohorts, especially those who came of age during World War II, viewed periods of unemployment as crises. A linear, continuous work career was rarely part of the reality in working-class life. Until World War II, "disorderly careers"—in which people experienced frequent discontinuities over their work lives—were accepted as the norm.

Although economic crises and business cycles affected the parents' cohort in Manchester uniformly, these same external events affected the younger cohorts differentially. The older children's cohort (2a) encountered the Great Depression when they were about to launch their careers. Unemployment and economic deprivation were, therefore, closely tied to their transitions to adult work life. The majority of people in this cohort never completed their high-school education. They had to wander in search of work and did not achieve stable employment until after World War II. Even after the postwar recovery, their early careers were erratic and subject to frequent interruptions.

The members of this particular cohort (2a) were coached by their immigrant working-class parents to enter middle-class careers. But the children were unable to fulfill the life plans that their parents had drawn up for them because of the ways in which the Great Depression and the shutdown of the mills disrupted their careers. For this cohort, the fulfillment of the script of the American Dream, namely, the transition of the mill-workers' children into a middle-class lifestyle, had to be postponed until later in their lives and, in many cases, until the next generation (Hareven, 1982).

Members of the younger Manchester children's cohort (2b), by contrast, launched their careers during and after World War II. As detailed below, although the war caused delays and disruptions in the careers of the men who went into the service, it also had a positive impact in the long run, both on the men who stayed home and on those who went into the service. For those who did not enlist, war industries brought employment and eventually recovery from the depression. For those who joined the military, the war opened new opportunities for acquiring skills and competence with which to launch careers (Elder and Hareven, 1993).

In trying to account for the experience of turning points in the lives of these cohorts, it is important to explore whether the interviewees' subjective experience of turning points was in some ways related to the timing of transitions. The timing of the three main transitions to adulthood—achievement of economic independence, marriage, and establishment of household headship—was related to the experience of turning points. For Manchester's historical cohort (Cohort 1), it was the Great Depression that caused delays in the achievement of economic independence and the establishment of independent households.

In the Manchester children's cohorts, as in Shizuoka's oldest cohort, the delays in the children's launching of stable work careers and establishment of independent families rendered the parents more dependent on their children as the parents approached old age. In Manchester, for both the older and the younger cohorts, the timing of life transitions and the launching of careers were shaped by external economic and social constraints imposed by the depression and World War II. Not only did these events affect the timing of work-life and family transitions at the point of their lives when people first encountered them, but they also indirectly shaped the subsequent flow of careers and family patterns over their life course. The stage in their lives (early in their careers, in midcareer, or later) at which members of these different cohorts encountered the Great Depression and World War II influenced significantly the impact that these events had on their subsequent life transitions and on their perceptions of turning points.

Cohort Differences in Perceptions of Continuities and Discontinuities over the Life Course

While turning points are subjective road marks along the life course, formal stages of life are culturally defined and are often institutionalized and legally established. It is important, therefore, to examine differences between the cohorts in the individuals' consciousness of culturally defined continuities or discontinuities in their life course. In Manchester, we found considerable variation among the cohorts in their perceptions of continuity in their life course.

Members of Manchester's historical cohort (Cohort 1) perceived their life as a continuous whole rather than as segmented into externally defined stages. They expressed little consciousness of having gone through stages such as "adolescence" or "middle age" or the "empty nest." Nor did they tend to view normative life transitions as turning points as much as the children's cohorts did. Most of the members of this cohort considered external events, especially those connected with business cycles and migration, to be much more critical changes than individual transitions. They viewed the declining textile industry, the strike, and the shutdown of the Amoskeag Mills as more critical than turning points in their individual lives.

The children's cohorts in Manchester (Cohort 2), however, were much more conscious of the existence of culturally defined stages in their life course. Unlike the parent cohort, the children's cohorts (especially the younger one) had a clearer view of their life course as being structured around a sequence of normative transitions and as punctuated by turning points. When asked what had been the major crises in their lives, many of the people interviewed in the younger children's cohort (2b) mentioned "adolescence" and "middle-age crisis."

The difference among the responses of these cohorts in their perceptions of continuities and discontinuities in their life course could be a result of the stage of life at which they were interviewed, as well as of their location in historical time. Accordingly, the older cohorts may have viewed their life course as a continuum because they were interviewed in their old age, whereas the younger cohorts were still in middle age or in earlier old age at the time of the interview. The question of the relative significance of life stage during the interview versus cohort experience in the subjective interpretation of the life course represents an important methodological issue that requires further research. In this case, the "cohort effect," namely, the specific historical conditions encountered by each cohort at various historical moments, may offer a more plausible explanation for the differences in the point of view of the younger and the older cohorts than the life-stage explanation.

Comparisons of the Manchester Patterns with Those of Japan

A preliminary comparison of life-course patterns among the Manchester cohorts with their age counterparts in Japan has revealed considerable differences among cohorts in each country as well as similarities that cut across both societies. Both the Shizuoka and Manchester cohorts experienced turning points in relation to historical events—the Great Depression and World War II. In both societies, this experience of turning points was connected to off-timing as a result of these historical events (Hareven and Masaoka, 1988).[2] Although cultural differences in the timing of life transitions and the subjective construction of the life course are significant, the common experience of cohorts in response to shared historical events transcends cultural differences.

In each of the two communities, the older cohorts were more likely to claim having experienced turning points in their work life, whereas the younger cohorts had a greater propensity to cite having experienced turning points in personal and family life. In both communities, the location of a cohort in historical time was the most significant factor in defining the experience of turning points. Both in Shizuoka and in Manchester, the life stage at which a cohort encountered such external events was most significant in causing turning points, as well as in determining an individual's ability to carry out "course correction" (i.e., to take the necessary steps for adapting their life course to these changes). Even though Shizuoka's oldest cohort were age contemporaries of Manchester's children's cohort, their patterns of timing and perceptions of turning points parallel those of Manchester's historical cohort.

The similarities as well as the differences in the experience and attitudes of the Japanese and American cohorts can be explained from a historical and cultural perspective. Both societies idealize linear, continuous work careers and uphold occupational advancement as the ideal script. Both societies introduced mandatory retirement during the early part of this century, thus imposing institutionalized discontinuities on the work life. The surface similarities between the two societies should not, however, obscure the cultural differences affecting the timing of life transitions and the social and subjective construction of the life course.

Historical and Comparative Implications

The differences among the three Manchester cohorts' perceptions of timing reflect the historical changes that have affected the life course in American society since the turn of the century, especially the demographic changes in the timing of life transitions and in the synchronization of individual time schedules with the collective timetables of the family unit (Uhlenberg, 1978).

The younger cohorts' consciousness of discontinuities and stages in their life course may reflect the societal recognition of life stages as well as more marked discontinuities in family life, such as the empty nest. In the United States, the empty nest concept had become sufficiently widespread to account for the younger cohorts' perception of specific stages in family life, especially in the later years of life. However, the older cohort's perception of the absence of marked stages in their life course is consistent with the demographic realities of the first two decades of this century—a time when members of Manchester's oldest cohort (Cohort 1) were immersed in their parenting roles. Typically in this cohort, the youngest child (usually a daughter) remained in the parental household even if old enough to leave home. As will be explained below, it was commonly the youngest daughter who delayed marriage or gave it up altogether in order to remain in the parental home and support aging parents (Hareven, 1982; Chudacoff and Hareven, 1979).

The younger cohorts' perceptions of discontinuities in the life course may reflect increasing societal recognition of life stages. The historical trend in the timing of life transitions in American society has thus become more regulated in accordance with socially accepted age norms. The very notion of embarking on a new stage of life and the implications of movement from one stage to the next have become more firmly established. Both in the United States and in Japan, the establishment of legal age limits for school attendance, child-labor legislation, and formal retirement all served as official landmarks for such societal and legislative supports for these life stages.

The social and cultural attributes of life stages have by no means been subject to universal definition across time and across cultures even within the same time period. Since the turn of the century, the definition of life stages in American society and their appropriate developmental tasks have become progressively more related to age norms. Thus, the private as well as the public consciousness of normatively marked life-course transitions was a much more prominent factor in the earlier life history of the children's cohorts in Manchester. It was, however, less clearly formulated in the counterpart Japanese cohort.

The historical changes affecting the life course were most clearly expressed in the timing of transitions to adulthood. In American society over the past century, the timing of these transitions has become increasingly more age related (Modell, Furstenberg, and Hershberg, 1976). Since World War II, transitions have become more rapidly timed and are following a more orderly sequence. Prior to the beginning of this century, by contrast, transitions from the parental home into marriage, to household headship, and to parenthood occurred more gradually and were timed less rigidly. The time range necessary for a cohort to accomplish such transitions was wider and the sequence in which transitions followed was more flexible and erratic. The increasing age-uniformity in the timing of transitions reflects a long-term historical process leading to the individualization of life transitions: Age norms have become more crucial in dictating timing than are the needs of one's family or kin.

A similar pattern has also emerged for the timing of later life transitions—into the empty nest and out of household headship. The timing of these later transitions has always been more erratic than that of early ones. Even after the timing of transitions to adulthood had become more compressed and orderly, the later transitions continued to follow a considerable age spread (Chudacoff and Hareven, 1979). Eventually, the later-life transitions have also become more age related.

Although in the United States orderly and age-related sequencing of transitions is a recent phenomenon, in Japan the strict timing of life transitions and sequencing in relation to age norms has been the modal, historical pattern. In Japan, even when familial considerations predominated, the timing of individual life transitions adhered to strict time schedules and sequencing, which had been dictated separately by each local community. Marriage and the birth of the first child as well as the succession to household headship were more uniformly timed. Similarly, the departure of the second and third child from the parental home was synchronized with the marriage of the heir. Hence, there existed a delicate balance in the age norms of each local community and family (Morioka, 1985).

In both societies, family considerations and needs initially took priority over the individual timing of life transitions. In Japanese society, however, family considerations of timing were traditionally consistent with age-stratified norms governing the timing of life transitions; in the United States, age-related timing of transitions emerged at the expense of familial control. Whereas timing dictated by family needs was at odds with timing in relation to age norms in the United States, in Japan the two were mutually reinforcing.

7

The Generation in the Middle

Cohort Comparisons in Assistance to
Aging Parents in an American Community

Introduction

The gerontological literature has generally treated patterns of support from adult children to aging parents from a contemporary perspective that is limited to one point in time (Bengston, Kasshau, and Ragan, 1985; Bengston and Treas, 1980; Shanas, 1979; Antonucci, 1990; Cicirelli, 1981). Rarely have these studies addressed the question of how the caregiving relationship was formed over the life course. With some exceptions, contemporary studies of intergenerational assistance have not examined how adult children's support to aging parents changes over time, nor have they considered caregiving children in the context of their social historical times.

In this chapter, Kathleen Adams and I approach intergenerational supports from a life-course and historical perspective (Hareven, 1981b). By comparing two cohorts of adult children, we aim to identify changes both in the practices of caregiving in aging parents' and in adult children's attitudes toward caregiving. By following a historical and developmental approach, we examine the ways in which patterns of support among generations developed over the life course and were revised or adapted in the later years of life. A life-course perspective provides a way of understand-

*This chapter is coauthored by Kathleen Adams. Hareven gratefully acknowledges the support from the National Institute on Aging for the Manchester study "Aging and Generational Relations: Cohort Change" under a Research Career Development Grant #5 K04 AG00026 and with Research Grant #1RO1 AG02468.

This chapter first appeared as "The Generation in the Middle: Cohort Comparisons in Assistance to Aging Parents in an American Community," in Tamara K. Hareven, ed., with Kathleen Adams, *Aging and Generational Relations over the Life Course* (Berlin: Walter de Gruyter, 1996).

ing how relations of mutual support are formed over people's lifetime and how they are reshaped by historical circumstances such as migration, wars, or the collapse of local economies. The earlier life-course experiences of each cohort—as shaped by historical events—also affect availability of resources for their members, modes of assistance, coping abilities, and expectations. Exploration of these earlier life-course experiences enables us to relate patterns of support in the later years of life to the social and cultural conditions that the respective cohorts encountered over their lives (Elder, 1978; Hareven, 1978e; Riley, 1978).

A life-course perspective, therefore, provides a framework for understanding variability in supports as well as changes in the expectations of both recipients and caregivers, who are influenced by their respective social and cultural milieux. Our research examines adult children who were caring for aging parents in the context of the opportunities and experiences characteristic of their respective cohorts at various periods in their lives. We view behavior and expectations for receiving and providing support as part of a continuing process of interaction among parents and children and other kin, over their lives and as they move through historical time. Attitudes toward generational assistance in the later years of life are influenced by values and experiences that evolve or are modified over the entire life course. Ethnic values rooted in premigration culture call for a more exclusive dependence on filial and kin assistance than do the attitudes in the dominant American culture, which relies on supports available from government programs and community agencies.

This study is based on extensive life-history interviews with former textile workers in Manchester, New Hampshire, and two cohorts of their adult children. The parent generation, on whom *Family Time and Industrial Time* (Hareven, 1982) is based, migrated to Manchester in order to work in the Amoskeag Mills between the turn of the century and World War I. Most of them came from Quebec, Poland, and Greece, and in smaller numbers from Scotland, Ireland, and Sweden. During the period of their arrival, the Amoskeag Company—the world's largest textile mill complex—was at the peak of its production. Following World War I, the Amoskeag Company entered a precipitous decline that finally shut down the mills in 1936, a disastrous event that paralyzed the local economy for almost a decade. Since Manchester was a one-industry town, the shutdown's effect on the workers' lives was particularly severe (Hareven, 1982; see Chapter 2; Hareven and Langenbach, 1978).

In examining the interaction of adult children with their aging parents, we compare the ways in which two cohorts of adult children who belong to the same generation have differed both in caregiving and in their attitudes toward providing assistance to their parents. We explore the range of life-course paths of adult children who were caregivers for their frail, elderly parents. In doing so, we try to identify the ways in which the care-giving relationship emerged over the life course and the price that care-giving children paid in this relationship.

The "generation in the middle" on whom this chapter focuses consists of the children of immigrant textile workers. The parents and some of the older children were textile workers in the Amoskeag Mills. Most of the children were born in the United States to immigrant parents or were brought there in their childhood by their parents. Several characteristics set them apart from their parents. Whereas the parents often moved back and forth between Manchester and their communities of origin or around New England to seek factory work in various other communities during business slumps, most of the children grew up in Manchester in the "shadow" of the Amoskeag Mills. These children were too young to have worked in the mills, but were not old enough to have experienced the pre–World War I period of prosperity in Amoskeag's history that had in-duced their parents to work there. The older members among the chil-dren's cohorts were old enough to have experienced directly the negative effects of the shutdown of the mills and the Great Depression on the fam-ilies of Manchester. The children were slated by their parents to escape mill work and to fulfill the American dream. The parents' ideal was for sons, especially, to get a high-school education and work their way up to middle-class occupations or to own a grocery store or a restaurant. As one member of this group put it: "My father said to me: 'No mills for you down there.' So my brother was a postal inspector, I was a cost accoun-tant . . . we went to school. In those days there was a very small percent-age that went to college or had a high-school education."

Most of the members of the children's cohorts, however, were unable to fulfill their parents' scenario. The shutdown of the Amoskeag Mills dur-ing the Great Depression blocked this means of escape, especially for the older children, who encountered economic crises in their teenage years. The younger children came closer to fulfilling this dream, but only mar-ginally. The children were the first generation in their families to speak English as their first language and to "Americanize" in any significant way through their schooling. About half of the children's generation had actually married outside their ethnic group, although they remained within their faith. They represent a transitional group. While adhering to some of their parents' traditional values, they also accepted American middle-class values and aspired to that lifestyle. In contrast to the par-ents' erratic migration patterns, most of the children grew up within a single American community.

From a demographic point of view, the children were the first cohorts to experience their parents' survival beyond their seventies and to en-counter the problems of caring for "old old" parents. Even though most families had large numbers of children, the primary responsibility of caring for an elderly parent usually fell upon one child. Members of these cohorts were the first, therefore, to experience a "life-cycle squeeze." They had to care for aging parents at a point in their lives when they themselves were approaching old age and needed to prepare for their own retirement (Cantor, 1983; Brody, 1981). In addition, they needed to launch their own children. The squeeze was intensified especially for women, who had performed the traditional roles of mother and wife while holding full-time jobs.

For the purpose of life-course analysis, we divided the children's generation into two cohorts according to the historical events they encountered as they reached adulthood: The children's earlier cohort was born between 1910 and 1919 and came of age during the Great Depression (Cohort 2a), and the later cohort was born between 1920 and 1929 that came of age during World War II (Cohort 2b). This chapter uses the historical data set that Hareven constructed for the parents' generation, on which *Family Time and Industrial Time* is based. We linked the data on the parents' generation with a new set on the children's cohorts, which we generated from intensive life-history interviews during the period 1981–1985, combined with demographic histories, work histories, and migration histories, which are included in the new data set on the children's cohorts.[1]

Intergenerational Supports over the Life Course

For the ethnic working-class families studied here, the expectation that adult children care for aging parents was embedded in the traditional patterns of kin assistance and family values that the parent generation had brought with them. Immigrants carried over their kinship ties and customs for assistance from their communities of origin and adapted them to the needs and demands of the urban-industrial setting in the United States. Most members of the parents' generation came to Manchester in their teens or as couples with young children. Many of them had left their own parents behind but maintained consistent kinship ties with their communities of origin. In some instances, parents followed and joined them later. Those who came from Quebec, especially, were enmeshed in kinship networks across the industrial landscape of northern New England and Quebec (Hareven, 1982).

Assistance among the generations stretched across the life course and tended to be mutual, informal, and recurrent under normal circumstances as well as during critical life situations. In the regime of economic insecurity characteristic of the late nineteenth century and the first part of the twentieth century where kin assistance was the only constant source of support, family coping necessarily dictated that individual choices be subordinated to family considerations and needs. Mutual assistance among kin, although involving extensive exchanges, was not calculative. Rather, it expressed an overall principle of reciprocity over the life course and across generations.

Individuals who subordinated their own careers and needs for those of the family as a collective unit did so out of a sense of responsibility, affection, and familial obligation rather than with the expectation of eventual gain. Such sacrifices were not made without protest, however, and at times involved competition and conflict among siblings as to who should carry the main responsibility of support for aging parents. The sense of obligation toward kin was a manifestation of family "culture"—supported by a commitment to the well-being and self-reliance or survival of the family—which took priority over individual needs and personal happiness. Family autonomy, essential for self-respect and good standing in the neighborhood and community, was one of the most deeply ingrained values (Hareven, 1982).

Various types of assistance to the elderly grew out of the daily exchanges between parents and children over the life course. Children, especially daughters, helped their aging parents by taking them shopping or to the doctor, by doing household chores and providing supplies, and by visiting frequently. Such ongoing assistance set the stage for coping with subsequent crises, such as widowhood, serious or chronic illness of a parent, and dependence. These helping patterns revolved principally around the generational axis of parents and children. Despite the long tradition of kin assistance among these families, there is only scattered evidence that other kin (the aging person's siblings, nieces and nephews, or grandchildren, for example) cared for an elderly relative. Other kin provided sociability and occasional help for an elderly relative, but the major responsibilities for regular care fell primarily on adult children.

Patterns of assistance to parents that were formed early in life generally carried over into old age. Children who had experienced a closer day-to-day interaction with their parents during their own child-rearing years were more likely than their siblings to take responsibility for parental assistance in the later years, except when the relationship was disrupted by migration, death, early impairment, or family conflict. Even in cases where children in the later cohort (primarily daughters) had left Manchester, they tended to return to the parental home if they lost their spouses. Some of these daughters left home again after they reconstructed their lives; others stayed on and later took care of their parents or widowed mothers.

Martha Smith McPherson (born 1918) is a classic case of the continuity of kin assistance embedded in several generations and reaching back to the family's origin in Scotland. Her father came from Scotland with his widowed mother and then arranged for his siblings to join him one by one. Martha's mother, an Irish immigrant, one of ten children, became a lifelong "kin keeper" after she married Martha's father: She took care of a young nephew who came alone to the United States and also took her own father into the household. Later, Martha's parents took in her father's mother and one of Martha's father's brothers, who was an alcoholic: "Rather than put him any place else, we took him in." Eventually, the responsibility for caring for these dependent kin fell on Martha when both her parents became sick. In order to care for her relatives, Martha dropped out of school. While caring for various relatives over a forty-year period, she hired nurses and continued to work at her job. "I made my own decision, because my folks could have sacrificed more, but I felt they sacrificed enough, because they took my grandmother in, and they took my uncle in. . . . and I couldn't see them sacrificing any more, so I made my own [sacrifice]."

In fact, caring for her aged relatives gave Martha a nurturing role as her marriage disintegrated due to her inability to have a child. After her husband fathered a child with her girlfriend, she divorced him and returned to Manchester. She stayed with her parents: "I loved to be with them." After her father and uncle died, Martha sold the family home in order to pay for her father's cancer treatment and her father's and uncle's funeral costs. Her eighty-seven-year-old mother moved with her into an apartment, then died shortly thereafter. In retrospect, Martha said her compensation was "peace of mind." "I haven't got a home, but I have got peace of mind . . . because I never wanted my mother to go to a [nursing] home, I never wanted my father to go, or my uncle. I wouldn't put him out on the street." At the time of the interview, Martha expected she might live together with her sister and her sister's husband in the large house that her sister owns. Martha intimated, however, that she and her sister had different lifestyles and that there would need to be some adjustment. Martha figured that they would be most likely to live together in the event that her sister's husband died.

In another case, two sisters, Marie Bouchard (born 1917) and Joan Riley (born 1914), grew up in a close relationship to their mother, rendered more interdependent by their father's death when they were young children. The mother actually placed the two daughters in an orphanage for day care—a pattern quite common among Manchester's working mothers whose husbands were absent, sick, or dead. Following the shutdown of the Amoskeag Mills, their mother was unable to find another job because she was considered "too old" and because her eyes were worn from many years of textile work. The two daughters supported their mother for the rest of her life. Joan left Manchester after her marriage, but Marie brought her husband into the household. Her mother wanted to leave and said: "Well, I'm going to get a place of my own. You're married now, you have your life to live." But Marie insisted that her mother stay: "We couldn't see it. We just wanted her with us. You couldn't help it. My husband . . . was closer to my mother than he was to his own mother."

During the 1940s, Marie and her husband left for Connecticut to find work there and then moved around to various places, including Florida, because of the husband's military career. Meanwhile, Joan returned to Manchester after her husband's death and stayed with her mother. She did not remarry because her mother "was getting along in years then, and I knew darn well that if ever we got married again, she wouldn't mind, but she would feel." Marie and her husband returned from Connecticut after her husband's brother died so that they could take care of her husband's father. Following her husband's death, Marie continued to take care of her father-in-law for another decade. Her father-in-law, grateful for Marie's support, left her his house. Joan and Marie, both widowed and childless, lived in separate apartments in the same building at the time of the interview. They had only each other as sources of support.

Coresidence Among the Generations

In Manchester as in most other American urban communities, the pervasive residential pattern was one of nuclear households. The older generation rarely resided with their married adult children in the same household. Newlywed children or young families occasionally lived in their parents' household for short periods. They tended to find housing nearby and often received assistance from their parents, especially in establishing a new household or in caring for young children (Chudacoff and Hareven, 1979).

For most of the people interviewed and for the population in general, "intimacy from a distance" seemed to be the preferred formula for married adult children's interaction with their parents. When both parents survived into old age, the children were more likely to try to maintain them in the parental home. As already noted, when elderly parents were able to cope on their own, the children made an effort to reside nearby—in the same building or the same block—but not in the same household.

In cases of illness or need, daughters visited their parents daily and often stayed over in the parental home rather than moving their parents into their own household. After the death of one parent, children initially took in the surviving parent temporarily or for recurring visits. If the widowed parent was able to take care of himself or herself, the children tried to move the parent to a nearby apartment. Adult children were often willing to financially maintain their parent's home. In some cases, several siblings contributed jointly to hiring a nurse to take daily care of a frail parent who was still living at home.

The ideal model of residence for aging parents who were still able to care for themselves is represented by the Duchamp family: Solange Duchamp's mother moved into the upstairs apartment in the home of her husband's (Guy, born 1928) parents' home.

'Course my mother lives alone and I feel that with Mom and Dad C. downstairs, of course, they have always been good friends anyway, and since we've been married it's like she's in the family and when I come home from work, oh, once, twice, and you know. . . . sometimes during the week, I'll drop by and I'll visit upstairs and I'll visit downstairs. Everybody's there all at once, and sometimes I'll come in and my mother will come down, or they'd come upstairs or anything, and talk and it's reassuring so that everybody cares so much for each other in this household, that if anything happens upstairs I know that I don't have to worry that Mom and Dad C. downstairs would call, or vice versa. If anything happened downstairs, my mother would call. So it is a worry-free type of situation.

In cases where the parents could be left alone for part of the time, daughters tried to juggle a career and care for a parent; some commuted considerable distances in order to maintain a balance between their own family and their parents' needs. Some daughters tried to lead double lives in order to fulfill obligations to parents while not diminishing their contribution to their children's advancement.

Especially in the earlier cohort, the most consistent pattern of assistance was that one child assumed the main responsibility for caring for the parents. Usually, other children contributed to the effort through financial support, visiting, or taking turns keeping the parent in their home. One child, however, carried the primary responsibility for parental care and tried to mobilize and coordinate the efforts of the other children as the need arose. This was not always accomplished without strain.

In one case, the sibling, who was the backup to help his father, found that his part in providing assistance jeopardized his own health. Pierre Bergeron (born 1914) explained: "While John [Pierre's brother, caring for the father in his home] was working, I lived across the road, and I would have to go over there two or three times and sometimes four or five times. . . . It was getting so that I was getting sick myself." Pierre's own adult children insisted that the burden of worrying about his father, who was not safe alone, was too much for Pierre.

The people studied here transcended or modified the pervasive custom of the residential separation between generations in American society only in cases of dire need, when aging parents experienced chronic illness, handicap, or dementia, and needed help with their daily activities (Chudacoff and Hareven, 1978a). In such cases, an adult child, most commonly a daughter, took the parent into her home. In some cases, a daughter who was widowed, divorced, separated, or incapacitated moved in with her parents in order to receive other types of assistance, especially for child care. If that daughter continued to stay in the parental home, she subsequently took on the responsibilities of caring for her parents (see Matthews, 1987).

Although it was a common pattern for daughters to take in a dependent parent, daughters-in-law also often took on the responsibility of caring for a husband's parent, sometimes even after the husband's death. Women provided the same effort for a parent-in-law as for their own parent. The most common pattern, however, was that a mother moved into her daughter's house. In some cases, a daughter-in-law cared for parents-in-law in their home. Occasionally, however, when couples had to care for a parent from each side simultaneously, they established priorities as to which parent to take in and worked out alternative arrangements with other siblings.

Bringing a frail, chronically ill, or demented parent into the household required considerable readjustment of the household space and of the family's daily routines. In some instances, limited space made it necessary for the couple or the grandchildren to give up their bedrooms. Helena Debski Wojek (born 1913) first commuted from Manchester to Massachusetts General Hospital in Boston to take care of her mother, who was being treated there. (The mother's second husband refused to take care of her.) "I'd go out of work and run right to Boston, because she could not speak English at all." Then her mother lived with her for six months. "We gave up our bed, and we slept up in the attic on a couch. And my son gave up his bed." The family had to get up many times during the night to keep the elderly woman from choking.

The greatest problem of adjustment in caring for an aging parent at home fell on the daughter or daughter-in-law, especially when she had a job. With some exceptions, women carried the major burden of daily care, while the men provided primarily financial assistance and sociability. Most women were in the labor force and were caught, therefore, in the squeeze between caring for an aging parent and their own work and family responsibilities. Many of the caregiving women reported conflicts resulting from the need to spend almost the entire day caring for a live-in aging parent and at the same time continue their careers. Some had to work during the day and take care of the parent at night. Some had to give up their full-time job or replace it with part-time and less satisfying work. Such changes in the wife's career deprived the family of the supplementary income necessary in order to own a home or provide a better education for their children (Brody, 1981).

Suzanne Lacasse Miller (born 1916) held two jobs while caring for her sick husband and having her mother in the household. She was married in 1941 and had four children. During her childbearing years, she had worked intermittently in the smaller textile mills that had opened up just before World War II in the empty buildings of the Amoskeag Mills and had another job at Dunkin' Donuts. Her husband's illness made her the main supporter of her family. Suzanne's father and her older brother both died in 1955; her younger brother died two years later. After his death, her mother moved in with Suzanne, who was then the only surviving child in Manchester. Suzanne's sister lived in Center Harbor, New Hampshire (one hour's distance by car), but her mother did not want to move: "She wanted to stay here [in Manchester] 'cause her friends were here."

Initially, Suzanne's mother provided child care after moving in. But in her last years, she was sick, "and I'd have to run home from the job and get her to the hospital, get her into oxygen. She didn't want anybody else." In 1964, the same year her mother became ill, Suzanne's husband, who had been ill for some time, died. In 1966, Suzanne's mother died as well, and her last daughter married and left home. Suzanne lived alone for only a short time before she took on the care of an elderly male relative in her parents' generation and provided extensive babysitting for her grandchildren.

The Making of a "Parent Keeper"

An only child, especially an only daughter, fell naturally into the role of "parent keeper." Ellen Wojek Mitchell's (born 1922) mother had a stroke at age fifty; she had two more strokes and died at age fifty-seven. Ellen's father remained alone while Ellen was raised by relatives in Vermont. Her father remarried, but when her stepmother died in 1946, Ellen was fetched back by her brother to take care of her father. (Apparently, the brother was not capable of taking on this role himself.) "Well, I wasn't married, and it was only right that somebody should stay with him," recalled Ellen. She married in 1955, after her husband's mother died. Then Ellen's husband moved in with her and her father. Her father helped babysit his granddaughter while Ellen worked.

A caregiving daughter's intention to marry caused a great deal of tension between the generations, and many couples sometimes waited decades for parents to die before they could marry. Marianne Trudeau Wiznewski (born 1912), the oldest daughter, was forty-seven when she finally married. Up to that time, she lived with her mother. As a young girl, she and her sister witnessed an ongoing conflict between their mother and their father, which was intensified by her mother's belief that her husband had fathered an illegitimate son. Marianne became protective of her mother: "I was afraid to leave my mother alone. My father was quite . . . and I was afraid to leave her." (She never explained what the source of fear was.) When Marianne finally decided to get married in middle age, her mother objected. "She didn't like him [the fiancé]. He was a widower and, I don't know, she didn't trust him." Marianne's husband was commuting from Massachusetts, and finally he moved in. Marianne's mother died six months later of diabetes. "And Mama didn't like him. And then she died in December. I felt so bad . . . makes you feel awful."

Even when a daughter tried to make up for lost time by marrying in middle age, she still encountered her mother's protest. Lucille Martineau Grenier (born 1915) was forty-eight when she married a sixty-two-year-old widower, a father of five married children. Her sixty-eight-year-old mother was upset about the marriage "cause her right arm was gone. . . . I was living with her and I provided for her until I got married. She expected to have me for the rest of her life." Lucille put her mother in a nursing home because she was "really sick." Later, when her husband became sick, Lucille requested his children's help to put him in a nursing home as well. Both her mother and husband died shortly after entering the home.

Young women, aware of the cultural expectation that one daughter remain at home to care for aging parents, followed various strategies to escape early. Sister Marie Lemay (born 1926) was warned in her youth that if she was to avoid being saddled with the care of aging parents, she would have to pay attention to her own timing in her desire to become a nun. Her two older sisters, who were getting married, warned her: "If you don't enter [the convent] now, when we're all gone, you'll find it difficult to leave."

> So they told me their plans so that in a way, three of us left in the same year. Father was always saying, "We have this French saying that someone stays home to be the support of the elderly parents." . . . Most of the time it seemed to be the youngest of the family or the youngest girl. The oldest grew up and got married, and the parents were getting on in age. By the time the youngest grew up, the parents were getting old enough. . . . So, instead of settling down, that one was almost like naturally left to take care of the family.

Daughters who returned to the parental home due to disruptions in their own lives often fell naturally into the role of parent keeper. Joan Riley (born 1914), who returned from Providence, Rhode Island, after her husband's death to live with her mother, explained why she never married again: "I had my mother to take care of. She came first, because she was getting along in years, and she had to have somebody."

In cases where the parent keeper was not already living with the parents, the main factors dictating the selection of a parent keeper were governed by that particular adult child's ability and willingness to take the parent in, by such other responsibilities as a sick child or spouse in the parent keeper's own family, by the consent or support of the parent keeper's spouse, and by the readiness of the parent to accept the plan. If the other children were already too old and needing care themselves, they were unable to take in and cope with an aging parent. Frank Kaminski's (born 1921) seventy-three-year-old sister did not marry because her salary as a shoe-factory worker was needed to help the family keep their home during the Great Depression. Long after their father's death, this sister, who was by then frail herself, continued to live and take care of their mother, who was in her late nineties. The family considered new arrangements, but these plans failed: "They were thinking of having my other sister take care of them." In the meantime, her sister's husband died, and she was bedridden. "So she can't do it anymore. So, you know, that took care of that solution to the problem."

Most parent keepers evolved into that role over their entire life course; others were pushed into it through family crises. Earlier life-course experience was an overwhelming factor in the designation of a parent keeper. The most significant factor was the continued or recurring proximity of residence of a child and the parent and the corresponding mutual assistance. Daughters who maintained close contact with their parents after marriage fell into the role of parent keepers, especially when the other siblings "bailed out" by marrying early. Sometimes this was accomplished by eloping. The risk of siblings' bailing out increased if the father's early death necessitated a child's support for a widowed mother and the remaining siblings.

The emotional bond between a parent and a certain child often meant that that child was considered the most appropriate one to care for an aging parent. The bonds frequently grew stronger during the parent's last period of chronic illness; some children reported loneliness following a live-in parent's death; some caregiving children remarried or intensified their relations with their own children in order to maintain close family ties. Parents expressed their preference about which child to join, even if that child, usually a daughter, resided outside of Manchester. These mothers went a distance because they preferred to live with a particular daughter rather than with other children in Manchester. When Anna Charboneau Lessard (born 1928) and her family moved to New York City to manage an apartment building, her mother first lived with Anna's sister in Manchester. "Then she came up to me and asked me if she could live with us." The mother moved to New York and took care of Anna's and her husband's four children. Sandra Kazantakis Wall (born 1921), who lived with her second husband in Maryland, brought her mother from Manchester after her father died, even though other siblings lived in Manchester, because her mother insisted, "I want to come and live with you." Sandra's mother lived with her for the last five years of her life. "Dick [her husband] was very good to mother, and she loved him like a son. . . . In fact, she liked him better than some of her children sometimes."

In both cases, the mother's choice of the geographically distant child was related to earlier life experiences. For example, Sandra had been particularly close to her mother. She had eloped with her first husband at age twenty; because her husband was in the military, she lived in various places overseas and in the United States; she and her husband adopted a son in Germany. She returned home from time to time, usually when she had marital problems. "My mother and father, yes! that was the home, that was my life, and that's where I found the answers, at my mother's and father's." In 1959, after her husband was killed in a plane crash in Alaska, Sandra and her adopted son moved back to Manchester to her parents' home. After this respite, Sandra remarried and again moved with a new husband to Maryland. When her mother became widowed, she went to live with Sandra.

In another case, a son had to accept reluctantly his parents' decision to leave his home in Manchester and move in with his sister in Rhode Island. Jonathan Fournier's (born 1926) parents insisted on making their move even though his father was working for him in Manchester: "Why do you want to go back down there, you have been up here with me for fifteen years?" asked Jonathan. His parents replied that they could be better taken care of in Rhode Island. "How the hell are they going to take care of you any better than I have?" But Jonathan's mother insisted on moving. After the move, his father commuted from Rhode Island to Manchester. He continued work with Jonathan and stayed with him from Monday to Thursday, then returned to Rhode Island.

In summary, parent keepers' careers followed several trajectories: Some children remained as adults with the family in which they grew up and gradually took over the care of parents. The caretaker was usually the youngest daughter. In other cases, children returned home due to their own disrupted life course or in response to a parent's need for assistance. This was usually a contingency act, provoked by events and needs that had not been anticipated earlier in the life course. The returning adult child was usually single, divorced, or widowed and could divert his or her own life more easily than could married siblings. More daughters than sons returned home as adults. Another pattern was that some children did not coreside with their parents but handled the main responsibilities of caregiving. These children, usually daughters, shuttled between their own homes and those of their parents, often carrying the burden of a job as well.

In the fourth pattern, the parent moved into the adult child's home in cases of extreme need for personal care. Adult daughters were willing to give care, even to a bed-bound and incontinent parent; they resorted to a nursing home only in cases where total care was required. In some cases where the sick parent's spouse was still alive, the spouse continued to live separately in an independent household or with another child. If both parents needed care, sometimes each was taken into the home of a different sibling—a concept alien to our times but one that is quite common to immigrants. Some families, especially with all members pitching in, were able to accomplish care for an elderly parent in their home. These adult children were squeezed between their obligations toward their parents and their desire to provide for their own children. In other cases, changes in the relations within the family and the women's commitment to work made the expectation of providing care for an incapacitated parent unrealistic.

The struggle of adult children, often approaching old age themselves, to keep a parent in their own home exacted a high price from them. The extra work of caring for frail parents changed daily life and, for some, led to a disrupted life course. Some children's own health declined because of the strain; others suffered tensions in their marriage or experienced economic loss because of the wife's withdrawal from the labor force; and others were unable to prepare for their own retirement and old age because of the financial strain and the demands on the wife's time. Some parent keepers worried about limits on the life plans of their own children (Ory, 1985).

It is not surprising, therefore, that all the children interviewed who had taken care of aging parents in their own homes expressed a strong desire never to have to depend on their own children in their old age. They considered living with their children the greatest obstacle to maintaining their independence. Sarah Butterick, who had taken care of her father in her own home after he had a stroke, said she would never consider living with her own children: "I hope not; I hope I drop dead. . . . [I] hope I just don't wake up some morning." Helena Debski Wojek (born 1913), whose mother lived with her for six months when she was ill, explained why she lived alone (after her husband's death). "Well I try to, because I know what it is to take care of people that are really sick, and I wouldn't want to see my children go through that. . . . I wouldn't want to live with one of my children because they've got lives of their own, and I've got a life of my own."

In some cases, members of the children's cohort did not want to have to live with their own children in the future because of the aspects of parental control they had experienced firsthand. Stephen Livak (born 1911), who had lived for several years with both his mother and his wife's mother, said he would never want to live with his son: "I knew what I had to go through living tied with the apron strings. I wouldn't want him to be tied to my apron strings. I would want him to be free, and I wouldn't want to be obligated to him."

Yves St. Pierre (born 1910) and Cora Lemay St. Pierre (born 1910) helped care for Yves's father in the first three years of their marriage, after the father was paralyzed from a stroke. "That was a long three years, I'll tell you." Both Yves and Cora rejected the notion of living with their children in the future: "We've always been independent and we'd feel if we lived . . . with our children we wouldn't be independent. I'd rather live with myself as long as I can, and when I can't I'd go into a home." Even though they upheld their own independence and placed their mentally retarded thirty-four-year-old daughter in an institution, the St. Pierres, when asked what was different about families today, replied: "They're too independent each on their own side." Yvonne Lemay Gagne (born 1916) and Pierre Gagne (born 1916) both agreed that they would rather live in a nursing home than with their children: "I wouldn't be happy anyway. When you know you're in somebody's way, you don't feel right." Yvonne was less definitive at first: "I'd be lonesome in a nursing home first. I'd feel: They don't need the old lady around!" But then she concurred with her husband, and the couple proclaimed their preference for a nursing home almost in unison.

When assessing the children's strong pronouncements about their desire for independence in their own old age, one must keep in mind the life stage at which they were interviewed. There is no telling whether their attitude will change when they reach dependent old age. As fifty-two-year-old Raymond Champagne put it: "I think I would still try to make it alone. Ten years from now, I might think differently."

The Shadow of the Nursing Home

The unsatisfactory alternative to keeping parents at home was placing them in a nursing home. Parents most commonly went to nursing homes in cases of extreme physical sickness, paralysis, or dementia. For example, when parents wandered around, were irrational, impulsive, and unpredictable, or could not be managed by the adult child, then children sought another solution. Indeed, in several cases elderly couples faced this dilemma with regard to their own spouses and committed them to nursing homes.

In cases where children lived in another town and were not able to care for a parent on a regular basis, the nursing home was the only solution.

Susanne Robert (born 1927), for example, had a close relationship with
her parents since childhood. After her marriage in 1950, her husband's father rented a nearby apartment for the new couple. Susanne's parents
also helped with a loan to buy a car, and her mother took care of her children once a week. When Susanne's mother became ill, after Susanne and
her young family moved to Maine in 1955, her mother entered a nursing
home, while her father continued to stay in his own apartment.

> My intentions were to take care of them, but my mom ended up in a nursing
> home because my dad couldn't take care of her and we were living in Maine
> at the time. My sister was in California and my youngest was only two
> months old. . . . So she was paralyzed for weeks and she did end up in a
> home which kind of broke our hearts, but there she got good care and she
> was in about three years. Then he [father] died before her. He had one heart
> attack and that was it.

Almost simultaneously, Susanne encountered other needs for parent care
in the family. Susanne's husband placed his father in a nursing home and
tried to place his mother in subsidized housing for the elderly. According to
Susanne's husband, his mother, however, followed her own plan.

> Well, my father was the one that got sick first and she [his mother] tried as
> much as she could to take care of him, but it was too much. So we had to
> place him in a home. This was done by my mother. She was about eighty
> years old and she was still living in an apartment. And my brother had con-
> nections with politics, to put her in those high rises that were being built in
> Manchester, and while waiting for one to be built, she went and placed her-
> self in a nursing home on the west side where the old hospital used to be.

Most elderly parents who went to a nursing home did so during the final period of chronic illness and died shortly thereafter. Children who
lived in Manchester regularly visited their parents in nursing homes, often daily. Daughters did laundry, provided haircuts, bought delicacies,
and took the elderly parent on "outings." If the children lived in a distant
community, the day-to-day care was left to a local sibling. Jonathan
Fournier, whose parents, at their own choice, left his house and moved to
Rhode Island, lost contact with his mother. After his father's death,
Jonathan's sister placed his mother in a nursing home in Rhode Island.
Jonathan deferred to the judgment and planning of his sister, who took
charge of their mother's care, but he felt guilty:

> I am ashamed to tell you. I haven't seen my mother for a year and a half, two
> years. I feel bad about it. Really, I should get myself up and get there. . . . It's

only the last six months its been bothering my conscience about going down there. It isn't because I have no respect or love for her; I got other things turning all the time. . . . I think it's wrong, but the decision was made to put her in a nursing home. I'm not gonna fight over it.

In some cases, the parent's impaired safety awareness resulted in a long period of anxiety among the siblings before seeking another solution to the home environment. Pierre Bergeron (born 1910) described the problems his brother John had in caring for their father at home. "One day John came home and found all the water faucets on full-strength. And another day he came home and found all the burners on, on the electric stove." Their father decided to take trips using the public buses; on one of these trips, he fell and broke his hip. This was the final straw for the children; they decided to send their father to a nursing home. Pierre felt that was not his decision to make: "I said I would not give him [John] any decision because I thought that he took care of them all their lives, and he's the one who should [make the decision]." In other instances, the children believed in a commonly accepted plan that their parents should enter a nursing home when required. Vincent Duchamp (born 1922) explained: "Arrangements have been made already. If something does happen to one or the other [parent], they can't sustain themselves, then they'll be put automatically into a nursing home." But his mother (born 1899), who was caring for her husband and a retarded daughter, had another point of view: "We didn't think of that yet . . . when that time comes, we will see."

Another case of conflicting accounts concerning a parent's entry into a nursing home occurred when we interviewed Alice Robert St. Martin's (born 1925) eighty-seven-year-old mother in a nursing home, with Alice present. The interview ended because the mother burst into tears, prompted by her feelings of being abandoned in the nursing home. Alice had maintained in an earlier interview that her mother had been placed into the nursing home at her own request:

My mother wanted a nursing home and we never knew, she told us when she was going in the next day. She made arrangements with people that worked in the hospital. I guess, I don't know if Donald [son] knew. I know I didn't. She called me and she said, "I hope you won't be mad but I am leaving, you know." She sold her furniture. What could I say. It was the best way, you know, because she couldn't today at eighty-seven.

Even though nursing homes had come into common use by the late 1960s, a stigma remained attached to having a parent in a nursing home. Those interviewed, without exception, felt compelled to provide an excuse or justification for having had a parent in a nursing home. The theme that parents had entered a nursing home on their own initiative, presenting their children with a fait accompli, recurred in the children's retrospective narratives. Mary Grzwinski Petrowski (born 1918), for example, who had placed her eighty-two-year-old mother in a nursing home after she was unable to live alone, said she had done so "simply because she [her mother] requested it. . . . She didn't want to live with us; she felt we had our own life to live, and she said, 'Why don't you put me in a nursing home?' And so we did." Her mother stayed in the nursing home for six months until her death. "But it was her choice, because I was going to take a year off [from teaching school]. My mother was very intelligent, she was very independent and she felt, 'This is your life and why should you stop working just to sit with me.'" Had Mary stopped working, her and her husband's plans for retirement would have been financially jeopardized (Scharlach, 1987).

Florida St. Honoré Rouillard (born 1926), whose mother lives with her youngest brother, expressed the prevalent ambivalence toward the nursing homes: "[In the past] you took care of them, there was no thought of nursing homes, today there is one on every corner. . . . In a way, they are probably getting better [care] but, of course, it's a much more distant feeling. I visit nursing homes. I know what I'm saying." Florida expects that she and her husband will end up in a nursing home rather than with their children. "Because of the beautiful facilities they have there now; they did not have that then. They have nurses, the best care, professionals today."

Cohort Location in Historical Time

The pervasiveness of the children's involvement with the care of their aging parents was closely related to their earlier life-course patterns, over which they had different degrees of control, and to the ethnic and cultural traditions that governed their family relations. A fuller understanding of the differences in their attitudes depends on our identification of the changing social and historical contexts that affected the lives of the respective children's cohorts.

Members of the parent cohort had been the major supporters of their aging parents. They viewed kin as their almost exclusive source of assistance over the life course. For that very reason, they also expected their main support in old age to come from their children. They tried to remain self-reliant as late as possible, however, and viewed all support from their children as part of the family's self-reliance. As Andrew Proulx (born 1922) put it:

Well they didn't have the old folks homes those days like they have today. In those days, it was the kids that took care of the parents. Today, the old folks they place them some place. Get rid of them! Well, the kids want their liberty a little bit more, and they don't want to be straddled to the parents that are senile or sick or whatever.

The older members of the parent cohort (in their eighties and nineties at the time of the interview) were especially articulate on this issue. Having spent the prime of their lives in an era preceding the welfare state, the very concept of relying on public agencies was alien to their principles and upbringing. Their belief in the self-sufficiency of the family led them to view public support as demeaning. These were the values they had taught to their children. Ranking their preferences for sources of assistance, they saw assistance within the nuclear family as their highest priority, followed by assistance from extended and more distant kin. As expected, they cited public welfare as a last resort. The parents proudly claimed to have avoided public relief even during the Great Depression. Those who resorted to welfare agencies did so surreptitiously and later denied having received help (Hareven, 1982).

The parents' preference for support from kin rather than from public agencies was also shaped by their ethnic backgrounds. Their ideology of kin assistance was part of their tradition and formed a survival strategy carried over from their respective premigration cultures. After settling in the United States, the parents modified this ideology to fit the needs, requirements, and constraints imposed by the insecurities of the industrial environment. Their involvement in mutual kin assistance thus represented both the continuation of an earlier practice of family caregiving among the generations and an ideology that shaped their expectations of each other and of the younger generation.

Both children's cohorts were socialized with expectations and ideologies of kin assistance similar to those of their parents, but they were challenged to implement these norms under different historical and social circumstances. The children were caught in a bind and were ambivalent toward the obligation to be the almost exclusive caretakers of their aging parents. The coping strategies they worked out were intended to meet the values of kin assistance passed on by their parents, but new pressures, new aspirations, and the emergence of bureaucratic agencies led them to modify these ideals. The desire to meet their parents' expectations and at the same time launch their own children added to their generation's sense of conflict due to their obligations to them. These children prioritized obligations, worked overtime, reframed the meaning of family obligations for caregiving, and did not expect that their life-course squeeze would be repeated in their own children's middle years.

While the parents expected their children to assist them in old age, the children did not expect (or want) to have to rely on their own children for economic support. They prepared for old age through pension plans, savings, and home ownership and expected to rely on social security and, if needed, on assistance from the welfare state. In cases of illness or disability, they expected to be in a nursing home. The most they expected from their children was emotional support and sociability. This attitude also resulted from their cohort's becoming accustomed to agency public assistance and to interacting with bureaucratic institutions.

Both children's cohorts shared a deep involvement with the care of aging parents. As discussed above, their commitment was rooted in their life-course antecedents and was reinforced by their ethnic traditions and family culture. There were, however, significant variations within this common theme. Members of the earlier children's cohort had resigned themselves to staying within their social class, because of the devastating impact of the Great Depression and the shutdown of the Amoskeag Mills. Toughened by the depression, they assigned the highest priority to recovering from the depression and staying afloat economically. In order to achieve this, they pooled resources among kin, doubled up in housing, and moved around among various relatives within Manchester and sometimes around New England or other parts of the United States. For them, survival of the family as a collective unit remained the highest goal rather than the pursuit of individual careers. Within that context, children were expected to stretch their resources in order to keep aging parents within the family and to support them as long as possible. They held to the traditional ideologies of relying on kin rather than on public agencies (Hareven, 1982).

The later children's cohort, however, came of age during World War II. Having experienced the Great Depression and the shutdown of the Amoskeag Mills less directly, they were exposed to a lesser degree to the strong interdependence among kin that was dramatized most during the depression. Obviously, a majority of the later cohort had younger parents; for many, their trial period was yet to come. In this cohort, generational assistance still flowed more commonly from parents to children than the reverse. Parents helped newlyweds rent nearby housing, loaned them money to purchase a car, and provided child care. In some cases, the younger children's cohort still benefits from parental assistance, which has continued over their lives.

Taking advantage of both the economic recovery brought about by World War II and the career training and educational benefits that the young men had gained in the military service, the children's cohort was devoted to building new lives and improving their housing conditions. They tried to pull themselves out of a depressed, unemployed, working-class situation into a middle-class lifestyle (see Chapter 8). Realizing their limitations, they also assigned a high priority to the educational opportunities for their children. Ironically, members of the later children's cohort had been coached by their own parents to aspire toward occupational advancement and to develop a middle-class lifestyle. But as they attained these aspirations, they were also less available to their parents, especially to those who needed assistance in old age. Florida Rouillard (born 1926) explained how her daughter had realized the dream she had been unable to implement for herself: "I never did become a nurse. My daughter did, though. It's funny, how it worked." William Silvers (born 1927) observed, "I'd like all my children to have more than I have, and we parents try to push them that way."

The later cohort had a higher individualistic orientation. They drew firmer boundaries, both between the nuclear family and extended kin and between the younger generation and the old. They valued a more private life for married couples. Their primary energies were directed toward their children and their own future rather than toward their parents. Members of this cohort expressed ambivalence about carrying economic obligations for aging parents or taking them into their homes when they became unable to care for themselves. At the same time, they helped their parents, principally by providing services rather than regular financial support. They were also less inclined to take a frail, elderly parent into the household than were members of the earlier children's cohorts. The ambivalence of this younger cohort may have resulted from the erosion of values of interdependence among kin and from an expectation of assistance from the public sector. Although they had been raised with strong values of familial responsibility, the later children's cohort made the transition to a more individualistic mode of thinking and into a greater acceptance of public welfare as an extension of kin assistance. They expected this change to continue in the lives of their own children.

In some respects, members of the later children's cohort were also more emotionally distant from their parents. Unlike members of the older cohort, who stayed home until their marriage, those members of the later cohort who stayed on in Manchester tended to leave home before marriage and reside separately, although near their parents. Many children left home because of World War II. Men (and sometimes women) went into the service; the women often followed husbands who were stationed in other places. Children's departure from the home in early adulthood produced an earlier separation between the generations than in the earlier cohort. Living away from home also increased psychological separation. Alice Robert St. Martin (born 1925) explained that after her marriage, she felt more separate from her parents. "When I went to my mother's and father's it was like I was visiting. I felt that way."

The later children's cohort expressed a clearer preference that the generations reside separately: Pierre Gagnou (born 1926) explained, "It wouldn't be a family [rather than a couple's] life if they would have their father or their mother living with them." Thinking of the children, he continued, "If for some reason they would have an argument, it would make it hard for them." Raymond Champagne (born 1926) upheld the need for separate residence of the couple:

> I believe that marriage is something very sacred. It should be a husband-wife situation, nobody else. . . . and I have listened when I was younger that families who took in the old people, I always felt that those people [taking in elderly parents] were not fully leading a married life. . . . I just wouldn't want to be in their shoes, and I wouldn't want to put my children through it.

Members of the later children's cohort had far less experience caring for elderly parents in their own home than the older cohort. They were more likely than the older cohort to place their physically or mentally impaired parents in nursing homes or seek institutional help. Those who most commonly took care of an adult parent in their own home were only children, usually daughters. In other cases, the parent was often shuttled from one home to another among children in the later cohort. These younger adult children were either less willing or less able than the earlier cohort to make a full-time commitment as a parent keeper.

Viewing themselves as separate from their family origins, members of the later cohort upheld their own nuclear family as a separate entity. Some of them contrasted their own life-styles with those of their parents, setting themselves apart from the values of the previous generation. Marlene Bertram Kaminski (born 1925), for example, said that she exercised greater detachment from her own children, as a reaction against her mother's demanding attitude:

> I mean, when I look back, I say, "My gosh, I never had . . . a life, really, of my own." Because I went from my mother bossing me to my husband bossing me, and [laughs] I never knew what it was to really be on my own. And now Marsha [her daughter] has moved to Merrimack, which is not far from here. But I'm not mad or angry that she isn't calling me every day, because I feel that—for me, my mother was so hurt if I didn't call every night and tell her what kind of a day I had, that it got to be sort of a drag that you have to do this. So my—some day, some weeks I don't hear from my daughter all week. And I don't resent it at all. I really don't. And I, I didn't try to tell my children what to wear, and this and that.

Marlene did try, however, to manage her mother's life. When her twice-widowed mother wanted to leave Marlene's house and marry again, Marlene warned her against it. "You've gone through so much—two husbands with illnesses and being upset; now you have a reasonably good job, you can support yourself, you can live here. . . . You have a home here." But her mother insisted on her independence: "You have your husband, you have your family, and even though I'm in the house, I don't have anyone that really belongs to me."

Neither the earlier nor the later children's cohort was free, however, of the complexities involved in handling the problems of generational assistance. Although the earlier children's cohort had a more clearly defined commitment to collective family values and kin assistance, its members who had actually cared for elderly parents in their own home or had sacrificed their own marriage for parental care did not do so without ambivalence, doubt, bitterness, or the specter of a lonely old age for themselves. Their posture had often been one of resignation to familial norms and acceptance of "fate" rather than free choice. Members of the later cohort, by contrast, who followed a more individualistic course, were not free of guilt over the way in which the support of their aging parents had been worked out.

Both cohorts were, to some degree, transitional between a milieu of a deep involvement in generational assistance reinforced by strong family and ethnic values and one of individualistic values that emerged after World War II. In this historical process, the earlier cohort's lives conformed more closely to the script of their traditional familial and ethnic cultures, whereas the later cohort, as it Americanized, gravitated toward individualistic middle-class values. The transition was by no means completed. Members of the later cohort had not entirely freed themselves of their traditional upbringing. Both cohorts were the middle generation: They still expressed their parents' values, but the later cohort felt less able or inclined to implement them.

Our comparison of the cohorts of the children's generation suggests differences in the practice of caregiving and in the attitudes of each of the two cohorts toward the care of aging parents. Both cohorts were transitional in that they were still strongly bound by their parents' values and expectations that children should serve as the major caretakers. Both cohorts attempted to fulfill this script, often at a high price to their own marriages, to their ability to help their grown children, and to their preparation for their own "old age." Members of the earlier of the two children's cohorts were more inclined to live by their parents' cultural script, despite the fact that they were more vulnerable as their own "old age" approached. The later cohort was more ambivalent and more conflicted about a commitment to long-term care for a frail or chronically ill parent; its members were especially hesitant about caring for such a parent at home.

The difference between the two cohorts thus reflects a historical process of increasing individualization in family relationships and an increasing reliance on public agencies and bureaucratic institutions for the care of dependent elderly. The historical process is well known, but the detailed analysis of the interviews of the members of these cohorts provides first-hand testimony about how this change was perceived and experienced by the women and men who were caught up in it. The caregivers studied here revealed a commitment to their parents, as well as ambivalence about their roles, inner conflicts, and strategies that have resulted in various compromises as they tried to meet their obligations. When confronted with the burden of caregiving, they were also attempting to redefine their obligations, as assistance from the public sector became more widely used and accepted.

When identifying these differences among the cohorts, we need to keep in mind that their testimonies are derived principally from interviews with the parents and the children. Their statements derive from their own subjective reconstruction of their life course and from their perceptions of their current situations.

The very historical circumstances that influenced behavior and attitudes toward caring for aging parents among members of the later and the earlier children's cohorts also shaped the ways in which they remembered and interpreted these patterns in the course of the interview. The ways in which members of the two cohorts articulated their problems were shaped, therefore, by their own historical experiences over their life course. Thus, not only were the maps of the cohorts' respective life-course patterns charted by their earlier life experiences but also the coordinates that they superimposed on these maps, in order to make sense of their own lives, were a product of their location in historical time (Hareven, 1986).

8

Rising Above
Life's Disadvantage

From the Great Depression to War

In one life span, Americans had moved from scarcity to abundance, from sacrifice to the freedoms made possible by prosperity.
—**Glen H. Elder Jr.**
Children of the Great Depression, 1974, p.296

Life-course continuities from childhood across the adult years seem all too expectable in American life, a predictable outcome without mystery. Until recently, social scientists have given little attention to the timing of historical events in lives and their biographical influences. As Everett Hughes

*This chapter is coauthored by Glen H. Elder Jr.

The first part of this chapter is based on Glen Elder's program of research on social change in the life course within the Carolina Consortium on Human Development and the Carolina Population Center. Elder acknowledges with appreciation support from the National Institute of Mental Health through Grant MH41827 and a Research Scientist Award (MHOO567). He is indebted to the Institute of Human Development, University of California at Berkeley, for permission to use archival data in the Oakland Growth Study and the Berkeley Guidance Study.

Hareven's research for the Manchester data has been supported by two research grants from the National Institute on Aging. Hareven is indebted to Kathleen Adams for managing the interviewing in Manchester, to Michael Weiss for qualitative data analysis, and to Nancy Wilson for valuable assistance and editing. An earlier version of this chapter was presented at the annual meeting of the Social Science History Association in Chicago, November 1988. The authors are grateful for the comments of Karl Ulrich Mayer presented at the session.

once noted (1971a, p. 124), "Some people come to the age of work when there is no work; others when there are wars." For others, the timetable may offer a better match between life stage and historical stage, whether increasing or decreasing hardship or prosperity. At issue here is the synchronization between life history and social history and the subsequent ripple effects of that match or mismatch through adult life.

The synchrony between individual life stage and historical time for Americans born during the *early* 1920s minimized vulnerability to the Great Depression; those cohorts were too old to be wholly dependent on hard-pressed families in the 1930s and too young to face a stagnant labor market when they were coming of age. However, they were just the right age to be mobilized into World War II and to experience the economic recovery it prompted (Elder, 1974). This global war counteracted the impact of the Great Depression for members of this cohort, just as it ended the depression generally.

In our examination of several cohorts who came to adulthood during the depression, we asked the following question: Why did the Great Depression not produce a "lost generation" as had been generally assumed? In an effort to answer this question, we examine the impact military service had on the subsequent lives of men (born during the late 1920s and early 1930s) who experienced deprivation as young children during the Great Depression. We compare, in particular, the experiences of two cohorts of young men who were members of two very different communities—the textile-mill community of Manchester, New Hampshire (Hareven, 1982), and the California cities of Berkeley and Oakland in the San Francisco Bay Area (Elder, 1979). In each case, the long-term impact of the war on the lives of young men encountering it depended on life chances that were structured by class, community setting, adversities inflicted by the Great Depression, and options provided by World War II. Of special interest are the children of working-class families and their life chances within a declining textile-mill community and the vibrant urban setting known as the Bay Area. How did community differences in opportunities affect the ability of young men to overcome the devastating effects of the Great Depression? How were those differences expressed in responses to military mobilization and its subsequent impact on careers?

Depression Children in the
Bay Area and in Manchester

The influence of historical times on life experience generally depends on the point in people's lives when they first encounter new situations. According to this life-stage concept, adolescents in the 1930s were too old to be wholly dependent on their highly stressed families and too young to be looking for a job in a stagnant labor market. By comparison, younger children experienced the harshness of depression losses through their family—through heavy drinking and withdrawn behavior of father or frantic concern of mother.

Hitting the Great Depression

Members of Oakland and Berkeley cohorts encountered the Great Depression at different ages, which entailed an important difference in risks of lasting impairment. The Oakland cohort experienced the depression during early adolescence, well after the early years of development, whereas members of the Berkeley cohort were still highly dependent on parents at the time of family misfortune.

Consistent with this life-stage difference, members of the younger Berkeley cohort, especially the boys, were most likely to be disadvantaged by family strains and conflicts associated with heavy income loss. The Oakland boys were least harmed by the experience. Hardship markedly increased a lack of self-confidence for the younger boys, but not among the older ones. Similar differences in adolescence appear in assertiveness, social competence, and aspirations. Young women in the two cohorts ended up in the middle on psychological well-being in adolescence.

In much the same fashion, the younger Manchester men, who were born from about 1925 to 1934, were more adversely influenced by depression hardship than were the community's older men, born before 1924. All of these men were the children of former workers of the Amoskeag Mills. As already noted, the Amoskeag Company, once the world's largest textile mill, reached its peak of prosperity in the early 1900s and shut down in 1936, after a precipitous decline (Hareven, 1982). The children's generation, whose careers are being discussed here, consists of two cohorts: Those who reached adulthood in the Great Depression (similar to the Oakland cohort), and those who reached adulthood in World War II or in the immediate postwar era (this younger cohort matches the historical time of the Berkeley cohort). Data on the Manchester children's cohort include extensive open-ended interviews gathered between 1980 and 1983 and demographic, career, and migration histories constructed from the interviews and other vital records. Data on the children's life histories were linked to those of the parents, thus making comparisons across generations possible (see Chapter 6).

Manchester was a one-industry town (see Chapter 2). The Amoskeag's shutdown left the entire labor force stranded. The shutdown deprived entire families of jobs and tore these families apart, as their members wandered around New England or returned to Quebec in search of work. The blow of unemployment on Manchester's laborers was particularly severe because these immigrant workers had already been deprived through low wages and the ups and downs typical of textile industry prior to the depression (Hareven, 1982). The first opportunity for relief in Manchester came with the arrival of war industries, following the entry of the United States into World War II.

Considering all aspects of the depression experience, we have many reasons to expect an impaired future for the younger sons of hard-pressed parents in the California cohorts. Nevertheless, studies show (Elder, 1979) remarkably little evidence of such impairment on socioeconomic achievements. With adjustments for class origin and IQ, men from deprived homes were just as likely as the nondeprived to be in the upper middle class by their forties and fifties. War may have pulled some of these younger sons toward greater opportunity in both the Berkeley and Manchester studies. We focus on these groups, but with some comparisons to the older men in both studies.

The Community Context

Berkeley was a city of approximately 82,000 residents in 1930, and the local campus of the University of California loomed over the economic and cultural scene. Scattered evidence suggests that a university education for offspring attracted families to the city. As able children passed through the public schools, they were shaped by an ever-present standard of achievement and opportunity represented by the university. At the time, the state offered all residents a tuition-free higher education if they had a high-school diploma. But only the most talented had access to the research universities, such as the Berkeley campus. The message for ambitious and able children of the working class was clear enough. An educational route to a better life was available and manageable.

Just as the University of California at Berkeley ranked as one of the finest public universities in the land, the Amoskeag Mills in Manchester was the world's largest textile mill at its peak of prosperity in the early 1900s with a labor force of more than 19,000. In 1907, the *Manchester Mirror* (cited in Hareven, 1982, p. iii) vividly described the enormous flow of humanity that left the great gateways of the mill at 6:00 P.M.: "The first to leave the plant were men and boys, some with dinner pails and some with bicycles. Then came a steady stream of men and women, boys and girls. . . . The great majority of the younger of the toilers were chatting amiably, and appeared to be thoroughly happy and contented with their lot."

A workday from 6:30 A.M. to 6:00 P.M. for teenage Manchester boys and girls was clearly another world from the experience of working-class youth in Berkeley, and Amoskeag's demise in the Great Depression increased the difference. By the end of 1935, fewer than 1,000 workers were still employed by Amoskeag—a hundred-year-old institution had come to an end for the Manchester working class. In 1936, the mills shut down completely, devastating the economy of this one-industry town and leaving the entire community of 100,000 stranded. Only the economic recovery resulting from the unparalleled mass mobilization of a global war put an end to the crushing effect of this event.

Considering these contextual differences, the opportunity function of military service most certainly varied between the two communities and populations. Two questions, then, are central to our exploration.

1. Did military mobilization open up opportunities and the possibility of a better life for children of the Great Depression in the two communities?
2. How did military mobilization vary by community, especially among members of the working class?

Keeping in mind the life stage of each cohort at the beginning of World War II, the story of mass mobilization applies mainly to the older men— the Oakland and Manchester men who were born around 1920, the older cohorts. We begin with this account because it left a powerful impression on the minds and military aspirations of the younger men, who were teenagers during the war. Some of these teenagers managed to get into the war before it ended, though most entered in the postwar era and through the Korean War. Empirical evidence of the military pathway to greater opportunity comes from the younger cohorts in the two urban areas, the Bay Area and Manchester. These young men were especially vulnerable to depression hardships and thus had much to gain through the social advantages of the military. The two studies, Bay Area and Manchester, rely on different types of data, and we attempt to integrate them as much as possible in the analysis.[1]

Recasting Men's Lives Through Military Service

A major explanation for these unexpected developments centers on the positive effect of war mobilization in reversing the adversities of the Great Depression, from World War II through the Korean War. In view of maturing opportunities during World War II and the educational benefits of duty in the armed forces, military service represents a promising source of clues to the worklife accomplishments of the depression cohorts, despite the adversity they experienced during the 1930s.

In the nation as a whole, four of five American men born in the 1920s served in the armed forces of World War II (Hogan, 1981). Approximately nine of ten men from the older Oakland cohort (birth dates 1920–1921) were inducted into the armed forces (Elder, 1974). The young Berkeley men (born 1928–1929) were generally too young to be mobilized in this war, although 73 percent entered the service through the Korean War. In both the older and the younger Manchester cohorts, 75 percent of the men served in World War II or shortly thereafter. Taking all of these figures into account, we have good reason to view military mobilization as a prime influence in changing the life-course direction and prospects of men reared during the Great Depression.

The military has long been seen as a pathway to opportunity for youth from disadvantaged backgrounds, but the full meaning of this statement requires examination of the impact of service experiences on the careers of young men from the working class who were caught in hard times during the Great Depression in communities such as Berkeley and Manchester.

The outbreak of war in Europe in September 1939 spurred America's initial mobilization for war—the draft in the fall of 1940. Between the surrender of France to Germany in 1940 and Japan's surrender in 1945, the number of men and women in the armed forces increased to over 16 million. By pulling tens of thousands of young men from diverse and highly insular communities and placing them on large training bases, service mobilization established conditions that favored dramatic life changes, breaking the hold of family hardship, frustration, and vanishing opportunity caused by the Great Depression.

This account applies only to men who survived their term of service and wartime events. Thankfully, war casualties were relatively light in these cohorts, and consequently, we must weigh this fact and the legacy of combat with the recasting influence of mobilization. Only one-fifth of the Berkeley veterans faced combat, compared with nearly one-half of the Oakland veterans, but the impairing legacy of heavy combat can still be observed in the later lives of some men in both cohorts.

Symptoms of post-traumatic stress disorder are still reported by one-fifth of the heavy combat veterans (Elder and Clipp, 1988), including sleep disturbances, depression and anxiety, and flashbacks of combat scenes. Whether pathogenic or health promoting, the service experience and war events clearly have long-term implications across the life course. The effect of wars reverberates across lives and generations in human populations. War mobilization promoted social independence, a broadened range of knowledge and experience, a legitimated time-out from age-graded careers and their ever-present expectations, and greater access to the means of educational and work-life achievement. The war experience also exposed young men to other areas of the United States and other countries.

Entry into the service also meant separation from family influences and a measure of social independence coupled with establishment of new social relationships. Induction "knifed-off" (Brolz and Wilson, 1946) the recruit's past experience. In particular, basic training fostered peer equality and comradeship among recruits by separating them from their pasts. It provided, at least temporarily, new identities (except where race was concerned), required uniform dress and appearance, minimized privacy, and viewed performance on the basis of group achievement or failure. An Oakland veteran spoke about "the unforgiving environment" in which the consequences of personal failure were felt by the entire unit.

A second feature of the military experience is the extent to which service time represents a clear-cut break with the conventional expectations of an age-graded career—a time-out or moratorium from "adult" responsibilities. Military duty provides a legitimate time-out from educational, work, and family pressures in a structured environment. As a rule, presence in the service is not questioned, and neither is the lack of career progress or work plans resulting from being in the service. The very act of military service provides adequate justification for nonconformity with age-related expectations of career development. Indeed, Samuel A. Stouffer and his associates (1949, p. 572) note that for many soldiers in World War II, "perhaps for a majority, the break caused by military service [meant] a chance to evaluate where they had gotten and to reconsider where they were going." For individuals deprived of job opportunities and the normally expected transition into careers, the service provided a temporary respite from the desperate, often circular, search for employment.

Especially among men from deprived circumstances—the older Oakland and Manchester men—military service and its situational imperatives provided an escape from daily poverty by promoting independence and exposing recruits to new ideas and models. It offered a legitimate time-out or moratorium for those unsure of the course to follow in life. For deprived youth lacking self-direction and a sense of adequacy, military service also offered developmental alternatives to the course charted by their families—separation from maternal control through involvement in a masculine culture and the opportunity to sort things out in activities that bolstered self-confidence, resolve, and goal setting. Some of these themes appear in the life reviews of veterans from deprived households. The break from a confused and painful family situation is a recurring theme (Elder, 1987). One man recalled that he "finally realized what was happening and broke away." He entered the navy. Another described the time he joined the army at eighteen as the end of his mother's domination and the start of independence.

Several men recalled the novel and rewarding experience of mastery of military tasks or of skills learned in the military, of doing something well and on their own. Across this period, we see a contrast between descriptions of self before and after time in the military, from the implication of being "such a flop" in adolescence—"I couldn't do anything"—to the claim that from "the day I went into the service, I was almost on *my own* [an extraordinary statement from someone regimented into military discipline] . . . figured out my own situation and went on from there."

A third feature of mobilization entailed a broadened range of perspectives and social knowledge. Mobilization increased the scope of awareness of oneself and others through an expanded range of interactional experiences, including encounters with new people and places that promote greater tolerance of social diversity. Willard Waller once likened the process to "stirring soup; people are thrown together who have never seen one another before and will never see one another again" (1940, p. 14). Out of this experience comes greater awareness of self and others, an expanded range of interactional experiences with their behavior models and social support, and possibly a greater social tolerance of diversity. A veteran interviewed just after World War II in the study by Robert J. Havighurst and colleagues (1951, p. 188) spoke about the incredible diversity of his acquaintances in the service and their influence on his views. As he put it, the experience "sort of opens up your horizons. . . . You start thinking in broader terms than you did before."

Similarly, for young men who had never left Manchester before, military service provided an opportunity to "see the world," to experience for the first time other parts of the United States as well as foreign countries. As one former serviceman from Manchester put it, "Part of the change is people getting to know and experience other people from different parts of the country and maybe different parts of the world." A veteran of the Pacific theater explained, "a man's life can't help but expand when you go through things like that. You see things from a different perspective than you ever had before" (Havighurst et al., 1951, p. 172). This access to greater opportunity stems from some of the personal changes we have noted and from service training and G.I. benefits that encouraged efforts to get ahead.

Finally, the educational opportunities presented by the G.I. Bill of Rights enabled veterans to expand their education and acquire new skills after the war. Remembered now for its educational and housing benefits, the G.I. Bill was prompted by fear of the social and political danger of widespread unemployment among returning veterans. In many respects, the bill was a "child of 1944; it symbolized the mood of a country immersed in war, recalling the depression, and worrying about the future" (Olson, 1974, p. 24). At least in the area of education, the G.I. Bill became a primary factor in the life opportunity that veterans from the California studies experienced. For example, nearly one-half of the California veterans reported having completed an educational degree on the G.I. Bill. The education portion of the bill was designed for men in their early adult years—men most likely to want to complete an undergraduate education. Thus, the usual structure of the life course made the bill and its benefits more attractive to the younger men who lacked the competing alternatives to higher education, such as marriage and a family or a full-time job.

Typically, military mobilization seeks young men not involved in families and careers. However, the enormous workforce needs of World War II prevented strict adherence to this standard. As the recruitment boundaries included larger numbers of older men, the personal disadvantages of service also expanded. Beyond the formative times of adulthood, older recruits experienced more of the costs, through career and family disruptions, and fewer benefits (e.g., the G.I. Bill) when compared with early entrants. By comparison, early entry into the armed forces minimized the costs and increased the benefits. For these men, military service was truly a timely event, especially if they came from hard-pressed families. By enhancing opportunity and achievement for men who grew up in the depression, military service functioned as a turning point, or change, in the life course.

There are thus two parts to our interpretation of military service as a turning point. One links Great Depression hardship to military service and especially to an early entry into the military. In this scenario, deprived boys who lacked achievement options as well as feelings of personal worth are attracted to military pride and self-respect and the masculine appeal and status of military dress. They could, it seems, become someone of note merely by joining. The second part of the interpretation assumes that military service diminishes the persistence of prior disadvantage. From this perspective, the adult disadvantage of a deprived childhood in the 1930s would be least among men who entered the service at a relatively young age. Not surprisingly, the evidence shows that early mobilization was a major pathway toward life achievement and away from depression hardship among veterans in the California and Manchester cohorts.

The best single test of the turning-point thesis is provided by the younger cohort of Berkeley veterans (born in 1928–1929) and their counterparts in the Manchester working class. Members from the Berkeley cohort enjoyed higher status before the Great Depression than did members from the Manchester cohort, but they also had more to lose. We begin with the Berkeley cohort and then consider the life histories of the Manchester cohort.

Escaping Hard Times in the Bay Area

When war mobilization started, the younger Berkeley adolescents were in high school. A midwar survey found them surrounded by symbols of war

mobilization (Elder, 1986). Signs of mobilization and consciousness-rais-
ing were everywhere in Berkeley. A local radio series entitled *My War* dramatized "the wartime contributions of every man, woman, and child on
the home front." Children at Saturday matinee movies saw war's reality
through newsreels. Troop trains from nearby army bases chugged constantly through Oakland, and warships moved in and out of the bay.
Families worked victory gardens on vacant plots—over 40,000 were reported in the East Bay Area during 1943. The energetic role of young people in the war effort and their resulting sense of significance are strikingly
documented through the seemingly endless round of collection drives for
fats, wastepaper, scrap metal, and even milkweed pods.

Among the Berkeley boys, "the war" became the most popular conver-
sational topic with peers, outranking girls, school, parents, and "things I
want." As military events began to shift in favor of the United States and
the Allies, the boys were asked what they most often talked about with
friends. The list included aspects of popular culture (such as movies), relations with girls, family and school affairs, and war items—the war in
general, the armed service one would choose, the new defense workers
and their families, and postwar planning. Over one-half of the boys
claimed that they often talked about the war with other boys, and the preferred branch of military service was only slightly less popular (53 percent versus 41 percent) as a topic. For many boys, a major concern was
getting into the armed forces, even though they were underage.

These preferences are revealing concerning the boys' future life course
and reflect disadvantages extended back into the Great Depression.
Slightly more than 70 percent of the Berkeley boys eventually served in the
armed forces, and those who found the war an especially salient experience
were likely to join up at the first opportunity, frequently during the last
months of World War II. Early joiners entered the service before age
twenty-one; later entrants, at age twenty-one or older. Nearly 70 percent of
the early joiners selected at least one military occupation on a "things-to-be
inventory" in 1943–1944, as did over one-half of the late joiners. Fewer than
40 percent of the men who never served also chose a military occupation
during their high-school career in World War II. Conversation (in the interviews) on this topic shows corresponding differences among these groups.

Disadvantage is a factor in the military preference of the Berkeley boys
and in their mobilization. Frequent talking with peers about military roles
during World War II is linked to disadvantages of one kind or another,
such as low family status, deprivation, poor high-school grades, and feelings of personal inadequacy. This background of disadvantage was more
relevant to the timing of service than to entry itself. From all perspectives,
the stronger the disadvantage, the *earlier* the military induction (Elder,
1986). Boys who entered the service early turned out to be the most disad-

vantaged group in the cohort. They were most likely to have grown up in hard-pressed families during the 1930s, and their school performance was less than promising. They were less goal-oriented, less confident, and less assertive than other adolescents in this cohort.

But did the life disadvantage of entering recruits carry over to their postmilitary lives (Elder, 1986)? To answer this question, we must distinguish between veterans who entered the service relatively early and late. The early joiners stand out on family and personal disadvantage relative to late entrants. Regarding family disadvantage, the early recruits have more in common with the Berkeley men who did not enter the service at all. But they were actually more successful in terms of education—70 percent completed at least some college, compared with 58 percent of nonveterans. For many early joiners, the G.I. Bill made college possible and a reality.

Consider the life experience of two men who came from deprived families in the 1930s. The first young man, from a working-class family, expressed a positive attitude toward the military during World War II. He listed a variety of military occupations; however, becoming a marine remained his primary goal. As his mother said at the time, "He'll be a marine regardless of what I want him to be." He followed through on this objective by quitting high school at age seventeen and persuading his parents to let him join the marines. After a four-year stint in the Middle East, he returned to civilian life, launched an apprenticeship in printing on the G.I. Bill, and married his high-school sweetheart. The other young man, with similar aspirations for military service, dropped out of high school and joined the navy. After the service, he became a member of the air reserve and earned a high-school diploma. Eventually, his fascination with flying led to his enrollment in a university electrical engineering program on the G.I. Bill.

Not all of the Berkeley veterans went on to higher education and took advantage of the G.I. Bill in the 1940s and 1950s. Three observations are relevant here. First, military service did not reinforce or increase the educational aspirations of all men. Some with strong vocational skills (e.g., electricians) entered corresponding jobs after demobilization. Second, the experience of combat left some men psychologically impaired, and typically, these were men who ranked lowest in ego resilience in adolescence. Third, some men who returned to demanding family responsibilities were discouraged from entering or completing their higher education. From another perspective, those men did not receive the support from wives, children, and parents that would enable them to take advantage of the G.I. Bill. The time for personal sacrifice had passed.

Occupational experience provides more conclusive evidence that military service became a turning point in the life course of men with backgrounds of disadvantage in the Great Depression. By the age of forty, men who entered the service early ranked slightly higher on occupational status than nonveterans. The two groups are evenly matched on family social class in 1929, although early entrants were far more likely to come from hard-pressed families, by a difference of three to one. More notably, we even find increasing similarity up to the middle years in the occupational rank of early and late entrants, despite their markedly different backgrounds and preservice educational achievement. For example, slightly more than one-half of the late entrants were college graduates, compared to one-third of the early joiners. Status differences of this sort tend to diminish as we follow the men into their later years, but how does this occur?

Are there developmental gains over the life course, from an ineffectual pattern of behavior in adolescence to greater mastery and self-direction during the middle years? Consider a comparison of the early entrants and nonveterans (in California) on four measures of psychological functioning in adolescence and at midlife (approximately age forty): self-inadequacy, goal orientation, social competence, and submissiveness. The content of each measure is identical for the two periods. In general, the data point to a convergence of psychological functioning by midlife, with veterans who joined the service early showing a pronounced shift toward greater competence. However, these men still have not completely closed the gap with nonveterans; at midlife, they still rank slightly lower in all areas.

Our concept of military service as a potential turning point for children of the Great Depression is based in part on the assumption that service experiences markedly reduced the persistence of initial disadvantages. As noted, military service did weaken the usual cross-time correlation between adolescent and midlife competence. In this case, adolescent disadvantage should be more predictive of military service than the latter is predictive of adult disadvantage. The data favor this interpretation, but other interpretations (such as regression to the mean) warrant consideration.

Developmental growth among men entering the service at an early age suggests another perspective on the service as a recasting mechanism. Military service may enhance life opportunities by enabling men to *use their personal resources* to good effect in education, work, and family. Motivation is part of the explanation, along with personal qualities that veterans frequently cite as benefits of their service experience (Elder, 1987). Especially prominent among these qualities are self-discipline, ability to cope with adversity, and skill in managing people. Such qualities are most likely to be put to a test among children of the Great Depression, who had to use all they had to be successful in life. Neither a quality education nor a rewarding job is a given for this cohort.

Building on this account, we assume that military service is more predictive of occupational achievement among men from deprived families than among the nondeprived and, further, that the service effect occurs primarily through higher education. To put these ideas to a test, Glen Elder and Avishai Caspi (1990) set up the same prediction equation for men from deprived and nondeprived backgrounds: childhood IQ and military service as antecedents of midlife occupational status. The analysis shows that military service has a significant effect only among the economically deprived, whereas IQ is generally predictive in both groups. Second, the service effect occurs primarily through higher education. With education in the model for men from deprived families, military service no longer has any effect on adult occupational status.

These results suggest that some children of the Great Depression broke the cycle of disadvantage by entering the service and, if not mobilized, by virtue of their own intellectual ability. By contrast, the attainment of men from nondeprived homes most clearly hinges on their own abilities. Military service in young adulthood neither aided nor hindered their life success, in large part because these veterans generally entered the service later in life, often in response to induction processes.

Many years after the Great Depression and World War II, the director emeritus of the Berkeley Guidance Study, Jean Macfarlane offered some reflections on the lives of the Berkeley men that summarize in many respects the turnaround we observe in the life course of veterans who grew up in deprived families. She noted that some of the Berkeley boys turned out to be more stable and effective adults than any of the research team, with its differing theoretical biases, had predicted. Most noteworthy, she observed, are the number of men whose poor adolescent scholastic records "completely belie the creative intelligence demands of their present position." A large proportion of the "most outstandingly mature adults in our entire group . . . are recruited from those who were confronted with very different situations and whose characteristic responses during childhood and adolescence seemed to us to compound their problems" (Macfarlane, 1963, p. 338; 1971, p. 413).

These reflections are not scientific observations by any means, but they are remarkably attuned to the results we have presented. Macfarlane sought explanations for the disparity between early experience and the adult life course in the psyche and proximal world of the individual. First, she noted a common failure to recognize the potential maturation value of hardship experiences. As she put it, "We have learned that no one becomes mature without living through the pains and confusions of maturing experiences" (1971, p. 341). Second, she decried our insufficient appreciation of experiences in late adolescence and early adulthood, including the potential of later events for altering life trajectories. According to Macfarlane, a large number of the Berkeley boys did not achieve a sense of ego identity and strength until later situations "forced them or presented an opportunity to them to fulfill a role that gave them a sense of worth" (Macfarlane, 1971, p. 341). Thus, developmental gains may be associated with departure from home and community, changes that provide an opportunity to "work through early confusions and inhibitions" (p. 341).

Indeed, historical features of the transition to young adulthood offer promising explanations for the disparity between early deprivation and adult fulfillment among the Berkeley men as children of the Great Depression. After a decade of depression hardship, these men experienced the new prosperity of full-scale mobilization in World War II, followed soon after by the Korean War and postwar era affluence. Paradoxically, mobilization for World War II and the Korean War converged in ways that improved life choices or altered forever the depression's legacy of disadvantage, placing young boys of the Great Depression on a more promising route to personal growth.

Military service *and* higher education emerge in the lives of the Berkeley men as events that turned their lives around by enabling them to surmount childhood disadvantages in the 1930s. Another event of significance for changing life course of lives is marriage. Lee N. Robins (1966) underscored the critical support a spouse provides in enabling the young to overcome problem behaviors in the transition to adulthood, and we find similar benefits of wife support in the lives of Berkeley and Oakland veterans from World War II and the Korean War (Elder and Clipp, 1988). Mobilization frequently brought the veterans in these cohorts together with their prospective wives on army bases or in hospitals; in some cases, the prospects of wartime separation led to hasty or early marriages. For men who had lost confidence and hope in their future, an optimistic wife could turn their dysphoric outlook toward greater vitality and ambition for a new day. Judging from available evidence, husbands and wives are likely to change in similar directions over time, far more so than unrelated men and women (Caspi, 1989).

From another angle, we find that the young women who managed to escape the hardships of the 1930s generally did so through marriage to a young man of potential. Indeed, the depression experience itself tended to orient women to life accomplishment through marriage by increasing the importance of interpersonal ties and reducing the value of higher education for daughters, who, as one father put it, "are only going to marry." A middle-class mother from the Berkeley sample expressed aspirations for her daughter as "college, social popularity, and an early marriage." This young woman met her upwardly mobile spouse at college and promptly left school to marry (Elder, Downey, and Cross, 1986). Women of this generation frequently sacrificed both education and occupational careers for the work of husbands and the presumed domestic claims of the home.

Wartime employment, the college campus, and population mixing through wartime demands played important roles in shaping the marriage experiences of the Berkeley women. By midlife, these women of deprived childhoods had gained more through marriage than through personal accomplishments. Marriage turned out to be a more prominent route to high status for them than for women from more privileged backgrounds.

Respite from the Great Depression in Manchester

The coming of wartime imperatives to the depression-weary community of Manchester set in motion general change processes that drastically altered the lives of young people from working-class families. War production on the home front sharply increased job opportunities and earnings just as military recruitment siphoned off the young men for basic training and overseas duty. Both types of mobilization opened up a future of greater opportunity, if only within the working class. War pressures also increased the incentive to marry before the expected separation during overseas duty; the rate of marriage actually accelerated during the war. Finally, the loss of workers from the community and the opening of war industries expanded women's roles in particular, both within the household and in the community. Each of these developments is part of the mobilization experience for Manchester's children of the Great Depression.

Following the decision of the United States to join the war, the city's atmosphere was permeated with patriotic drives and appeals to Manchester's citizens to do their best in the war effort. Public buildings were plastered with recruitment posters from the military and the War Production Board, and churches acted as clearinghouses for information and as recruitment stations to the military and for various aspects of the war effort. The patriotic atmosphere was heightened by the Office of Civil Defense, which warned about the presence of submarines off the coast. Manchester residents' sense of connection with a distant war abroad was reinforced by the constant movement of troops through the city on their way to the adjacent Grenier Airfield, where they took off to Newfoundland and on to England.

The feverish excitement of the war and its patriotic effort was especially significant in a city such as Manchester, where former mill workers still suffered from the double blow of the Great Depression and the shutdown of the Amoskeag Mills. The war effort united community members with a new sense of a common purpose and a commitment to the joint effort for survival. Sons and daughters who had left in search of jobs outside Manchester returned to find employment in the new industries mushrooming in the city. A new feeling of hope overcame the sense of despair and loss of purpose in the wake of the shutdown of the mills.

The first stage of Manchester's recovery during the war entailed the opening of various war-production factories in the empty buildings of the Amoskeag Mills—a sweater factory for the military, a rubber plant for producing rafts and life jackets, a metal factory that made bullets, and a parachute factory. These industries restored the beat of life and activity to the desolate mill yard and recruited men and women of all ages. In addition, the Portsmouth Navy Yard, only an hour's drive from Manchester and nearby Grenier Airfield, attracted young working men in large numbers.

Jobs were available again after a hiatus of about eight years. (Even though the Amoskeag Mills had shut down officially in 1936, the company actually employed only a rump labor force from about 1933 on.) Manchester's teenage boys and girls and even their older siblings were surprised at the sudden return of opportunity: "And they paid well. Boy, did they pay," reminisced one of the Amoskeag's young workers who had remained unemployed after the mill's devastating shutdown.[2] Manchester youth who had been wandering around in other parts of New Hampshire and New England, working in occasional, temporary jobs, began to return home and start regular employment at unprecedented high wages.

For Manchester's young men, the war counteracted the deprivation imposed by the Great Depression in two stages. First, war industries provided employment, some of which involved learning professional skills. These opportunities benefited the entire community and provided new employment for women as well. Second, the war opened up new opportunities for young men through military service. When the war industries were first inaugurated, people were seized with excitement: "You could make yourself three to four hundred a week, no problem at all. Big money!" recalled a former shipyard worker. "My father was working for $54 a week for that job he had all his life. I told him 'Quit it, Pa! Quit it. Come down to the shipyard and we will get you in there.'"

For some of Manchester's young men, the jobs that opened up in the initial war industries had a more lasting impact on their subsequent careers than military service by itself; but the military experience provided young men with excitement and a stage for heroic performance. Those who went to work in the war industries before military service felt for the first time a sense of self-respect as workers and enjoyed the kind of sociability with fellow workers that their parents had enjoyed in the Amoskeag Mills. These young men had missed that experience entirely because of the shutdown of the mills and the Great Depression. In many cases, the military also taught young men new skills they could use after the war.

Manchester's young men and women, born between 1920 and 1924, were the cohort that came of age to work when there was no work (Hughes, 1971a, p. 124). They were the "lost generation" of the Great Depression, the children of the shutdown of the Amoskeag Mills. As they were growing up, their parents dreamed that they would escape mill work by graduating from high school and entering "middle-class" occupations. The decline and the shutdown of the mills in the midst of the Great Depression set this cohort's progression into the middle class back by one generation. Not only were they unable to escape blue-collar occupations, but they felt fortunate to have a chance to return to or enter such occupations once the war industries opened in Manchester.

One long-time resident, Carl (born 1922), was able to embark on a steady job in a textile mill in Manchester in 1941 because of employment opportunities created by the war. The availability of textile work enticed him to quit high school. Carl got his job because his father was a foreman.

> So he got me the job with the intention that by September I'd go back to high school. Well, my intentions were all the time that I'd never go back to school, because I hated it. . . . [S]o come September I really fussed about going back to school and my mother forced me or tried to force me and, ah, from one thing to another my father said, "Look, he's old enough to know what he wants, he's eighteen, almost nineteen years old, it's up to him to make his decision. If he wants to work in the mill, he can work." Which is what I did.

Pete, also born in 1922, was first able to improve his chances by entering the war industries after a long period of floundering and unemployment during the depression. "In those days (I'm talking about 1939) there was no work . . . and I was happy to work even for nothing, to learn something." Pete first worked as a plumber's apprentice to learn a trade. He subsequently worked in a shoe company gluing soles and finally found a job assembling typewriters at the Royal Typewriter Company in Hartford, Connecticut. After nine months Pete was laid off because the company was being converted to produce Colt firearms. He was finally saved from unemployment by the war industry at Pratt and Whitney Aircraft. "It was good work and it was a lot more money than I'd ever made in my young years."

The draft diverted Pete from the chance to make money in the war industries: "As a patriotic American I had to enlist. I was actually drafted into the army, but I didn't want to go into the army, so I volunteered to go into the navy." Because he was making aircraft engines, Pete did not have to enter the service if he preferred to continue working. But he said, "I would not hear any of this" and volunteered.

Pete was sent for training to the submarine school in Newport, Rhode Island. He became a torpedo man and served on a submarine in the Pacific until the end of the war: "I enjoyed serving my country. I enjoyed every minute of it. If I had to go back in the service that's what I'd want. Of course it wasn't a picnic, but you had to be doing something to save your country. And to me that was what I did and I enjoyed it!"

After Pete's return from the service, he sold hardware in Manchester. Two years later, he joined the family beauty supply company his brother headed. Family ties eventually proved to be more critical in finding Pete a steady career than his navy experience: "My brother was after me to go to work for him, so I decided to start working for him, on a basis that I would be looking for something else later. And obviously I didn't find anything else better because I've last[ed] for thirty-five years." Pete's large family could stay together in Manchester because of the availability of jobs: "I think the big factor that the family stayed here so close is that we all found work here. That's what it amounts to, we all found a job and something to do and the something that we had in common, the beauty business."

The war industries were also extremely significant for those family members, especially wives and daughters, who did not join the military and who were able, therefore, to work and support the family members who remained at home while the men were away.

Helen, one of the women in the Manchester study (born 1924) worked in several war industries and managed to support herself, her children, and her mother-in-law during her husband's four-year absence. At Manchester Metal Products Company, she said, "We were making 15-millimeter bullets. I was inspecting bullets—I was a little squeamish in there. I was afraid if you don't do it right it might backfire. It might kill your own man." Helen soon quit to work in a sweater factory for military supply as a hand cutter. "I was the only one who could cut army sweaters; fifty dozens a day, by hand."

The war provided Manchester's young men with an escape from parental and societal pressures to attend college or obtain steady work. As noted for the Oakland and Berkeley men, it offered a moratorium from the usual expectations that young men move through orderly sequenced transitions, such as graduating from high school and embarking on a continuous, stable career or continuing with higher education or technical-professional training. The war provided an excuse for the men's delay in following such regular career patterns, especially where deprivation during the Great Depression had rendered regular careers impossible.

For some young men, the war also offered an escape from oppressive employment conditions. Consider an eighteen-year-old working in a shoe factory. He had a conflict with his boss: "I had damaged a shoe. And he came over about nine-thirty in the morning, started chewing me out. Well, I shut off my machine and told him where he could shove his job, and I took off, and I went downtown, and I enlisted in the army." His wife remarked during the interview, "That's a patriotic way of going in the army."

For Manchester's young men, as for their California age counterparts, the war provided an opportunity to regain their self-respect, acquire skills, demonstrate their aptitude, and perform well even under trying circumstances. For Jerry (born 1920), the service provided such an opportunity. It also counteracted to some extent his educational deficiencies resulting from lack of a high-school education. During technical training in the navy, Jerry felt under a severe disadvantage for not having graduated from high school. "I had to work three times as hard as anybody who had finished high school to get the same passing grade."

Before going into the service, Jerry could find only casual jobs (such as dishwashing in a grill or delivering for a meat market where his brother-in-law worked). He enrolled in a Civilian Conservation Corps camp for unemployed youth in the White Mountains, where he worked in a forestation project for six months. After that, Jerry could find work only in Vermont, where he buffed leather for the International Shoe Company. As he put it: "Work was very hard to get in Manchester" before the war. The period just before the war was "the hardest time in my life."

Jerry joined the navy in 1941 and trained as a radio operator. He reminisced: "That training made my subsequent advancement in the area of electrical technician possible. When I went in the service, I joined the navy and became a navigation radioman. I knew absolutely nothing about radio and electronics." After the service, he enrolled in a technical school under the G.I. Bill, where he learned to repair electrical motors. Following graduation from the technical school, Jerry worked steadily as a turbine tester for General Electric until 1955, when he became a supervisor, a position he still held at the time of the interview in 1983.

In assessing his own progress, Jerry speculated on how far he actually might have gotten had he started with a high-school education: "I picked myself up by my bootstraps as you might say, because I came out of the navy as a chief petty officer and worked my way into General Electric to a supervising position. So I think if I had had an education, I might have been dangerous."

The war had such a profound impact on his life that when asked to describe the main periods in his life, Jerry designated the war years as a distinct period:

Well, I'd say the start of my life, when I was a child in the city of Manchester would be one period of life—very stable. And then the Second World War which is a period of turmoil, trials, tribulations, separation. . . . and then I'd say the third period was bringing up the children . . . which is a period of responsibility. Now we are coming to the fourth period, which I'd say would be leisure.

Another cohort member (born 1923) viewed the military as an opportunity for education before the war broke out. Raymond grew up in Greenfield, Indiana, and married a Manchester woman. While in high school, he worked at various odd jobs.

I started passing newspapers . . . at four in the morning; and then I started working in the soda fountain at the local drugstore, naturally. All of us kids went through that I believe. I worked at the swimming pool, at the park. I also helped take care of the clay tennis courts in the summertime. And I hoed corn for a dollar a day from sunup to sunset and believe me that was tough, but I was tickled to death to make a buck.

After Raymond graduated from high school, his parents wanted him to train as a butcher. "And I says, 'Forget it.' So I went into the service hoping to get some education, so I could maintain a job. And I didn't realize that we were so close to war." After his release from the service four years later, Raymond went to Tri-State College in Indiana under the G.I. Bill. He then made his career as a civilian employee for the military. In the 1960s, Raymond worked at a satellite tracking station in New Hampshire. The war provided him with a critical turning point for his education. It also enabled him to meet his bride in Manchester and eventually to settle in New Hampshire.

Beyond teaching specific skills, military service also expanded the horizons of many young immigrant men in Manchester, by enabling them to learn the English language. One member of the Manchester cohort study, Henri (born 1927), who grew up in Manchester's "Little Quebec" on the West Side, attributed his acquisition of English and the ensuing benefits to his subsequent employment to his military service: "We spoke French outside, we spoke French inside, and when I went to the service this is where I learned [English]. Grammar school was all French even in the English class. I learned the hard way so I didn't want my kids to go through what I went through." After eight years of grammar school, Henri worked in a shoe shop. He entered the service at age seventeen and left after four years. Next came work in a canteen for two years, a job made possible only by Henri's knowledge of English. After that, he worked as a bread salesman. (His military pay, $20 a week for fifty-two weeks, enabled Henri to search for a job after he left the service, while contributing to his family.) He has continued to work as "a bread man ever since."

As it did for the California young men, the service opened new social and psychological horizons for the Manchester men and provided them with a new experience and an understanding of the world. "The war made me a better person," said Paul (born 1926), who had enlisted at age seventeen. "The war opened up my eyes. I learned a lot." As a gunner's mate on a ship, he went to France, England, and Africa, "all through the invasion," and then to the South Pacific and Japan. These travels were his first time outside Manchester. After observing conditions in Asia, Paul came to idealize the United States:

> It made me appreciate the United States more than I ever did [before]. I feel that we're living in the greatest country in the world. Actually you can get away with everything here. Really it's so free. It's unbelievable. . . . And what I saw out in Japan and in that area there . . . I feel that we're very fortunate. Well, the way the people were living and they weren't as free as we were.

He was deeply moved by the poverty he encountered in Asia. By contrast, he welcomed "coming back here and having a nice home."

Despite his having grown up in abject poverty in Manchester and his disrupted childhood family life, Paul gained a new perspective on poverty and suffering from his observations in Asia beyond those of his family background. His father had deserted his mother, who was left struggling with work in the mill and rearing her children without outside assistance: "We were a poor family, because mother was left alone with all the family. She was working in the mills. She was all alone to take care of the whole family. That's why she died young [at age fifty-one]. She died right after we came out of the service. Six of us were in the service during World War II."

Paul gained no special skills from the military to apply directly to subsequent work. The war did provide him, however, with a sense of self-respect, maturity, and a perspective on the world that enabled him to assess his own poverty and unfortunate childhood experience in the context of a broader world scheme. In addition, the service also facilitated Paul's marriage. He met his spouse on the train from Boston to Manchester, the very day he was mustered out of the navy. He was returning home, and Arlene was returning from a day's excursion with "a bunch of the girls." "I got married young because I needed a home. I had no home. My mother had died and we were all alone. So I wanted to make a home for myself."

For most members of Manchester's war cohort, as for their California counterparts, the war reversed some of the disadvantages imposed by the

Great Depression on community and individual levels. However, the pattern of reversal and the ensuing levels of achievement were different. Whereas most of the California men started from a middle-class base, the Manchester men were from the working class, and many of them had grown up in poverty or on its margins during the depression. They had few resources to fall back on.

Members of the Manchester cohort were textile-mill workers, shoe workers, metalworkers, and semiskilled laborers. Their fathers had been textile workers or shoe workers and their mothers had been textile workers, maids, and waitresses. The war did not afford these men opportunities to advance to the next rung of the occupational ladder or to escape their family's working-class status. At best, the World War II experience saved them from falling below the economic level of their parents prior to or during the Great Depression. It gave them a chance for a "new start" within their own class.

Accelerating the Timing of Life Transitions

As it did in other places in the United States, for most of the members of the Manchester cohort, the war had a direct impact on the timing of marital decisions (Modell and Steffey, 1988). The war hurried the process along among couples who already knew each other. It also exposed Manchester's young men and women to new potential marriage partners from other parts of the United States and even to local ones whom they met through war activities. Marriages in this cohort typically occurred in the early stages of the war or at its end.

Those who married during or at the beginning of the war eloped with their sweethearts before they left for duty. Most of the people interviewed, husbands and wives, admitted that the timing of their marriage (the husbands age twenty to twenty-one, the wives usually three years younger) was early by comparison even with the immediate prewar years and that elopement had been common. Thinking back, they were conscious of this early timing; those who married during the war did so in the face of the emergency and threat of separation for an indefinite period. Postwar affluence encouraged marriage after a service member's return. By contrast with depression times, the men who were returning now had prospects for a job and felt they could afford to marry and establish a family.

A Manchester resident who married in 1947 explained that depression hardships and obligations to one's family of orientation had caused delays in marriage. Conditions changed after the war "because then everybody was in the money . . . not lots of money but everybody had a job.

There was work all over the place." The war, as he pointed out, also exposed people to the opportunity of meeting spouses from other places in the United States and other parts of the world. But the shutdown of the mills had already started the process of sending Manchester's laborers afar.

Consider a Manchester couple married in 1941. The new husband was already in the service, and he planned to take his bride from Manchester to a Florida military base. However, he was sent overseas a day and a half after the wedding. "Got married on a Friday night," reminisced his wife, "and on a Sunday morning I was all alone again for two years. . . . Never, never saw him [during those two years]. I had quit my job, packed my bags and everything." She stayed with her mother in Manchester and worked in a textile factory folding parachutes.

Another woman eloped at age seventeen just before the war and eventually suffered through four years of loneliness. Even though the war precipitated young marriages, elopement was not unusual for Manchester's working class. "[Eloping] was an accepted thing to do in those days, because nobody had any money for weddings. Everybody was very poor before World War II, that big depression, it was terrible."

Many of the youth in Manchester had little family backing or control, anyway:

> Well, he didn't have any father; he was on his own, and I didn't have anybody either. I was on my own more or less. He was a mechanic, but he had lost his job. He was A-1 in the draft, so after this it was Pearl Harbor. So every eligible man was called. He was twenty-two, so he was called right away. He forgot to inform them that he had gotten married.

Left alone when she was seven months pregnant, this bride reluctantly decided to return home to Manchester. "I swallowed my pride and I asked my folks if I could come there until the baby was born . . . so my father took me in, and I had the baby alone."

Another young Manchester woman, Ellen, was attracted by the presence of large numbers of servicemen in Manchester. "We had a whole bunch of men at first in Manchester. And then I met my husband there . . . my first husband." Both were age twenty. "I remember when it happened, too. It was December 7, 1941. I was listening to the radio when it happened [Pearl Harbor]. I didn't quite understand what they were talking about." Ellen's fiancé then called her from North Carolina and said "he wouldn't be able to see me for a while . . . and from then on we wrote letters, and finally we eloped." They were married despite her parents' objection. Karl was German, and Ellen's parents wanted her to wait. They said, "We don't know too much about him and we have to wait until the war is over in case something happened to him." Ellen took her fate into her own hands: "Well, when you're in love, everything seems great and you just take a chance because you don't think of tomorrow; you want to do it right now; because tomorrow is too far away, at that time." Ellen then became a "migrant" army wife through the war.

The war thus precipitated two transitions to adulthood for Manchester's youth. For young men, it facilitated and accelerated the transition to a regular adult work life, preceded by skill acquisition and completion of high school or a technical education under the G. I. Bill. Similarly, the war enabled young women to enter into regular, well-paid employment in the war industries after they had been deprived of that role by the Great Depression and the mill's shutdown. The war also accelerated the transition to marriage and, in many instances, the transition to parenthood. Sequencing of the transitions to work and to marriage was erratic, however. Prior to the war, the young couple's economic self-sufficiency was a precondition for marriage; however, during the war, marriage often preceded regular employment (especially the husband's steady employment).

Customarily, marriage would lead to the couple's establishing a separate household (one of the main conditions for independent adulthood in American society; see above). In Manchester's working class, despite the high incidence of immigration and poverty, the residential separation of the new couple from their families of orientation was consistently respected, except in cases like the Great Depression, when temporary "doubling up" became frequent. During World War II, marriage placed young couples in a status of semidependency; the bride usually continued to stay in her parental home or with other relatives. While the groom was in the service, even among those who married at the end of the war, the wife continued to reside, at least temporarily, with parents or relatives until her husband returned. In many cases, the young couple continued to reside with parents until they were able to establish a separate household. Thus, although the war accelerated the transition to adulthood, on the one hand, it also slowed down the establishment of independent nuclear families, on the other.

The nature of this adult transition undoubtedly reflects the age at which men were mobilized. Entrants out of high school were seldom married, and their service frequently entailed overseas duty. We find marital delays in this subgroup. Older men involved in serious dating relationships often turned intimate friends into marital partners over a weekend.

A persistent historical theme in the study of the life course has been the interdependence of individual life transitions and collective family ones (Hareven, 1978e). The common pattern among the families of Manchester's young people had been that of a strict subordination of individual members' career choices to the family's collective needs and strategies. This traditional pattern governed the early lives of Manchester's war cohort and cramped their chances for achieving greater occupational mobility by leaving home and seeking new opportunities elsewhere. The war partly counteracted this pattern of individual members' subordination to the family of orientation by providing opportunities for young men's separation from their families of orientation and by thrusting them into new environments and circumstances. That many young men enlisted voluntarily at age seventeen, even when they were not drafted, suggests their view of the war as an opportunity to break away from home and familial control. Both the Manchester and California cohorts' experience suggests that this desire to break from home was rooted in family hardships during the 1930s.

The war thus imposed a new pattern of timing on the transition to adulthood: It accelerated departure from the family of orientation and, at least temporarily, offered young men a chance to become "independent" without having to support themselves or their brides and without having to carry the usual responsibilities for kin support at home. The situation was somewhat different, however, for young women. Their entry into the labor force as part of the war-industry effort enabled them to contribute to their families of orientation while continuing to live at home. In this way, daughters' work made up for the absence of income from sons who were in the army and cushioned the family from deprivation during wartime.

Any discussion of the career advantages that war opportunities and the service offered to the California or New England young men would be incomplete without viewing these individual men as part of a family configuration. In terms of careers, the war promoted a certain degree of individualism, expressed in the servicemen's temporary independence from their family of orientation. That independence was mitigated, however, by a persistent commitment on the part of servicemen to their families of orientation or to their new spouses and these women's families of orientation, as the case may be. All the men interviewed emphasized their efforts to send remittances back home, meager as they were. From a life-course perspective, it would be inaccurate to interpret the young men's career accomplishments as strictly individual achievements. Their educational and career development during the service was backed up by the efforts and sacrifices of family members who stayed on the home front (most commonly women).

Despite the relief brought about by war industries, the families left behind were still coping with the ripple effects of the Great Depression, while being deprived of the economic contribution as well as personal support from loved sons, brothers, husbands, or fiancés. "He could have stayed home," reminisced a Manchester son about his father, "but he didn't want to, so he joined the merchant marines. We missed him terribly, and my mother kept writing letters." The division of labor was very clearly defined, as one woman put it:

> The war came shortly after my father died, and the boys were all in the service and we girls [mother and three daughters] stuck it out until they all came home. And you pulled together. I think that's where your basic pulling together of families is. It was the hardship that everybody went through. You don't have that today to keep your families together.

Women served as a matter of course as backup for male relatives who were in the service. One Manchester woman stayed home and worked in a newly reopened textile mill in the old Amoskeag building while her brothers were in the service. She left school after eighth grade: "So my high-school years were mostly the war years. I had no choice when I came out of grade eight, I was only thirteen or fourteen. There was no question of going to the mill then." Emma went to work because "I wanted to help my parents and the boys were gone, and I didn't want to leave home until the boys came back." She contributed her earnings to her family. "Well, you paid board, you know; you helped with the food and you were given a certain allowance."

A full understanding of men's ability to avail themselves of the challenges and opportunities presented by the service and to realize their potential depended on the support of family members on the home front. The backup services family members provided at home by caring for young children and older relatives were crucial not only for the family's survival but also for the servicemen's ability to concentrate on resettling when they returned.

The careers of these men by themselves do not provide the whole picture, unless one takes family configurations, needs, and supports into consideration. Even the servicemen's ability to find a job often depended on kin connections after their release from the army. Several returnees entered their relatives' businesses, and many who acquired a house did so because their relatives, taking advantage of low prices, had already purchased one for them. Mutual assistance among kin had been a strong tradition among Manchester's working class all along. Members of the cohort studied here were raised in that tradition and retained a commitment to kin despite their transition to a more individualized career during the war.

Discussion

We set out originally to ask: Why did the Great Depression not produce a "lost generation" as was generally assumed? By placing the careers of the young men in Berkeley and Manchester in the context of World War II and the Korean War, the significant role of military mobilization becomes apparent in reversing or mitigating the injuries of hard times. The service had a positive impact on both the Berkeley and Manchester cohorts, but it did not affect the two communities uniformly.

In both cohorts, the service turned around the lives of men from disadvantaged backgrounds by enabling them to reverse the impact of the Great Depression. The extent of this reversal and its impact on their subsequent careers differed considerably by community. Most of the Berkeley men who started from a lower middle- and working-class base were able to advance far into the middle class. Their advancement, facilitated by the service, enabled them to move beyond the status of their parents.

In contrast to the experience of the men from the San Francisco Bay Area, the war did not have the same "elevating" impact on the lives of the young Manchester men. Although it considerably redressed the adverse impact of the Great Depression by enabling Manchester men to enter relatively stable careers, the war made it possible for them only to remain floating and to keep their heads above water. Few members of the Manchester cohort managed to rise above their class origins. The Manchester men were more likely to start from a working-class base and did not rise much beyond their level. Rather than propelling them into the next level, the service prevented them from slipping below their parents' working-class status.

Other contrasts by place revolve around the fate of dominant institutions in the 1930s. In Manchester, the Amoskeag Mills shut down in the depths of the Great Depression, literally paralyzing the community and leaving an entire labor force unemployed. In Berkeley, however, despite the severe impact of the Great Depression, a variety of employment opportunities were still available because of Berkeley's diversified economy and the presence of the university.

Berkeley's young men, even within the working class, were better equipped to cope with adversity than the Manchester men when they encountered the Great Depression. The mill workers' families in Manchester had survived marginally even before the Great Depression and depended, therefore, on the labor of their children. Thus, even when military service offered veterans new opportunities, such as the G.I. Bill, the Manchester ex-servicemen were less prone to take advantage of them than were the Berkeley young men. Manchester men could not afford to take the time out for an extended education, whereas the G.I. Bill became one of the main avenues of advancement for the Berkeley men.

The positive impact of military service on these young cohorts was closely related to the community contexts in which the men lived. The differences in the life trajectories of young men in Berkeley and Manchester were thus the products of the interaction of time and place. Life in the working class has different meanings in historical time and in different places.

It is a tragic commentary on American society that an entire generation caught in the Great Depression had to wait for a global war to escape the lasting effects of economic deprivation. Nevertheless, even the effects of war industries and war mobilization on the cohorts of young men encountering them in Berkeley and Manchester differed in the two communities.

9

Changing Images of Aging and the Social Construction of the Life Course

Introduction

Concern with old age in our time has tended to focus attention on this stage of life in isolation from the entire life course. Without denying the unique problems of this period of life, it is important to interpret it in a life-course and historical context. The "discovery" of old age as a unique stage of life in the twentieth century is part of a larger historical process involving the emergence of new stages of life and their societal recognition. It is also part of a continuing trend toward age segregation in the family and in the larger society (Hareven, 1976a). A historical perspective is useful, therefore, because it sheds some light on long-term developments affecting "middle" and "old" age.

The first part of this chapter discusses the emergence of "old age" as a new stage of life in the context of the discovery of other stages of life; the second part addresses the emergence of discontinuities in the life course; and the last part discusses the contribution of historical changes in the family and the life course to age segregation.

It was probably no coincidence that G. Stanley Hall, who had formulated the concept of "adolescence" in the 1880s, offered a synthesis of "senescence" as his last creative opus in 1920, when he himself was eighty years old: "To learn that one is old is a long, complex, and painful experience. Each decade the circle of the Great Fatigue narrows around us, restricting the intensity and endurance of our activities." Whereas his con-

---

*This chapter first appeared as "Changing Images of Ageing and the Social Construction of the Life Course," in Mike Featherstone and Andrew Wernick, eds., *Images of Ageing* (London: Routledge, 1995).

temporaries focused on the deterioration and decline characteristic of old age or sought the secrets of longevity, Hall emphasized the unique psychological processes connected with aging and their societal significance. Rather than viewing old age as a period of decline and decay, he saw it as a stage of development in which the passions of youth and the efforts of a life career had reached fruition and consolidation: "There is a certain maturity of judgement about men, things, causes and life generally, that nothing in the world but years can bring, a real wisdom that only age can teach" (Hall, 1922, p. 366).

The interest in the meaning of aging in the early part of the twentieth century had not sprung merely from idle curiosity. It was related to questions about the limits of usefulness and efficiency on the job that had arisen with industrialization and to the movement for providing social insurance for the aged. In 1874, psychologist George Beard had already begun to ask questions about the limitations of old age: "What is the average effect of old age on the mental faculties?" and "[T]o what extent is the average responsibility of men impaired by the change that the mental faculties undergo in old age?" Analyzing the record of "human achievements," he tried to determine at what age the "best work of the world" had been done. He found that 70 percent of creative works had been achieved by age forty-five and 80 percent by the age of fifty. Within this range, he identified thirty to forty-five as the optimal period of life. Although he was emphatic about the need for setting a retirement age for judges, he did not recommend an automatic retirement age for laborers (Beard, 1874). Beard's investigation represented the first attempt at a scientific inquiry into the relationship between aging and efficiency, and it set the stage for the concept of the "superannuated man" that was to come.

In the late nineteenth century, American society passed from an acceptance of aging as a natural process to a view of it as a distinct period of life characterized by decline, weakness, and obsolescence. Advanced old age, which had earlier been regarded as a manifestation of the survival of the fittest, was now denigrated as a condition of dependence and deterioration: "We are marked by time's defacing fingers with the ugliness of age" ("Apology from Age to Youth," 1893, p. 170). Writers began to identify advancing years with physical decline and mental deterioration. Beginning in the 1860s, the popular magazines shifted their emphasis from attaining longevity to discussing the medical symptoms of senescence. By the beginning of the twentieth century, geriatrics emerged as a branch of medicine. In 1910, I. L. Nascher, a New York physician, became the first to formulate the biological characteristics and medical needs of senescence as a life-cycle process. He drew on the work of his predecessors to conceptualize its medical treatment and thus laid the foundation for geriatrics (Nascher, 1914).

The gerontological literature approaches the problems of aging from several directions: The developmental perspective has focused on biological and psychological changes connected with aging; the institutional approach has stressed the socioeconomic status and the roles of old people; and the cultural perspective has concentrated on stereotypes and perceptions of the elderly. Some of these approaches have also led to the confusion of the "aged" as an age group or as a social class with aging as a process. Little effort has been made to integrate these views or interpret them as interrelated processes over the life course.

The emergence of "old age" as a social, cultural, and biological phenomenon can best be understood in the context of other stages of life. The social conditions of children and adolescents in a given society are related to the way in which adulthood is perceived in that society. Conversely, the role and position of adults and the aged are related to the treatment of children and youth. The formidable task of investigating the synchronization of individual development with social change requires an approach that would take into account the entire life course and various historical and cultural conditions rather than simply concentrating on a specific age group. As Erik Erikson put it:

> As we come to the last stage [old age], we become aware of the fact that our civilization really does not harbor a concept of the whole of life. . . . Any span of the cycle lived without vigorous meaning, at the beginning, in the middle, or at the end, endangers the sense of life and the meaning of death in all those whose life stages are intertwined. (Erikson, 1964, pp. 132–133)

The Discovery of Stages of Life

Age and aging are related to biological phenomena, but the meanings are socially and culturally determined. "Social age" is a relative concept and varies in different cultural contexts. In trying to understand the societal conditions affecting adulthood and old age, it is important to realize that the definitions of aging, as well as the social conditions and functions of every age group, have not only changed significantly over time but have also varied among different cultures. In Western society, we are accustomed to referring to stages of life such as childhood and adolescence as socially recognized stages of development that encompass specific age groups and are accompanied by certain cultural characteristics.

From the middle of the nineteenth century on, American society had gradually begun to acknowledge at least the existence of various stages of life and to develop a corresponding series of institutions to deal with them. As we have seen, childhood was "discovered" in the first half of the nineteenth century and adolescence was "invented" toward the end of the century. Both stages of life emerged into public consciousness as a result of the social crises associated with those age groups in a manner similar to the emergence of old age later on. However, despite the growing awareness of childhood, adolescence, and youth as preadult stages, no clear boundaries for adulthood in American society emerged until much later, when interest in the "middle years" as a distinct segment of adult life arose out of the need to differentiate the social and psychological problems of "middle" from "old" age. The social and cultural conditions of the past half century have since contributed to the sharpening of the boundaries between those two stages. More recently, even old age has been divided into stages such as the "young old" and the "old old" (Neugarten and Datan, 1973).

The "discovery" of a new stage of life is itself a complex process. First, private individuals become aware of the specific characteristics of a given stage of life as a distinct condition among certain social classes or groups. This recognition is then made public and popularized on a societal level. Professionals and reformers define and formulate the unique conditions of such a stage of life, and then it is publicized in the popular culture. Finally, if the conditions peculiar to this stage seem to be associated with a major social problem, it attracts the attention of public agencies, and it becomes institutionalized: Its needs and problems are dealt with in legislation and in the establishment of institutions aimed directly to meet its needs. Such public activities, in turn, affect the experience of individuals going through the stage. They clearly influence the timing of transitions in and out of such a stage by providing public supports and, at times, by imposing constraints.

As mentioned above, in American society, childhood emerged as a distinct stage first in the private lives of middle-class urban families in the early part of the nineteenth century. The new definition of childhood and the role of children was related to the retreat of the family into domesticity, the segregation of the workplace from the home, the redefinition of the mother's role as the major custodian of the domestic sphere, and the emphasis on sentimental rather than instrumental relations at the very base of family interaction. Having emerged first in the life of middle-class families and having become an integral part of their lifestyle, childhood as a distinct stage of development became the subject of the voluminous body of child-rearing and family-advice literature. These advice books and magazine articles popularized the concept of childhood and the needs of children and prescribed the means to allow them to develop as children. The moralists who became advocates of children and for compulsory school attendance called for the regulation of child labor.

The discovery of adolescence in the latter part of the nineteenth century followed a pattern similar to that of the emergence of childhood. Whereas puberty in itself is a universal biological process, the psychosocial phe-nomena of adolescence were only gradually identified and defined, most notably by G. Stanley Hall in the latter part of the nineteenth century (Hall, 1922). There is evidence that the experience of adolescence, particu-larly some of the problems and tensions associated with it, was noticed in the private lives of individuals reaching puberty during the second half of the nineteenth century (Demos and Demos, 1969). Educators and ur-ban reformers began to observe the congregation of young people in peer groups and styles of behavior that might be characterized as a "culture of adolescence" from the middle of the nineteenth century on. Anxiety over such conduct increased, particularly in large cities, where the reformers warned against the potential threat of youth gangs.

By the beginning of the twentieth century, Hall and his colleagues artic-ulated adolescence as a new stage of life. This new stage was also widely popularized in the literature. The extension of school age through high school in the second part of the nineteenth century, the further extension of the age limits for child labor, and the establishment of juvenile refor-matories and vocational schools were all part of the public recognition of the needs and problems of adolescence (Bremner et al., 1970, 1971). The boundaries between childhood and adolescence, on the one hand, and be-tween adolescence and adulthood, on the other, became more clearly de-marcated over the course of the twentieth century. The experience of childhood and adolescence became more pervasive among larger groups of the American population, as immigrant and working-class families made their entry into the middle class.

Beyond adolescence, Kenneth Keniston (1971) has suggested that in the twentieth century, the extension of a moratorium from adult responsibili-ties has resulted in the emergence of yet another stage of life—that of youth. Despite the growing awareness of these preadult stages, no clear boundaries for adulthood in America emerged until much later, when "old age" became prominent as a new stage of life, and with it, the need to differentiate the social and psychological attributes and problems of "middle age" from those of "old age."

There are many indications that a new consciousness of "old age," along with institutional definitions and societal recognition, emerged in the latter part of the nineteenth and early part of the twentieth century. The convergence of an increasing volume of gerontological literature, the proliferation of negative stereotypes about old age, and the establishment of mandatory retirement represent the first moves in the direction of a public and institutional formulation of "old age" as a distinct stage of life (Fischer, 1977).

Whereas the recognition of childhood and adolescence generally came as a response to external pressures and to a fear of the potential disorganization that might otherwise ensue from societal neglect of a particular age group, little apprehension of this sort was initially expressed toward the elderly. In the nineteenth century, this apprehension was particularly dramatic as it was manifested in attitudes toward treatment of children and adolescents, where undisciplined and unsocialized young people were regarded as the "dangerous classes."

The elderly received comparatively little attention because they were not considered dangerous to the social order. The argument against the neglect of children was that they would grow up into dangerous, socially destructive adults. No parallel argument applied to the aged. In a society in which the fear of the afterlife was not central and in which awareness and contact with death were not integrated into everyday life (because in public belief, the dead no longer held a mythical power over the living), there was no reason to fear any potentiality of revenge from among old people. Consequently, the first demonstration of organized political power on the part of the aged was not manifested until the Townshend movement in the 1930s, which, along with other pressures, succeeded in pushing the federal government into instituting social security.

It is clear, however, that in American society, "old age" is now recognized as a specific period of adulthood. At least until recently, it had a formal beginning—age sixty-five, so far as an individual's working life is concerned. It was institutionalized by a rite of passage—retirement and the commencement of social security. Since so much of adult life has been contingent on work, especially for men, retirement also often involves migration and changes in living arrangements. More recently, mandatory retirement has been revised, following new legislation regulating retirement. At the same time, business corporations and universities instituted policies of a "golden handshake."

In the beginning of the twentieth century, public concern for and interest in old age converged from various directions. In addition to physicians, psychologists, and popular writers, efficiency experts and social reformers were instrumental in attracting public attention to old age as a social problem. A variety of medical and psychological studies by industrial-efficiency experts focused on the physical and mental limitations of old age. At the same time, social reformers began to expose the deprivation and dependency suffered by many old people as part of a general investigation of poverty and to agitate for social security and social insurance (Douglas, 1936; Epstein, 1922).

Government recognition of old age evolved more gradually and emerged on the state level first. By 1920, only ten states had instituted some form of old-age legislation; all programs were limited in scope, and most of them were declared unconstitutional by the Supreme Court. Nevertheless, agitation for old-age security continued and finally culminated in the Social Security Act of 1935. It was not until the 1940s, however, that gerontology was recognized as a new field and even more recently that social scientists identified old age as constituting a new and pressing problem for Western society. Social definitions of age limits and public treatment through institutional reform, retirement legislation, and welfare measures represent the most recent societal recognition of this stage of life (Tibbits, 1960; Philibert, 1965).

The popular and social-science literature has recently devoted a great deal of attention to the social and economic plight of older people and to their isolation. The major developments that have been cited as explanations for these problems are: the overall impact of urbanization and industrialization; demographic changes arising from increases in life expectancy in childhood and early adulthood and from prolongation of life in old age due to advances in medical technology; the increasing proportion of older people in the population resulting from the decline in fertility and increase in life expectancy; the decrease in productive roles that older people are allowed to play as the result of the shift from a rural to an industrial economy; the technological revolution; and, finally, the denigration of old age, which has been explained by the "cult of youth."

Without denying the importance of these explanations, stereotypes of aging and the problems of old age and aging in American society can be more fully understood in the context of changes in the social and cultural construction of other stages of life and in fundamental historical discontinuities in the life course, in relation to the emergence of age segregation in work life and in the family.

Because age boundaries and criteria for adulthood vary significantly across cultures, classes, and historical periods, the meaning of adulthood cannot be defined merely in terms of a specific stage in the life course. Unlike adolescence, which represents a person's passage through puberty, adulthood is not clearly defined in biological terms. Even within the same age group, the social meaning of adulthood and the functions associated with it vary among cultures and according to psychological conditions. For these reasons, it is important to determine to what extent and in what ways individuals in the past have perceived their entry into adulthood and transitions to old age under varying historical conditions.

The Emergence of Discontinuities
in the Life Course

The social experience of each cohort is influenced not only by the historical conditions it encounters currently but also by the cumulative impact of past historical events over the life course of its members. Consequently, the position of the elderly in modern American society has been shaped in part by social and economic conditions that have combined to isolate their family and productive life when they enter their sixties or seventies and in part by their previous experience along their life course. For example, individuals who reached the age of sixty in the 1890s and were still working had commenced work at an earlier age and continued to work until the end of life, or as long as they were able to. Having grown up in periods when life transitions were less rigidly marked or institutionalized, they would have found imposed retirement at a set age far more traumatic than a cohort who had come of age in the early twentieth century, when both entry into and exit from the labor force were more clearly timed according to age. The response of an older cohort to changing social and economic conditions is therefore significantly different from that of a younger one, because it is based on very different individual and social experiences (Hareven, 1986; Riley, 1978). In trying to understand those differences, it is necessary to view both the contemporary social milieu in which members of a cohort reach that age and their cumulative experience over their entire lives.

In preindustrial society, demographic, social, and cultural factors combined to produce only a minimal differentiation in the stages of life. Childhood and adolescence were not regarded as distinct stages; children were considered miniature adults, gradually assuming adult roles in their early teens and entering adult life without a moratorium from adult responsibilities. Adulthood flowed into old age without institutionalized disruptions. The two major adult roles—parenthood and work—generally stretched over an entire lifetime without an "empty nest" and compulsory retirement (Chudacoff and Hareven, 1979). In rural communities, the insistence of older people on self-sufficiency and their continued control over family estates delayed the assumption of economic independence by adult children and afforded aging parents a bargaining position for support in old age (Greven, 1970; D. S. Smith, 1973).

The integration of economic activities with family life also provided continuity in the usefulness of older people, particularly for widows, even when their capacity to work was waning. One should not, however, idealize the condition of the elderly in preindustrial society. John Demos has pointed out that although they were venerated publicly, they were insecure in private life. Some of the symptoms of insecurity and uncertainty are reflected, for example, in wills where support for a widowed mother was made a condition for the inheritance of family estates (Demos, 1970, 1978). Nevertheless, old people experienced economic and social segregation far less frequently than they do today, and they retained their familial and economic positions until the end of their lives (D. S. Smith, 1973). If they became "dependent" because of illness or poverty, they were supported by their children or other kin or were placed by the town authorities in the households of neighbors or even nonrelatives. They were placed in institutions only as a last resort (Greven, 1970).

Discontinuities in the Life Course

Under the impact of industrialization and the demographic changes of the nineteenth century, however, a gradual differentiation in age groups and a greater specialization in age-related functions began to emerge, although it was by no means complete by the end of the century. Discontinuities in the individual life course were still not marked, and age groups were still not completely segregated in accordance with their functions. As explained above, even age configurations in the family were considerably different than today.

Prior to the turn of the twentieth century, parenthood was not segregated to certain periods in the life course. Whereas today parents generally complete their child-rearing functions with one-third of their lives still ahead, nineteenth-century parenthood was a lifelong career. The combination of relatively late marriage, short life expectancy, and high fertility rarely allowed for an "empty nest" stage. In addition, marriage was frequently broken by the death of a spouse before the end of the child-rearing period. Because women married earlier and lived longer than men, this pattern was more common among them. Widowed or not, however, the extension of motherhood over most of the life course continued to engage women in active familial roles into old age (Uhlenberg, 1978).

Under conditions in which the life course was compressed into a shorter and more homogeneous span, major transitions into adulthood, such as leaving school, entering the labor force, leaving home, establishing a separate household, marrying, and having children were not so clearly structured as they are today. Except for marriage and the formation of households, these transitions did not even necessarily represent moves toward independent adulthood. The order in which they occurred varied significantly rather than following a customary sequence. Children and youth shuttled back and forth from school to work depending on the seasons, the availability of jobs, and the economic needs of the family. Departure from school did not mark a definite turning point, nor, at a time when child labor was an established practice, did entry into the labor force necessarily imply the onset of adulthood. Leaving home, a phenomenon typically associated with the commencement of adulthood today, did not have such significance in the preindustrial and early industrial period (Modell, Furstenberg, and Hershberg, 1976).

In nineteenth-century rural and urban working-class families, sons and daughters often continued to live at home until well into their twenties and to contribute their income to the common family budget. Some children left home in their early teens to become servants or apprentices, while others continued to live on the family farm and to postpone marriage and the assumption of adult responsibilities until much later. Irish immigrant families in Massachusetts, for example, customarily kept the youngest son at home through his late twenties. Among other immigrant industrial workers in New England, the last remaining daughter at home was expected to postpone or give up marriage and continue living at home to care for her parents as long as they lived. When unmarried children did leave home, they often spent transitional periods as boarders or lodgers with the families of strangers rather than setting up their own households (Modell and Hareven, 1973; Hareven, 1976a; 1981b).

Even marriage, which is usually regarded as an "adult" act in twentieth-century society, much less often marked the transition to autonomous adult life in the nineteenth century. In urban communities, where immigration produced both scarcity in housing and unemployment, it was difficult to set up an independent household, so newlyweds often brought their spouses to live in their parents' households for a transitional period. Even when they lived separately, it was usually nearby, often in the same neighborhood. In the early years of marriage and especially after the birth of the first child, young couples were willing to sacrifice privacy for the luxury of parental assistance and support, a willingness that increased during periods of economic crisis and depression or during family crises brought on by unemployment, sickness, or death (Chudacoff, 1978). The most significant historical change in the timing of life transitions since the beginning of this century has been the emergence of greater uniformity in the pace at which a cohort accomplishes a given transition. This is particularly evident in the transitions to adulthood (leaving home, getting married and establishing a separate household). Over the past century, life transitions have become more clearly marked, more rapidly timed, and more compressed in their timing. In contrast to our times, in the late nineteenth century, transitions from the parental home to marriage and to household headship were more gradual and less rigid in their timing. The time range necessary for a cohort to accomplish such transitions was wider, and the sequence in which transitions followed one another was flexible. In the twentieth century, transitions to adulthood have become more uniform for the age cohort undergoing them, more orderly in sequence, and more rigidly defined (Modell, Furstenberg, and Hershberg, 1976). The consciousness of embarking on a new stage of life and the implications of movement from one stage to the next have become more firmly established.

The historical changes over the past century, particularly the increasing rapidity in the timing of transitions and the introduction of publicly regulated and institutionalized transitions, have converged to isolate and seg-regate age groups in the larger society. These changes have generated new pressures on timing within the family as well as outside its confines. Among these, the major historical change over the past century has been from a timing that is more closely articulated to collective family needs to a more individualized timing. Timing has become more regulated accord-ing to specific age norms rather than in relation to the family's collective needs.

Changes in the Family

In earlier time periods, the absence of dramatic transitions to adult life al-lowed a more intensive interaction among different age groups within the family and the community, thus providing a greater sense of continuity and interdependence among people at various stages of life. But as greater differentiation in stages of life began to develop, social and eco-nomic functions became more closely related to age and ages of family members became more streamlined. This, in turn, contributed to the emergence of a greater segregation between age groups.

The major changes that have led to the isolation of older people in soci-ety today were rooted not so much in changes in family structure or resi-dential arrangements, as has generally been argued, as in the transforma-tion and redefinition of family functions and values. Among these changes, the erosion of an instrumental view of family relationships—and the resulting shift to sentimentality and intimacy as the major cohe-sive forces in the family—have led to the weakening of interdependence between members of the nuclear family and extended kin. Affective rela-tionships have gradually replaced instrumental ones.

The ideology of domesticity that emerged during the first half of the nineteenth century enshrined privacy as a major value in family life. The home was glorified as a retreat from the world and, at the same time, as a specialized child-nurturing center.

This shift first occurred in the middle class, around the middle of the nineteenth century, but it soon affected the working class and various eth-nic groups, as increasing conformity introduced middle-class values into working-class lives. Since then, the emphasis on domesticity and child rearing as the major preoccupations of the middle-class family—and es-pecially on the role of women as custodians of the domestic retreat—has tended to insulate middle-class urban families from the influence and participation of aging parents and other relatives. This transition added to the loss of power and influence of the old people in the family.

Under the impact of industrialization, the family surrendered many of the functions previously concentrated within the household to other social institutions. The retreat and growing privatism of the modern middle-class family led to the drawing of sharper boundaries between family and community and intensified the segregation of different age groups within the family, leading to the elimination of older people from viable family roles. The transfer of social-welfare functions, once concentrated in the family, to institutions in the larger society further contributed to the segregation of older people. The care of dependent, sick, delinquent, and elderly members of the community, which had been considered part of the family's obligation in the preindustrial period, was gradually transferred to specialized institutions such as asylums and reformatories. The family ceased to be the only available source of support for its dependent members, and the community ceased to rely on the family as the major agency of welfare and social control (Bremner, 1956; Rothman, 1971).

Conclusion

The characterization of the aged as "useless," "inefficient," "unattractive," "temperamental," and "senile" has accompanied the gradual ousting of people from the labor force at age sixty-five since the beginning of the twentieth century. The development of what Erving Goffman (1963) has called the "spoiled identity" or what others have referred to as the "elderly mystique" (Rosenfelt, 1965) had already begun to appear in popular literature in the United States during the later part of the nineteenth century. The emergence of such negative stereotypes should not be misconstrued as causing an immediate decline in the status of older people, but it did reflect the beginnings of an increasing tendency to denigrate the aged in society.

Some people have attributed the emergence of a negative image of old age to a "cult of youth" in American society. Although there is undeniably a connection, one cannot be construed as an explanation of the other. The glorification of youth and the denigration of old age are both aspects of far more complicated processes. They are results of the increasing segregation of different stages of life—and of their corresponding age groups—in modern American society.

The socioeconomic and cultural changes of the past century have gradually led to a segregation of work from other aspects of life and to a shift from the predominance of familial values to an emphasis on individualism and privacy. Child-labor laws and compulsory education to age fourteen (or sixteen) tended to segregate the young, increasingly so from around the middle of the nineteenth century (Bremner et al., 1971). Similarly, the gradual ousting of older people from the labor force at the beginning of the twentieth century and the decline in their parental functions in the later years of life tended to disengage them from their offspring. One of the most important changes affecting the elderly, therefore, has been the increasing association of functions with age and the formation of segregated, age-based peer groups. This segregation by age occurred first among the middle class and was only later extended into the rest of society.

These changes have affected each stage of life: They have resulted in the segmentation of the life course into more formal stages, in more uniform and rigid transitions from one stage to the next, and in the separation of the various age groups from one another. The problems of older people in American society are in some respects unique to this age group, but they also reflect the most acute problems experienced by people in other age groups and in other stages of life.

Part Three

Comparative Perspectives

10

Between Craft and Industry

The Subjective Reconstruction of the Life Course of Kyoto's Traditional Weavers

Introduction

Some of the key questions in the study of the life course are: How do individuals reconstruct their life histories, and how do they interpret their lives in relation to the historical events they encounter and in the context of their own culture? The subjective reconstruction of one's life history is shaped by the individuals' interaction with the interviewers, by the life stage of the

*This chapter is part of a larger project on the traditional silk-weaving industry in Kyoto. It will result in the forthcoming book *The Silk Weavers of Kyoto: Family and Work in a Changing Traditional Industry*. I am indebted to the Japan Society for the Promotion of Science; the Japan Foundation; the Joint Committee on Japanese Studies, cosponsored by the Social Science Research Council and the American Council of Learned Societies; and the Japan-U.S. Educational Commission for their support of the research for the larger project. I am also indebted to Seijo University for an initial grant for interviewing, in 1982; to Doshisha University's Institute for the Humanities and the Social Sciences, where my research project was based while I was visiting professor in 1984, 1985 and 1987; and to Keio University, where I was the Harvard YenChing Exchange Professor in 1986–1987. I am extremely grateful to Professors Kamiko Takeji and David Plath for their initial help and encouragement, to the late Professor Kokichi Masuda, to Professor Ken Nakamura, to Professors Kiyomi Morioka and Akira Hayami for their continuing support and inspiration, to Professors Masato Tanaka and Michiharu Matsumoto for help and guidance, and to Emiko Ochiai and Toshiko Sumizawa, who were the first interpreters on this project, for their great help and continuing interest. I am indebted to Professor David Plath for his constructive comments on an earlier draft of this chapter and to Rona Karasik for editorial help.

This chapter first appeared as "Between Craft and Industry: The Subjective Reconstruction of the Life Course of Kyoto's Traditional Weavers," in Susanne Formanek and Sepp Linhart, eds., *Japanese Biographies: Life Cycles and Life Stages* (Vienna: Ästereichische Akademie der Wissenschaften, 1992, pp. 179–207), reprinted by permission of the Österreichische Akademie der Wissenschaften.

people interviewed at the time of the interview, and by the social-structural conditions and historical events that shaped the individual's life (Hareven, 1982). The cultural values influencing people's own perspectives on their lives provide the context within which they interpret their life history and attribute meaning to their experience. From a life-course perspective, individuals' reconstruction of their life history is intertwined with that of their family members and other "consociates" who travel the life road together or who interact at various points over their lives (Plath, 1980). Individual lives are best understood, therefore, in their synchronization with those of family or community members and in relation to historical time (Hareven, 1988; Elder, 1978; Hareven and Masaoka, 1988).

This chapter examines Kyoto's traditional silk weavers' perceptions of their worlds of work and family and of themselves as craftspeople, in light of the economic and technological changes affecting their industry and their work and family lives. It is based on extensive life-history interviews that I have conducted over the past nine years with weavers and manufacturers in Kyoto's Nishijin weaving district.

I encountered the Nishijin district early in 1981, during my first visit to Japan. With the help of an interpreter, I visited several highly skilled weavers who were operating traditional hand looms. Some of the older weavers with whom I talked said that they were the last generation to weave on hand looms. Shocked by this revelation, I wanted to examine the Nishijin problem in depth and find out why these highly skilled craftspeople had this sense of impending doom. Since my own research as a social historian in American society was heavily based on the relationship between the family and work in a declining textile industry (Hareven, 1982), I wanted to understand what the Nishijin industry was experiencing in a comparative context.

I returned to Kyoto in the fall of 1982 and spent three months interviewing various manufacturers and weavers in Nishijin. My first contacts were with manufacturers *(orimoto)*, to whom I was introduced by colleagues in Doshisha University, and with several demonstration weavers in the Nishijin Orimono Kaikan (the Nishijin Textile Center). After I won the trust of the first people I interviewed, they introduced me to their fellow manufacturers and weavers and to their relatives and friends. Following along these networks, I was fortunate to gain access to more groups of weavers and manufacturers in Nishijin, representing various forms of production of Nishijin *obi*, such as woven on the hand loom or power loom, and various forms of employment—such as factory weaving or cottage weaving. I interviewed individual weavers initially, but whenever an original person interviewed had a spouse or another relative who was also a weaver, I repeatedly interviewed them as well, sometimes in tandem with the original interviewee, and other times separately.[1]

I returned to Kyoto every year from 1982 on and spent three to four summer months and periodically two winter months interviewing in Nishijin. I also spent my sabbatical year interviewing in Nishijin in 1986–1987. From 1982 to 1990, I repeatedly interviewed the same people, as well as new ones, whose acquaintance I had made over the years. The group of interviewees consists of about 200, including about 110 women and 90 men. After I discovered that over half of Nishijin *obi* are woven in the cottages of farmers and fishermen near the Japan Sea, I also started interviewing the cottage weavers in this area in order to compare their experience with that of the urban artisans.[2]

My interviews, two to three hours long, were typically open-ended, with free-form questions that developed with the conversation. I interviewed each person numerous times over the years. As my friendship with the Nishijin people grew, the interviews gained greater depth, and the "formal" sessions were extended into longer social occasions that often continued in the interviewees' houses late into the night. In addition to answering my questions, the people interviewed talked about the issues of greatest concern to them. Some of my questions, which emanated from my earlier research on the textile industry in New England, surprised some of the interviewees. Assuming that my questions were based on inside information in Nishijin, they asked me, "How do you know to ask these questions?" I showed them the book *Amoskeag: Life and Work in an American Factory City* (Hareven and Langenbach, 1978). Looking at the photographs in the book, Nishijin weavers were struck by the similarities between their experiences as textile workers and those in remote America. They were also impressed by the differences between the traditional, small-scale enterprises they engaged in and the large textile factories in the United States.

Initially, Nishijin weavers were puzzled as to why I should want to interview them about their own lives and families rather than talking to more "famous" and "important" people. Similar to the former workers of the Amoskeag Textile Mills in Manchester, New Hampshire, whom I had interviewed in the early 1970s, Nishijin weavers initially felt that their lives were of no relevance to an understanding of the historical process (Hareven, 1982). Both in Manchester in the 1970s and in Nishijin in the 1980s, the interviewees graciously agreed to talk with me even though they were not convinced initially of their centrality to an understanding of the process. As the interviews progressed, the Nishijin people became gradually immersed in the interview process. They shared information about their lives enthusiastically and with a deep involvement. Partly, this was in response to my deep interest in every detail of their life history and their current experience and my returning regularly to see them again and again, and it was partly because my research background in the textile experience in the United States and England enabled me to speak "textile language." Another major reason for the Nishijin weavers' responsiveness was the fact that they felt angry and frustrated about the decline of their industry at the very time when I interviewed them. They found in these interviews an opportunity to discuss the meaning of the transitions they were experiencing with a deeply interested foreigner and with each other.

The Nishijin Context

Nishijin is the name for three interrelated entities: the district of Kyoto in which silk-brocade weaving has been carried on for some five centuries; the weaving process, which is complicated and requires the finest skills in silk weaving in Japan; and the unique product—the brocade used for priestly garments and for *obi* (kimono sashes) that are worn on the highest ceremonial occasions in Japan, such as weddings, tea ceremonies, No plays, and traditional festivals. Over its long history, Nishijin cloth has become one of the cultural symbols of Japan.

For the weavers, artisans, manufacturers, and tradesmen who work and live there, Nishijin *mura* (village)[3] represents a way of life—a tradition of family-based craftsmanship and a mode of production that has been embedded in the community for centuries. For many generations, the manufacturers, craftspeople, and shopkeepers associated with this traditional industry have developed a strong identity as "Nishijin men and women."

In many respects, Nishijin is representative of the contradictions inherent in contemporary Japan. On the one hand, Nishijin remains an enclave of traditional craftsmanship and aesthetics in the midst of the world of Sony and Mitsubishi. On the other hand, the weaving craft in Nishijin itself has undergone many profound technological and social changes over its long history. Although Nishijin weavers participate in most aspects of modern Japanese life, their methods of weaving, internal organization, and division of labor, as well as their aesthetic values and view of themselves, demonstrate the survival of traditional craftsmanship. Changing tastes and fashions have affected the style and colors of Nishijin cloth, yet the product has remained consistent in its basic motifs and design. A Nishijin *obi* is still instantly recognizable. More important, Nishijin has maintained its traditions of craftsmanship, even though the process of weaving has changed into a partly mechanized "industry."

Nonetheless, Nishijin has been affected by modernization. The craftspeople and manufacturers are caught in the crosscurrents of old and new, of modern technology and traditional culture, and of bureaucratic organizations and lingering family traditions, all of which are representative of the complexity of contemporary Japan. Whereas recent Western literature in praise of modern Japan has extolled harmony, conformity, and efficiency as the secrets of Japan's being "number one," Nishijin represents another side of Japan—one too frequently overlooked by Western commentators (Vogel, 1979). Its current problems highlight the contradictions hidden beneath the surface of the "streamlined" modern Japan. Within Nishijin, the tensions between lingering tradition and the pressures of modernization are now being played out.

In Nishijin's narrow streets, the planning and production of cloth have been closely integrated with traditional *machiya* (town house) architecture. In this setting, work and family life have been almost inseparable for centuries. Many weavers still live and weave inside the typical Nishijin wooden houses, which are nicknamed *unagi no nedoko* (sleeping place of eels) because of their long, narrow shape. Rooms are arranged in a narrow sequence and are entered directly from one to the next. The weaving workshop in the back of the house has an unpaved earthen floor into which the loom is sunk, to ensure sufficient humidity for the silk. In some houses, the skylight in the roof still survives, similar to those in the historic weavers' cottages in Lancashire, England.

The tightly integrated houses flanking the narrow streets and lanes form a textured urban landscape. The unique sense of place is most striking in northwestern Nishijin between Horikawa Street and Daitokuji Temple, and in the Kashiwano area behind the Kitano Shrine. Recently, multistory concrete buildings, some with neo-Spanish colonial facades, stand out like false teeth amid the rows of classic wooden buildings. Some are the manufacturers' new headquarters, built to express pride and affluence; others are "mansions" (the Japanese word for apartments), built as investments by manufacturers who have liquidated their weaving companies because of the depression that Nishijin has been experiencing over the past six years.

When walking in Nishijin's streets, one cannot help being caught up in the hustle-bustle of the community's ancient industry. Almost every house carries a sign, called a *noren*,[4] denoting its particular craft. Glimpses through the semiopen screen doors reveal the array of activities on which weaving depends: the dyeing and winding of the thread, tying of the warp, and pattern making and punching of the Jacquard cards. The sound of clicking looms fills the air into the early evening.

The Nishijin industry is currently undergoing an unprecedented crisis threatening it with extinction, caused by the declining consumer market for kimonos and intensified by internal problems in the organization of production and marketing. The waning popularity of the kimono, and its replacement by Western fashions in Japan, has caused a serious depression in the manufacturing of Nishijin *obi*. This has led to a curtailment of production and consequently to increasing unemployment and insecurity for Nishijin weavers (Kyoto-fu, 1983; Hareven, 1985b).

Economic decline in Nishijin started with the energy crisis ("oil shock") of the early 1970s, which affected the Japanese economy as a whole; but a steadier, more painful decline became visible in the early 1980s. Nishijin manufacturers were particularly vulnerable to the oil shock, because many had overproduced during the preceding boom period in the 1960s and some had even expanded beyond capacity. "A Nishijin company is like a pimple," goes one saying. "When it gets too big, it bursts." An average of forty-five to fifty manufacturers have shut down in Nishijin each year since 1983. Most surviving firms have severely curtailed production. There is little doubt that there will continue to be a market for the very specialized expensive *obi*. But the disturbing question is: How many of the current manufacturers will be able to survive in such a limited market?

The current crisis also threatens the relationship between the family and traditional weaving, which has been at the base of this historic industry. The manufacturers' family business is increasingly insecure, making the entire family vulnerable to economic depression. The uncertainty of the future has discouraged sons from continuing the family business. The crisis undermines the weavers' security even more dramatically. They have begun to experience increasing unemployment and uncertainty.

In addition to shrinking markets, Nishijin's crisis is intensified by several factors. The price of silk thread in Japan is artificially high because the Japanese government, in its effort to protect domestic silk growers, has imposed a high tariff on imported Chinese silk thread. Nishijin manufacturers are forced to pay the same price for otherwise cheap Chinese silk as for Japanese-grown silk. Another problem is the traditional power that the Muromachi *tonya* (wholesalers) still wield. (Kimono wholesalers have long been concentrated southeast of Nishijin, along Muromachi Street above Shijo.) The wholesaler imposes a high margin on the retail price of Nishijin *obi*. This contributes to pricing it out of the consumers' market. Even people who would like to wear a fine *obi* often cannot afford to buy it. The fortunes of the manufacturer are tied to those of the wholesaler. If the wholesaler goes bankrupt, the manufacturer sinks with him. The dependency of manufacturers on wholesalers reaches far back into Nishijin's long history. Even now, during this crisis, most Nishijin manufacturers are unable to circumvent the wholesalers, because they lack the know-how for developing independent distribution routes and direct communications with the retail markets.

The impact of declining markets on Nishijin weavers has been intensified by having Nishijin *obi* woven in remote villages along the Japan Sea, and in China and Korea. "Yes, I think that by sending products to be made in the countryside in Korea, the manufacturers in this Nishijin business are choking their own necks like a suicide," said one of the very skilled hand-loom weavers (Mr. K.). The availability of a cheaper and ready labor force among the wives of farmers and fishermen in the countryside has led Nishijin manufacturers to employ rural cottage weavers. Approximately 60 percent of all Nishijin *obi* are now woven outside Kyoto, primarily in the villages of the Tango Peninsula, about four hours by car to the north of Kyoto city. Cottage weavers in Tango produce *obi* commissioned by Nishijin manufacturers, using Nishijin designs and raw materials. Their product is sold, therefore, under a Nishijin label, although they generally have no direct contact with the manufacturer in Nishijin.[5]

Nishijin weaving is fundamentally a family industry on the level of the manufacturers, the weavers, and the craftspeople in related processes. The manufacturers' family business is the backbone of the industry. Some weavers and their descendants have worked for the same manufacturers' families for several generations. All stages of production are closely integrated and family based. The manufacturer plans the design and production of *obi* and commissions a design on the basis of a sketch. He then orders the pattern makers to translate the design into precise patterns that are used for the punching of the cards *(mongami)* for the Jacquard loom. The manufacturer buys the yarn, sends it to the dyer, sends the dyed thread to the warp maker, and then sends the warp, the yarn, and the punched Jacquard cards with the designs to the weaver. Finally, the manufacturer sends the finished *obi* to the wholesaler for distribution to retail stores. The manufacturer is at the center of the process: At each stage of preparation, the yarn or patterns are sent back to the manufacturer, who then sends them on to the next craftsperson.

The larger family manufacturing concerns were incorporated after World War II and started paying salaries to family members working in the company. Even these "modern" corporations, which have larger numbers of employees, are at the core family businesses, in which several family members work together and the eldest son is usually the successor. In one company, for example, that makes the most traditional hand-woven *obi*, three generations work together: the president, his son (vice president), and his grandson, who is now training. The three wives work together with their husbands in the family enterprise. The craftspeople for the various auxiliary operations have also functioned in Nishijin as small family businesses for generations. Unlike the weavers, the other craftspeople in Nishijin (pattern maker, dyer, warp maker, and so on) are not the manufacturer's employees. They service various manufacturers on a subcontract basis *(shitauke)*.

The weavers, who form the essential base of Nishijin's industry, work either as factory weavers *(uchibata)* or—the great majority—as cottage weavers *(debata)* in their own homes. Nishijin "factories" are small workshops employing no more than ten to twenty workers on the premises. Most manufacturers follow both systems—they run one or more small factories, but they rely primarily on a large network of cottage weavers, most of whom are now located in the countryside (Chujo, 1984).

Since the late Meiji period, the bulk of Nishijin weaving has been increasingly produced in a cottage industry system, *kanai kogyo*. The cottage weavers are employees of the manufacturer even though they own their looms, engage their own family members, and weave in their own homes. The manufacturer supplies the raw materials and the design. The weaver delivers the finished *obi* to the manufacturer and receives payment by the piece. The weavers' livelihood depends on an even flow of orders from the manufacturer. During boom periods, the weavers used to rush to the manufacturer's house (or send their wife or child) to deliver a finished *obi* as soon as it was ready, in order to obtain the next order (Hareven, 1988).

Contrary to the stereotype of the streamlined permanent careers that are often cited as characterizing work lives in modern Japan, the careers of Nishijin weavers have been fluid and fragile under the impact of various forces. Their careers rose and declined under the impact of war and peace, business cycles, changing fashions, changing technology, world markets, and Japanese government tariffs on imported silk yarn. For Nishijin weavers, "disorderly" work lives were the norm rather than the exception (Wilensky, 1961; Plath, 1983). As for Manchester textile workers, disorderliness in itself provided a form of continuity from one generation to the next (Hareven, 1982). As Mr. N. (seventy-five years old) put it:

> So many changes have happened. Every time we had a war, the business became brisk all of a sudden and then became dull again. Such things happened so many times that in my life I can't count them all. After the war (World War II) the business became gradually stabilized and is balanced now. The worst up-and-down period was about the time when I was twelve or so. Only old persons like me can tell the history from the Meiji period and deep personal history of the Nishijin industry. My life was full of "ups and downs." It was really *sono hi gurashi* (a "hand-to-mouth" or "live for the day" existence). The hardest time I remember in Nishijin was in my childhood, when I was about fourteen to fifteen years old, in my school age, about sixty years ago. At that time, after delivering the product to the *orimoto* [manufacturer] on my way home, I could only buy one *sho* or two *sho* of rice. Yes, sixty years ago, all of us, my father and I also, all of us worked together. I started from age fourteen or fifteen. We could not eat unless we worked; so I had to leave sixth grade in the second term. Before the war we had a rest day only twice a month. We even worked in the night until nine or ten o'clock. We worked until late, even after the war.

Within this framework of disorderly work lives caused by the "ups and downs," Nishijin men and women organized their careers and charted their family strategies in order to maximize opportunities for work and income in good times, adapt to constraints in bad times, tide over depressions and disasters, and maintain their craft and their family's livelihood in the fickle world of industry and trade on which they depended. To accomplish these goals, they used every possible resource available to them—their skills and those of their family members, their ties with their distant kin, and their former village ties (for those who had migrated to Kyoto City). Individual skills, resourcefulness, perseverance, and diligence, as well as a collective family effort, were all essential in responding to changing opportunities and constraints.

The Interweaving of Family and Work

The Nishijin weaving industry was family intensive both in the manufacturer's enterprise and in the weavers' cottages. The work of individual members was part of the family's collective effort and was valued as such. Almost all members participated in the family's collective enterprise. Even weavers who worked individually in a factory usually belonged to a family where most members engaged in the cottage industry (Kyoto-fu, 1933). Cottage weaving emerged in Nishijin at the beginning of the twentieth century. It gained momentum as the dominant form of production from the early 1920s on and has continued to be the most characteristic organization of production in Nishijin to the present.

Increasing numbers of cottage weavers engaged in this household industry and began to weave for the manufacturer in their own homes, employing their own family members rather than weaving as individual employees in the manufacturer's house. The cottage industry putting-out system gradually replaced the historic *totei* labor system that had prevailed in Nishijin since the Edo period (Honjo, 1930; Yasuoka, 1977). In the *totei* system, apprentices lived in the manufacturer's house and worked there. After the completion of their apprenticeship, they continued to live and work in the manufacturer's house as journeymen. The more enterprising among them opened small branch weaving establishments of their own, with the support of the manufacturer, who permitted them to use his trademark as affiliates *(noren wake)*.

By contrast, the cottage weavers live and weave in their own household and employ their own family members. Originally, they rented looms from the manufacturer; hence their name, *chinbata,* meaning "borrowed loom." Since World War II, most cottage weavers own their looms; their name has changed, therefore, to *debata,* meaning "putting out" weaver. The *debata* are not self-employed entrepreneurs. Rather, they are employees of a capitalist manufacturer and produce Nishijin cloth for a nationwide market. The *debata* receive the silk yarn and the designs for each *obi* from the manufacturer, deliver the finished product to the manufacturer, and are paid for each finished *obi*. During periods of high demand for cloth, the *debata* employ occasional outside workers in addition to family members.[6]

The emergence of the *chinbata* system in the 1920s was brought about by two important technological developments in the Meiji period, both of which had a significant impact on women's work. The first was the introduction of the Jacquard mechanism into Nishijin in the 1880s; the second was the spread of the power loom *(rikishoki)*, which was first introduced into Nishijin early in this century. The Jacquard mechanism freed women's time from serving as a "human Jacquard" and made them available as potential weavers. The power loom actually made it possible for women to become weavers, because its manipulation required less physical strength than the hand loom (Hareven, 1990b). The use of power looms spread in Nishijin during the Taisho period, even though the hand loom *(tebata)* still predominated. Both the power loom and the hand loom had Jacquard attachments in order to produce the desired designs. The power loom was used essentially for weaving the same type of cloth as the hand loom, but it required less skill and less physical strength. The cottage industry has become the dominant form of production in Nishijin. It has coexisted with small factories (operating twenty to thirty looms at the most), which emerged beginning in the early Showa period (Honjo, 1930). Most Nishijin *obi*, however, have continued to be produced in the cottage industry. Power looms still coexist with hand looms, but power looms have gradually come to predominate (Nishijin Ori-kogyo Kumiai, 1980).

From the late Meiji period on (as a result of the introduction of the Jacquard loom), women could become weavers and could acquire the same type of skills as men. Particularly significant in this respect is women's involvement in the family's collective enterprise, not only as menial assistants but as full-fledged weavers (Kyoto-fu, 1933), generally using the power looms rather than hand looms. As the power loom spread through Nishijin, the division of labor between hand looms and power looms followed along gender lines. As Mr. T. recalled:

When power looms were introduced, women immediately replaced the men as if they had been waiting. After all, the hand loom required hands and feet. Power looms do not. They require just watching. They have to use their hands only. Power loom weaving is not men's work anymore. Men continued to weave on *tebata*, while women became specialists on the power loom.

(Mr. T. exaggerated the easiness of power-loom weaving. It does not involve "just" watching. It also requires special skills, because the shuttle is still put through by hand and the weavers use a multiplicity of colors in the weft in order to achieve a complex design. Power-loom weaving is physically less demanding, but it still requires high skill).

From the cottage weaver's point of view as head of the household, the advantage in household production was to employ as many of his own family members as weavers and helpers under his own supervision and thereby maximize the family's collective income. Cottage weaving in Nishijin has been continuously a collective family enterprise. In the context of a household industry, the weaver's household is paid as a *unit* for production of the individual *obi*. Even though family members work individually, each at a separate loom, they are not paid as individuals. By engaging their wives and young adult sons and daughters in weaving, many cottage weavers actually aspired to own one or more looms and, eventually, to become independent small manufacturers *(jimae)*. Only a few achieved this goal, however, because of the severe fluctuations in Nishijin's industry (Hattori, 1948). Many never became *jimae*, and those who were temporarily able to establish independent operations temporarily lost their independence during business slumps or depressions. Many of the cottage weavers did perceive themselves as a "fallen *jimae*"—a self-employed small entrepreneur who did not make it because of fickle markets.

Among cottage weavers before World War II, the entire family was engaged in the weaving enterprise. Husband and wife and older sons and daughters were usually working side by side, as were the husband's parents, with whom they usually resided. Prior to the introduction of the power loom, the men did most of the weaving, and the women and aging parents carried out preparatory and auxiliary tasks. Children were initiated into the craft by assisting their parents in tasks such as winding the thread or changing bobbins and in various menial tasks *(shita-shigoto)*.

"The young people today don't know about the life in Nishijin" claimed Mrs. F. (fifty-three years old). "We couldn't even receive compulsory education. If we didn't stop going to school in the sixth grade and didn't have work, the parents and children couldn't eat. Even before we entered the sixth grade we had to wind the woof." Following the introduction of compulsory junior-high attendance and child-labor laws in the post–World War II period, children ceased to be central in household production, but husbands and wives and aging parents continued to weave together.

Nishijin weavers trained their own family members as well as young migrants from the countryside in informal apprenticeships and helped launch them as weavers. Before World War II, children apprenticed with

their parents or with other relatives from about age ten. At the conclusion
of the apprenticeship period, the young weavers could either remain to
work for their masters, return to work for their parents, or find jobs with
other weavers. (In the postwar period, the age at which apprenticeship
began was moved up to fourteen). As Mr. T. observed: "Second and third
sons were kicked out [from their parents' farm] to apprenticeship." Mr. T.
recalled his being sent by his father to apprentice in Kyoto, during early
Showa:

> And my father said, what about my son? He decided without asking me, be-
> cause at the time we obeyed our parents. Without thinking anything, when
> my father told me to go, I went to Kyoto. I learned to weave with a relative.
> Based on a contract they promised me some money after ten years. So I
> stayed at his house for ten years. After the term was up, they said I could
> somehow earn a living by working independently. I went out to rent a house;
> I had a small house where I worked with a loom which my former boss give
> me. That was when I was twenty-four. When I was twenty-five I got married.

Poorer families, however, bound their children out to other weavers'
houses in exchange for loans. This was called *nenki boko* (indentured apprenticeship). As Mr. T. recalled:

> In the old days the kids had an education only up to the fourth grade. After
> that they were forced to leave for *nenki boko*. During the *nenki boko* they could
> not leave their master by any means, because the parents borrowed money
> in advance from the master in exchange for their kid's service. It's like selling
> human beings. You know how young people won't listen to parents now?
> Nowadays if they were sent as *nenki boko* they would say it's illegal. In those
> days they must have been so impoverished.

The collective familial character of Nishijin weaving, especially its predominance as a household industry, had serious implications for marriage patterns and the relations between the generations. As Mr. S. (eighty
years old) put it in a joint interview with his wife: "It was a common
thing, especially in Nishijin, for husbands and wives to meet in the factory, because both men and women worked in factories. Marriages resulting from factory courtship were usually referred to as 'love marriages,' as
opposed to *miae* [arranged marriages]." Underlying these courtships
were important strategies. "It was to the advantage of a Nishijin weaver
to marry a weaver, because when we marry a wife who is a weaver, she
can help when we need help at home in weaving. Women continued to
work in the factory after their marriage, usually until they got pregnant
and babies were born. After they had babies they couldn't go out." Mrs. S.

(seventy-five years old) added: "After the baby was born, I was also weaving at home."

Nishijin families tried to maximize their household labor force in periods of high demand for *obi* and, conversely, divested themselves of "extra mouths to feed" during periods of idleness by sending children out for *nenki boko* or for adoption. They tried to subsist or remain solvent by pressuring sons and daughters to become weavers, even when these children preferred to leave for other occupations. As Mrs. F. recalled:

> My family was a weaving family and I was urged to weave against my will. I grew up with the weaving sounds. My mother died early, and I had to help my father: I was ten years old when my mother passed away. I had one older sister and three younger brothers. My grandmother took care of us. She was living with us. I was seventeen years old when I started weaving. Even before that, when I was in school, I still helped my parents to spin threads. I did many errands for them. My father is still weaving *tsuzure* [fingernail weaving][7] at age seventy-five. My grandmother lived to age ninety-two. She was also a weaver, but she said she did not like it very much and finally gave it up. I had a resistance to weaving. Eventually I came to like this role. I am proud of my job now.

Nishijin mothers tried to discourage their own daughters from marrying Nishijin men, because they knew "how difficult the life" of a Nishijin wife was. Families that had no connection with Nishijin work were particularly wary about their daughters' taking on the exacting tasks of a Nishijin wife's life. Mrs. K. (forty-five years old), who was the daughter of a salaryman and a housewife, was "deceived" by her future husband during their courtship. She met him in a dance hall twenty-two years ago, and he initially disguised his occupation. "We didn't know at the beginning that my husband was a weaver. He didn't reveal to us that he was, either. I myself did not know exactly what weavers do. My parents didn't, either." Mr. K. (fifty years old), explained apologetically: "Some people, you see, have looked only at the bad aspects of Nishijin. Women in Nishijin have to work from morning to night; this is the tradition." His wife added:

> He thought that I wouldn't go out with him anymore, so he did not mention that he was weaving in Nishijin. When we went out, he would be properly dressed. He looked neat when we would go out, so my parents or I couldn't tell where he was from. He was very responsible about such matters as time, too. He would ask me in the midday, for example, if I wanted to go to the movies or something in the early evening. So I was impressed that he was so free, and also that he seemed to have a lot of money. In fact, he had a lot of

money. He used to buy me all sorts of things like shoes. If I said I wanted a dress, he would buy me one right away, so I really liked that (laugh). He had a lot of money before our marriage.

Whether they weave on the hand loom or power loom, women have developed a consciousness as artisans *(shokunin)*. They work with the same meticulousness and expertise as men. Like men, they are dedicated to making a perfect product and view their entire lives as a continuous quest for perfection in their skills and their product. At the same time, however, women weavers view their husbands as the main breadwinners. They describe their own roles as weavers as ancillary to their husbands' but as integral parts of their overall contribution to the family economy. Wives who are weaving at home tolerate interruptions in their work as an inevitable (although not welcome) aspect of their domestic roles. While protecting their husbands' weaving schedules, wives, who are highly skilled weavers in their own right, take it upon themselves to run errands. They deliver the finished *obi* to the manufacturer and pick up the new orders and yarn, as well as help with the preparatory work (winding the yarn, tying the warp, and so on) and the cleanup. They carry out all these tasks as well as the housework and child care. Even when they receive assistance from their mothers-in-law in child care and housework, their weaving is still interrupted for various tasks.

Glorifying his wife's domestic role, Mr. S. (eighty years old), said: "Women have to do many miscellaneous things in housework when compared to men. And that kind of work is more worthwhile than weaving. For instance, she has to clean around the house, go shopping, everything depends on her. That's why we can concentrate on our jobs." His wife (seventy-five years old), insisting, however, also on the significance of her contribution as a weaver to the family's economy, said: "Well, unless I worked we couldn't have eaten." Her husband added: "Our livelihood depended on that, so to speak." Their daughter-in-law (forty-seven years old), who was present at the interview, claimed that she was weaving both "for joy and for money," but the older woman insisted: "I just follow what is necessary—nothing special." Her husband retorted: "My wife acquired sophisticated skills and when she looks at her product, I think she likes it the more for her commitment to weaving."

As dutiful wives, Nishijin women acknowledged their role as weavers as being secondary and supportive to that of their husbands or other adult male weavers in their family. As weavers, however, they expressed the sense of expertise and standards of perfection similar to those articulated by male craftspeople. As Mrs. F., a fifty-three-year-old expert hand-loom weaver, who was initially reluctant to take on this craft, said:

I am proud of my role now. Some wives do the preparatory work for their husbands. My husband does the same work as I do. He is also a weaver on a hand loom. I wanted to accomplish something for myself. I also love domestic work. I never use instant food, and I knit and sew for my family with my own hands. I even educate my children in that way. It is all right for them to work outside, but also, they should take care of their families.

Once again, she emphasized, however: "Women who have skills cannot be satisfied with the work only [meaning with their craft only]."

Even though their "female" language was more modest and understated, women described the actual process of their weaving in great detail, including the intricate techniques involved, and talked with pride about their work. Since wives also acted as their household's external agents (delivered the *obi* to the *orimoto*, or manufacturer), they were more directly in touch with the *orimoto*'s world and were familiar with the broader context in which Nishijin's *obi* were produced. Women often brought home the news about changes in the marketplace and in production policies, curtailments, and other problems concerning production policies of *obi*. Men obtained such news from exchanges of information with other men in the evenings while drinking, playing mah-jongg and gambling, or at the Nishijin Textile Labor Union meetings. (Very few Nishijin cottage weavers, however, belonged to the union.)[8]

Nishijin women viewed their life paths as interwoven strands of work and family obligations, with little separation between the two. They continued weaving all their lives, intermittently during the early years of child rearing but continuously over their life course. When they were too old to weave, they worked in subsidiary roles, helping the other weavers in the household. Some of the older women weavers who still retained sharp eyes and nimble fingers worked as *tatezunagi* (tying the threads of the new warp to the frame of the loom). As "experts" on call to weavers' households, *tatezunagi* women went from house to house carrying their delicate bamboo rods—the tools of their trade—which are used for pulling the threads through their knots. *Tatezunagi* women are paid handsomely and are treated to tea and sweets in each house they visit. Weavers treat these women with awe because they depend on their timely arrival and also because these women are notorious for carrying gossip from house to house.

Similarly to the wives of other traditional craftsmen (potters, for example), Nishijin women view their various supportive tasks as an integral part of their family responsibilities (Kleinberg, 1983). In contrast to the potters, however (except for industrial potteries), Nishijin women weavers work as artisans, often commanding the same, or even higher, skills as their husbands. Nishijin women's sense of competence and understanding of their craft was even expressed in the style of their participation in the interview. Unlike the wives of traditional potters, whose houses I had visited in Bizen, Tatchikui, Karatsu, and Mashiko, Nishijin wives sat side by side with their husbands at the *kotatzu* (the low table with a foot warmer underneath, around which family members and guests gather in the cold season) and participated actively in the discussions, except when they disappeared briefly to prepare and serve tea. They often spoke in tandem with their husbands, each completing the other's sentences, and sometimes contradicted or corrected their husbands' accounts.

Nishijin women also experienced greater flexibility than their husbands in moving back and forth between household weaving and factory weaving, especially during periods of depression and after World War II, because they were more willing to change assignments or take on part-time work than men. Most Nishijin women weavers had done both household weaving and factory work. Following the spread of the power loom during the Showa period, women weavers often shuttled back and forth between the cottage industry and the factory. They learned to weave in their own homes or as apprentices in another weaver's or the manufacturer's household; they then worked in small factories or in another weaver's cottage until their marriage. After marriage, they started to weave side by side with their husbands at home.

In contrast to men, however, women weavers who had experienced factory work preferred it to weaving at home. Many of the women whom I interviewed in the small factories in Nishijin expressed the preference for working there, rather than at home. As Mrs. I. (forty years old) put it:

> When I come in here to the factory my time is my own. When I worked at home, we all worked together: my mother-in-law, my husband and me. But my husband kept interrupting me and asking me to help him, and I had to help him, and I had to do things around the house. Also, there is no one to talk to at home, except my husband and my mother-in-law. When I come here I talk with all the people while drinking tea.

Like Mrs. I., many Nishijin women of her generation viewed the factory as an opportunity to express themselves as individuals. They were paid individually for their work; their product was evaluated and judged as their own rather than as the household's collective product; their work time as weavers was defined and respected without interruptions for household chores, child care, and assistance to their husbands. Women weavers also valued the sociability of the workplace—the opportunity to learn from fellow workers and the tea-break chats.

The Identity of Nishijin Weavers

Nishijin weavers are acutely aware of themselves as Nishijin "men" and "women," as members of Nishijin *mura* (village), in which daily life and interaction is governed by its own internal codes (often unspoken ones). Even their language differs in some respects from the standard *Kyoto-ben* (dialect). At times, Nishijin people describe feelings or situations in metaphors borrowed from the world of spinning and weaving, for example, the word for confusion is the same as "the threads are all entangled." Their identity rests on their being craftspeople, on their making a special product that is famous for its characteristic quality and design, and on their being members of a community in which all aspects of life are deeply interwoven with the production of Nishijin cloth. Their sense of place and location in Nishijin *mura* is inseparable from their work and ways of life. Nishijin weavers have a strong sense of themselves, not only as members of a particular craft engaged in making a nationally-famous product but also in their feeling part of a community, the existence of which has been identified with the production of magnificent ritual cloth over the past 500 years. As will be seen below, their strong identification with Nishijin has also become a source of tension and ambivalence in their lives, especially after their traditional industry began to decline.

Conformity to Nishijin's unspoken codes of behavior governs all aspects of life in Nishijin, including the regulation of production. Because of the proximity of weavers' houses to each other in Nishijin's narrow lanes, there is little that escapes the neighbors' attention. Following the introduction of the Fair Labor Standards Act after World War II, the pressure to enforce an eight-hour workday was increasingly felt in Nishijin. When some weavers continued to work late into the evening, others complained and requested that their neighbors stop their work earlier. The clicking of the looms during late hours was gradually silenced by community pressure. Nishijin wives often complained about the subtle pressure from neighbors to keep the wooden slats of their houses polished regularly. Despite their heavy workloads as weavers, Nishijin wives rose at dawn to polish the slats with soy bean oil in order to please their neighbors.

The pressure for conformity in Nishijin is so powerful that Mr. K., for example, would not dare be seen on his narrow Nishijin street helping his wife carry grocery bags from the bus. When the two of them return from shopping at the market, Mr. K. usually helps his wife with the bags as far as Horikawa Street (the main traffic artery that runs through Nishijin). Once they enter their neighborhood, his wife takes over the bags. Nishijin residents who were born and raised there have lost their sense of perspective on whether the behavior and attitudes they have witnessed in Nishijin are peculiar to this community. They tend to identify certain types of behavior as being unique to Nishijin, even though these can be found among other traditional craftspeople in Japan as well. For example, many of the Nishijin weavers attribute their fathers' conduct in the past, in activities such as gambling, playing with geisha, or having a "second wife" (mistress), to Nishijin customs rather than to a more widespread Japanese form of male conduct.

Similarly, disgruntled weavers who criticized their employers' unfair treatment of their employees attributed this behavior to the characteristic atmosphere of Nishijin rather than to a more widespread pattern of labor relations in Japan. Some of these behaviors were, indeed, rooted in Nishijin's paternalistic traditions of the relations between *oyakata* and *kokata*. Other strategies that the manufacturers followed, however, such as cutting wages, curtailment of production, layoffs of weavers, and pressure on older weavers to retire early, were by no means unique to Nishijin, though many of the weavers interviewed perceived them as such.

Nishijin craftspeople see in weaving their main identity, reinforced by the continuity of their craft over several generations in their families. Even though most of them did not choose this occupation, they had come to identify with it as their way of life. Their quest for perfection is the key element in their self-perception. Over their entire lives they strove to improve their skills and to perfect their product. In addition to learning from each other, they went to museums and temples to study the surviving fragments of ancient Japanese and Chinese textiles in their collections.[9] They often express their regrets that some of the older techniques had already been forgotten and lost to their generation. They share a broad understanding of the larger context of Japanese culture in which their craft, their products, and the aesthetic symbols used in the textiles they weave are embedded. Even the poorer of the weavers, who lacked a high-school education, were familiar with the tea ceremony, flower arrangements, the No play, and the religious rituals in which the cloth they weave has a central role. Similarly, they are knowledgeable about the meaning of the design symbols woven into Nishijin fabrics and their origins and significance.

For seventy-five-year-old Mr. N., weaving has continued to be "a spiritual exercise."

> I cannot do it [weave] easily. I have been doing this for sixty years but still it is impossible. I still enjoy weaving. Let me see, if I don't weave I have to babysit my grandchild, right? Then if I weave, I'm weaving. Since I've been weaving for sixty years, my lower back is bent out of shape. It is an occupational disease. I have had X-rays taken. So, although I feel pain, I am okay when I start to work. Even this low back pain, too, goes away. Because over

sixty years, I have been doing this. So, my spine has got to be bent. So, I feel comfortable when I am weaving like this. Although I have been weaving for sixty years, I really don't know everything. And weaving this cloth requires deep knowledge. I still study this weaving, and I haven't done anything so perfect that I can say, "This has been done without any mistake." There always is some part that I don't like really. So that is the spiritual exercise: I want to make weaving so perfectly without any mistake. This is what keeps me going.

Mr. F., his son-in-law, (forty-eight years old), a highly skilled weaver, added:

And this spiritual condition is not easy. We can't measure our product in meters. I'm hardly able to find even one piece that I like from the beginning to the end. I can't be completely satisfied somewhere, though, even if there is no flaw. I don't make any flaws but the pattern of the design cannot come out perfectly. It always happens. I set my own standards. Even if I don't make any actual mistake, I still wish this part could be perfectly done in this way. So, it is difficult.

Mr. S. expressed a very similar commitment to perfection:

When I look at the product which I successfully made, I feel really happy. Well, Nishijin people have repeated that our work requires practice all the way until we die. We deal with different designs all the time, and we make samples whenever we get them. We examine our products and seek reaction to samples. At his age, I can take any orders. When a weaver feels confident about his product, he can accept orders for new designs and changes, because designs change. We still face some difficulty even at this age which laymen wouldn't recognize, but, we cannot say that we cannot make some kind of thing.

Like many other accomplished Nishijin craftspeople of his generation, he regrets the recent decline in the quality of the product:

I think you may say that the quality has declined in certain aspects. In the past, people could tell just by spreading the cloth and feeling its surface which part was hard or soft and they criticized us. But now such a response is rarely seen. Even if you think you have woven a very fine cloth, you feel somewhat sad when others treat it without much care. Nowadays, the treatment for quality products is the same as for nonquality products, too. In the past, people cared for the quality of a product more than for efficiency in production. Nowadays, the manufacturer seeks profit by asking weavers to produce more, and faster. We elderly weavers cannot compete with younger people in terms of this kind of efficiency. So, younger weavers who may lack in advanced techniques but weave faster are more welcome. This is the tendency of today. It is hard for a quality weaver to be welcome for his techniques only. In this respect, you may well talk about the decline in quality.

Despite their deep commitment, Nishijin weavers are conscious of the ambiguities and internal contradictions in their roles. They are on the interstices between traditional craftsmanship and industrial work. As artisans, they are executing the manufacturers' designs as specified in the orders and in the patterns punched into the Jacquard system. They have no control over the designs or the colors they use. Their main challenge is in translating the designs into a flawless weave. They are not independent artisans or artists. Even the finest craftspeople among them could never aspire to becoming a "living national treasure," unless they started developing and weaving their own designs. In this context, it is significant that in the Japanese language, Nishijin weaving is not defined as an art or a craft but rather as a "traditional industry"—*dento sangyo*.[10]

Origins of Conflict

As employees of the manufacturer, Nishijin weavers have little control over the type of *obi* they are making or over their terms of employment. They are employed by a capitalist manufacturer who provides them with the raw materials, the design, and the punch cards for the Jacquard and who pays them for the finished product. Nor do Nishijin weavers have much control over their working conditions and their pay rate. If they are dissatisfied, their only recourse is to change manufacturers. In the past, weavers were able to exercise such choices, however, only during periods of labor shortage (compare Haak, 1975). Even when they weave in their own household, they are not independent artisans or small entrepreneurs.

Nishijin weavers' ambivalence and internal conflict derive partly from these ambiguities in their status. They feel betrayed and exploited by the manufacturer, especially during Nishijin's decline over the past decade. As Mr. F. put it:

Nishijin is feudalistic. The factory where I work [one of the richest and most traditional manufacturers in Nishijin] does not give us holiday with guaranteed pay and retirement pension *(taishokukkin)*. Labor pay *(kochin)* is not stable at all. We get no bonus either. When there is a big gap between what I demand and what the employer pays, it becomes difficult to make a living.

Mr. F.'s career was atypical for Nishijin, because he changed employers many times within the same community. As one of the most outspoken weavers in Nishijin, he was frequently fired, because he spoke his mind to the *orimoto* (manufacturer) or because he insisted on the rights of the union. He was also blacklisted several times and was able to obtain employment again, only because of the manufacturers' recognition of his exceptional skills. Now, in a period of labor surplus in Nishijin, he has become more subdued, but he still speaks his mind, despite his wife's anxiety that he might lose his job again.

> The employer does not like what I say, and I feel that I am discriminated by him. Ways of thinking in Nishijin are old. They speak about fairness, but we also have our own pride as craftspeople. When they pay so little, we feel they do not appreciate our skill. The union is nothing at all. The union is nothing where I work. Everything is the way the *oyakata* [old paternalistic term for manufacturer] says. They prevent us from having a union.

The weavers perceive a dual attitude on the part of the manufacturers. On the one hand, the manufacturers appeal to the weavers' sense of aesthetics and skill and to their loyalty. On the other hand, they violate the paternalistic bond between manufacturer and craftspeople by subcontracting out Nishijin weaving to be done in the countryside on the Tango Peninsula and in China and Korea. As a result, Nishijin's traditional weavers have been losing their jobs to weavers outside the city and outside Japan who are willing to work for lower wages. As Mr. F. put it: "There exist many ugly things behind such beautiful *obi*. If you visit the *orimoto* (manufacturer), they would speak beautifully about their business, but it is false. The *orimoto* are short-sighted. The *orimoto* do not make any effort to sustain success in Nishijin and they just keep awarding work outside Nishijin for lower wages."

Nishijin weavers also feel angry over the breakdown of the paternalistic relationship between manufacturer and weaver, especially when the manufacturers use various tricks to curtail production by slowing down the weavers, without fully laying them off long enough to justify having to pay them unemployment compensation. Mr. F. explained the sly way in which the manufacturers curtail production by putting cottage weavers on hold:

> To keep a weaver waiting, they use the excuse that the work is not ready. Sometimes they keep them waiting for days. Companies play games. Weavers do not have any idea of the color they should use. They come to the company to get the silk and the design, but the *orimoto* (manufacturers) de-

lay telling them the color arrangements. The *orimoto* plan these underhanded maneuvers on purpose. They can't just give anything to a weaver and tell him to go home. It would become a social problem. So they keep them waiting.

Similarly, Mr. and Mrs. K. are bitter about their manufacturer's shrewd techniques:

They are not really telling us that they are reducing production, but they are reducing our work time by changing the orders or asking us to wait for just a short while [because] they are now having the threads dyed. They do this to us from time to time. They don't ask us to stop weaving or anything like that. This is characteristic of Nishijin. This sort of thing is unthinkable in other businesses—there lies the peculiarity of Nishijin (laugh).

And his wife added:

They do it very cleverly. If they tell us in advance and ask us to wait for a whole day—then we would know it; and we could hope that we would get 60 percent of the pay for the day; but when they say they will bring an order soon, and they want us to wait just for two or three hours; or when they ask suddenly if we could change the colors, we would have to stop for a while. We don't really complain about that sort of little thing, you know. Well, that is, suppose we've woven a big piece today, and the next day when we have to do the next one they tell us that they want to change the colors this time. So they ask us if we could wait until they finish preparing the new threads; so we agree to wait. They say, if the time is about now 4:00, that they will have the threads ready the first thing in the morning. Because it's only 4:00 now, we expect to have them at 7:00 or 8:00 in the morning, and we plan to start working at 8:00. But for them, "the first thing in the morning" was meant to be 10:00 or 12:00, you see. Then after we receive the threads, we have to wind them and so on, so we can finally start weaving only after lunch. These hours are almost a whole day for us, but for them, "the first thing next morning" was delayed just little by little (laugh).

Mr. K. explained that the fundamental problem in Nishijin is the dead hand of the past: the paternalistic relationship between the manufacturer and the weaver. He uses the old terms, *oyakata* and *kokata*, which literally mean parent and child. The main problem that Mr. K. and the other weavers have confronted is the survival of the servile, exploitative aspects of paternalism, without the benefits and protection that were inherent in this system in the past: "There is a hierarchical line between *oyakata* (manufacturer) and *kokata* (weaver) in Nishijin; so if the *oyakata* says,

'Would you please wait for a while?' and taps on my shoulder, I have to accept this." "It means that I make less money now, because I am paid by the hour," explained Mr. K. And his wife added: "That's the point. They don't make us wait long enough to qualify for compensation. If we were unemployed for one day, we would get 6,000 yen. But they say, 'Just wait a little while,' so we don't receive anything." The manufacturer is thus taking advantage of the paternalistic relationship. "That's the peculiarity of Nishijin," emphasized Mr. K. "*Oyakata* and *kokata* always see each other. So, the *kokata* has to comply."[11]

Nishijin weavers' sense of frustration is enforced by their inability to exercise their one form of escape, to which they had resorted in the past— to change employers. They feel trapped in nonnegotiable working conditions, because during periods of decline in production, it is impossible to change manufacturers. "If we quit this role, there would be no place for us to go. What they are doing to us is just like beating babies," said Mr. Y., a seventy-year-old weaver. In the past, selecting another employer was their only recourse if they were dissatisfied with their working conditions. As Mr. K. recalled: "It used to be that if we didn't like the wages or conditions of one *oriya* [manufacturer], we would walk around Nishijin with a pair of scissors in our hands. We used to look for the sign on the houses, 'Weaver wanted,' and we'd find another *oriya*. Now we have nowhere to go, nowhere!"

Witnessing the precipitous decline of their craft and the erosion of their source of livelihood, Nishijin weavers feel betrayed by the industry they and their ancestors had served loyally over several generations. "But now young people do not want to succeed to our work, because this industry has no future," said Mr. F. "I belong to the 'young' generation. I am forty-eight years old. Some weavers are older than seventy. Real good *tebata* work will disappear from Nishijin when my generation gets old." As Mr. T. put it:

> I did not ask my son to be a weaver. He now thinks that it would be better not to be a weaver. I imagine. At the present time we cannot make a living unless we do something extra and ordinary. In comparison with what I did, nowadays they must work twice as much. After all, fabrics have become difficult to weave. Weaving is not men's work anymore. It is a work for women, to tell the truth. I cannot imagine weaving as men's work. . . . After all, women are patient in work. Men soon get tired. Women now do detailed work. [Mr. T. exaggerated his point.]

Over the past decade, Nishijin weavers' family strategies about succession have changed considerably. Faced with a declining industry and an insecure future, weavers who are currently in their fifties or older have discouraged their sons from inheriting their parents' craft in a declining industry. "Once I started helping with the preparation for weaving, I found that weaving is quite hard," said Mrs. K., "so we decided to let our children go to the university. Also, I wouldn't want my daughter to marry a weaver. The most important thing is for them to get out of the Nishijin *mura*." Accordingly, Mr. and Mrs. K. sent their son to a technical school and their daughter to a college. After graduation, the daughter married a salaryman and lives in a middle-class suburb.

In their efforts to interpret their world and explain their lives to me, Nishijin people expressed their frustration about their inabilities to understand their own world in Nishijin in all its complexities. Worst was their sense of helplessness in coming to terms with the frustration resulting from the sense of betrayal they felt from their employers. After having interviewed Mr. K. for many hours, he asked me: "Have you come to understand Nishijin?" Mrs. K. followed up: "It is also hard for us weavers to understand each other's feelings." And Mr. K. added: "Maybe that's one of the uniqueness in Nishijin." Part of the bewilderment, Mr. T. claimed, emanated from the wage system:

> There is no stable wage system except that people talk with each other and draw the minimum line to base on. I think this is why it's so complex and hard to understand. Everybody in this business wants to survive no matter what happens. Even if others go bankrupt, people want to serve at the expense of others. No matter how bad the economic depression might be, the people pretend with smiles that everyone is getting along well on the surface, and yet they are very competitive at the bottom of their hearts. I think that this is the major cause of complexity. I was born in Nishijin and my wife has been involved in Nishijin work over twenty years and it is still hard for us to understand.

Reflections

The reconstruction of the work lives of the Nishijin weavers and of their self-perception reveals several patterns that call for cross-cultural comparisons. The cross-stitched and "disorderly" character of their work careers resulting from fluctuations in the market, business cycles, and production policies is historically characteristic of textile work in Europe and the United States as well. The weavers in the Amoskeag Mills in Manchester, New Hampshire, had experienced disorderly careers as a norm (Hareven, 1982). Both in Nishijin and in Manchester, New Hampshire, at times, the workers themselves contributed to the disorderly character of their careers by changing employers in order to improve their conditions.

Textile workers experienced disorderliness and insecurity imposed by the system during periods of contraction in the industry and labor surplus. Conversely, the workers themselves initiated career changes during periods of expansion accompanied by labor shortage.

Similarly to the industrial weavers in Manchester, Nishijin weavers had a strong commitment to their craft and identified both with the product they were making and with its special function and fame. Even the weavers in Manchester who were making mass-produced cloth on power looms had an intense pride and a strong commitment to the quality of their product and to its fame. This type of identification of weavers with their products is characteristic of the textile industry at large, because textile workers produce a whole visible product rather than a part in an assembly line. For that very reason, even semi-skilled or low-skilled industrial workers in the United States described their product with a sense of pride and identification similar to that of the artisans in Kyoto.

The strong integration between family and work in Nishijin's traditional industry also evokes parallels in the textile industry historically in Europe and in the United States. By its very nature, textile work is family intensive. Whether it is performed in a weaver's cottage or in a factory, textile work engaged the entire family unit or at least a major portion of the family. The cottage industry that emerged in Nishijin early in the twentieth century had its strong parallel in proto-industrial production in Western and Central Europe in the eighteenth and early nineteenth centuries. Similar to Nishijin's system, the proto-industrial household production involved the making of cloth or other products. Like Nishijin weavers, these artisans and their family members were employed by capitalist manufacturers, were producing for external markets, and were paid collectively by the piece (Medick, 1976). Proto-industrial production in Europe was eventually superseded by the factory system. In Nishijin, by contrast, the cottage industry continued to coexist with a modern factory system and retained its traditional character, even after the introduction of new technology.

The integration of family and work persisted in the textile industry in Europe and the United States even in the modern factory. As discussed above, workers were recruited into the textile factories in family groups and retained strong kinship ties with other workers within the factory (Smelser, 1959; Hareven, 1982). The strong integration of individuals with the family's collective identity was evidenced in Nishijin, as well as among European and American factory workers, even when the latter were employed as individuals rather than in family groups (Tilly and Scott, 1978; Hareven, 1982). It is precisely this strong integration that led to an ambiguity in the roles of women weavers. Both in Nishijin and in Manchester, New Hampshire, women who followed continuous careers and developed skills as men did viewed their work as supplemental to their various domestic activities rather than as individual careers.

Finally, the ambivalence and the sense of betrayal that Nishijin weavers have experienced during the dramatic decline of their industry over the past decade was matched by a similar sense of betrayal that the Amoskeag workers felt when the factory in which they had invested their trust and energies let them down during its decline and final shutdown in 1939. The stronger the sense of identification with an industry, the stronger the feeling of betrayal during its decline. Both Amoskeag and Nishijin weavers were bitter about the decline in their employment security and wages. But what they resented most was the apparent lack of a concerted effort on the part of their employers to find a constructive solution and save the world of work to which the weavers had committed their loyalty.

Even though the Nishijin weavers were in a transitional state between artisans and industrial workers, they held many attitudes and self-definitions in common with the industrial workers in Manchester, New Hampshire. In this case, the textile experience and the "textile language" transcended the cultural differences between Japan and the United States. Cross-cultural comparisons often generalize on common traits and differences for entire populations, without distinction by occupation, class, or ethnicity within each of the societies compared. In the case of the Nishijin weavers and the Manchester textile workers, the commonality in the experience of producing textiles and of being artisans in a specific industry cut across the two cultures. In some respects, Nishijin weavers hold more in common with the textile workers in Manchester than they do with salarymen or white-collar professionals in Japan. In many other aspects of their lives, Nishijin weavers hold more in common with other Japanese than they do with textiles workers in the United States.

Any cross-cultural comparison carries its own risks of generalizing on superficial similarities at the expense of fundamental cultural differences. Now that the similarities in the worlds of Nishijin weavers and American textile workers have come so clearly to the surface, it is necessary to distinguish these apparent commonalities from aspects specific to each of the two cultures. One needs to explore, therefore, those features that set apart the ways in which Japanese culture provides special meaning to the Nishijin craftspeople's view of their world and the sense that they made of their lives.

11

The Festival's Work as Leisure

The Traditional Craftsmen of the Gion Festival

Introduction

The debates about the role of work in modern society and about the relationship between work and leisure have dominated thought and scholarship in Western society since the industrial revolution. These issues have become especially acute in "postindustrial" society. A more complex view toward these issues draws on the anthropology of work and on social history, rejecting the dominant view of work in modern society as dehumanizing and emphasizing the constructive role of work in identity formation and in providing self-esteem and honor. When viewed as distinct from "labor," work is being recognized as having a positive impact on the formation of individual and social identity. My own study of textile workers in New England has also demonstrated laborers' strong attachment to their industrial work as part of their identity and sense of community (Hareven, 1982).

The role of work in identity formation is particularly significant in Japanese society, where the organization of work has become regimented to an extreme and where *work* and *leisure* in large enterprises have become highly regulated and controlled by management, in order to shape a collective group identity that conforms to the company's ideals and dic-

Reprinted from *Workers' Expressions: Beyond Accommodation* by John Calagione, Doris Francis, and Daniel Nugent (eds) by permission of the State University of New York Press. © 1992 State University of New York. All rights reserved.

tates. Under these circumstances, leisure is not an antidote to work but rather part of the company's control over the workers' entire time budget.

This chapter examines a highly traditional festival in modern Japan, where workers are able temporarily to reverse their streamlined roles and achieve once a year a self-identification in a nonregimented work process. Although festivals usually serve as occasions of leisure and joyous transgression, their organization and successful execution requires exhausting work, elaborate organization, synchronization of delicate time schedules, and extraordinary skills (Abrahams, 1982). Even traditional festivals that are enacted in contemporary society are regulated or controlled by state and municipal bureaucracies, insurance requirements, traffic regulations, and police. Thus, although festivals are intended to provide a release from the pressures and routines of daily work, they generate work pressures of a different character, which bring to the foreground the leadership and skills that are essential for their successful production and maintenance.

Festivals in Japan have had the special role of enforcing the status quo and upholding the existing hierarchy of class or age through their special rituals. Festivals have also provided, however, certain groups or social classes with the opportunity of temporarily reversing their roles and of expressing their group identities (Bestor, 1989; Soeda, 1973). Such role inversions were controlled or initiated in the past by the ruling classes. They were used as occasions that enabled peasants or members of lower classes to vent their frustrations in a controlled, ritualized way and then acquiesce to the authorities.

In contemporary Japan, class divisions are less rigid than in prewar Japan, but boundaries based on occupation, income, and social status are still clearly observed. The Gion Matsuri, as this festival is called, provides the craftsmen engaged in its production with the opportunity to transcend, at least temporarily, the boundaries of their class, to gain a sense of identification with the community, and to achieve honor and self-respect through their use of their indispensable traditional skills in producing the festival.

The festival's work is no ordinary labor, and the service of the community members and the craftsmen is no ordinary service. The festival is homage to the gods who visit the community during these celebrations. The craftsmen's labor, and the community members' labor, is *o'kamisamano shigoto* (labor for the gods). Even though the craftsmen receive some pay for their services, this pay is considerably lower (by about one-third to one-half) than what they would be receiving for their usual work. In this sense, the craftsmen view themselves as volunteers. They take their vacation time from their regular jobs during the festival and intensely contribute their time and labor to the festival. Since vacations in

Japan are extremely short, the craftsmen actually forgo their main vacation for the sake of the festival.

This chapter discusses the role of the traditional craftsmen in Kyoto in constructing and moving the Gion Festival's giant floats, *yama* and *hoko*. It examines their relationship to each other and to the community members who employ them once a year, as they utilize their special skills during the festival.

The Moving Museum

The Gion Festival, one of Japan's three biggest and nationally famous festivals, has been celebrated annually by the residents of the Muromachi district of Kyoto since the ninth century (Yoneyama, 1973). During the festival, each neighborhood sponsors and produces one "float" (a *hoko* or a *yama).* The festival culminates in a procession of thirty-two giant floats. They consist of two types: The *hoko* are three-story, towering structures that are moved on giant wheels and pulled along the streets by close to 100 pullers for each. The *yama* are smaller one-story structures and are carried through the procession by twenty to thirty pallbearers. The *yama* and *hoko,* which resemble miniature shrines, are decorated by magnificent carvings in wood, lacquerware, and metal and are hung with ancient tapestries, rugs, and dyed fabrics. As the *yama* and *hoko* move in the parade through Kyoto's main downtown streets, Kyoto people refer to them as the "Moving Museum."

The townspeople in the Yama Hoko Cho district who have produced and maintained this festival were traditionally the wholesalers of kimonos. Since World War II, the district's population has become considerably diversified in occupation and businesses, but wholesalers of kimonos and related accessories still keep their shops and residences in certain subneighborhoods of this district.

Following World War II, most of the traditional houses and shops on Shijo Street were replaced by tall, modern office and bank buildings. There are hardly any dwellings left on the corner of Shijo and Karasuma Streets—the focal point of the Gion Festival. The former residents moved out to the suburbs, and the older ones died carrying their knowledge with them. In several of the thirty-two neighborhoods, a few original families still reside in their historic houses, or at least they keep shops there. Even in these communities, though, the exodus to the suburbs continues. Soaring land values in this central area of Kyoto have attracted real-estate speculators, who drive out the local residents, sometimes through pressure and threats of violence. They replace the traditional two-story wooden houses with high-rise "mansions" (apartment buildings) and parking garages. The Yama Hoko Cho is thus embroiled in a continuing struggle to maintain its traditional streetscapes and its original community.

The Gion Festival was already recognized as one of Japan's major festivals in the Edo period. In exchange for the festival's cultural and religious contribution to the nation, the Tokugawa emperor recognized Kyoto's maintenance of this festival as a form of "tax." Kyoto was exempt, therefore, from certain national taxes. Because of the festival's national importance, the other districts of Kyoto City that were not involved in the festival were obligated to contribute to the Yama Hoko Cho (the Gion Festival's district) through a fixed tax in money or labor for the maintenance of the festival. This obligation was eliminated during the Meiji period (Yoneyama, 1986). Nevertheless, residents of the Gion Festival districts as well as those of other districts, the merchants, and the hotel and tourist service associations have continued to contribute to the Gion Festival on a voluntary basis, because of the festival's importance to Kyoto's cultural life and tourism. The Yama Hoko Cho district, which puts on and maintains this festival, struggles financially, and the festival's Central Committee (Gion Matsuri Rengo Kai) are engaged in a continuous effort to raise financial and volunteer support from various associations within the city.

Even though the Gion Festival is produced in one district of Kyoto only, it is shared and celebrated by the entire city and by hundreds of thousands of visitors who watch the parade on July 17 on Kyoto's main downtown streets. Since its early origins, the Gion Festival has therefore attracted numerous visitors from other parts of Japan. (Until World War II, there had actually been two parades: one on July 17 and one on July 27, each parade encompassing the *yama* and *hoko* of one-half of the district. Because of traffic problems and the financial efforts involved in producing two parades, they were merged after World War II into one that is held annually on July 17.)

In recent years, the Gion Festival has become one of Kyoto's main tourist events. Among Kyoto's three nationally famous festivals—Aoi Matzuri, Jidai Matzuri (Festival of Ages), and Gion Matsuri, the Gion Festival stands out as Kyoto's greatest tourist attraction. The festival brings hundreds of thousands of tourists (domestic as well as foreign) into Kyoto and serves as an important source of income for the city's tourist industry.

According to tradition, the Gion Festival's initial purpose was to avert a plague that was devastating the population of Kyoto. In this respect, the Gion Festival is one of numerous summer festivals in Japan, which occur after the various spring festivals and before the Bon Festival (ancestor worship) in August. When the Gion Festival first started, the townspeople paraded a primitive *hoko*—a symbolic weapon that was intended to fight evil. Initially unadorned, it was shaped as a metal pole with a pointed end on the top and was carried around in religious processions. The primitive *hoko* used for the Gion Festival were subsequently enveloped and embedded in fancy ornaments and were finally surrounded by the structures of the towering floats that are used in the procession today.

What had originally been a magical weapon intended to fight the evil that besets the community was transformed into a display of the merchant bourgeoisie's pride and wealth, expressed in an elaborate display of artistry. The tapestries and carpets that are used to cover the four sides of the towering structures have become symbolic of Kyoto's connection with China and Western Europe. From the seventeenth century on, the *hoko* and *yama* were decorated with carpets imported from Iran and India and with tapestries woven locally, as well as imported ones from Belgium, France, and China. (One of the magnificent Belgian tapestries depicting scenes from Homer's *Iliad* has survived as a unique specimen of that genre and cannot be found in Belgium anymore.) Since the Yama Hoko Cho district's main merchandise had been Kyoto's handwoven brocade, the display of tapestries and precious rugs on the *hoko* and *yama* is one of the festival's main characteristics and claims to fame.

The construction of the festival's floats requires a variety of traditional skills that are gradually becoming extinct. These towering floats are built from wooden beams that are knitted together only by an elaborate rope mesh. No nails or pegs can be used. Magnificent lacquerware, bronze, and gold ornaments are fitted together as in a jigsaw puzzle and mounted upon the skeletons of the floats. The tapestries and various artistically dyed fabrics are then hung and fixed with metal clasps. Finally, the wheelmen mount the huge wooden wheels, so that the *hoko* can be moved in the procession. The turning of these wheels around street corners requires the kind of special skills used for maneuvering carriages in the Middle Ages. During the parade, the *yama* and *hoko* move through the streets of Kyoto as a result of the coordinated efforts of the carpenters, wheelmen, conductors (who signal when to move and when to stop), and men who pull the *hoko* forward with heavy ropes.

Before World War II, residents from surrounding villages, who were tied to the townsmen in the Gion Festival district by various obligations, used to perform these highly skilled services. Today, the community members who produce the festival have to hire the few craftsmen who have retained these skills or who learned them from the older generation. During the year, these craftsmen work in ordinary occupations such as high-rise construction jobs and factory work or as salarymen or farmers. Once a year, they leave their regular jobs and carry out the festival's labor. Despite its arduous and dangerous character, these craftsmen consider the festival's work as a form of leisure. The festival offers them a special opportunity to practice and display their skills in front of millions of viewers on the streets and on television. Their reunion during the festival with fellow craftsmen and community members enables them to socialize together once a year and to maintain a sense of the festival's community.

Since the skills needed for the festival are becoming exceedingly rare in modern Japan, the craftsmen use their knowledge as a means of managing the procedures and social events of the festival beyond what would be considered their usual status. The community members who are responsible for the festival depend increasingly on these craftsmen's knowledge and performance. Without them, it would be impossible to construct the *hoko* and to move them safely. Even the slightest mistake in the turning of the wheels or in the coordination of the rope pulling could cause severe accidents. In view of the delicate coordination and balancing required to hold up and move the giant structures, these craftsmen are indispensable during the festival. The power of knowledge also enables craftsmen to participate in special social events, such as the final party following the festival from which members of their class would have been excluded in the past because of their lower social status.

This chapter is based on extensive interviews of the craftsmen as well as the community members and leaders in the various neighborhoods involved in the festival, conducted from 1986 to 1991. My original purpose in studying the Gion Festival was to understand how the communities that are responsible for the festival produce it and carry on its traditions, despite the pressures of rapid modernization. I have thus conducted repeated, open-ended interviews of the community members and leaders in six of the thirty-two districts of the festival and of the various craftsmen who work with them. I have followed the preparations in each community, starting each year on July 1, when the festival's work is officially launched.

The Festival's Work

The entire festival's work is carried out by three groups: the community members, the hired craftsmen, and the volunteers. The community members are obligated to contribute fixed amounts of money and a certain amount of labor each year in carrying out the festival's work and in managing it. They take turns in carrying the responsibility for various tasks and the management roles. In the community, members contribute both financially and by investing their time way beyond their required share. Most family businesses in the community close down after July 1 and barely reopen by the beginning of August. Men and women work day and night on all the details and the preparations. The craftsmen, however, are hired as "experts" for a specific time period to carry out their specialized tasks. They are paid at least a minimal fee for their labor.

The construction of a *hoko* or a *yama* involves three teams of craftsmen, each with its specialized skills and responsibilities: The carpenters *(daiku)* construct the *hoko* from wooden beams and poles that they knot together with elaborate heavy ropes. As mentioned, they use no nails or any other type of pegs in this process. The carpenters' work culminates in the construction of the roof, which is made of elaborate carved wood and lacquer segments, fitting together as in a puzzle. The construction of the *hoko*'s skeleton always begins on July 10 and is completed within two days.

The "helpers" *(tetzudai)* work closely with the carpenters. They assist the carpenters in the construction of the *hoko*, in building the roof and tapestries and the various ornaments, and finally in moving it through the streets. The carpenters as well as the helpers have special tasks during the parade itself, as will be described below. The third group, the wheelmen *(kururnakata)* are in charge of mounting the giant wheels of the *hoko* and moving the *hoko* during the parade. After the parade, they are responsible for dismantling the wheels and preparing them for storage.

The three groups of craftsman work in close coordination with each other. They all take their instructions from the *oyakata*, the contractor who is responsible for all three groups to the community leaders. Under the main *oyakata* there are usually two subcontractors, one for the carpenter and helper groups and one for the wheelmen. The subcontractors are responsible for recruiting the workers in their group and for supervising their respective tasks directly. In some cases, the two subcontractors also negotiate and communicate directly with the community leaders.

The organizational structure of the craftsmen thus varies from one community to another. In some cases, one main *oyakata* of the carpenters is in charge of the entire production and the two subcontractors are responsible to him. In other cases, each *oyakata* carries out his respective tasks in coordination with the others but is responsible to the community leaders independently and controls his own men.

Each *oyakata* seals his contracts for his work with the community leaders on July 1 each year. It has been customary for the chief *oyakata* and for the two subcontractors to attend the Kippuiri—the opening meeting for the preparation of the festival's work on July 1. Even where there is a chief *oyakata*, the two subcontractors appear at the Kippuiri. In that ceremony, the community leaders, dressed in *haori*, the formal black kimono that is customarily worn during special celebrations, kneel in front of their deities. The *oyakata* and the subcontractors wear business suits rather than their usual working clothes. Each subcontractor presents his contract to the community leaders, detailing the amount of work to be accomplished and the price for materials and labor. The community leaders and the contractors bargain over the fees. Since the same *oyakata* serves the same community year after year, the fees were actually agreed upon long ago. They involve only a slight increase each year due to the increases in the cost of living or in the price of materials. Once the community leaders and craftsmen reach an agreement, they consecrate it in an *o'miki* ceremony in which sanctified sake is drunk in front of the community's deities.

The community members' promise to each other and the craftsmen's promise to the community is no ordinary promise. It represents a sacred promise for a sacred task—service for a festival that celebrates the special presence of the deities from the Yasaka Shrine in the community. The community leaders and the contractors promise each other that they will do their best to produce the festival as effectively this year as in the past: *"Kotoshi mo yoroshiku onegai shimas"* ("This year, please do your best again"). The promise is then consecrated with the communal drinking of sanctified sake. The community leader in charge of the festival's organization for that particular year (they take turns), carries a small lacquer-ware table with a silver sake flask and cup. He kneels in front of each member in turn. He then bows and hands the member a cup and pours the sake. The member drinks the sake, returns the empty cup, and bows. The leader then provides him with a snack of dried squid. The member eats part of it, wraps the remainder in Japanese paper, and tucks it into the pocket inside his kimono sleeve, for good luck. The leader moves on to the next person and the next, including the contractors. All participants kneel in the typical Japanese position until the ceremony is completed.

The Craftsmen's Performance

The craftsmen's activities could be roughly divided into four stages: construction, rehearsal, parade, and dismantling. The first stage, the *hokotate*, entails the construction of the *hoko*, the mounting of the ornaments, the attachment of the wheels, and finally the hanging of the tapestries on the *hoko* in preparation for the parade. This entire operation, starting from the bare beams and ropes to the erection of the *hoko* with its sacred pole, is accomplished in three days. The second stage *(hikizome)* involves the rehearsal for the parade on July 13, during which the *hoko* is pulled only a short distance within the neighborhood. Next comes the climax of the festival, the parade on July 17, and finally the dismantling and putting away of the various parts of the *hoko* and treasures in storage for another year.

During the first stage, the carpenters and the assistants construct the skeleton of the *hoko*. They then assemble the *shimbo* from its parts. It consists of a tall pole that is topped by a young pine tree. A small effigy of the deity is attached to the pole. The *shimbo* represents the most sacred section of the *hoko* and is, in fact, a metamorphosis of the original *hoko* into ultimate splendor. Following the mounting of the *shimbo*, the community members assemble around it. They decorate the pole with branches of the *sakaki* tree (a sacred tree used in various Shinto rituals), which are bundled into two large bouquets. Community members and guests each pay homage by tying numerous small pieces of sacred white Japanese paper to the branches, which symbolize the presence of the deities. (Women are also allowed to participate in this ritual.) By the time this task is completed, the branches look as if they were covered with snow. An elderly community member then purifies the pole by scattering salt over it and by pouring sake over the deity's effigy. The *hoko* and its *shimbo* are now ready to stand up.

The chiefs of the carpenters' and assistants' teams pull up the *hoko* to its erect position while the people assembled around the *hoko* watch in awe. This process, requiring delicate balancing, is accomplished with the help of a winch and a metal cable. As the chief carpenter coordinates the pulling, the *hoko* rises slowly. It then rests temporarily suspended at a 45-degree angle to the ground. Then it continues to rise higher and higher, until it stands perpendicular to the ground, soaring three stories high. Community members and bystanders all applaud. The craftsmen then prop the *hoko* with the necessary stabilizers and guards in order to support it in its standing position.

Next, the wheelmen attach the giant wheels to the *hoko* and fasten them with metal screws. They then cover the screws with brass caps, on which the emblem of the *hoko* is engraved on the center of each wheel. They also attach the ropes required for the pulling of the *hoko*, one on each side. After that, the carpenters, the assistants, and the community leaders attach and hang the various ornaments in preparation for the trial run, or *hikizome*.

Hikizome is the rehearsal for the parade, two days before the event, carrying important ritual meaning in its own right. Technically, it is to test whether the *hoko's* operations work smoothly and whether the *hoko's* tower and pine tree will clear the electrical wires overhead. However, *hikizome* also provides an opportunity for the community members and the craftsmen to enter the festival's mood and to anticipate the main celebration yet to come. It is the first chance in the festival's proceedings for the craftsmen to display their accomplishments to the public, although the audience is quite small at that time. During *hikizome*, the craftsmen still wear their work clothes, and the community leaders wear ordinary clothes. Only the main community leader *(chonai kaicho)* is dressed in a formal black kimono. *Hikizome*, unlike the parade on July 17, is truly a community event, in which women and children and old men participate in the pulling that moves the *hoko*. During the parade, however, the *hoko* is pulled by teams of young men (mostly university students who are paid for their services or by volunteers, in some instances).

The musicians, wearing their *yukata* (traditional summer kimono) with their *hoko*'s emblems printed in blue and white, climb into their special space on the top of the *hoko* and start playing the festival's processional music with their flutes, cymbals, and drums. The helpers and carpenters, assisted by community members and children, seize the long ropes and pull the *hoko* as the wheelmen, using metal levers curved at the edge, start prodding the wheels from behind. During *hikizome*, the *hoko* travels only a short distance, at the most one and a half city blocks. Then it is pulled back to its original location.

Most of the neighborhoods in the festival's district have very few, if any, children residing in the area. Numerous children are therefore brought from other neighborhoods by their teachers or parents, especially for *hikizome*. The adults tug on the rope together with the little children, their faces transformed with the pleasure of pulling the *hoko*. *Hikizome* on July 13, much more than the parade four days later, is truly a folk event. In a sense, it *is* the festival.

After *hikizome*, the carpenters and helpers stabilize the *hoko*, prop it up, set the rail guards, and construct the special wooden platforms adjacent to the *hoko*. From these platforms, community members and volunteers will be selling good-luck tokens and various memorabilia during the three days preceding the parade, especially during the evenings. While the carpenters construct the platform, the electrician mounts numerous lanterns strung on ropes like pearls. These illuminate the *hoko* at night with soft, ornamental lights. When walking in the Gion Festival's district at night, I would suddenly see the soft glow of these tapestries of light, like fantasy ships in the night.

Following the successful rehearsal, the wheelmen and carpenters return to their regular jobs. They reappear again in the festival's district at the crack of dawn on July 17, when the preparation for the parade begins. During the three days between *hikizome* and the parade, the *hoko*, adorned with most of its ornaments and hung on its four sides with its ancient tapestries and carpets, stands on display in the center of its neighborhood. Each *hoko* usually stands in front of the community house, where the neighborhood's deities are stationed during the festival. The community members place the statues of the deities on an altar surrounded by the display of the communities' festival treasures, especially the tapestries and carpets that will be hung on the *hoko*. Many of the textiles are too old and too fragile to be carried in the parade, but the public can still enjoy viewing them in the exhibition.

During these last three days before the parade (the days are called Yio-yoi-yoi Yama, Yoi-yoi Yama, and Yoi-Yama) hundreds of thousands of visitors wander from one community to the next to watch the exhibitions of treasures in each *hoko* and *yama* and to buy good-luck tokens braided from bamboo leaves *(chimaki)*, blessed by the priests of the Yasaka (Gion) Shrine, and various other memorabilia. During these three evenings, the traditional musicians play their haunting beat on the upper tier of the *hoko*. Thousands of people walk the short distances from *hoko* to *hoko*. They listen to the lively rhythmical performance of the musicians, climb into the top of the *hoko* through a special stairway, admire the ancient ornaments, and buy the memorabilia and good-luck tokens.

The streets are lined with hundreds of peddlers' carts, selling fast food such as broiled squid, candy, octopus pancakes, sweet-bean cakes, and corn on the cob, along with various trinkets and toys, beetles, goldfish, and ornaments for children's aquariums. The entire district of Yama Hoko Cho takes on the character of a carnival. The climax of these festivities occurs on Yoi-Yama, the night of July 16—the third night, and the last one before the parade. On that evening, the crowds are so thick that the streets connecting the various *hokos*' locations and even Shijo, Kyoto's main wide street, look like a sea of people.

During these three days, the *hokos* and the sales tables are staffed almost completely by community members and volunteers. (In recent years, however, neighborhoods whose population has been depleted are hiring students to help in the sales.) Children dressed in summer kimonos chant songs in unison, inviting the passersby to buy the good-luck tokens. Communities that have no resident children left "borrow" children from other districts in Kyoto in order to keep this ancient atmosphere alive.

The Parade

The climax of the festival also sets the grand stage for the craftsmen's performance. In the early morning, prior to the parade, the carpenters and the assistants mount the final ornaments on the *hoko*, hang the tapestries on its four sides, and prepare it for movement. They then change into their parade outfits: narrow breeches, white *happi* jackets with the symbol of their *hoko* printed on it, and special bands tied around their foreheads. The *oyakata* of the carpenters and his main assistant climb to the top of the *hoko*'s tower, where they sit on the roof during the entire parade, each on one side of the pine tree. Clutching onto the ropes, they issue orders to the conductors *(ondotori)* and to the wheelmen, instructing them when to move and when to stop. From their lofty positions, they also watch the electrical wires overhead and signal to the *ondotori* each time the *hoko* tower is likely to be engaged in the wires.

Six of the carpenters' and helpers' team dress up in the conductors' special *yukata*, adorned with the dramatic designs and symbols of their particular hoko and serve as conductors. Uninformed viewers who see the two *ondotori* in their dramatic kimonos directing the movements of the hoko with their rhythmic and skillful movement of the fans, imagine them to be the highest-ranking community leaders. In reality, they are carpenters and helpers. The two conductors are perched on a narrow platform in front of the *hoko*, directly above the wheels. With one hand, they hold onto a rope, suspended from a canopy above their heads, and with the other, they signal to the wheelmen and the rope pullers, directing their movement. Each *ondotori* holds in one hand a large gilded fan with the *hoko*'s symbol engraved on a silver background on the other side. The silver and gold colors flash in the bright light so that the leader of the procession can see the signal. The *ondotori* move their fans in unison, in incisive and stylized rhythms. As in a Kabuki dance, they signal the *hoko*'s movement and stopping. At the same time, they chant the orders "*Yoi-yoi-ya-ma.*" The wheelmen respond to the instructions and start pushing or stopping the wheels as directed. The *oyakata* of the wheelmen, who walks on the street in the middle in front of the two wheels, transmits the orders to the pullers, who then proceed to pull in synchrony as the wheelmen prod the wheels.

The wheelmen wear narrow black pants and the typical Japanese workmen's black cloth boots and black ornate *happi* jackets with the symbol of their *hoko* imprinted on the back. They flank the wheels on each side, as well as behind and in front of the *hoko*. Except for the *oyakata* of the carpenters, who rides on the very top of the tower, the wheelmen's tasks are the most complicated and dangerous during the parade. They have to push and prod the wheels with great precision or else the *hoko* might roll backward or forward unexpectedly and run over the wheelmen or the community members who march in front of their *hoko* dressed in samurai garb *(kamishimo)*. The chief wheelman has the dangerous task of crawling under the *hoko* between the two front wheels, just as the *hoko* is set in motion, while two or three other wheelmen prod each wheel forward from the side. The chief wheelman jumps out just as the pullers begin to pull the *hoko* forward. The slightest miscalculation in timing could cause him to be run over by the giant carriage.

The parade starts sharply at 9:00 A.M. on the corner of Shijo and Karasuma Streets—the heart of the downtown, and currently Kyoto's main banking center. At 8:50 A.M., Naginata Boko (the most sacred *hoko* that always leads the parade) begins to move backward from its home position to the corner of Shijo and Karasuma Streets. *Ochicosan*, a young boy consecrated as a messenger to the gods, is carried up the ladder to the top of the Naginata Boko. This sacred child is positioned on the top tier of the *hoko* in front of the musicians. He signals the beginning of the parade with his drum. Immediately thereafter, the other *hoko* on Shijo Street begins to move toward Naginata Boko and line up on Shijo Street. Next, the other *hoko* from the side streets each emerge into Shijo street in the order prescribed by the lots that their leaders drew in Kyoto's City Hall on July 2. The order of the *hoko* and the *yama* in the procession changes every year in accordance with the lots, except for Naginata Boko, which always goes first, and for several other hoko, which for historic reasons have a fixed place in the parade. Once all the *hoko* and *yama* are lined up on Shijo Street, the procession begins.

The *yama* and the *hoko* advance on Shijo Street, which is lined with spectators on both sides, until they reach the checkpoint for *kuji aratame* (the "inspection of lots"). At that point, Kyoto's mayor, dressed in the purple robe and tall hat of a historic nobleman, and various dignitaries sit on a platform erected specially for the ceremony. When each *yama* or *hoko* nears the mayor's station, it stops and awaits its turn. Three community leaders of the first hoko march forward in a line. Two deliver to the mayor's assistant a bunch of the good-luck tokens that had been blessed for that *hoko*. The chief community leader steps into position facing the mayor, who stands under a parasol.

The community leader, dressed in samurai garb and following the stylized steps and arm movements of a Kabuki dance, thrusts the lacquer box containing the certificate, which affirms this *hoko*'s or *yama*'s place in the order of the parade, toward the mayor's face. The mayor reads the certificate aloud and grants the *hoko* permission to move on. The community leader then displays his acrobatic skill—waving the handle of his fan, he ties the silk string around the lacquer box containing the certificate. He bows to the mayor and then has to face his community representatives and *yama* or *hoko*. Again, with the movements of a Kabuki dance, he waves his fan to signal to the head wheelman to move forward. The next *hoko* arrives, and so on, until all *yama* and *hoko* have passed the mayor. *Kuji aratame* is one of the most media-attractive events in the parade. Television and press cameramen swarm at this station. The community leaders as well as the craftsmen, conscious of the broad coverage, display their skills and magnificent costumes to millions of viewers.

The most important test for the craftsmen and the most dramatic opportunity for displaying their skill occurs, however, at the two points where the *hoko* has to turn the corner to the next street: one on the corner of Shijo and Kawaramachi Streets, about one-third of the way through the parade, and again on the corner of Oike and Shinmachi Streets, just before the end of the parade, when all the *hoko* and *yama* go down narrow Shinmachi Street back to their home neighborhoods.

The turning of the corners (*tsujimawashi*) on those two occasions requires the greatest concentration, skill, and fine coordination among the carpenters, helpers, pullers, and wheelmen. The slightest error in turning can cause the *hoko* to lose its balance and topple over. Each *hoko* carries on its top about forty musicians, most of whom are young children and teenagers. The success of this operation rests on the coordination of all groups of craftsmen involved, but it depends most definitely on the wheelmen. The turning of the wheels around the corners is accomplished by using the ancient technique of wet bamboo slats. As the *hoko* reaches the intersection, it stops. The wheelmen line up the bamboo slats on the pavement in the direction toward which the *hoko* is expected to turn. They then pour water over the polished bamboo, so that the wheels can slide over it. Next, the master carpenter on the roof issues instructions to the *ondotori*. They, in turn, signal with their fans to the master wheelman, and he orders the wheelmen to turn. The wheelmen, with their feet planted firmly on the pavement and their palms pressed against the side of the wheel, push the wheel; simultaneously, the pullers rush across to the opposite corner and pull the ropes in the direction the *hoko* is to turn.

The wheels slide over the wet bamboo slats, and the *hoko* turns the corner. Usually the hoko is led only by two *ondotori*, but because of the formidable task of turning, their number doubles during this operation. While the *hoko* is waiting to be turned, the musicians play merrily the most rhythmical pieces of the festival's music. During the turning, the musicians stop their music and beat the drums only, as thousands of viewers lined up behind the ropes hold their breath. At the moment of turning, even the drums stop; the only audible sound is that of the *ondotori* chanting their orders rhythmically to the wheelmen and rope pullers and the creaking of the wheels as the *hoko* turns. Once the turning is accomplished, the musicians resume their music and the *hoko* is on its way. The energetic but controlled thrust of the wheelmen against each giant wheel of the *hoko* has become one of the most popular photographic poses of the Gion Festival. "I only wish that sometimes they would take the picture of our faces," said the *oyakata* of the wheelmen of one of the *hoko*. "They always take our picture from behind."

The first *hoko*, Naginata Boko, reaches the corner of Oike and Shinmachi Streets by approximately 11:30 A.M. From there, it takes about another hour and a half until the *hoko* returns to home base. "For us there are really two parades," said one of the craftsmen. "The real parade is on Shijo Street; there we do everything carefully and in style. The second parade is on Kawaramachi and Oike (the two main streets lined with seats for the tourists). There we just take it easy and get it over with."

Following the brief lunch rest, each *hoko* moves toward the street corner awaiting its moment for turning. As the *hoko* moves down narrow Shinmachi Street, one can have a glimpse of the festival's historic atmosphere that has been lost on the wide streets. On Shinmachi Street, there is hardly any space between the *hoko* and the doorways to the houses on each side.

From their second-floor windows, the residents hand out beer and juice cans to the musicians on the second tier of the *hoko* and receive in return *chimaki*—the good-luck tokens that are hung on door handles to protect one's house from evil. By the time the last *hoko* turns down Shinmachi Street around 2:30 P.M., most of the community members and craftsmen have marched and exerted their efforts on Kyoto's hot streets for about four to five hours. The craftsmen started three hours earlier, and their tasks are not yet finished. The task of dismantling the *hoko* is still ahead of them.

Dismantling

Despite the exhausting march in Kyoto's humid heat, no one rushes to dismantle the *hoko* immediately upon its return to its home neighborhood. Elated by a sense of accomplishment and saddened by the realization that the *hoko* is about to vanish for another year, the craftsmen slow down the *hoko* as it reaches its home street. Community members who did not participate in the parade, especially women, children, and older people, applaud the *hoko* when it arrives: "*Gokurisama! Gokurisama!*" ("You did a great job!") The wheelmen and pullers now move the *hoko* up and down the block, as they did during *hikizome*, and the musicians play with renewed energy. Gradually, the *hoko* comes to a stop. Despite the arduous task accomplished, no one seems to be in a hurry to stop. The musicians continue to play for the benefit of their community members. Finally, the music stops, and the last beat of the drums and cymbals echoes in the quiet street (no traffic is permitted yet on the street). The musicians climb down the steep ladder. Everybody on the street welcomes the musicians and the community members and the craftsmen who have returned from the parade. The women hand them cups of cold green tea. After the public performance in the parade, the community now has its private celebration.

The festival is successfully over—and "Thanks to the shadow of the gods, no one was hurt!" Everyone voices their sense of relief and satisfaction with the year's accomplishment. The community members unburden themselves of their samurai hats, and the wives rush to sort the mushroomlike hats and the straw sandals to pack them in preparation for next year. The community members and the musicians go to the traditional restaurant on their street or to the community hall to have their communal lunch and cold beer first, while the craftsmen embark on their next arduous task—the dismantling.

First, they take down the statues of the gods and carry them into the nearby community member's house, designated as a temporary shelter for the gods. The gods stay there until the next day, when they are un-

dressed and they and their costumes are safely tucked away into the cam-
phor-wood boxes and stored for another year. After that, the craftsmen
strip the *hoko* of its finery—the carved wood, gilded metal, and lacquerware ornaments and the magnificent tapestries. Some of the community
members assist the craftsmen by receiving these parts and storing them
temporarily on the elevated floors of the nearby houses or stores, in
preparation for packing.

Next, the wheelmen remove the wheels and with the help of a crane,
they hoist the wheels onto a truck and drive them to the municipal warehouse, where they are stored until next year. Kyoto's municipal government has built a special complex of warehouses that look like mau-
soleums with their giant safe-type iron doors for the storage of the *hoko*
and *yama* parts and for all the festival's treasures. Each community has
one warehouse in this complex in Maruyama Park. In the next step, the
carpenters and the helpers dismantle the *hoko's* roof, which consists of
finely carved wooden lintels and magnificent hand-painted lacquer panels. Community members, including women, help put these treasures in
the temporary shelter until the next day.

At this stage, it is almost 4:00 P.M. The community members emerge
from the dining hall, slightly swaying from the long exertion and the beer.
The craftsmen, followed by the wheelmen, enter for their meal and cold
beer. (This is their first meal since 7:00 A.M. In 1989, the festival's Central
Committee banned the eating of boxed lunches during the parade.) After
the meal, the wheelmen return home, but the carpenters and their helpers
still continue the festival's labor. If the weather is good and no rain is fore-
cast, they cover what is left of the *hoko* and return to their homes until the
next morning. If the weather is bad or there is a possible threat of rain,
they stay into the evening and continue to dismantle the *hoko*, until only
its skeleton is left.

Early the next morning, the carpenters and the assistants return to the
hoko site. They complete the dismantling while the community members,
men and women, dust off each piece of wood, polish the lacquerware and
the added panels, and remove the smudges from the tapestries and other
textiles. They then wrap each piece for its designated wooden box and
prepare it for the municipal warehouse.

Meanwhile, the carpenters and helpers disassemble the *hoko*. They cut
down the young pine tree that was the crowning glory on the *hoko's* roof.
Next, they slash the rope work that they had knotted so painstakingly
during the construction. Anyone walking through the Yama Hoko Cho
district between 11:00 A.M. and 12:00 A.M. on July 18 can see piles of cut
rope on the pavement surrounding remaining beams of the *hoko*. The
heavy beams are the last ones to be transported on the truck to the municipal warehouse. The craftsmen complete their work, put away the last

pieces, and change their clothes. They submit their bills to the community leader and go off to lunch together.

On July 19, however, the *oyakata* of the craftsmen and wheelmen meet again with the community members for their final celebration. The *uchiage*, or final party, sometimes nicknamed *ashi arai* (literally "washing your feet"), takes place in a famous traditional Japanese restaurant. On that occasion, the beer and sake flow from "bottomless" containers and the meal is lavish. (Prior to the festival, each *hoko* amasses a huge number of sake bottles that are donated by various individuals and companies and are dedicated to the gods. The sake is consecrated during the festival and is drunk during that final party in order to "make the gods happy.") During the party, the men enjoy the company of *maico* (young geishas), something the craftsmen could never afford today in their own circles. The craftsmen thus consider the party a much higher reward than the modest financial compensation they receive from the community.

The Festival's Pillars

Ennoshitano chikaramochi is a Japanese expression that has no precise counterpart in English. It means the "power from below that upholds a house, an institution, or the entire society." The craftsmen who construct, maintain, support, and move the giant floats of the Gion Festival in Kyoto are often perceived as "the power from below." Their contribution is indispensable to the production and effective performance and maintenance of this festival. Who are the craftsmen of the Gion Festival? Most of them do not reside in Kyoto City, and none of them reside within the Gion Festival's district, Yama Hoko Cho. They are recruited from the suburbs and villages in the periphery of Kyoto. Many of them are engaged as construction workers on high-rise buildings *(tobishoku)* and travel around in Western Japan from one construction site to the next. Others are carpenters, metalworkers, farmers, factory workers, and self-employed craftsmen. Some of them work together year round in the same carpentry team and under the same *oyakata* as during the festival. But the majority see each other only once a year, when they meet for the beginning of the festival's work. "We are like Tanabata" (the two legendary stars that meet only once a year; they had once been lovers on earth but after their transformation into stars, they meet on each July 7, the first day of the preparations), said one of the carpenters. "Our paths cross only once a year during the Gion Festival."

For many of the craftsmen, the Gion Festival thus provides a special form of continuity and permanence. The same team members meet once a year for the festival. During my five years of study of this festival, I have met the same craftsmen each year. (By my fifth appearance on July 1, they had also come to view me as a permanent participant, as one on whom they could count for the annual reunion.) The community leaders do not maintain any contact with the craftsmen and their *oyakata* during the year. "We do not know his address," said one community leader about the *oyakata*. "He will show up for the Kippuiri on July 1, just the same as for the past twenty years."

Some of the craftsmen who are now in their sixties or seventies have been working for the festival for forty or fifty years. Many are second or third generation in the same family, serving the same *hoko*. Most of them have learned the festival's traditional skills from their fathers or uncles or from their fathers' friends. The younger members of the teams active in the festival today are still learning from their older relatives. Mr. Aotani— the *oyakata* of the carpenters and the helpers in Iwato Yama, a *hoko* south of Shijo Street—is second generation in that capacity. His father had been the *oyakata* for the same *hoko* until his death. Aotani had accompanied his father in the festival's work since his childhood and apprenticed with his father in his youth. He learned the festival's skills from his father along with his ordinary carpentry skills. Now Aotani leads the carpenters' and helpers' teams for the same community and also employs his own son and nephew.

Aotani's wife recalled an incident concerning Aotani's mother, when his father was serving as *oyakata* for Iwato Yama in his time. The senior Mrs. Aotani was appalled that her husband was riding on the top of the *hoko* during the parade. That meant that he rode higher than the deities (whose statues were immediately under the roof on which he was sitting). Mrs. Aotani dealt with the problem by preparing each year a completely new set of clothes for her husband, including underwear and socks, to be worn during the parade only, so that he would be pure when he was close to the gods. The current Mrs. Aotani continues to follow the same practice. "I do my best," she said, "and if an accident happens, at least I know I did all I could."

The *oyakata* of the wheelmen for the same community, Mr. Wada, now in his early fifties, is the oldest son in his family. His grandfather was the first generation in his family to work for Iwato Yama. Wada lives in Shiga prefecture, one hour's drive by car from Kyoto. He is the contractor of a team of highly skilled plasterers, who construct and repair the walls of the traditional gardens, homes, and temples, including the Imperial Palace in Kyoto. The team consists of Wada, his three brothers, and his two sons. During the festival, Wada, along with one brother and his two sons, works on the wheelmen's team for the community of Iwato Yama. Two other brothers work for Tzuki Boko—four blocks away, on Shijo Street.

When the Tzuki Boko team experiences difficulties, Wada runs over to Shijo Street and advises his brothers; conversely, when Wada is short-handed, his brothers come over to help him. Usually, only Wada's oldest son worked in the festival. In 1989, Wada initiated his younger son (twenty years old) to the festival's work. Wada introduced the shy young man to me with great pride. He told me that his wife, anxious over her younger son's exposure to danger, made his costume with her own hands rather than have him borrow one of his brothers' or uncles' costumes. This was in order "to please the gods." During the parade, the young man assisted the wheelmen by handing them tools and by carrying bamboo slats and water. He was not yet allowed near or under the wheels.

The *oyakata* for the carpenters and helpers at Kanko Boko, Mr. Nakamura, in his late fifties, works normally as a construction worker. An orphan since his early teens, Nakamura was "adopted" by Mr. Sugiyama, the chief *oyakata* for Kanko Boko, and was trained by him in ordinary construction and carpentry work. Sugiyama also trained him in the festival's work, and since then, they have been working together for Kanko Boko. Sugiyama claims that Nakamura was a juvenile delinquent in his teens and was tempted to join a gang. His initiation into the work gave Nakamura a sense of continuity and permanence. The commitment he formed toward the festival then led him to embark on a more regular work life on Sugiyama's construction team. Last year, Nakamura introduced two of his sons to the carpenters' team. Now all three work together, and Sugiyama is grooming Nakamura as his successor as chief *oyakata* for Kanko Boko.

Even the other members of the teams who are not related to each other or to the *oyakata* through kinship ties have known each other for many years through their regular jobs or by living in the same neighborhood. The festival's work has placed them in a strong in-group relationship—in a symbolic community that is reconstituted without fail each year, once the festival's work begins. The festival's work provides the craftsmen with a special community that transcends the boundaries of neighborhood, territory, and status. Many of the older craftsmen and the community members have known each other's fathers and have known each other as young men. "We have watched each other grow older year after year."

A sense of continuity is not only an important factor in the craftsman's satisfaction and motivation but is also the key to the festival's survival. The initiation of young men into the festival's work and the transmission of skills to the next generation is one of the main concerns of the festival's older craftsmen, especially the *oyakata*. Those who are unable to recruit their own sons or who have no sons or nephews encourage unrelated but promising young men to join. "It was after the war [World War II], and life was still very dull around here. We were living here in the countryside and we were looking for some entertainment in the city," recalled Mr. Kida, *oyakata* of the wheelmen of Kanko Boko:

At that time they revived the Gion Festival for the first time since the war. My former classmate told me that he is helping an old man with the wheels of Kanko Boko. He said it was fun and it gives you a chance for entertainment in the city. I went along and I started to learn from him. Here I am, still doing it. But nowadays it is difficult to interest young men in this kind of work. They now earn enough and they can go on their own into the city and play around as much as they like.

Kida has no sons. After the old wheelmaster who trained him died, Kida started recruiting young men from his own village. Mr. Yamamoto, now in his early forties, was trained by Kida in this manner and is second in command. The wheelmen's most intricate work during the turning of the street corners now rests primarily on Yamamoto, a slender, short man with enormous strength and the agility and the grace of a ballet dancer.

The older craftsmen and the *oyakata* have few incentives to offer to the young men whom they recruit, other than sociability and the chance to perform in public. The sense of loyalty and the religious devotion, which are important to the older men, are less appealing to the younger ones. Perhaps the greatest incentive for the younger men is the speeding up of the training period, so that they will have a chance to perform in public during the parade.

Traditionally, apprenticeship in Japan took a long period out of a young man's life, during which he had to perform only menial tasks while learning from the master by observation or osmosis. Since the rapid modernization following World War II, the apprenticeship process has been accelerated in all areas, except in the very traditional crafts such as weaving and the potteries. In the Gion Festivals' teams, the older men teach their young recruits with great dedication and care. They enable them to try to perform on their own within a short period after their initial training. They teach young carpenters and helpers the complicated conductor's (*ondotori*) movements and chants, so that the young men will have the more glamorous role of wearing flamboyant costumes and performing on the *hoko* during the parade.

Two young men who trained for this role in early July were allowed to perform as *ondotori* while the *hoko* moved on Oike Street. "We are giving the younger men a chance this year," said one of the middle-aged *ondotori* who was walking on the street behind the *hoko*.

Of course, we wouldn't let them do it on Shijo Street [where the more solemn and formal part of the parade takes place]. It is a good chance for them. After we turned the corner to Oike Street, we handed the fans over to them, and said, "You do it, now." We are walking behind the *hoko* so that the young men wouldn't feel that we are looking over their shoulders. But Mr. Nomura is there watching from the corner of his eye in case there is any trouble.

The following year, the two young men were allowed to be *ondotori* during the turning of the street corner—when four *ondotori* were leading together, along with their veteran teachers. After the parade, the *oyakata* of the carpenters of that particular *hoko* asked me if I would send him copies of the pictures of the young men performing as *ondotori*. He made it a special point to request the pictures of the young men, even though he was aware of my habit of sending him every year multiple prints of the pictures of his team members' work, which I took on various occasions of the festival.

The Power of Knowledge

Sugiyama, Nakamura, Aotani, and Wada, and their many colleagues in other *hoko*, carry the keys of the survival of the Gion Festival. In their knowledge of the traditional skills also lies their sense of confidence, which allows them to rise beyond the confines of their class in modern Japanese society. Their special knowledge and skills are disappearing rapidly from modern Japan, as are other traditional crafts.

Most of the technical knowledge needed for the Gion Festival is based on the oral tradition. There are, of course, historic documents describing various organizational or traditional aspects of the festival, but there are no technical manuals illustrating the details of construction, manipulation, and movement. Some of the older *oyakata*, such as Mr. Sugiyama, have developed their own manuals and diagrams consisting of informal notes that they modify and revise over the years. But there is no standard manual offering systematic guidelines. All the training of new apprentices takes place through observation and personal explanation. Prior to World War II, the community leaders themselves carried a good deal of the knowledge about the construction, decoration, and movement of the *hoko*, as well as knowledge of the history, symbolism, and rituals of the festival, as part of an oral tradition. This knowledge has diminished considerably because of the erosion of the original communities in Yama Hoko Cho.

In every community, however, there are still some old men who carry on the oral tradition. These men work together with the master craftsmen and share their knowledge. In the Kanko Boko neighborhood, on Shijo Street for example, where not even one original dwelling or shop has survived, five old men, former residents of this community, return every year from the suburbs and cooperate with Mr. Sugiyama, the *oyakata*, with whom they have worked for over forty years. They pool their knowledge and offer him advice; but they always accept his decision on all technical matters as the final word.

Sugiyama and the other *oyakata*, who carry the vanishing skills and knowledge required for maintaining this festival, exert special influence within the Yamahoko district—an influence and respect that transcend the usual status in Kyoto society. Some of the *oyakata* stretch this power by trying to control various ceremonies connected with the festival that are not central to the construction or maintenance of the *hoko*. Mr. T., for example, the *oyakata* for one of the major *hoko*, expects complete submission from all the craftsmen under his command. He also gives orders to the community members and leaders who carry out supportive and ceremonial tasks. Some of these members are the wealthiest men and heads of the most prestigious shops and families in Kyoto. Mr. T. also dictates to the firemen when they should visit the *hoko*'s exhibition space for inspection and sometimes keeps the priest from the Yasaka Shrine waiting on the street while decoration of the *hoko* is in progress. In daily life, Mr. T., a building contractor, would never have had a chance to give orders to the leaders of this *hoko* and would have had virtually no social contact with them. Mr. T. has also become a favorite media subject. His face frequently appears in the newspapers and on television as the man who "single-handedly carries the burden of that *hoko*."

Other *oyakata*, such as Sugiyama, Kida, Aotani, and Wada, are more modest in their exercise of power. They use their knowledge and skills as a resource to be shared with the community leaders rather than as an instrument of self-aggrandizement. The community members collaborate with them and adhere to their judgment, especially on matters of safety and efficiency. One of the remarkable characteristics of the work procedures of these craftsmen and the community members is their style of collaboration and communication. An outsider approaching a *hoko* during its construction process could distinguish the craftsmen from the community members mostly by the fact that the craftsmen are wearing helmets ("hard hats") and baggy pants, with the tight leggings and boots characteristic of the construction trade. Otherwise, it would be difficult to tell apart the wealthy kimono wholesaler from the construction worker, as they work side by side. The *oyakata* stands or sits next to the work area and supervises every activity. However, one rarely hears an *oyakata* or a community leader utter direct orders or instructions. Most of the work is carried out implicitly, based on mutual understanding of the tasks and procedures. New workers or volunteers watch carefully until they find their own tasks.

Most of the exercise of power by the traditional craftsmen is subtle but firm. Whereas the younger craftsmen enjoy the opportunity to display their power and prowess, the older ones enjoy their special role in providing the continuity necessary for keeping the festival alive, despite the hazards of modernization and the pressures of bureaucracy. For these older craftsmen, the chance to serve in the festival also fulfills an important religious function: It is their opportunity to serve the gods.

Discussion

The Gion Festival thus provides the rare opportunity of witnessing the temporary status reversal brought about by the special needs and challenges that the community members encounter in producing and maintaining the festival. The transformation of the traditional Yama Hoko Cho neighborhoods into a district of banking and business companies and the accompanying depletion of the neighborhoods of their former residents and small shops has made the community members who still reside in this area dependent on the service of craftsmen from outside the district.

The community members who produce the festival once a year are "modern" men and women, people who work and live in modern settings and who utilize modern technology (cars, telephones, electricity, for example), even for the festival's work, whenever possible. The festival's organization and events are timed precisely by modern schedules and comply with the rules of contemporary bureaucracies, such as the municipal, prefectural, and national government, insurance regulations, and police.

To the uninformed eye, the relationship between the craftsmen and the community members could be considered an ordinary form of subcontracting in normal business relations. In such terms, it would mean that the community members hired the craftsmen to perform a certain job on an annual basis, in exchange for pay. Their relationship would not be different from that of other organizations or individuals who contract with craftsmen directly or with an *oyakata* for certain services. In reality, however, the relationship between the craftsmen and the community members is of a highly symbolic nature. It is deeply intertwined with the festival's rituals, with labor for the gods, and with the symbolic community that emerges during the festival and recreates itself each year. Once a year, the craftsmen identify with the festival's community, in which they achieve symbolic membership and status (Turner, 1969). They become part of this community by different means than the ordinary membership in an urban neighborhood *(chonai)* in Japan; they achieve temporary membership through work and participation in the festival's effort.

The craftsmen who work in the Gion Festival are not, however, fossils from another age. They are "modern men" who function under the constraints of the streamlined world of work and the bureaucratized society of modern Japan. They employ their traditional skills as a means of counteracting, at least temporarily, the larger processes of modernization and bureaucratization. Through their work in the festival, they express their identities as traditional craftsmen with special skills.

12

Divorce, Chinese Style

The Case of Zhenhua and Shuqin

Zhenhua and Shuqin were sitting on opposite sides of the aisle, their backs to the audience, facing a long empty table. Shuqin was fiddling with a piece of paper—her marriage certificate. She was suing Zhenhua for divorce. One September day, Shuqin had taken her clothes and her quilt and, with her sister's help, had moved out of her husband's family home. Now, two years later, her case was about to be heard in the Hongkou People's District Court in Shanghai, one of thousands of local courts of this type. A slight twenty-eight-year-old woman with short black hair, Shuqin worked as a statistician in a government office. She came to court wearing beige slacks and a patterned blouse. Zhenhua, Shuqin's slim, tall, thirty-one-year-old husband, worked as a laborer on Shanghai's waterfront. Wearing khaki pants and a blue cotton Mao jacket, he sat slouching forward, as if folded into himself. On the floor next to him rested a thick black plastic bag with two handles, of the type that men all over China carry with them.

Noise generally fills public places in China, but the austere courtroom of the Hongkou ("Mouth of the Rainbow") district was silent. The leaders of the couple's neighborhood committee sat along the wall to the right of the official table. Representatives of their work units sat along the opposite wall. Three judges entered. The scales of justice were embroidered in gold on their military hats and the epaulets of their dark-gray cotton uniforms.

The judges positioned themselves behind the table, facing the couple. Almost in unison, they took off their hats and placed them on the table in a neat row, each hat in front of its owner, with the visor and the emblem facing the public. First, the chief judge, a woman in her fifties, sat down. A somewhat younger male judge took his place on her right, and a female

---

*This chapter first appeared as "Divorce, Chinese Style," *Atlantic Monthly* (April, 1987).

judge in her late twenties sat on the chief judge's left. The trial was ready to begin.

The judges' theatrical entrance underscored the solemnity of the divorce proceedings and the importance attached to them in the People's Republic of China. Divorce was effectively made legal in China by the Marriage Law of 1950, which was designed to liberate men and women from forced marriages and to provide relief for women being abused by their husbands and in-laws. The law was passed one year after the Communists came to power, and since then, about 70 percent of divorce petitions have been filed by women. In 1953, the number of divorces granted reached a record 1.17 million. The number fell dramatically during the Cultural Revolution, but following the introduction in 1981 of a new marriage law, it has been rising again. The new law, for the first time in Chinese history, recognizes alienation of affection as grounds for divorce (providing that mediation has failed). By 1984, when I carried out this research, about 500,000 divorces had been granted each year since the new law went into effect—still a relatively small number when considered in proportion to the population, which is 1 billion. (In the United States, which had a population of 240 million in 1984, there were around 1.2 million divorces each year.) Despite the unprecedented liberality of the new law, divorce proceedings remain arduous. The drawn-out mediation process and the constant pressures to which a couple is subjected by local leaders and the courts are in themselves sufficient to discourage many couples from considering divorce.

The integrity of the family is a cornerstone of Chinese social policy. "Society and family in China depend on each other like a larger river on a little one," a leading authority on Chinese family law told me recently. "When the little rivers are full of water, the large river is also full. When the little rivers are polluted, they also pollute the larger one." In the case of Zhenhua and Shuqin, and in another recent case that I was given the rare privilege of observing, the court hearings illuminated Chinese family and community life, caught as it is between the forces of individualism and those of community, during a period of rapid social change.

The chief judge opened the proceedings with an announcement that the judges, along with the neighborhood-committee leaders and the work-unit representatives, had done all they could to mediate and bring about a reconciliation. But they had failed. The judges had worked closely with the local leaders, and the chief judge certified that she and her colleagues were familiar with all the details of the case.

The chief judge asked Shuqin why she wanted a divorce. Shuqin told her story: When she and Zhenhua met, they were both very poor. Zhenhua had just returned from forced labor in the countryside. They were introduced by a go-between and fell in love. After a yearlong courtship,

Zhenhua and Shuqin were married, in April 1981, and Shuqin moved into Zhenhua's crowded household, which included his parents and four sisters. Since their marriage, Shuqin said, she had tried to get along with her husband, but they had experienced numerous "contradictions." She said that she had repeatedly asked the leaders of her work unit and the neighborhood committee for help but that she had been unsuccessful in resolving the contradictions between herself and Zhenhua.

The judges explored the nature of these contradictions by questioning both Shuqin and Zhenhua. The first conflicts had occurred over the wedding itself. Zhenhua wanted a simple wedding, but Shuqin wanted to invite many friends to a large dinner, according to the current fashion. Shuqin had her way, but as a result they had to borrow 1,000 yuan (ten times the average laborer's monthly wage) from one of Zhenhua's sisters to pay for the dinner. After their marriage, Zhenhua used his wages to repay the debt, but Shuqin kept her own pay. The fact that Shuqin did not contribute her wages to the common kitty became a sore point with the family, especially since she gave ten yuan a month to her mother, despite Zhenhua's insistence that she give only five yuan.

Next, the judge brought up the matter of an abortion that Shuqin had had and asked Shuqin to tell the court about it. Her voice trembling with embarrassment, Shuqin said that she had gotten pregnant by Zhenhua before their marriage. In China, premarital sex is still considered a serious transgression, and until several years ago, it was severely punished. After her marriage, Shuqin wanted to get an abortion. Although his mother approved of it, Zhenhua objected. Shuqin went ahead anyway. Zhenhua never forgave her. But the abortion was not the cause of their estrangement, Shuqin insisted.

The fight that precipitated the breakup of the marriage resulted from Shuqin's struggle to maintain some privacy in her husband's home. Privacy is rare in China, not only because of overcrowding but also because of the traditional Chinese view that individual lives do not exist separately from the life of the community. Shuqin and Zhenhua, like the majority of other Shanghai residents, lived in cramped quarters. Many couples actually postpone marriage because they cannot find a room of their own. The Hongkou district, once the "concession" area controlled by the Japanese, is one of the most densely populated in Shanghai. In its narrow alleys, old Japanese wooden houses and dilapidated European stucco mansions, now subdivided into multiple dwellings, stand side by side with mammoth tenements and small shacks. Several unrelated families often share the same kitchen, which may consist of little more than a stove and a wok. They may also share a toilet and a water faucet in the common entry hall. Bathing is often done at public baths or at the place of work. In warm weather, family life spills out onto the sidewalks and into the alleys. People bring out small stoves, tables, chairs, and cots. They cook and eat out-side, play with their children, sew, and do repair work, all in close proximity. Under these conditions, family fights can hardly remain private.

Zhenhua and Shuqin began by quarreling over the television several months after their wedding. One evening, much to Zhenhua's chagrin, Shuqin locked the door to their room in order to keep his oldest sister out. The sister, who had been accustomed to sewing and watching television in that room, continued to do so after their marriage. Shuqin requested that she stop using the room because she habitually "left it in a mess." The sister threatened to take "her" TV away. Shuqin insisted that the TV stay, believing that Zhenhua owned it. The sister claimed that the TV was her own. Shuqin kept asking her husband who really owned the TV, but he never responded. As long as it was not clear who owned it, Shuqin said, she would not part with it.

Watching TV is almost the only form of entertainment available to a typical family in China. Until recently, the TV was the star of the "three technologies," its supporting cast being the electric fan and the radio-tape deck. (The brightest stars now are the washing machine and the refrigerator.) A TV is still considered so precious that in most households it is clad in an embroidered velvet or silk cover when not in use.

The argument escalated. One evening, Zhenhua's sister came home, pounded on the table, and shouted at Shuqin, "If you don't like to stay here, you can go back to your parents!" Neighbors rushed in "to help." Shuqin's mother and sister, who lived down the block, also came to her rescue. Several days later, Shuqin hid the TV. After Zhenhua found it, Shuqin hid its plug. When Zhenhua found the plug, Shuqin hid the activating button. Zhenhua asked for the button four times, but Shuqin refused to give it to him. Zhenhua openly sided with his family.

The next day, Shuqin's mother-in-law gave her two months' worth of food coupons: She was being expelled. Food coupons are given to each registered family, or *hukou*, for the purchase of subsidized rice and grain. After Shuqin joined her husband's family, her registration was changed to *hukou*. Giving the coupons to Shuqin meant: "Go away and do your own cooking." Shuqin sought the help of the neighborhood leaders. On their advice, she returned to her mother-in-law and said, "If you want me to do the cooking by myself, give me the coupons for two persons, and I'll cook for my husband." Her mother-in-law said nothing. When Zhenhua returned from work, Shuqin gave him her coupons and said, "You should take a stand." But Zhenhua kept silent.

Next, Zhenhua's mother and sister came into Shuqin's room and scolded her for not contributing her wages and for wanting to borrow money in order to buy a wedding present for her sister. They used "dirty words" and ordered her to leave. Shuqin rushed to Zhenhua's workplace and told him that his mother and sister had ordered her out of the house. Zhenhua said nothing. That evening, Shuqin's father came to see Zhenhua. He asked Zhenhua why he and his daughter were quarreling. Again Zhenhua was silent. Shuqin's father reaffirmed that he was not responsible for his daughter anymore. He told Zhenhua that when he had permitted Shuqin to eat at his home occasionally, he had been unaware of the couple's conflicts. "Now that I know you have a quarrel, I will not allow my daughter to eat in my house anymore." But despite her father's seeming resolve, the following day Shuqin moved back to her parents' home.

"Your conflict was with your husband's family, not with your husband," the chief judge said to Shuqin. "Why did you leave him?"

"Because my husband did not make an effort to solve the contradictions," Shuqin said.

The male judge, reminding Shuqin that her family consisted of *two* persons, asked, "Why did you leave if your husband did not want you to?"

Shuqin said that she knew Zhenhua did not want her to leave but that she had no choice. "Because my husband's family ordered me to," she said.

There were discrepancies between Zhenhua's and Shuqin's testimony that made it impossible to determine how persistent Zhenhua had really been in trying to get Shuqin back.

"Your husband wanted you back, so he came to your workplace and to your home at night," the male judge said. "Your husband did not completely sit with folded arms. Why did you not return after he asked you to?"

Shuqin replied that in fact Zhenhua was sitting with folded arms. During the quarrels, she had told Zhenhua in tears: "Your family has a quarrel with me. You should not sit with folded arms. If I was mistaken, you should criticize me, or if they are wrong, you should tell them."

Zhenhua told the court that on the advice of the neighborhood leaders, he took a gift to Shuqin's family during the midautumn festival. He and the leaders arrived at her home around 8:00 P.M. Shuqin's father was not there, and Shuqin was asleep. Zhenhua said: "I want to take my wife home. I have nothing to do with her parents." But the leaders advised him that given the late hour, he should try another time. After that, Zhenhua and Shuqin met for two hours at the Huangpu River Park. On Sundays and summer evenings, the park teems with young couples. Several couples share each bench and seek to maintain a discreet distance from one another. According to Zhenhua, Shuqin asked him whether she could return to his home, and he said yes. But Zhenhua recounted that she never came. Zhenhua and Shuqin did not meet again for two years.

Finally, the judges tried to pin Zhenhua down as to who actually owned the TV. After many evasive replies, Zhenhua admitted that his sis-

ter had bought the TV with her own money. The chief judge now held
Zhenhua responsible for the escalation of the fighting because he had
kept the truth from his wife.

The judges indicated that the time for their decision had arrived. The
chief judge asked Shuqin whether she wanted a divorce.

"Yes," Shuqin said.

"You have lived apart for two years," the chief judge said. "Can you
still be reconciled?"

"No," Shuqin said. She said she had attempted a reconciliation for a
long time. The work unit and the neighborhood leaders had also tried
their best. But Zhenhua was "cold-blooded." While insisting that she admit her mistakes, he refused to take a stand on his family's conduct.
Bursting into tears, Shuqin told the court that when her father-in-law
died—this had happened about a year earlier—she had asked Zhenhua's
permission to return, but Zhenhua's family refused. She had even asked
the leaders of Zhenhua's work unit to intercede on her behalf. But his relatives stood firm. They blamed Zhenhua's father's death on Shuqin and
said that his last words were not to let her come back.

Did Shuqin still wish to be reconciled? the judge asked again. "No," she
replied in a tearful voice. The judge then addressed the same question to
Zhenhua. In his evasive style, Zhenhua said that they had lived apart for
two years and some months. "Do you still have feelings?" asked the
judge. There was no basis left for the marriage, Zhenhua replied; the feelings were lost.

In their testimony, the leaders of the neighborhood committee and the
work units confirmed that all hope was gone. They had done everything
they could but all mediation routes were exhausted. The role that the
neighborhood committees and the work units play in the court is an extension of their function as moral guardians and mediators in the community. They implement government policy in the workplace, neighborhood, and family. The work-unit committee registers marriages, provides
some housing, and distributes food coupons and contraceptives. The
neighborhood committee, consisting primarily of retired workers, mostly
women, serves without pay. It enforces birth-control policy and investi-
gates disputes among neighbors and within families. Both committees
mediate cases and bring them to court as a last resort.

This type of mediation, which has its origins in ancient Chinese practice, is frequently used in China to settle disputes. In 1983, 7 million domestic disputes of various kinds were settled through mediation by local
committees. The committees wield considerable power over people's
lives in cases of internal family quarrels, adultery, and pregnancy. Since
people cannot change jobs and housing on their own initiative, falling out
of grace with committee leaders is tantamount to being ostracized. The

committees can intervene, unsolicited. They "persuade" people through persistent moral pressure and public shaming. During a visit to a neighborhood in Beijing, I asked a committee member in charge of family planning how it was possible to force a woman to get an abortion. "We don't force her," the leader said. "We talk to her again and again until she agrees."

Following the testimony from the committee leaders, the chief judge announced that the court would be prepared to grant a divorce once the matter of property was settled. In the division of property, the judges followed the principle that each person should keep those objects that he or she had brought into the marriage or paid for during the marriage. The judge established that Shuqin had brought to Zhenhua's house her own clothes, eight quilts, four pillows, two blankets, and a lamp. Zhenhua said that at the time of the marriage he had owned a bed, two bed boxes, a writing table, a sofa, two small tables, two chairs, and a glass box. Zhenhua, who had been passive and evasive in discussions of personal relations, became suddenly aggressive regarding property issues.

In a dispute over who had paid for quilt covers, Shuqin finally admitted that Zhenhua had. The judge ordered her to return the covers. Zhenhua also insisted that Shuqin return three wooden buckets that he had bought in the countryside. "Do not raise such a small thing," Shuqin responded with embarrassment. But the judge intervened: "Don't say this is a small thing." In response to Zhenhua's demand that Shuqin return the wedding photos, Shuqin proposed to cut each photo in half. "Don't do that," the chief judge said. "You have to continue to live as good neighbors." She also advised Zhenhua to instruct his mother and sister to stop quarreling with Shuqin. Zhenhua insisted that Shuqin pay the three-yuan court fee, because she had initiated the suit. It was irrelevant who sued, the judge said, but Shuqin had already offered to pay.

The chief judge announced the verdict. According to the marriage law of 1981, the couple would be divorced by mutual consent. Neither party could be married again until after receiving the certificate of divorce. The judge commended the neighborhood and work-unit leaders for their efforts, asking again for their opinions. The leaders concurred with the verdict. They also advised Shuqin not to rush back into marriage. As silence descended again over the courtroom, the judges picked up their hats in unison and walked out, followed by the local leaders. The audience, consisting of relatives and neighbors, erupted into loud conversation.

Shuqin and Zhenhua walked out separately. As Zhenhua passed the front row, he cast a curious glance at me, the foreign observer, who had, he knew, been sitting behind his back but whose face he had not seen. He smiled in embarrassment, revealing his buck teeth. He then moved on, carrying his black bag. Shuqin was free now from oppression by her husband's family and from a marriage that had lost its meaning. In reality, though, she had gained very little freedom. She would continue to live in poverty in her parents' home. Given the stigma attached to divorce in China and the competition from younger women, she would find it almost impossible to remarry. As a single person, she had no place in the community's social life. She was now part of the large pool of women whose inability to find a husband has recently become a source of anxiety to the Chinese leadership.

The social and economic circumstances over which Zhenhua and Shuqin had little control and which eventually figured in the destruction of their marriage were not unique to their lives. Their poverty and dependence on Zhenhua's family locked them into conflict. From the beginning, they were deprived of the opportunity to nurture their separate existence as a couple. By joining her husband in his family home, Shuqin continued a time-honored Chinese tradition. While the socialist regime has attempted to replace the patriarchal family with one based on equality and mutual respect, regardless of sex or age, the ghost of the "feudal" family relationship has lingered.

A considerable number of sons in China still bring their brides into their parents' households. This practice is especially common in the countryside, where arranged marriages and other traditional family customs have persisted despite the communal organization of production. Recently, the introduction of the new "individual responsibility" system—a limited free-market system for small farmers and craftsmen—has encouraged the return of married sons and their families to the parental home, because their labor can be essential to maximizing family profit.

In urban areas, residential patterns are more diverse: Some couples live with the wife's parents instead of the husband's, depending on housing space, proximity to a workplace, and compatibility. In the large cities, young couples increasingly tend to reside near their parents rather than with them. A recent survey of households in Beijing, Tienzin, and Shanghai found that about half the couples in each of these cities live in "nuclear" families. In such cases, however, nuclear families do not reside in separate, private housing. Because of housing shortages, the young couples typically share a flat with several other families who are not relatives.

Most of the older couples I interviewed in Beijing and Shanghai said that today, married children who stay with parents do so mainly as a convenience rather than out of filial piety. Several public officials with whom I spoke predicted that once housing and child-care needs are met, most young people will prefer to live separately, in the hope of avoiding the predicament that drove Shuqin and Zhenhua apart.

After the courtroom emptied, I met with the judges and the president of the district court to discuss the case. As the evidently customary bottles of orangeade were served, the judges relaxed and unbuttoned their uniform jackets, the women revealing colorful blouses underneath.

First, the judges wanted to assure me that they and the local leaders had worked very hard to save Zhenhua and Shuqin's marriage. Judges in China interpret divorce law conservatively. They distinguish carefully between the use of divorce to liberate people from bondage and its "abuse" in the service of individual whim or a new romance. Accordingly, one judge explained, the courts are guided by four major criteria for divorce: whether the conflict followed a "rash" marriage; the quality of the relationship; the causes and depth of the conflict; and the prospects for reconciliation. The courts are particularly conservative when children are involved.

The case of Zhenhua and Shuqin, the male judge said, was clear-cut before it even came to court. It could have been settled in the work-unit committee's meeting room and then registered with the Marriage Division of the Bureau of Civil Affairs, as is customary for uncontested divorces. Why, then, the lengthy testimony about painful personal matters? The chief judge replied that since Shuqin had seen fit to bring suit, the court had wanted to affirm in public that all reconciliation efforts had failed. Thus, the court served as a theater for public education—as it also had in traditional China. In a society where public shaming continues to be a method of social control, the story of Zhenhua and Shuqin would be a lesson to others.

Because the judges had determined early on that the quarrel was primarily between Zhenhua's family and Shuqin rather than between the husband and wife, I asked, had the local leaders, during their efforts to save the marriage, considered finding separate housing for the couple? "No, this is not done here," one of the judges said. "We could not separate the son from his family." The new ideology and traditional customs can make strange, uncomfortable bedfellows.

Couples in China are caught between the authorities' traditional commitment to the integrity of the family, on the one hand, and the rather more recent and limited emphasis on individualism and affection, on the other. Personal feelings are respected only as long as they serve the higher goals of family and community. Happiness is not a goal in itself.

The Case of Fuchang and Liyin

In this respect, the case of Fuchang and Liyin, in the Changning district of Shangai, provides a counterpoint to that of Zhenhua and Shuqin. Fuchang, twenty-nine years old, was suing his wife, Liyin, two years his junior, for divorce. Both were laborers, and they had met by chance at a movie. They were married in April 1981, after a six-month courtship.

They had a twenty-two-month-old son. Fuchang had just been discharged from the military when he met Liyin. She was "plain-looking" and did not wear fine clothes. But he decided to marry her, over his parents' objections, because he was "too poor to choose." Liyin said that she had seen marriage as an opportunity to have her own family after a hard life in her parents' home. She had lost her mother when she was six and had had to raise her younger brother, who ended up a delinquent.

Fuchang accused Liyin of deceit: At the time of their marriage, she had promised him a certain sum of money and a good apartment from her work unit. Neither had materialized, and they lived in a run-down apartment in an industrialized, working-class area. He said also that Liyin was a poor housekeeper and that she had gone to the movies with a male coworker. Liyin denied these accusations. The major problem, she said, was Fuchang's unwillingness to treat her as an equal. When she obeyed him, all was fine, but when she expressed a contrary opinion, all hell broke loose. Fuchang had been sympathetic to her family problems during their courtship, but after their marriage, he did not allow her to invite her father to dinner. He also prevented her from giving some money to her brother, who had just returned from a reform camp.

In February 1982, following a violent quarrel, Fuchang took the television set and moved to his parents' house, while Liyin and her infant remained in the apartment. The quarrel had broken out when Liyin returned from work one evening and found a "girlfriend" of Fuchang's visiting their home. Fuchang had brought this woman along to visit Liyin in the hospital after their child was born. At that time, the woman in the neighboring bed had told Liyin that she had seen Fuchang's companion place her hand on his thigh. When Liyin saw the guest "girlfriend" in their apartment, she concealed her jealousy and chastised Fuchang, ostensibly for not serving "proper dishes" to company. Fuchang told her to mind her own business; he was master of this house, and it was his responsibility to look after his guests. Liyin then asked the woman to leave. In response, Fuchang threw a bowl at Liyin, and blood started gushing from her forehead. Fuchang moved out that evening. The couple had been living apart ever since.

According to Fuchang, Liyin visited him several times after this. Each visit ended in a quarrel. On one occasion, Liyin stormed into Fuchang's workplace and broke a window. Another time, when their baby was sick, she left him at Fuchang's parents' house and poured the baby's medicine out on the floor. On a third occasion she showed up clutching a bottle of DDT and threatening to commit suicide. At this, Fuchang called the neighborhood committee. Mediation commenced.

Liyin told the court that she would not consent to a divorce. She still had feelings, she said. She was sure that if she and Fuchang could develop mutual trust and respect, the marriage could be saved. If they were reconciled, she would do her best to keep house. Nor could Liyin believe that Fuchang's feelings were all gone. Once after their separation, when Fuchang had fallen and hurt his arm, he had allowed Liyin to hold his hand and to comfort him. But when she asked him to move back home, he refused. Overcome by the memory, Liyin broke down crying in the courtroom. The child could not live without his father, she said between sobs. In his sleep he often cried out, "Papa! Papa!"

Fuchang's lawyer (lawyers were provided because the divorce was contested), a balding middle-aged man, used the only point of law he could latch onto: The couple should be granted a divorce on the grounds of a rash marriage. Liyin's lawyer, a wiry woman in her fifties, delivered an animated speech in reply. "In our country, women have equal rights in political and cultural life," she said. But Fuchang had not treated Liyin as an equal. Liyin's lawyer recommended that both partners undergo self-criticism and try to revive the good feelings that they had once had.

Fuchang insisted again that his feelings were dead. But Liyin said she was convinced that he still had some tenderness left. Fuchang turned to Liyin directly and shouted, "I have no more feelings for you!" Facing the judges, he said, "You cannot force me to feel a certain way." Even if they denied him a divorce, he said, he still would not have any feelings for Liyin. "Why should he say such insulting things to me?" Liyin asked, and she broke down crying.

The chief judge declared a recess in order to offer the couple one more opportunity for a reconciliation. During the recess, with the crowd milling around them, Liyin and Fuchang exchanged only a few words before Liyin started screaming and rushed out of the courtroom. Some relatives and work-unit leaders followed Liyin and ushered her into the far corner of the courtyard, where they spoke intensely with her, in the presence of one judge.

Meanwhile, inside the courtroom, Liyin's lawyer verbally assaulted Fuchang. "You must embark on self-criticism! You must admit your own shortcomings!" She shouted repeatedly. Fuchang kept saying that he had no shortcomings, that it was all his wife's fault. Two older women from the neighborhood committee kept trying to protect Fuchang: "Leave him alone. He is a good boy. He is a good boy."

The court reconvened after forty-five minutes. The judge accused the husband of violating the principles of equality, warned him against wife beating, and ordered him to continue to support his child. The court denied Fuchang a divorce, because in its view there were no grounds. Fuchang was charged the three-yuan court fee. Both parties had the right to appeal the case to a higher court. Fuchang's lawyer said later that he intended to do that.

Did the judges feel that they had accomplished anything by denying a divorce when one party so emphatically wanted one? They explained that they were unable to grant a divorce because Liyin still claimed to have feelings. Even though the judges had some doubts as to her sincerity, the law was on Liyin's side, especially because of the child.

Could they really get this couple to live together again? I asked. "Yes!" the judges said, so long as the couple was not divorced, they would have further opportunity for mediation. Even if there is a mere 1-percent chance, the judges said, the court will make a 100-percent effort to reconcile the couple.

Like Zhenhua and Shuqin, Fuchang and Liyin had not had the opportunity to establish an independent marriage. Familial obligations and economic constraints kept them from developing an egalitarian love relationship. They were barely able to spend time alone.

Young people in China are now facing a paradox. The socialist regime wants to foster marriages based on free choice, love, and equality. But the young men and women have neither the experience nor the role models to develop such relationships. The custom of dating is not yet widespread in China. Most couples still meet through parentally arranged introductions. Their relations are formal, even when they are alone. The many young couples hugging in public are already engaged. Otherwise, they would not be embracing in broad daylight. The Communist Party has launched an appeal to various local organizations to introduce matchmaking facilities. Meanwhile, the Young Socialist League and the All China Women's Federation have established "marriage introduction centers," which are supported by the municipalities as well. But these "marriage factories" in Beijing and Shanghai have not been notably successful, in part because potential candidates are often too shy to register.

According to Li Cheng, the presiding judge of the civil division of the Beijing Supreme People's Court, a recent poll indicates that 60 percent of China's young married people lack "real and spontaneous" love for their spouses. Among their reasons for marriage, the respondents said, were that they had "reached the age" and that "one had to be married sooner or later." These are, perhaps, traditional reasons. But there are also signs of change. The All China Women's Federation has embarked on a nationwide campaign to teach young people the meaning of love and equality in marriage, through film and study sessions. The honeymoon, meanwhile, is becoming popular for the first time, and honeymooners can be spotted at many of the major tourist sites, especially in favorite resorts like Suchou and Hangchow. Wearing a colorful suit with a corsage, and a lacy hat, the new wife poses for her husband's black-and-white snapshots in front of famous fountains and pavilions. Even the materialistic rewards of marriage have changed. The dowry chest is back in fashion (along with the wedding veil), but the dowry now comes from both sets of parents, and marriage partners typically have definite expectations as to what each side should contribute—expectations that at times may undermine "feelings."

Contemporary attitudes toward the family in China—among ordinary people and those who rule them—remind one somewhat of the Puritans' attitudes in seventeenth-century New England. The Puritan family was viewed as a "little commonwealth"—a miniature version of an ideal society. Like the Puritan elders, the rulers of the People's Republic consciously use the family as an agent of reform and morality. They endorse public intervention in family affairs, and they subordinate, to the extent that they can, the individual to the larger community. At the same time, the government has come to recognize the importance of "feelings" in maintaining social cohesion and strong family ties.

No one can predict precisely how the constellation of forces in China— of long-standing tradition and conformity, on the one hand, and of emergent individualism, consumerism, and romance, on the other—will change the dynamics of the Chinese family. It remains to be seen whether China can succeed in having it both ways.

Part Four

Broader Perspectives

13

Family Change and Historical Change:

An Uneasy Relationship

Introduction

Through much of the American past, the family has been seen as the linchpin of the social order and the basis for stable governance. Thus, the family, unique among the social structures discussed in this book, serves as a broker between individuals and other social processes and institutions. Yet the role of the family and the values governing its comportment and relationship to the community have been subjected to various paradoxes that have rendered adaptation to change and realization of the family's responsibilities to individual members exceedingly difficult (Demos, 1970; Hareven, 1977b).

The concept of structural lag, defined by John Riley and Matilda Riley (1994) as the mismatch between changing lives and changing social structures, is remarkably applicable to understanding the social changes involving the family and the anxieties surrounding its future. The conceptual framework helps identify the dilemma the family is facing in contemporary society in light of the contradictions surrounding its role. Because of the power of these contradictions, I will differentiate between a structural and a cultural lag.[1] The cultural component concerns the myths and stereotypes in American society that govern expectations from the family and that are used as a yardstick for the assessment of "normal" or "deviant" family behavior. Since these myths and stereotypes about the family have had a strong impact on individuals, institutions, and policy, it is important to examine how the cultural, as well as the structural, lag is exacerbating the

*The author acknowledges with gratitude the valuable editorial suggestions from John and Matilda Riley, Anne Foner, and Jennifer Dolde.

This chapter originally appeared in M. W. Riley, R. Kahn, and A. Foner. eds., *Age and Structural Lag: Society's Failure to Provide Meaningful Opportunities in Work, Family, and Leisure* (New York: John Wiley & Sons, 1994). Reprinted with the permission of John Wiley & Sons, © 1994 by John Wiley & Sons, Inc.

misfit between social change and individual and familial needs (Hareven, 1981a). One of the main problems affecting the family's ability to discharge its responsibilities is a mismatch between social and economic change, on the one hand, and the pace of family change and the ideologies governing its role, on the other.

The lag affecting the family does not involve a simple linear change and a carryover of nineteenth-century patterns into the present. Those aspects of change at dissonance with contemporary social needs involve developments that have occurred since the late nineteenth century. By contrast, certain earlier family and life-course patterns (in the preindustrial era and in some periods in the nineteenth century) would be more compatible with complex social conditions in the 1990s. The late nineteenth-century family patterns that are at odds with contemporary societal needs include the ideal of domesticity, involving the view of motherhood and homemaking as full-time pursuits; the ideal of privacy, enshrining the segregation of the family from the community and the larger society; and the diminution of interaction between the nuclear family unit and the wider kin group.

At the same time, earlier historical patterns more compatible with contemporary needs and developments are still surviving in certain groups of the population. If those were to be recognized and supported, a better fit between other contemporary structures and the family could be achieved. Such patterns include flexible and creative use of household arrangements involving coresidence with nonfamily members as well as with kin; instrumental relations among nuclear family members and extended kin; diversity in family forms; kinship networks including complex configurations of kin and surrogate kin; acceptance and facilitating women's work patterns as full-time careers; "erratic," flexible timing of life-course transitions; and a closer integration between family and community. A historical consideration of such family patterns helps us to assess the uniqueness of contemporary conditions and to distinguish between long-term trends and temporary aberrations.

From a historical perspective, this chapter explores family patterns in American society that have been affected by both a structural and a cultural lag resulting from the social and cultural construction of the role of the family. It examines changes in the family in relation to cultural and structural lags in the following areas: the organization and role of the household; interdependence among kin; privacy and sentimentality in family relations and the family's relationship to the community; women's work and the ideology of domesticity; and the timing of life transitions.

Myths About the Past

A series of myths about family life in the past cloud popular understanding of contemporary problems. According to these myths, three generations lived together happily in the same household, families were intimate and close-knit units, and single-parent households rarely existed. This belief in a lost "golden age" has led people to depict the present as a period of decline in the family. Nostalgia for a nonexistent past has handicapped policymakers in assessing realistically the recent changes in family life (Hareven, 1990a). For example, the efforts in the late 1970s and early 1980s to legislate changes in family behavior that would return the family to "the way it once was" are a striking example of policymakers' presumptions of what the family was like in the past (see *Family Protection Act*, 1979, 1981).

Despite persistence of this stereotype, historical research has dispelled the myths about the existence of ideal three-generational families in the American past. A nuclear household structure has predominated since the seventeenth century. There never existed in American society or in Western Europe an era when coresidence of three generations in the same household was the dominant pattern. The "great extended families" that became part of the folklore of modern society were what Goode (1963) referred to as a product of "Western nostalgia" (p. 6). Early American households were simple in their structure. Three generations seldom lived together in the same household. Given the high mortality rate in preindustrial societies, most grandparents could not have expected to overlap with their grandchildren. It would thus be futile to argue that industrialization destroyed the great extended family of the past, when such a family type rarely existed (Demos, 1970; Greven, 1970; Laslett and Wall, 1972).

Internal household arrangements in early American society differed, however, from those in our times. Even though households did not contain extended kin, early American households did include unrelated individuals, such as boarders, lodgers, apprentices, and servants, as well as dependent members in the community (Demos, 1970; Modell and Hareven, 1973). The tendency to include nonrelatives in the household was derived from a different cultural concept of family life. Unlike today, when the household—the "home"—serves as a private retreat for the family and is, therefore, primarily a site of consumption, the household in the past was the site of a broad array of functions and activities that transcended the more restricted circle of the nuclear family. In this respect, the historical households would be more suitable to serving today's social needs, as explained later in this chapter.

The Malleable Household

Despite an overall commitment to residence in nuclear households, which was practiced by members of various ethnic groups and native-

born Americans alike, the nuclear households included other kin in times
of need or at the later stages of the life course (Anderson, 1971; Hareven,
1977a). Household space was an important resource to be shared and exchanged over the life course. Members of the nuclear family shared
household space with boarders and lodgers in exchange for services or
rent or with children who had already left home and married but who,
during economic crises or housing shortages or when the parents became
too frail to live alone, returned with their spouses to reside with their parents in exchange for services or supports. Since the household was considered an economic resource, its membership changed in relation to the
family's economic opportunities and needs over the life course. Households were like a revolving stage on which different family members appeared, disappeared, and reappeared at their own initiative or under the
impact of external conditions such as migration, labor markets, or housing shortages (Hareven, 1982).

Household members engaged in direct exchanges across neighborhoods, as well as over wide geographic regions. As some members went
out into the world, newcomers moved in. Individuals whose families
were disrupted by migration or death were often absorbed into other
people's households. Young people were able to move to new communities, confident that they would board or lodge with relatives or strangers.
Working mothers were able to place young children in the homes of relatives or strangers, and dependent elders, who had become too infirm or
poor to live alone, moved into their children's or other people's households. Such exchanges among relatives, neighbors, or complete strangers
were laced through the entire society, as the family performed its function
as broker among individuals and other social structures (Hareven, 1982,
1990a).

The greatest flexibility in the use of household space was in the taking
of boarders and lodgers. Throughout the nineteenth century and the early
part of the twentieth century, one-third to one-half of all households took
in boarders or lodgers at some point during the life course of the head of
the household. In the later years of life, boarding and lodging served as
the "social equalization of the family," a strategy by which young men or
women who left their parents' home communities moved into the households of people whose own children had left home (Modell and Hareven,
1973). This practice provided young migrants to the city with surrogate
family arrangements, middle-aged or older couples with supplemental
income, and families with young children with alternative sources of income and child care. The income from boarders and lodgers provided the
necessary supplement for new homeowners to pay mortgages and for
wives to stay out of the labor force. The taking in of boarders and lodgers,
a practice more widespread than admitting extended kin, thus made it

easier for families to adhere to their traditional values without slipping below the margin of poverty.

Despite preferences for nonkin, families also took kin into the household, though usually for limited periods during times of need or at specific stages in the life course. Only about 12 to 18 percent of all urban households in the late nineteenth and early twentieth centuries contained relatives other than members of the nuclear family (Hareven, 1977b). The proportion of households taking in kin increased to 25 percent over the twentieth century and declined to 7 percent by 1950 (Ruggles, 1987). Sharing the family's household space with kin was nevertheless an important migration and life-course strategy. In urban industrial communities, which attracted large numbers of migrants from the countryside or immigrants from abroad, there was a visible increase in coresidence with extended kin over the nineteenth century. Newly arrived migrants usually stayed with their relatives for a limited time period, until they found jobs and housing. Then they set up separate households (Glasco, 1977; Hareven, 1982). They, in turn, took others into their own households when the need arose, but again on a temporary basis. Coresidence with extended kin was most common in the later years of life, when aging parents shared their coveted household space with their newlywed children, who delayed establishment of an independent household because of housing shortages (Chudacoff and Hareven, 1978b, 1979).

Continuing to head their own household was an almost sacred goal in American society among native as well as foreign-born couples. Older people, especially widowed mothers, avoided at all cost living in their children's homes. Parents usually prepared for old age by requiring their youngest daughter to postpone her marriage and stay with them; if that was not possible, they took in boarders and lodgers. Only if all these failed did they move in with a child or another relative. In these cases, the child who took in the parent headed the household, whereas in the case of the newlywed couples, the parents continued to head their own household (Chudacoff, 1978; Chudacoff and Hareven, 1978b, 1979). For older people in urban society, holding on to the space and headship of their household in exchange for future assistance in old age was a life-course strategy, reminiscent of the contracts between inheriting sons and rural older people in preindustrial Europe and Colonial New England (Demos, 1970). In the past, these types of accommodations encouraged greater flexibility in household arrangements than are present in contemporary society.

Interdependence Among Kin

As noted above, the role of kin in the past has been central in individuals' functioning and adaptation to new social and economic changes and in

coping with critical life situations. The viable historical patterns of kin assistance could provide an important model for the present, as new configurations of kin and surrogate kin have been emerging. Even though the
nuclear family resided separately from extended kin, its members were
enmeshed in kinship networks that provided reciprocal assistance over
the life course. As has been stated, kin served as the most essential resource for assistance and security and carried the major burdens of welfare functions for individual family members (see Chapter 2). Contrary to
prevailing myths, urbanization and industrialization did not break down
traditional kinship ties and patterns of mutual assistance. Historical studies have documented the survival of viable functions of kin in the nineteenth century, especially their central role in facilitating migration, in
finding jobs and housing, and in assistance during critical life situations,
particularly in the later years of life (Anderson, 1971; Hareven, 1978b,
1982; see Chapter 2). Patterns of kin assistance were pervasive in neighborhoods and extended back to the communities of origin of immigrants and
migrants. Contemporary research has documented continuity in the viable
roles of kin in modern American society (Shanas et al., 1968; Sussman and
Burchinal, 1962; Litwak, 1960).

In a regime of economic insecurity and in the absence of welfare agencies, kin assistance was the only constant source of social security. Kin carried the major burden of welfare functions, many of which fall now within
the purview of the public sector. Reciprocity among parents and children
and other kin provided the major, and sometimes the only, base for supports during the critical life situations, especially in the later years. Mutual
assistance among kin, although involving extensive exchanges, was not
strictly calculative. Rather, it expressed an overall principle of reciprocity
over the life course and across generations. Individuals' sense of obligation to their kin was a manifestation of their family culture—a commitment to the survival, well-being, and self-reliance of the family, which took
priority over individual needs and personal happiness (Hareven, 1982).
Autonomy of the family, essential for self-respect and good standing in the
neighborhood and community, was one of the most deeply ingrained values.

Individuals who subordinated their own careers and needs to those of
the family did so out of a sense of responsibility, affection, and familial
obligation rather than with the expectation of immediate gain. Such sacrifices were not made, however, without protest, and at times involved
competition and conflict among siblings on issues such as who should
carry the burden of support for aging parents. The salient role of kin,
and the strong sense of mutual obligations that kin carried toward each
other, have shaped these early cohorts' expectations for supports and
sociability in the later years of life. This type of integration with kin is

still present in the life experience of those cohort members who are now among the "old old" (Hareven, 1982). More recent cohorts, by contrast, have been more inclined to turn to new bureaucratic agencies rather than to kin as their major sources of economic support in old age (Hareven and Adams, 1996; see Chapter 7).

The increasing separation between the family of orientation and the family of procreation over the twentieth century, combined with a growing privatization of the family, occurred in the context of changes in the quality of relations with extended kin. The major historical change has not been in the decline of coresidence with kin but rather in the functions that kin fulfilled. The gradual erosion of the interdependence among kin has tended to increase insecurity and isolation in old age, especially in areas of need that have not been met by public programs. The difference lies in the extent of individuals' integration with kin and their dependence on mutual assistance. Although more intensive patterns of kin interaction have survived among first-generation immigrants and working-class families, an overall erosion of instrumental kin relations and an increasing focus on the private, nuclear family have occurred. This pattern differs, however, among various ethnic groups.

The historic shift of major responsibility for the material well-being of older people from the family to the public sector has generated some ambiguity in the expectations for support and assistance for aging relatives from their own kin. On the one hand, it is assumed that the welfare state has relieved children of the obligations of supporting their parents in old age. On the other hand, these public measures are often insufficient in meeting economic need, nor do they provide the kind of supports and sociability in areas that had been traditionally carried by the family. It is precisely this ambiguity, along with the failure of American society to consummate the historical process of the transfer of some major functions of welfare from the family to the public sector, that has become one of the major sources of the problems currently confronting older people. Even today, in the small fraction of families where the older person is severely disabled, most care is provided by the spouse, a daughter or daughter-in-law, or other relative, but at a high price to the caregiver (Brody, 1981). However, any kind of plans to return the major care for aging relatives to the family cannot be carried out realistically without providing supports to the family that would enable it to meet such expectations.

Despite the survival of some traditional patterns of kin assistance among certain ethnic groups, it would be unrealistic to expect that kin could carry the major burdens for the care of aging relatives, for several reasons. Except for the baby boomers, future cohorts will have fewer kin available to them when they reach dependent old age (Uhlenberg, 1979). Even if kin are available, several changes converge to reduce the potential efficacy of kin: The employment of women in full-time careers limits the pool of available traditional caregivers, and the extension of life has brought about the "life-cycle squeeze," where the children of the "old old" are old themselves and therefore unable to provide the necessary supports to their parents (Brody, 1981; Hogan, Eggebeen, and Smith, 1996). The only way in which kin could be utilized to aid aging relatives would be by providing them with public supports to carry out these tasks.

Alternatively, new, complex, and more flexible kinship and surrogate kinship configurations are emerging as a result of divorce, remarriage, the formation of blended families, and cohabitation. These new kinship ties could be strengthened and utilized in a constructive way for the care of aging relatives. As Riley and Riley (1996) point out, these new networks, including "step-kin and in-laws and also adopted and other surrogate relatives chosen from outside the family," form "a latent web of continually shifting linkages that provide the potential for activating and intensifying close kin relationships as they are needed" (p. 173). Such networks could make it possible to form new configurations of assistance at various stages of the life course.

Privacy and the Family's Retreat from the Community

The emergence of privacy as one of the central values governing family life has handicapped the family's effective interaction with other social institutions. Originating at first with the urban middle class in the nineteenth century, privacy has become an ideal of family life and of individual comportment in the larger society (Ariès, 1962; Lasch, 1977). Privacy gradually became pervasive with the triumph of middle-class values and their acceptance by working-class families and by the older waves of immigrants as they became Americanized.

The triumph of the values of privacy has led to an increasing separation of the nuclear family from extended kin and to the closing of the household to nonrelatives. The idealization of the family's role as a private retreat and as an emotional haven is misguided in light of our knowledge of the past. The loss of the family's sociability as a result of its function as a refuge from the outside world has rendered it less flexible and less capable of handling internal, as well as external, crises. According to Ariès (1962), family life in the past exposed children to a diversity of role models—friends, clients, relatives, and protégés—equipping them to function in a complex society. Paradoxically, as the society and the economy have become more diversified over time, the family has become more streamlined and segregated from the outside world. The tendency of the family to shelter its members from other social institutions may well have weakened its ability to affect social change or to influence the programs and legislation that public agencies have directed toward the family.

Closely related to the ideals of privacy in the family has been an excessive emphasis on individual rather than collective needs and on sentiment as the core of family relations. Over the past several decades, American families have been experiencing their members' increasing preference to follow individual priorities and preferences over collective family needs. The major historical change from a view of the family collectively to one of individualization and sentiment has caused a further lag in the family's adaptability.

This individualization of family relations has combined with an exaggerated emphasis on emotional nurture and sentiment as the crucible of the family's role. On the one hand, it has contributed considerably to the liberation of individuals from familial pressures; on the other hand, it has eroded the resilience of the family and its malleability in weathering crises and coping with change. Moreover, it has led to a greater separation among the generations and especially to the isolation of older people. One of the major sources of the crisis of the private nuclear family today may be its difficulty in adapting to the emotional responsibilities thrust upon it. Concentration on the nurturing and sentimental functions of the family has grown at the expense of another of the family's much-needed roles: preparing members to function in a complex bureaucratic society.

In the past, instrumental relations in the family and in the wider kinship group provided important supports to individuals and families, particularly during social and economic crises and critical life situations. Family members were valued not merely for providing emotional satisfaction to each other but for a wide array of services on their part for the family. A collective view of familial obligations was at the very basis of survival. From such a perspective, marriage and parenthood were not merely love relationships but partnerships directed to serve the family's goals and needs (Hareven, 1982). The relationships between husbands and wives, parents and children, and other kin were based upon reciprocal assistance and supports. Such "instrumental" relations drew their strength from the assumption that family members had mutual obligations and engaged in reciprocity. Although obligations were not specifically defined by contract, they rested on the accepted social expectation of what family members owed to each other (Anderson, 1971; Hareven, 1982).

The experience of working-class families in the nineteenth century and of ethnic families in the more recent past was drastically different from that of middle-class families, among whom sentimentality emerged as the dominant base of family relationships. Among the former, sentiment was secondary to family needs and survival strategies. Hence, the timing of children's leaving home and of marriage as well as the commencement of work careers were regulated in accordance with collective family considerations rather than guided by individual preferences. For example, as noted earlier, parents tried to delay the marriage of the last child in the household, commonly a daughter, in order to secure continued supports in later life when they were withdrawing from the labor force. Certain working-class and ethnic families continued to adhere to earlier ways of life by maintaining a collective view of the family and its economy (Hareven, 1982). In contrast to the values of individualism that govern much of family life today, traditional values of family collectivity have persisted among certain ethnic groups.

In the preindustrial period, the family interacted closely with the community in discharging responsibilities of welfare and social control for family members as well as for unattached members of the community. The family not only reared children but also served as a workshop, a school, a church, and a welfare agency. Preindustrial families meshed closely with the community and carried a variety of public responsibilities within the larger society (Demos, 1970). Over the nineteenth century, however, the family surrendered many of the functions previously concentrated within it to other social, economic, and welfare institutions. The family's retreat from public life and the commitment to the privacy of initially the modern middle-class family have drawn sharper boundaries between family and community at the very time in historical development when families could have benefited from various forms of interaction with the larger society in areas such as care for family members during critical life situations, as well as for children and for aged relatives. The community has ceased to rely on the family as the major agency of welfare and social control, and the family has ceased to be the primary source of support for its own dependent members. Nevertheless, no adequate substitute agencies for the care of elderly dependent people have been developed.

The Ideology of Domesticity and Women's Work

Married women's entry into the labor force and their pursuit of a career have been handicapped by the structural and cultural lags between women's changing roles and the tenacity of older institutional and ideological practices. While married women, especially mothers, have been assuming full-time careers, institutional adjustments have not kept pace with these developments. First, child-care facilities in contemporary society have not fully met the needs of working mothers, especially in low-income groups. Second, mothers have had to carry out their work in a climate where vestiges of the ideology of feminine domesticity still prevail. Appearing first in the early nineteenth century in middle-class families, this ideology has idealized motherhood and homemaking as women's full-time occupations, and consequently, it has constrained the opportunities for mothers to develop careers in paid work outside the home (see Chapter 4).

Women's labor force participation has also been at odds with the increasing need to provide care in the home for dependent and chronically ill elderly. Because the major responsibilities for the care of children and older people and various other aspects of kin assistance have historically been in the women's domain, it is not surprising that women have emerged as the main caregivers for elderly relatives today. The "generation in the middle"—consisting of stressed-out, caregiving women, usually daughters of dependent, frail, or chronically ill elderly—has become a well-known phenomenon of the aging society (Brody, 1981; see Chapter 7). Ironically, the burden of care for aging relatives has been thrust on certain cohorts of women just at the time when they were trying to pursue individual work careers, after launching their children into adulthood.

In preindustrial society, even though families contained large numbers of children, women invested relatively less time in fulfilling the duties of motherhood than did their successors in the nineteenth century, as well as in our time. Child care was part of a collective family effort rather than a woman's exclusive preoccupation. From an early age on, children were viewed not merely as tender objects of nurture but as productive members of the family and society. Responsibility for the tasks of child rearing did not fall exclusively on mothers; older siblings and other relatives living nearby also participated in this process. The integration of family and work allowed for an intensive sharing of labor between husbands and wives and between parents and children that was later diminished in industrial society. Housework was inseparable from domestic industries or agricultural work, and it was valued, therefore, as an economic asset.

Under the impact of industrialization, the family's functions of production were transferred to agencies and institutions outside the family. The workplace was separated from the home, and asylums and reformatories assumed many of the family's functions of social welfare and social control previously held by the family. Talcott Parsons (1955) wrote, "The family has become *a more specialized agency than before* . . . but not in any general sense less important, because the society is dependent *more* exclusively on it for the performance of *certain* of its vital functions" (italics in original; pp. 9–10). These include childbearing, child rearing, and socialization. The family has ceased to be a work unit and has limited its economic activities primarily to consumption and child care.

These changes in family life that accompanied industrialization were gradual, however, and varied significantly from class to class as well as among different ethnic groups. Preindustrial family patterns persisted over longer time periods among rural and urban working-class families. During the nineteenth century, most working-class families still considered their members' work a family enterprise, even when they were employed outside the home. The labor of wives, sons, and daughters was carefully regulated by the collective strategies of the family unit. Much of what we perceive today as individual work careers was actually considered part of a collective family effort. Women continued to function as integral partners in the family's productive effort, even when they worked in factories. Daughters were considered assets, both for their contribution to the family's economy during their youth and for the prospect of their support during their parents' old age (Hareven, 1982; Tilly and Scott, 1978).

This continuity in the family's function as a collective economic unit is significant for understanding the changes in the roles of women that industrialization introduced into working-class life. Industrialization offered women the opportunity to become wage earners outside the home. In the working class, however, it did not bring about immediate changes in the family's collective identity—at least not during the early stages of industrialization.

Among middle-class families, by contrast, industrialization initially had a more dramatic impact on gender roles. The transformation of the household from a busy workplace and social center to the family's private abode involved the exclusion of nonrelatives, such as business associates, partners, journeymen, apprentices, and boarders, from the household. It led to a more rigorous separation of husbands from wives and fathers from children in the course of the workday. Men worked outside the home; women stayed at home, and children went to school. The separation of the home from the workplace that followed in the wake of industrialization led to the enshrinement of the home as a domestic retreat from the outside world and to the development of the child-centered family (Demos, 1970; Welter, 1966; Wishy, 1968).

The ideology of domesticity and the new view of childhood as a tender stage of life requiring nurture combined to revise expectations of parenthood. The roles of husbands and wives became gradually more segregated. A clear division of labor replaced the old economic cooperation. The wives' efforts concentrated on homemaking and child rearing, while men worked outside the home. Time invested in fatherhood was concentrated primarily on leisure. This marked the emergence of the domestic middle-class family as we know it today. As custodians of this retreat, women were expected to concentrate on perfect homemaking and child rearing rather than on serving as economic partners in the family. Tenderness, gentleness, affection, sweetness, and a comforting demeanor began to emerge as the crucible of family relationships. Stripped of the multiplicity of functions that had been previously concentrated in the family, urban middle-class families developed into private, domestic, and child-centered retreats from the world of work and politics (Degler, 1980; Welter, 1966; see Chapter 4).

These patterns, which emerged early in the nineteenth century, formed the base of relations characteristic of the contemporary middle-class American family. Some of them have persisted to the present day and are the root of certain problems in the family and in the contemporary gendered division of labor. Because the prejudices against mothers' labor-force participation persevered at least until the 1960s and handicapped women's pursuits of occupations outside the home, it is important to understand their origin in the nineteenth-century cult of domesticity (Degler, 1980; Welter, 1966).

The ideology of domesticity and of full-time motherhood that developed in the first half of the nineteenth century relegated women to the home and glorified their role as homemakers and mothers. Ironically, this ideology was closely connected to the decline in the average number of children a woman had and to the new attitudes toward childhood that were emerging in the nineteenth century. The recognition of childhood as a distinct stage of life among urban middle-class families led to the treatment of children as objects of nurture rather than as contributing members to the family economy (Wishy, 1968; D. S. Smith, 1974).

Over the late nineteenth century and early part of the twentieth century, the ideology of domesticity was gradually adopted as the dominant model for family life in the entire society. Second- and third-generation immigrant families, which originally held a view of the family as an integrated corporate unit and which had earlier accepted the wife's work outside the home, began to embrace the ideology of domesticity as part of the process of Americanization (Hareven and Modell, 1980). In the early part of the twentieth century, after internalizing the values of domesticity, working-class families began to view women's labor-force participation as demeaning, compromising for the husband, and harmful for the children. Consequently, married women entered the labor force only when driven by economic necessity.

Until very recently, the ideology of domesticity has dominated perceptions of women's roles and has shaped prevailing assumptions governing family life. The consequences of this ideology have been the insistence on confining women's main activities to the domestic sphere and the misguided assumption that the work of mothers outside the home would be harmful to family and society. Only over the past few decades, as a result of the women's movement, have these values been criticized and partly rejected. But the cultural lag from the nineteenth century is still reflected in the censure of mothers' labor-force participation.

Changes in the Timing of Life Transitions

Paradoxically, although demographic and social changes over the past two decades have propelled families and individuals into more complex family configurations and into the erratic timing of life-course transitions, the normative and institutional ideal of a streamlined, uniform life course still prevails. One widely held myth about the distant past is that the timing of life transitions was more orderly and stable than it is today. The complexity that governs family life today and the variations in family roles and in transitions into them are frequently contrasted to this more placid past.

The historical experience, however, reveals a very different condition: Patterns of family timing in the past were often as complex, diverse, and erratic as they are today. From the late nineteenth century to the mid-twentieth century, however, the timing of life-course transitions in American society did become more streamlined, more uniform, and more closely articulated to age grading and age norms. Voluntary and involuntary demographic changes that started in the late nineteenth century resulted in a period of greater uniformity in the timing of transitions. Yet the developments of the past two decades have led to the reemergence of erratic timing of life transitions. As will be explained, however, the reasons for these contemporary patterns of timing differ from those in the past.

In the nineteenth century, the timing of life transitions to adulthood (leaving school, starting to work, leaving home, setting up a separate household, and getting married) was erratic, did not follow an established sequence, and took a long time to accomplish. Young people shuttled back and forth from school to work, moved in and out of the parental home, and did not set up a separate household until their marriage. Even after marriage, young couples returned to live temporarily with their parents if the parents needed assistance or during housing shortages (Modell, Furstenberg, and Hershberg, 1976). The timing of early life transitions was bound up with later ones in a continuum of familial obligations. Aging parents' needs for support from their children affected the latter's transitions into independent adulthood (Modell and Hareven, 1978).

In the nineteenth century, later life transitions were then timed even more erratically than earlier ones. In the absence of mandatory retirement, people worked as long as they could. When older men were not able to work any longer in their regular occupations, they alternated between periods of work and unemployment and took on downwardly mobile but physically less demanding jobs (Hareven, 1982). Women's work careers were erratic over their entire life course, in relation to marriage, childbearing, and child rearing. Older women experienced more marked life transitions than men, because losing a spouse was more the experience of women. The continuing presence of adult children in the household, however, meant that widowhood did not necessarily represent a dramatic transition into an empty nest (Chudacoff and Hareven, 1979).

Timing of early life transitions was "erratic" in the nineteenth century because it followed family needs and obligations rather than specific age norms. During the 1970s and 1980s, by contrast, age norms and individual preferences emerged as more important determinants of timing than familial obligations.

Over the past two decades or so, however, the erratic, more flexible patterns of timing of life-course transitions have emerged again. These new patterns depart from the earlier age-related rigidities in timing to reflect changes in family arrangements, values governing generational relations, a greater individualization, and new policies regulating the work life. For example, over the past decade, the age at first marriage has risen. Remarriage following divorce has resulted in a wide spread in the age at marriage, in greater age differences between spouses, and in later commencement of childbearing. There has also been erratic movement of young adult children in and out of the parental home, but their return after having left home differs from the same practice in the past in a fundamental way: In the late nineteenth century, children continued to stay at home or returned after they had left in order to meet the needs of their family of orientation—to take care of aging parents in some cases and of young siblings in others. In contemporary society, young adult children (including divorced or unmarried daughters with their own young children) return home in order to meet their own needs—because of their inability to develop an independent work career or find affordable housing or because they need help in child care (Cherlin, 1992).

The contemporary erratic style of family life coincides with changing patterns of retirement. The rigid end to a work career is becoming erratic once again, but for very different reasons than those in the past. The "golden handshake" to encourage or force early retirement does not solve the dilemma of the structural lag. As the Riley, Kahn, and Foner have stated it:

> Today by contrast [with the nineteenth century], survival into old age is commonplace and many years of vigorous postretirement life are the realistic expectation. . . . Nevertheless, the major responsibilities for work and family are still crowded into what are now the middle years of long life. . . . Despite the twentieth-century metamorphosis in human lives . . . the social structures

and norms that define opportunities and expectations throughout the life course carry the vestigial marks of the nineteenth century (pp. 1-2).

Reducing the Misfit

Currently, there are two sources of misfit between family and society: (1) Some societal institutions lag behind the changing needs of the family unit and of individual family members; and (2) the family has not always adapted to contemporary social and cultural changes. To achieve a balance that serves the family as well as individuals will require adaptive changes in the family, in other societal institutions, and in cultural attitudes governing the family comportment. In this regard, it is helpful to call on some of the historical patterns of family behavior in the past that have been outlined in this chapter. This is not to suggest that we turn the clock back or revive older patterns that are incompatible with the present. Rather, certain models from the past could be adapted to contemporary needs to overcome the structural and cultural lag between the family and other social structures. This task is rendered easier because some of these historical patterns still survive in the experience of certain ethnic groups.

American society is multilayered, containing significant differences in values and attitudes toward the family based on differences in class and ethnicity. Because of differences in the timing of the influx of various ethnic groups into American society, some of the historical family patterns that would be compatible with contemporary needs still survive. Such patterns were often denigrated because they did not conform to the stereotype of the nuclear, WASP family ideal (Hareven and Modell, 1980). Over the past two decades, however, these varieties of family and kin configurations and patterns of mutual assistance have gained increasing recognition and appreciation for their ability to negotiate the complexity of institutional change—to buttress the family as broker between individuals and other structures.

Now is the time to recognize these family forms and to foster their adaptation to contemporary needs. At the same time, institutions and cultural stereotypes upholding "ideal" family patterns and women's roles must be modified to meet the pressing needs resulting from changes in the family, in women's work careers, and in the life course. Now is the time to reduce both the structural and the cultural lag.

14

What Difference
Does It Make?

Almost thirty years have passed since the "new" social history and its related fields fired the imagination of historians and other social scientists,
particularly sociologists, anthropologists, and psychologists. Perhaps the
time has come to ask: What difference does it make? What has been the
impact of these new historical efforts on our understanding of more general patterns in history?

The new social history and its subdisciplines have become so established that they are not viewed as new anymore. Younger generations of
scholars take them for granted. Nonetheless, those of us who witnessed
their emergence and helped develop them still remember the sense of
promise and discovery and the frantic search for methodologies with
which to answer new questions. The excitement led to collaborations and
to an enduring sense of kinship among practitioners.

Since the early 1970s, the various subdisciplines of the new social history—such as labor history, urban history, family and women's history,
black and rural history—have developed their own topical and methodological coherence and diversity and their own linkages to the larger
processes of change. Research among these branches has also been closely
interrelated. Since work, family, and community are interlocked in people's lives, they should not be compartmentalized in historical research.
Indeed, the most exciting products of these scholarly enterprises have

*An earlier version of this chapter was delivered as the presidential address at the An-
nual Meeting of the Social Science History Association, November 18, 1995. When preparing
the text for this publication, I decided to retain the talk format rather than reconstructing it
as a book chapter. We have many opportunities to write in this style but few occasions to deliver presidential addresses. Hence, I retained the first-person style in this chapter.

This chapter first appeared as "What Difference Does It Make?" *Social Science History* Volume 20, (Autumn, 1996):317–344. Reprinted by permission of Duke University Press.

been those linking such dimensions as work, family, and community. At a later stage in the development of the field, the life-course approach has provided a framework for interpreting their interconnectedness.

An assessment of the impact of these historical efforts on our understanding of the larger processes of historical change needs to be done on two levels. First, what difference has the research of the past three decades made to our understanding of social history? Second, to what extent has this body of research and the resulting interpretations been woven into the larger fabric of history? Here, I can address only the first question.

My primary examples are for American society, with some comparisons with Europe and Japan. I first sketch the general contribution of the new social history. I then discuss the impact of the subfields with which I am most familiar—the history of the family and the life course—on the following areas: the reinterpretation of the process of social change; the role of human agency; family strategies; the subjective reconstruction of life history; and the rediscovery of complexity through the life-course approach. In doing so, I must generalize, and due to shortage of space, I cannot address the complexities and internal debates in these subfields. Since I provide examples from my own research, it is necessary for me to reiterate that following my study of family and work at the Amoskeag Mills in Manchester, (Hareven, 1982), I conducted comparative research on this topic among the silk weavers of Kyoto, Japan, from 1982 to 1993 (Hareven, 1990b, 1992a, 1992c, forthcoming). More recently, I extended the comparison to Lyon, France.[1] This type of research, especially the in-depth interviews that I have conducted in three cultures, has transformed me as a historian. I wish to acknowledge the contributions of the men and women who have shared with me their life histories and memories in Manchester, Kyoto, and Lyon.

My encounter with Mr. M. in Lyon in 1994 exemplifies some of my central themes here. In January 1995, I conducted several interviews with Mr. M., a highly skilled former hand-loom weaver, whose atelier is now on the visitors' itinerary in the former silk capital of France. When Florence Charpigny (a distinguished oral historian in Lyon) and I entered the atelier, Mr. M., then eighty-two years old, said immediately, "You are now in the last familial atelier in Lyon." After he had completed his standard account of the history of hand-loom weaving in Lyon, I asked him questions based on my research in Kyoto and showed him my photographs of the Japanese silk weavers. In an entirely different style, and with great feeling, he then told me about his struggles as a hand-loom weaver in a declining industry. Only in my third interview with him, however, did I learn that he had stopped weaving on hand looms twenty years prior to his retirement and that he had spent the last period of his working life setting up textile factories in Algiers, because hand-loom weaving had almost completely disappeared from Lyon. For Mr. M., the recovery and preservation of his atelier and its placement on the tourist route represented the restoration of an important segment of the world he had lost and reaffirmed his identity as an artisan.

Reweaving the Tapestry

The original objectives of the new social history were to reintegrate into the historical tapestry people who had been left out of it and to retrieve human experiences that had been neglected; to reconstruct and reinterpret historical experience from the perspective of the actors and the participants rather than from the vantage point of rulers, custodians, and overseers; to study entire communities; and to follow processes rather than static events. The new social history and its subfields have met these objectives and much more. The historical imagination and the research efforts brought to bear on this enterprise have produced an embarrassment of riches.

The new social history, continuing the tradition started by Marc Bloch (1954), advanced the notion that history is past politics (in fact, it vastly broadened the notion of what constitutes politics) and introduced everyday life as a central subject. It has reintroduced into the historical tapestry the experience of major groups that had been left out; it has reinterpreted the role of human agency; it has linked human development to institutions and structures and to the larger processes of change; and it has substituted a complex view of time and change for a simplistic linear view of change over time. Specifically, the new social history has succeeded in bringing women, children, youth, old people, laborers, slaves, serfs, peasants, farmers, immigrants, and other neglected groups into the historical arena. Focusing on private life as a subject that is important in its own right, the new social history has introduced human intimacy, sexuality, and emotions as legitimate areas of historical research and has provided important linkages between public and private life. It has integrated experiences such as growing up, marrying, parenting, widowhood, and death into the social context. By shuttling back and forth between the private and the public spheres, this type of research has highlighted the boundaries as well as the interconnectedness between the two (Ariès, 1962; Perrot, 1990; Stearns and Stearns, 1988).

Without becoming antiquarian and localized, the new social history has introduced the study of everyday life into the tapestry of history. The main reason the history of everyday life has had such a significant impact is that it has been preoccupied not merely with the nuts and bolts of how people did things (although this was important as well) but also with the interrelationships of such activities with household and family and with work and community. In all these areas, it has succeeded in linking social life with material culture.

The new social history has shown in a more direct way how social change impinges on the lives of people and how, in turn, human agency has affected social change. It has introduced a dynamic dimension into the study of the major processes of urbanization and industrialization and has examined their meaning to the people participating in them and coping with them. Ultimately, by revising stereotypes and myths about the preindustrial period, it has led to a break with a nonexistent past.

Time and Motion

Let us now consider a detailed example of how the contributions of the subfields of the new social history together introduced a sense of time and motion into the larger history. Many of us still remember the impact of Stephan Thernstrom and Peter Knights's work on historians and sociologists alike. When their article "Men in Motion" (1971) appeared, it jolted us into recognizing that in the nineteenth century, close to one-half of an urban population present at one moment was unaccounted for a decade later. Although Rowland Berthoff (1960) and others had already emphasized transiency and turnover as major characteristics of American society, Thernstrom and Knights provided a graphic, statistical description of who moved and why and what their movement meant to urban communities.[2]

Thernstrom and Knights posed a significant question: If American city dwellers were as footloose as our evidence suggests, how was any cultural continuity—or even the appearance of it—maintained? Somewhat later, the study of the family offered an answer: In most situations, migration was organized under the auspices of kin, even if individuals seemingly migrated alone (Bieder, 1973; Tilly and Brown, 1974; Hareven, 1978b). Kin acted as a conveyer belt for migrants from one community to the next and for back-and-forth migration. Through chain migration, family members and extended kin brought each other into the same neighborhoods (Bott, 1957; Hareven, 1982). Proximity of kin held urban neighborhoods together. But kin members did not do it alone; they overlapped with networks of former villagers and townspeople (Schwarzweller, Brown, and Mangalam, 1971). Another stabilizing force provided by the family was the absorption of young adult migrants or immigrants into the household. Boarding and lodging with families, moreover, offered some stability and continuity for young men and women who had left their parental homes and who joined the households of middle-aged or older adults while migrating (Modell and Hareven, 1973). In short, the family, the larger kin group, and the household fulfilled important roles in ordering migration and in stabilizing urban society.

Labor history has further enriched the picture by answering the question about why people moved. David Montgomery had emphasized that one of the very few sources of control that workers had over their working conditions was to quit. Underlying the massive labor turnover at the beginning of this century that bewildered industrial employers was the workers' desire to exercise some control over their lives (Montgomery, 1967). My study of the Amoskeag workers' careers, as reflected in the corporation's cumulative employee files, has shown, however, that quitting was by no means terminal. Quitters were often repeaters and were readmitted during periods of labor shortage (Hareven, 1982).

Labor turnover, voluntary or nonvoluntary, has dramatized the vulnerability of workers as a continuing social phenomenon. The discovery in American society throughout the nineteenth and during a major part of the twentieth century that what Harold Wilensky (1961) called "disorderly careers" was the norm has led us to consider the implications of this phenomenon for security and stability in the larger society. The instability of work lives was not limited to American society. Some of Lyon's silk weavers, whose work in this luxury industry had continued over several generations, referred to their careers as "transient." Similarly, the Kyoto silk weavers whom I interviewed over a decade repeatedly described their lives as *sono hi gurashi,* a hand-to-mouth existence, resulting from the fickleness of the silk industry. They thus experienced continuity in the discontinuity and precariousness of their careers (Hareven, 1992a). Once again, it was kin who bore the lion's share of the responsibility for coping with the change and adversity of laborers' disorderly careers.

Reexamining Social Change

As Charles Tilly (1987) expressed it, the main goal of social history is to understand the linkage between individual lives and small-scale experiences and the larger processes of social change. The family plays a central role in this because it is an arena in which many of the relations between individuals and social change are acted out. The family also serves as a broker between individuals, institutions, and social change (Hareven, 1994b). This is why some of us in the first generation of researchers on the history of the family viewed the family as a missing link. And this is why I first became interested in the historical study of the family. It was important to study the family in its interaction with these processes rather than in isolation (Hareven and Plakans, 1987). Not only has family history provided the missing link in our understanding of the relationship between individuals and social change, but cumulative findings in the field have led to reinterpretations of the pace and meaning of the "grand" processes and, consequently, of the standard periodization (Hareven, 1971, 1991a; Wrigley, 1972; Stone, 1977).

Specifically, findings in family history have challenged one of the major markers of periodization in West European and American history, namely, the industrial revolution and the ensuing dichotomy between "preindustrial" and "industrial" society. As John Demos (1970) stated, the family develops and changes at its own pace and does not necessarily conform to the standard historical periodization. The early findings of Louis Henry and the Annales group in France, the Cambridge Group for the History of Population and Social Structure, and historians of colonial North America—that preindustrial populations resided in small, predominantly nuclear households, married later than previously assumed, and practiced some form of family limitation—have led to a drastic revision of generalizations about the impact of industrialization on family and demographic behavior (Laslett, 1965; Wrigley, 1966a; Henry, 1968; Goubert, 1970; Laslett and Wall, 1972; Wheaton, 1987).

Since the industrial revolution did not produce the "Western European family pattern," E. A. Wrigley concluded that "it may prove mistaken to assume that the industrial revolution coincided with great changes," proposing instead that "earlier changes within a still rural society may have been as great or greater" (1977, p. 77). Significantly, Wrigley urged that industrialization be separated from modernization. By denying a simple cause-and-effect relationship between industrialization and social change, historical research on the family has raised new questions about the "phasing" of historical change in social life (Kertzer and Hogan, 1989). Consequently, it has led to a rejection of simplistic linear interpretations and has opened the debate as to whether the industrial revolution occurred at all.

Findings on the family's contributions to industrialization as well as its adaptation to it have shed light on how industrialization may have actually happened. These findings have reversed the stereotypes of family passivity and breakdown during industrialization and have documented the family's role as an active agent (Goode, 1963; Anderson, 1971; Hareven, 1982). Neil Smelser's (1959) discovery of workers' recruitment in family units into the textile factories in early nineteenth-century Lancashire demonstrated that the very success of the industrial system depended on a continuous flow of labor from the countryside to the industrializing centers.

My own research has challenged the stereotype of family breakdown and of the uprooting of kinship ties under the impact of industrialization and migration. As I found in my study of the textile workers in the Amoskeag Mills, the emergent as well as the mature factory system was dependent on kin for recruiting workers, organizing or assisting in migration, training young workers or newly arrived immigrants on the factory floor, interpreting, and supervising or disciplining the younger members of kinship groups. Workers carried their kinship ties and their traditions of reciprocity into the factory. They modified them in response to the pressures of the factory and addressed the industrial system on its own terms (Hareven, 1978b, 1982).

Earlier, Herbert Gutman and David Montgomery shed light on the active role that workers played in modifying the factory system to meet their needs by bringing their own customs and traditions to bear on this process (Montgomery, 1967; Gutman, 1976b). Family history has contributed an understanding of the extent to which the family and the kin group exercised job controls within the factory, disciplined new members not to exceed production quotas when they were pushed to do so, and protected their younger and new immigrant members on the factory floor (Hareven, 1982). The discovery of this interaction between the workers' families and capitalist enterprises has also shed new light on how industrial enterprises functioned, in several areas: their use of kin to recruit and stabilize a labor force; their employment of family metaphors and family ties to develop and sustain paternalistic regimes in order to foster the loyalty of a labor force; and their reliance on family loyalties to reduce labor turnover and break strikes (Hareven, 1978b; Smelser and Halpern, 1978).

Finally, as shown above, these findings have also provided a critique of modernization theory. The Amoskeag workers' encounter with the modern factory led neither to the abandonment of their premigration traditions nor to rigid adherence to them. Rather, immigrant laborers adapted their customs and social organization selectively to the new conditions they encountered. Modernization in the workplace did not automatically lead to "modern" family behavior, as Alex Inkeles and David A. Smith (1974) argued. Selectivity was the key principle in the workers' adaptation (Hareven, 1976b, 1982).

Proto-Industrialization

Even prior to the emergence of the factory system, the employment of family members in what Franklin Mendels (1972), Hans Medick (1976), Rudolph Braun (1960, 1978), and others called "proto-industrialization" in Europe led to a reinterpretation of industrialization itself (Levine, 1983). The demographic model of proto-industrialization, involving early marriage and higher fertility, has recently come under criticism (Gutmann and Leboutte, 1984; Mitterauer, 1992; Pfister, 1992).[3] Nevertheless, the concept of proto-industrialization has been an important contribution to our understanding of how transitions from one form of industrial production to another occurred. Proto-industrial production prepared a family labor force for the factory, even if the tasks and the skills required there were not identical. More important, the discovery of proto-industrialization as a phase preceding the factory system has directed attention to the diversity of urban and rural household-based production, whose origins preceded those of the factory system. Significantly, some of these forms of household production overlapped with the factory system.

Through the study of family work patterns, however, it has become clear that the factory did not succeed household production in a linear fashion; rather, the two systems coexisted over a considerable period, depending on the region. As Jane Quataert (1985) found in her study of the textile industry in nineteenth-century Saxony, behind this coexistence were the strategies of the workers' families. Exercising a "flexible family economy," some members tended to be employed in the factory while others worked in household production, depending on the availability of work and on the need for child care and for raising food on small garden plots. I found a similar coexistence of production in the household and in small factories among the silk weavers of Kyoto in the early twentieth century (Hareven, 1993a).

Women's history added a new dimension to the examination of the transition from proto-industrial production to the factory system by posing the "proto-industrial carryover hypothesis," namely, that the sex typing of women's occupations as secondary and lower-paying jobs originated in proto-industrial households and subsequently carried over into the factory and the larger society (Tilly and Scott, 1978; Hudson and Lee, 1990). Recent research has provided new evidence that the carryover was far more complex than portrayed in the earlier interpretation. Even though proto-industrial women found employment in factories, the type of work they did there was different from their work in the household industry. Their work depended both on the type of industry prior to the transfer of production to the factory and on changing technology (Rose, 1987; Jordan, 1989). The continuation of the debate over these issues is important in examining linkages between the gendered division of labor in the family and in the larger society (Hareven, 1994c).

The family thus played a central role in charting the transitions to various modes of industrial production by following diverse routes: from a rural economy to a proto-industrial and then to an industrial one or, alternatively, from a rural economy directly to an industrial one. The strategies of laboring families both facilitated the transition and maintained the coexistence.

Family Strategies

Historical research on family strategies has demonstrated that ordinary people had life plans of their own and made choices in response to the opportunities and constraints they encountered, for example, ups and downs in the economy, political upheavals, and discrete local changes (Hareven, 1990a). Such strategies can be best described as interrelated family decisions and plans governing household membership, marriage and family limitation, migration, labor-force participation, and consumption (Goldin, 1981). Family strategies involve explicit or implicit choices families make for the present, for the future, or for long-term needs. Central to this perspective is an emphasis on family action as a dynamic process, which involves a constantly changing interaction of personalities rather than a view of the family as a monolithic entity.

Recently, the concept of family strategies has been rightly subjected to a criticism that asks whose strategies were family strategies. To what extent and in what ways did family members participate in the collective decisions impinging on their lives? The concern has been that the emphasis on the family as a collective entity might obscure the roles of individual members in the decisionmaking process (Hareven, 1991a). These questions have opened the door to a continuation of empirical work that has led to the discovery of further complexity and diversity in family decisionmaking.

The focus on collective family strategies has proved its significance, nevertheless, because people's interaction with changing economic conditions and institutions is no longer viewed as strictly individual but as tied to collective family decisions. It has also made an important contribution to our understanding of the role of culture by demonstrating that the choices that families made were not guided strictly by economic need. Rather, they were driven by the interaction of economic and cultural factors. In issues such as children's or wives' labor or family expenditure patterns, even economically marginal families did not always make the most prudent choices, from a purely economic point of view, if such choices were inconsistent with their own cultural values (Engerman, 1978; Hareven, 1992a). Underlying family strategies, human agency is at work in various historical settings.

The Role of Human Agency

The emphasis on human agency as a central theme of the new social history has shifted the spotlight from the great heroes and elites to common people and has reversed the prevailing stereotypes that women, workers, slaves, immigrants, and the family itself were passive victims of historical and institutional change and that they succumbed to external pressures. When the historical investigation started from the vantage point of the people involved rather than from that of the institutions, it also shed new light on the ways the institutions functioned.

The cumulative body of research over the past three decades has provided splendid examples of the active role that individuals and families took. For example, findings in historical demography have shown that even in preindustrial society, couples tried to limit the size of their families by practicing birth control (Wrigley, 1966a; D. S. Smith, 1974; Laslett, 1977a). Recently, James Lee, Wang Feng, and Cameron A. Campbell (1994) have identified the significance of human agency to family limitation in China among the nobility of the Ching dynasty. As Herbert Gutman (1976a) eloquently demonstrated, slaves struggled to keep families together or to reunite them. Andrejs Plakans and Charles Wetherall (1995) have shown that serfs on Baltic estates achieved some control over their family lives through negotiations with the estate owners. In America, factory workers used their kinship ties to adapt to industrial work and to resist the pressure of speedups (Hareven, 1982). More recently, Linda Gordon (1988) has found that victims of child abuse and family violence, attempting to become the heroes of their own lives, struggled against their caretaking agencies and their abusers, and Theda Skocpol (1992) has documented the effectiveness of grassroots movements among mothers and soldiers in the introduction of pensions in the United States.

The discovery of individuals' and families' efforts to seize control of their lives has exorcised the ghosts of social breakdown from the study of migration, industrial workplaces, urban communities, and institutions of welfare and social control. This type of exorcism, however, could go too far by reversing the stereotype mechanistically and by claiming that families were always in control of their lives. There is one question—Under what circumstances was the family in control of its destiny, and under what circumstances did it lose control?—that continues to provide a theoretical and empirical agenda for the examination of a large range of social processes.

It is important to realize that individuals or families might be resilient at one point in their lives but not at another, depending on external circumstances and internal events. As William Thomas put it, "The family is both the product and the producer of its career" (in Volkart, 1951, p. 93). We also need to ask: What were the social dynamics of resilience? How could kin continue to assist each other if they were all rendered powerless by the same circumstances? At what price did people assist their kin? And at what price to whom?

Now that the historical literature has recognized the family's active response to opportunities and constraints, it has become necessary to examine what loss has meant to families and how they coped with war, unemployment, and insecurity resulting from business cycles and the shutdown of industries. The former workers in the Amoskeag Mills whom my collaborators and I interviewed in the 1970s were very articulate about the meaning of loss. Mrs. Skrzysowski, a fifty-two-year-old battery hand, expressed it eloquently on her last day in the Chicopee Mill, February 15, 1975, when the last textile mill closed in Manchester:

> You've worked all this time and now you see it shutting down. You go up the aisle and see one loom running here, back and forth, and then stop, all empty. You go up and down the aisle and say, "I used to have all these looms to fill." Now you don't have anything. Now it's so empty, you can almost hear the stillness come across the room. . . . People don't say very much when they're leaving. They're sad and a lot of them cry. It's a bad thing when there are no jobs to be had. (Hareven and Langenbach, 1978, p. 381)[4]

During my research in Kyoto and Lyon, I became even more attuned to the significance of loss and abandonment in the contexts of declining or vanishing industries. The former factory workers and artisans there, too, had experienced not only material loss but the loss of the world of work with which their identity had been strongly intertwined.

The Subjective Reconstruction of Past Lives

The life-course approach has provided a way of understanding how people perceive the relationship of their lives to historical events and their own roles as actors. The reconstruction of life histories by the actors themselves enables us to understand how they interpret the historical experiences that have affected their lives. Efforts in oral history in the late 1960s and early 1970s have focused the attention of social historians on the subjective nature of the interview process and its significances.[5] Oral history of ordinary people as a legitimate source of historical inquiry rather than the earlier use of the memoirs of leading figures became widespread and acceptable in the 1970s. More than a source of factual evidence or a reconstruction of reality, oral history is a recreation of people's memories and perceptions (Hareven, 1978d). It teaches us what people remember, why they remember, and how they remember. The recognition that interviews are sources of perception rather than of fact has been an important step in interpreting life histories and memoirs. Doing so in context, by linking subjective narratives to other documentary sources and by relating them to the social and institutional structures in which the people interviewed lived, has emerged as a significant development since the 1970s.

The former laborers and artisans with whom I conducted life-history interviews in the United States, Japan, and France expressed again and again their consciousness of occupying a special moment on the stage of history. When I approached these men and women initially, however, they hesitated and were ambivalent about their historical roles and their meaning (Hareven, 1992a). In all three societies, I had to explain to them why the stories of their lives, as opposed to the exclusive use of archival materials, were important for the reconstruction of the historical picture. In Lyon, Mr. L., a sixty-year-old weaver, said to me on the phone: "I have nothing to tell you. I just closed my atelier. I am finished." When I explained that that was precisely why I wanted to meet him, he acquiesced. When I arrived at his apartment on the top floor of a traditional weavers' building in La Croix Rousse (the former silk-weaving district) and introduced myself, he pointed to himself and said, *"Voilà le dernier Canut"* ["Here is the last Canut"]. ("Canut" is the historical nickname for the household weavers in Lyon. Many former weavers feel that it was once derogatory, but now it has become a mark of pride and identity.)[6]

Mr. L.'s self-characterization reminded me instantly of the Kyoto silk weavers, who, during my first visit to observe their work, in 1982, said, "We are the last generation to do this." As one highly skilled weaver put it: "Young people do not want to succeed to our work, because this industry has no future. I belong to the 'young' generation. I am forty-eight years old. Some weavers are older than seventy. Real good hand-loom weaving will disappear from Nishijin when my generation gets old." Once the people I approached were persuaded to talk, they became partners in the interview process. At the end of our last interview on that visit to Japan, one silk weaver said to me, "Be sure to return soon, because you are taking part of our lives with you" (Hareven, 1992a).

Research on the subjective reconstruction of lives has shown very clearly that individuals interpret their life history in relation to the social structures and the culture within which they function. They attribute meaning to their life stories by placing them in a larger context, and they employ their respective cultural backgrounds (LeVine, 1978, p. 290). For example, a former shoemaker in Manchester was eighty years old when we interviewed him. He said that he was nineteen when he got married and that his bride was the same age. When asked whether this would have been considered the right age to get married, he replied: "Oh no! For shoemakers that was not the general age, because you know, they never made too much money . . . so that was considered young. And I know that both sides of the family had tried to discourage us from getting married so young. But anyway we got married and brought up five kids." He proceeded to explain why he had insisted on getting married: "We grew up together, always had one another in childhood and even in our religious beliefs. We were baptized at the same time, had first Communion and Confirmation together and we got married not because we were obliged to, but we felt as though we'd been together so long in all kinds of sacraments we might as well get married."

Thus, how individuals interpret turning points, transitions, and stages in their lives is shaped by the historical events they experience and by their cultural orientation (Hareven, 1986). From a comparison of the subjective reconstruction of the life course of three cohorts in Manchester, it became clear that the cohorts' interpretations of continuities and discontinuities in their life course differed. As detailed above, the parent cohort composed the former textile workers on whose lives *Family Time and Industrial Time* was based (Hareven, 1982). They had come to adulthood at the turn of the century. The children's generation consisted of two cohorts, whose members had come to adulthood in the Great Depression and in World War II, respectively (Hareven and Adams, 1996). Members of the parent cohort attributed discontinuities and turning points primarily to external events, whereas the children's cohorts, especially the later cohort, interpreted them as emanating from personal and familial experiences. The parent cohort expressed little consciousness of having gone through stages such as "adolescence," "middle age," and the "empty nest." They considered external events, connected with wars, migration, and business cycles, especially the decline of the textile industry, the nine-month-long strike in 1922, and the shutdown of the Amoskeag Mills, to be much more critical than individual or familial transitions. The children's cohorts, by contrast, were highly conscious of culturally defined stages in their life courses. Unlike the parent cohort, the children's cohorts (especially the later one) had a clear view of their life course as being structured around sequences of normative transitions and punctuated by turning points. When asked what had been the major crises in their lives, some mentioned adolescence and middle-age crisis (Hareven and Masaoka, 1988; Hareven, 1991a).[7]

In the 1990s, historians have begun to view the process of reconstructing life histories and family histories as social phenomena to be analyzed in their own right, rather than merely as research tools. This has led to a redefinition of the subject of research itself. For example, historians in France study familial memory as a topic in its own right, not only as a source of factual information. Thus, some scholars analyze genealogies not as sources for reconstructing family patterns but as documents created by families to enhance their identities (Burguière, 1993).

The subjective reconstruction of past lives has also challenged us with new responsibilities as interviewers and interpreters of our data. Interviewing is a process of interaction between the interviewer and the person interviewed. We need to know who we are as interviewers and what our role is when people generate their life stories. We also need to know what we bring with us to the interviews and what we leave behind; what impact our séances have on those people revisiting their own lives and what we give back to them and to their communities. On my last visit to their house in Kyoto, Mr. and Mrs. K. expressed frustration over their inability to explain fully what was happening around them in the tragic decline of Nishijin, the traditional silk-weaving community, although they had provided thoughtful and incisive explanations for the work relations there: Mr. K. said: "It is also hard for us weavers to understand each other's feelings. I was born in Nishijin and my wife has been involved in Nishijin for over twenty years, and it is still hard for us to understand. And this is where the complexity lies."

The Life Course and the
Rediscovery of Complexity

The contributions of the new social history—time and motion, time and place, linked lives with the larger processes, human agency and family strategies, and the subjective reconstruction of lives—are all principles of the life-course approach and have become connected and elucidated through it. By focusing on the synchronization of various levels of timing—individual, familial, institutional, and historical—the life-course paradigm has provided a way of examining the interaction of lives with the forces of social history and an understanding of how external historical events impinge on individuals and families (Elder, 1978; Hareven, 1978b).

The life-course approach has offered a way of capturing the complexity of the impact of social change on people and, conversely, of the contribution of people to facilitating or modifying social change. As Everett Hughes (1971b, p. 124) put it: "Every man is born, lives, and dies in historic time. As he runs through the life-cycle characteristic of our species, each phase of it joins in the events of the world. . . . Some men come to the age of work when there is no work; others when there are wars." Our understanding of this interaction has been achieved largely by emphasizing the experience of cohorts as a dynamic process (Ryder, 1965). In life-course research, a cohort is defined as an age group that has shared common historical experiences. In this respect, a cohort is different from a generation (Kertzer, 1983).

Cohort experience should not be misconstrued, however, as cohort determinism. Sophisticated life-course analysis has paid attention to differences *within* cohorts in their reaction and adaptation to historical circumstances, along lines of gender, ethnicity, educational level, and class, for example. It has also shown that the impact of historical events on the life course is cumulative but not irreversible. This means that the negative impact of societal forces at one point in people's lives could be modified or reversed later. Glen Elder and I have examined the impact of World War II on the cohorts of young men in Berkeley, California, and in Manchester, New Hampshire, in answer to the question "Why did the Great Depression not produce a lost generation?" (Elder and Hareven, 1993). We found that military service had a major role in reversing or mitigating the negative impact of the Great Depression on the lives of these young men from disadvantaged backgrounds (see Chapter 8).

Another major contribution of the life course has been the recognition of life stage as an important determinant of the impact of historical events on individual lives. For example, the stage of life at which individuals felt the impact of the Great Depression was critical to their subsequent adaptation (Elder, 1995). Related to life stage is the concept of "disorderly cohorts," introduced by Joan Waring (1975) to explain the mismatch between the economic opportunities and the career plans of different cohorts entering adulthood in relation to changing opportunity structures. At the same time, life stage has warned us against what Matilda Riley (1978) called the reification of age, because life stage emphasizes social age rather than calendar age.

The life-course paradigm has directed attention to the dynamic interaction of time and place in people's lives and in institutions. Its very metaphors, such as "clocks," "trajectories," "transitions," and "convoys," emphasize dynamics and synchronization and reflect aspects of appropriate timing or ill timing in educational, work, and family careers. It has thus introduced a cultural dimension in defining the appropriate time clocks for being "early," "late," or "on time" when negotiating the transition to adulthood and other life transitions (Neugarten and Datan, 1973; Fry and Keith, 1982; Hareven and Masaoka, 1988; Modell, 1989; Hogan, 1991).

An understanding of the social and cultural construction of the life course helps explain why institutions, such as schools and juvenile reformatories, and legislation, such as compulsory school attendance and old-age pensions, that addressed different stages of life emerged when they did. The life-course paradigm has provided an important way of linking human development to institutional change. The timing of life transitions and the rhythms of life trajectories are relevant to our understanding of educational and work careers and to the juggling of such careers in relation to opportunity structures. Research on the timing of life transitions has identified the emergence of the institutionalization of the life course in Western society over this century. As Denis Hogan put it, "The emergence of a set of rules and preferences implicit in the organization of schools, labor markets, and retirement systems are viewed as creating a standardized life course, with which the subjective life course [of the individuals] resonates" (1989, p. 97).

Even though research on the life course started from the perspective of individual and family lives, it has led to an understanding that agencies and institutions have a life course of their own and that development within them takes place as part of a larger process of change and affects lives in turn. In my study of family and work in the Amoskeag Mills, for example, it was important to relate the life course of the workers to that of the factory. As the factory kept changing, the impact of its policies on the workers assumed new dimensions as well (Hareven, 1982).

A key concept of the life course is the interdependence of lives. Hence, the synchronization of individual timing with that of the family as a collective unit is a central aspect of life-course analysis (Hareven, 1991b). Far from being centered on the individual, the life-course paradigm has captured the complexity of the synchronization of individual time with family time and with larger societal spheres and institutions. In Glen Elder's words: "Much like an interactionist, the life-course analyst moves back and forth between the individual and the group level. The resulting portrait depicts 'family in people and people in family'" (Elder, 1981, p. 509). The pressure on individuals to synchronize transitions with those of the family was a potential source of family conflict. Understanding such pressures sheds light on how individuals and families relate to outside structures, such as labor markets and educational and welfare systems (Hareven, 1994a).

Central to the concept of linked lives are the questions "Who travels with whom over life, and how do these configurations change?" The life-course approach has directed attention to the fluidity of life trajectories and to the interlocking and separation of career paths of couples, siblings, parents and children, other kin, and unrelated individuals. Whether the networks of individuals who travel together over certain periods of their lives consist of kin, surrogate kin, friends, or other associates, a study of their changing configurations can provide an understanding of how social supports are shared and exchanged among generations and how networks formed early in life have an impact on the availability of supports later (Hareven and Uhlenberg, 1995; Hareven and Adams, 1996). An alliance between research on the life course and network analysis could thus be a powerful means not only to examine networks but to understand how they are formed and re-formed over lifetimes and historical time.

Looking to the Future

In summary, the new social history has introduced a dynamic dimension into the interpretation of social change. Although historians have traditionally viewed their tasks as searching for order and identifying the categories under which social phenomena could be effectively shelved and explained, the new social history has brought forth a beneficial, controlled chaos that does justice to the complexity of real life. It has focused attention on transitions rather than stages, on different time clocks ticking away simultaneously, on people moving into and out of households, on disorderly careers and fickle institutions, on the coexistence of various forms of industrial production, on the complexity of the timing of historical change, and on the selective adaptation of people to new social and cultural conditions. It has made fluid, multilayered phenomena acceptable.

Does recognition and acceptance of these patterns in the past call for a new synthesis?[8] It is still an open question. In his provocative article "Have Social Historians Lost the Civil War?" Maris Vinovskis (1989a) expressed the concern that a preoccupation with the topics of the new social history might lead to the neglect of more "traditional" ones. Since then, social history has shed new light on traditional topics by posing new questions, utilizing new methodologies and sources, and reinterpreting old explanations.

One important characteristic of historical scholarship is its tendency to revise itself. Many early findings in the new social history have already been challenged, revised, or modified (Berkhofer, 1995). As we continue to practice in these fields, it is important that we keep this dynamics alive, so that new findings and revisions in our subfields continue to infuse the larger field of history with new interpretations. It is also important, as Vinovskis has pointed out, that new generations of social historians continue to train in social-science methods or the skills to produce this kind of history will be lost.

Cross-Cultural Dimensions

The route that I have found particularly enriching and revitalizing for social history is cross-cultural research. My exposure to Japan has led to a great transformation in my role as an American historian. The decade during which I conducted comparative research on family and work among the silk weavers in Kyoto exposed me to what de Tocqueville described as turning the mirror onto ourselves. Part of my impetus was the conversation I had had with several highly skilled silk weavers in Nishijin before I actually planned to embark on research in Japan. As I described earlier in this book, I asked them certain questions that had emerged from my study of the Amoskeag Mills. The weavers were silent. Finally, one of them asked, "How do you know to ask these questions?" They thought I was familiar with unique and not generally known aspects of their work lives. For me, it was the beginning of a long engagement. Comparative research in Kyoto became important in its own right. It led to the turning of the mirror back and forth and, finally, after my research in Japan, inspired me to do research in Lyon.

Research in which we immerse ourselves in the societies we are comparing is more likely to render meaningful results than research conducted extensively in one society and then compared with secondary sources for another society. From a practical point of view, such research is not possible for most historians. But collaborative cross-cultural research projects are possible. Comparison is important not only for assessing uniqueness, an ongoing concern in American studies, but also for understanding how similar social forces affect people in various societies differentially as they encounter great transformations. To me, the most important lesson of cross-cultural comparison is that phenomena of social change that appear similar on the surface are not necessarily the same underneath. Grand social changes are mediated through local cultures.

Notes

Preface

1. A cohort is defined here as an age group that shared a common historical experience.

Chapter One

1. My own involvement in family history reflects these trends. In 1967, the United States Children's Bureau commissioned a collaborative documentary history of children in American society. Headed by Robert H. Bremner, that project led to a pathbreaking collection, *Children and Youth in America: A Documentary History* (Bremner et al., 1970–1974). While working on this project, I became interested in linking children's history to family experience, especially in the relationship between the family and industrialization. Two conferences I organized at Clark University (one in 1970 titled "Childhood and Youth in Historical Perspective" and a second in 1971 called "The Family: Social Change and Social Structure") aroused such widespread interest in this area that the Rockefeller Foundation offered to support a Family History Program at Clark University aimed at developing the newly emerging research through conferences and workshops, including a newsletter, *The Family in Historical Perspective*, which I started editing in 1973. The newsletter was published by the Newberry Library in Chicago, which also had an influential training program in quantitative methodology that included family history and historical demography. The second phase of the Family History Program at Clark was supported by the Education Division of the National Endowment for the Humanities. In 1975, I proposed to the National Council on Family Relations (NCFR) the establishment of a scholarly journal on the history of the family. With the support of the NCFR, Robert Wheaton and I launched the *Journal of Family History: Studies in Kinship, Family and Demography (JFH)* (first issue, fall 1976). The *Journal* was published by the NCFR, 1976–1986, and by JAI Press from 1986 on, under the sponsorship of the NCFR. *JFH* has published special issues on France, Latin America, Central and Eastern Europe, China and Japan, the Iberian Peninsula, and Sweden; thematic issues on family and sexuality in France, anthropology and family history, and spinsterhood; papers from the Rockefeller Foundation's conference on women, work, and the family, September 21–22, 1978, from the Shelby Collum Davis Center for Historical Studies, Princeton University, and from Old Sturbridge Village.

2. Swedish demographic data are exceptionally rich because parish registers kept track of members even after they had migrated elsewhere. The most elaborate reconstitution and data linkage project in Sweden is now being carried out in

Umeå; for analyses of the Umeå data base, see the special issue of *JFH*, Tom Erics-
son and Lars-Göran Tedebrand, guest editors, vol. 14, no. 3 (1989). Family reconstitution in Japan was pioneered by Akira Hayami, who from the early 1960s on
embarked on a massive data linkage project from local population registers.

3. Recently, Hajnal's thesis has been applied to Eastern Europe and to Japan,
and there is now serious question on how unique the model is for Europe and
how general it is.

4. The seminars were funded by the Mathematics Social Science Board of the
National Science Foundation under the mentorship of Charles Tilly. The resulting
analysis, accompanied by interdisciplinary essays on the life-course approach,
was published in 1978 in Hareven, ed., *Transitions: The Family and the Life Course in
Historical Perspective*. The volume contains five articles, by historians Bengt Ankarloo, Howard Chudacoff, Tamara Hareven, Karen Mason, John Modell, and Maris
Vinovskis, who collaborated in various configurations on the analysis of life transitions using the same data set from the census manuscript schedules of Essex
County, Massachusetts, 1880, and articles by Glen Elder on the life-course approach, by Peter Ulhenberg on demographic dimensions, by Stanley Engerman
on an economic perspective, and by Robert LeVine on a cross-cultural anthropological perspective.

5. Initially, the richest studies of kinship were based on peasant communities,
in the preindustrial period and in the nineteenth century. Robert Wheaton's reconstruction of kinship networks in seventeenth-century Bordeaux provides an
exemplary model of an analysis of urban kinship networks in the early modern
period.

6. Anderson documented the vital role of kinship ties in workers' migration
from rural Lancashire and from southern Ireland to the industrial town of Preston,
but he did not have data illuminating the role of kin inside the factories during
daily work situations.

7. William Goode urged the reversal of the stereotype of the family as a passive
agent to a view of the family as an active agent in the process of industrialization.
He challenged historians to produce the evidence.

8. Mendels coined the term "proto-industrialization."

9. Saito concluded that proto-industrialization in Japan was not accompanied by
demographic changes as in Western Europe.

Chapter Two

1. These patterns of residence were reconstructed from city directories and addresses listed in the Amoskeag Company's employee files.

2. For definitions and descriptions of traditional kinship systems, see Fox
(1967), Arensberg and Kimball (1968), Fortes (1969), and Levi-Strauss (1969). For a
historical analysis of legal changes governing American family and kinship organization, see Farber (1973).

3. For a theoretical discussion of the instrumentality of kin in modern society,
see also Bennett and Despres (1960).

4. Adjustment, June 26, 1920, Amoskeag Records, Baker Library, Harvard University.

5. Bott's model has been subsequently applied to a variety of neighborhood and community studies in England and the United States, most notably Michael Young and Peter Willmott's study of East London (1957) and Herbert Gans's study of Boston's West End (1962).

6. Compare also with Litwak's assertion that geographic propinquity is not an essential condition for the maintenance of extended kinship ties (1960).

7. Similarly, in his study of the impact of geographic mobility on middle-class kinship ties, Litwak demonstrated the persistence of kinship ties over a wider geographic space (1960).

8. Recently, the extent to which St. Denis is representative of most rural Quebec communities has been questioned. No comparable studies for other Quebec communities are available, however.

9. For a more detailed description of the reconstruction of kinship networks and the use of other sources (Amoskeag Corporation Records), see *Family Time and Industrial Time* appendices (Hareven, 1982) and "The Subjective Reconstruction of Past Lives" in the same book.

Chapter Six

1. In addition to the qualitative textual analysis of the interviews, we also reconstructed individual migration, educational, and work histories for each individual in the two cohorts from the interview data, as well as from city directories, employee files, and vital records. In Shizuoka, the Japanese researchers carried out a series of interviews between 1981 and 1983, using survey questionnaires. The last interview stage in Shizuoka in 1984 was an intensive, open-ended one, in which the men were encouraged to describe their turning points in detail.

2. I am indebted to Kanji Masaoka for his collaboration on the comparative study of the life course of American and Japanese men.

Chapter Seven

1. By tracing the children of the historical cohorts, their spouses, the siblings of the spouses, and other family members in Manchester, as well as in other parts of the United States, we followed relatives along kinship networks as far as possible (Hareven, 1982). We assembled this group of interviewees in a "snowball" method and interviewed all kin who responded. We interviewed each person three times, using open-ended questions in two-hour to three-hour sessions. The interview questions covered a broad range of areas pertaining to the interviewee's life history. Many questions focused in great detail on the issues of assistance over the life course and support networks in old age. Wherever possible, we elicited the perceptions of the children and the parents or of several siblings on the same issues covered in the interviews.

In addition to interviews, we also constructed a demographic history, migration history, work history, and family history for each individual. We then linked this sequential information into a "time-life line," reconstructing the individual's life chronologically, in relation to age and historical time. This enabled us to examine in each individual the synchronization of work-life transitions with family transitions and to relate patterns of timing to the interviewees' subjective accounts of the life course in the interviews. The time-life lines also enabled us to analyze differences within each cohort. (See also Chapter 6.)

The detailed reconstruction of the life histories and of the migration and work histories of these cohorts enables us to relate earlier life events to later ones and to identify life-course patterns as important variables in kin assistance in old age. A comparison of the two cohorts provides a perspective on changes over historical time and an understanding of the ways in which the patterns of assistance of each cohort were shaped by the historical circumstances and cultural values affecting their lifetimes.

Chapter Eight

1. The Berkeley and Manchester studies used different regimes in collecting and analyzing data. The Berkeley data are longitudinal records based on recurring interviews and observations that extend to 1928–1929 and follow an annual schedule across the 1930s up to 1945. Adult follow-ups were carried out in 1960, 1972, and 1982. Using these data, it was possible to construct life histories from early childhood to the later years of life. Much of the data analysis on which the Berkeley study is based is quantitative. By contrast, the Manchester study relies on retrospective data that Hareven and her associates gathered through extensive life-history interviews. These interviews were then augmented with demographic data on family histories and immigration and employment histories for each interviewee. The Manchester project uses both quantitative and qualitative analysis of the interview data. In preparing this chapter, we have sought to blend these two styles of research as much as possible.

2. Throughout the remainder of this chapter, we have used unpublished quotations from Hareven's Manchester data. Respondents' names have been changed to protect their anonymity.

Chapter Ten

1. I carried out all the interviews with the help of intepreters and recorded the interviews on cassette tapes. In preparation for the interviews, I familiarized myself with the various procedures and terminology in textile production in Nishijin. I also learned these terminologies, as well as terms of kinship in Japanese, in order to avoid mistranslation. During the interview, the interpreters translated longer narratives in summary form. We recorded both the English and the Japanese statements in the interview. Following the interview, I had each tape translated systematically into an English typescript. The translation was done by individuals other than the interview interpreters. This provided a complete translation of the entire interview, including a transcript of the English parts. It also provided an additional check on the translation.

2. This chapter is based only on the interviews of the urban weavers in Nishijin. The cottage weavers in the Tango Peninsula on the Japan Sea started weaving

Nishijin *obi* only about fifteen years ago. The majority of these weavers in the countryside have lower skills, weave less complex fabrics, and use power looms predominantly.

3. Nishijin people refer symbolically to this district as *mura*. Nishijin is a neighborhood within Kyoto, encompassed primarily in the Jamigyoku ward of Kyoto City. When the emperor established it as a weavers' settlement at the end of the Onin war, it was outside the Western Wall of Kyoto, hence its name "Western Camp."

4. *Noren* is a split curtain that hangs over shops, restaurants, and other establishments, with the name of the shop and its symbol woven into it or printed on it.

5. The manufacturers in Kyoto communicate with the cottage weavers in the Tango Peninsula through a middleman, who supplies the weavers with the orders and the raw materials and collects the finished product from them, which he transports to the manufacturer in Kyoto. By using middlemen, the manufacturers avoid the kind of traditional paternalistic involvement that they have with the weavers in Nishijin.

6. *Debata* (*de-hata*) means weaving for putting out. *Chinbata* was the historical term for the system when it was first introduced. The term used currently is *debata*. *Chinbata* is now considered a demeaning term, because a rented loom connotes greater dependency on the manufacturer. The terms that I will use to describe this system of household industry are "cottage industry" or "cottage weavers."

7. *Tsuzure* is fingernail weaving. It is carried out completely by hand on a traditional wooden loom. The weaver freely translates the design from a drawing and uses the fingernails, which are sharpened like a saw, in order to pull the threads through. This process requires higher skill, and the product resembles a tapestry.

8. The Nishijin Labor Union (Nishijin Ori Rodo Kumiae) consists primarily of weavers in factories. It is almost impossible to unionize cottage weavers.

9. The Shosoin Museum in Nara contains some of the oldest fragments of silk weavings in Japan. Some of the leading Nishijin manufacturers and designers, especially Tatsumura Heizo, restructured these designs from fragments and reintegrated them into contemporary Nishijin weavings.

10. There is no strict definition that distinguishes traditional "craft" from "industry." The word *sangyo*, "industry," in this case does not connote use of machinery or factories. *Dento sangyo* is used loosely to define various local crafts such as textile, pottery, lacquerware, metalware, paper, and so on.

11. *Oyakata* (meaning parent) and *kokata* (meaning child) are the traditional terms that define the paternalistic relationship between manufacturer and weaver in Nishijin. These terms are no longer used in Nishijin. Mr. K. was making a special point by reviving the old "feudal" terminology.

Chapter Thirteen

1. In this volume, cultural values and normative expectations as institutionalized in structures are treated, for parsimony, as components of structural lag.

Chapter Fourteen

1. I embarked on comparative research in Lyon during my sabbatical in the spring and summer of 1995 and have continued to interview former artisans and manufacturers in the silk industry there and in the surrounding countryside.

2. In 1963, Peter Laslett and John Harrison surprised scholars with their findings that in seventeenth-century Clayworth, 61 percent of the population found in the records at one point in time could not be found twelve years later (Laslett and Harrison, 1963).

3. For a more detailed critique see *Journal of Family History*, 1992.

4. The giant Amoskeag Mills had shut down in 1936. The Chicopee Mill opened after World War II in one of the Amoskeag buildings.

5. Oral history and the subjective reconstruction of lives overlap. However, oral history usually involves interviews centering on one or several specific events in a community, whereas life-history interviews reconstruct whole lives.

6. Canut has also become commercialized in the tourist industry. It is a popular name for restaurants.

7. This analysis of the differences between the cohorts is part of a larger study of generational relations and changes in the life course of the parents and the children of Manchester, based on extensive life history interviews of the children and their spouses, who were in their sixties and seventies during the interviews, and of those parents who were still alive. The interviews were carried out from 1979 to 1985 (Hareven, 1994a; Hareven and Adams, 1996).

8. Thomas Bender (1986) advocated a new synthesis in American history and proposed a framework for one, but the proposal was rejected at a roundtable discussion organized by the *Journal of American History* (Thelen, 1987). The reluctance to develop a new synthesis may stem from a fear of imposing an overarching framework at a time when new building blocks are still being made.

References

Abrahams, R. D. 1982. "The Language at Festivals: Celebrating the Economy." In V. Turner, ed., *Celebration: Studies in Festivity and Ritual*. Washington, DC: Smithsonian Institution Press.

Adams, B. 1968. *Kinship in an Urban Setting*. Chicago: Markham.

Adams, B. N. 1970. "Isolation, Function, and Beyond: American Kinship in the 1960s." *Journal of Marriage and the Family* 32: 575–597.

Ägrent, K., et al., eds. 1973. *Aristocrats, Farmers, Proletarians: Essays in Swedish Demographic History*. Stockholm: Essette Studium.

Anderson, M. S. 1971. *Family Structure in Nineteenth-Century Lancashire*. Cambridge, Eng.: Cambridge University Press.

_____. 1979. "The Relevance of Family History." *Sociological Review Monograph* 28: 49–73.

Andorka, R., and S. Balazs-Kovács. 1986. "The Social Demography of Hungarian Villages in the Eighteenth and Nineteenth Centuries (with special attention to Sarpilis, 1792–1804)." *Journal of Family History* 2: 169–192.

Angus, D. L., J. R. Mirel, and M. A. Vinovskis. 1988. "Historical Development of Age-Stratification in Schooling." *Teachers College Record* 90, 2: 211–236.

Antonucci, T. C. 1990. "Social Supports and Social Relations." In R. H. Binstock and L. George, eds., *Handbook of Aging and the Social Sciences*. 3d ed. New York: Academic Press.

"Apology from Age to Youth." 1983. *Living Age* 1903: n.p.

Arcury, T. A. 1986. "Rural Elderly Household Life Course Transitions, 1900 and 1980 Compared." *Journal of Family History* 11: 55–76.

Arensberg, C. M., and S. T. Kimball. 1968. *Family and Community in Ireland*. 2d ed. Cambridge: Harvard University Press.

Ariès, P. 1962. *Centuries of Childhood: A Social History of Family Life*. Translated by R. Baldick. New York: Knopf.

_____. 1980. "The Dead in the Early Middle Ages." Commentator at Annual Meeting of the American Historical Association, December. Washington, DC.

Armstrong, J. B. 1968. *Factory Under the Elms: A History of Harrisville, N.H., 1774–1969*. Cambridge: MIT Press.

Beard, G. 1874. *Legal Responsibility in Old Age, Based on Researches into the Relationship of Age to Work*. New York: Russells.

Becker, G. 1960. "An Economic Analysis of Fertility." *Demographic Change in Developed Countries*. Universities-National Bureau Conference Series No. 11. Princeton: Princeton University Press.

_____. 1981. *A Treatise on the Family*. Cambridge: Harvard University Press.

Bender, T. 1986. "Wholes and Parts: The Need for Synthesis in American History." *Journal of American History* 73: 120–136.

341

Bengston, V. L., N. E. Cutler, D. J. Mengen, and V. W. Marshall. 1985. "Generations, Cohorts, and Relations Between Age Groups." In R. H. Binstock and E. Shanas, eds., *Handbook of Aging and the Social Sciences*. New York: Van Nostrand Reinhold.

Bengston, V. L., P. L. Kasshau, and P. K. Ragan. 1985. "The Impact of Social Structure on Aging Individuals." In J. E. Birren and K. W. Schaie, eds., *Handbook of the Psychology of Aging*. 2d ed. New York: Van Nostrand Reinhold.

Bengston, V. L., and J. Treas. 1980. "Intergenerational Relations and Mental Health." In J. E. Birren and R. B. Sloane, eds., *Handbook of Mental Health and Aging*. Englewood Cliffs, NJ: Prentice-Hall.

Bengston, V. L., C. Rosenthal, and L. Burton. 1990. "Families and Aging: Diversity and Heterogeneity." In R. H. Binstock and L. George, eds., *Handbook of Aging and the Social Sciences*. New York: Academic Press.

Bennett, J. W., and L. A. Despres. 1960. "Kinship and Instrumental Activities." *American Anthropologist* 62: 254–267.

Berkhofer, R., Jr. 1995. *Beyond the Great Story: History as Text and Discourse*. Cambridge: Belknap Press of Harvard University Press.

Berkner, L. K. 1972. "The Stem Family and the Developmental Cycle of the Peasant Household: An Eighteenth-Century Austrian Example." *American Historical Review* 77: 398–418.

_____. 1975. "The Use and Misuse of Census Data for the Historical Analysis of Family Structure." *Journal of Interdisciplinary History* 5: 721–738.

Berthoff, R. 1960. "The American Social Order: A Conservative Hypothesis." *American Historical Review* 65: 495–514.

Bestor, T. C. 1989. *Neighborhood Tokyo*. Stanford: Stanford University Press.

Bieder, R. 1973. "Kinship as a Factor in Migration." *Journal of Marriage and the Family* 35: 429–439.

Bloch, M. 1954. *The Historian's Craft*. Translated by P. Putnam. Manchester, Eng.: Manchester University Press.

Bott, E. 1957. *Family and Social Networks: Roles, Norms, and External Relationships in Ordinary Urban Families*. London: Tavistock.

Brace, C. 1872. *The Dangerous Classes of New York*. New York: Wynkoop & Hallenbeck.

Braun, R. 1960. *Industrialisierung und Volksleben: Die Veränderungen der Lebensformen in einem ländlichen Industriegebiet vor 1800 (Züricher Oberland)*. Zurich: Erlanbach. Published in English as *Industrialization and Everyday Life*. Translated by S. Tenlson. Cambridge, Eng.: Cambridge University Press, 1990.

_____. 1974. "Early Industrialization and Demographic Change in the Canton of Zurich." In C. Tilly, ed., *Historical Studies of Changing Fertility: Quantitative Studies in History*. Princeton: Princeton University Press.

Bremner, R. H. 1956. *From the Depths: The Discovery of Poverty in the United States*. New York: New York University Press.

_____. 1976. "Other People's Children." *Journal of Social History* 16 (3): 83–103.

Bremner, R. H., J. Barnard, T. K. Hareven, and R. Mennell, eds. 1970. *Children and Youth in America: A Documentary History*. Vol. 1, 1600–1865. Cambridge: Harvard University Press.

_____, eds. 1971. *Children and Youth in America: A Documentary History*. Vol. 2, 1866–1932. Cambridge: Harvard University Press.

_____, eds. 1974. *Children and Youth in America: A Documentary History.* Vol. 3, 1933–1973. Cambridge: Harvard University Press.

Brody, E. M. 1981. "Women in the Middle and Family Help to Older People." *Gerontologist* 21: 471–480.

_____. 1990. *Women in the Middle: Their Parent-Care Years.* New York: Springer.

Brody, E. M., P. T. Johnson, M. C. Fulcomer, and A. M. Lang. 1983. "Women's Changing Roles and Help to Elderly Parents: Attitudes of Three Generations of Women." *Journal of Gerontology* 38 (5): 597–607.

Bronfenbrenner, U. 1969. "The Changing American Child: A Speculative Analysis." In J. N. Edwards, ed., *The Family and Change.* New York: Knopf.

Brotz, H., and E. Wilson. 1946. "Characteristics of Military Society." *American Journal of Sociology* 51: 371–375.

Brown, W. 1915. *A History of the Amoskeag Company.* Manchester, NH: Amoskeag Company.

Burguière, A. 1978. "Le rituel de mariage en France: Pratiques ecclésiastiques et pratiques populaires (XVI–XVIII siècles)." *Annales E.S.C.* 33: 637–649.

_____. 1987. "The Formation of the Couple." *Journal of Family History* 12: 39–56.

_____. 1993. "La mémoire du bourgeois-gentilhomme: Généalogies domestiques en France aux XVII et XVIIIe siècles." *Annales E.S.C.* 4: 771–788.

Burton, L., and P. Dilworth-Anderson. 1991. "The Intergenerational Family Roles of Aged Black Americans." In S. K. Pifer and M. D. Sussman, eds., *Families: Intergenerational and Generational Connections.* New York: Haworth Press.

Burton, L., and C. deVries. 1992. "Challenges and Rewards: African American Grandparents as Surrogate Parents." *Generations* 17 (3): 4–6.

Byington, M. F. 1910. *The Households of a Mill Town.* Vol. 5, *The Pittsburgh Survey.* New York: Sage.

Cantarella, E. 1987. *Pandora's Daughters: The Role and Status of Women in Greek and Roman Antiquity.* Baltimore: Johns Hopkins University Press.

Cantor, M. H. 1983. "Strain Among Caregivers: A Study of Experience in the U.S." *Gerontologist* 23: 597–604.

Caspi, A. 1989. *Mate Selection, Marital Relations, and Developmental Change.* Working paper, Harvard University, Department of Psychology, Cambridge, MA.

Charbonneau, H. 1975. *La vie et mort de nos ancêtres: Etude demographique.* Montréal: Presses de l'Université de Montréal.

Charbonneau, H., et al. 1987. *Naissance d'une population: Les Français établis aux Canada au XVII siècle.* Montreal and Paris: Presse de l'Université de Montreal and Presses Universitaires de France.

Cherlin, A. 1981. *Marriage, Divorce, Remarriage.* Cambridge: Harvard University Press.

Cherlin, A., and F. Furstenberg. 1990. *The New American Grandparent.* New York: Basic Books.

Chudacoff, H. 1978. "Newlyweds and Familial Extensions: First Stages of the Family Cycle in Providence, R.I., 1864–1880." In T. K. Hareven and M. Vinovskis, eds., *Family and Population in Nineteenth-Century America.* Princeton: Princeton University Press.

_____. 1980. "The Life Course of Women: Age and Age Consciousness, 1865–1915." *Journal of Family History* 5: 274–292.

Chudacoff, H., and T. K. Hareven. 1978a. "Family Transitions to Old Age." In T. K. Hareven, ed., *Transitions: The Family and the Life Course in Historical Perspective.* New York: Academic Press.

_____. 1978b. "The Later Years of Life and the Family Cycle." In T. K. Hareven and M. A. Vinovskis, eds., *Family and Population in Nineteenth-Century America.* Princeton: Princeton University Press.

_____. 1979. "From the Empty Nest to Family Dissolution: Life Course Transitions into Old Age." *Journal of Family History* 4: 69–83.

Chujo, T. 1965. *Keiei romu no kindaika: Nishijin chusho keidi romu kindaika ni yosete* [The modernization of management: A contribution toward the understanding of the modernization of management in the small- to medium-sized enterprises of Nishijin]. Kyoto: Sanwa Shobo.

_____. 1984. *Nishijin no chinbata rodo to sono kozo taisaku* [Cottage industry work in Nishijin and its organization]. Kyoto: Sanwa Shobo.

Cicirelli, V. G. 1981. *Helping Elderly Parents: The Role of Adult Children.* Boston: Auburn House.

Clark, M., and B. B. Anderson. 1976. *Culture and Aging: An Anthropological Study of Older Americans.* Springfield, IL: Charles C. Thomas.

Cornell, L. L. 1983. "Retirement, Inheritance and Intergenerational Conflict in Preindustrial Japan." *Journal of Family History* 8: 55–69.

_____. 1987. "Hajnal and the Household in Asia: A Comparative History of the Family in Preindustrial Japan, 1600–1870." *Journal of Family History* 12: 143–162.

Cornell, L. L., and A. Hayami. 1986. "The Shumon Aratame Cho: Japan's Populaton Registers." *Journal of Family History* 11: 311–328.

Corsini, C. 1976. "Materiali per lo studio della famiglia in Toscana nei secoli XVII–XIV: Gli espositi." *Quaderni Storici* 33: 998–1052.

_____. 1977. "Self-Regulating Mechanisms of Traditional Populations Before the Demographic Revolution: European Civilizations." *International Population Conference* 3: 5–23.

Cott, N. F. 1976. "Eighteenth-Century Family and Social Life Revealed in Massachusetts Divorce Records." *Journal of Social History* 10 (1): 20–43.

_____. 1977. *The Bonds of Womanhood: Woman's Sphere in New England, 1780–1835.* New Haven: Yale University Press.

Cox, C. A. 1988. "Sibling Relationships in Classical Athens: Brother-Sister Ties." *Journal of Family History* 13: 377–396.

Creamer, D., and C. W. Coulter. 1939. *Labor and the Shutdown of the Amoskeag Textile Mills.* Philadelphia: Works Project Administration.

Davis, N. Z. 1977. "Ghosts, Kin, and Progeny: Some Features of Family Life in Early Modern France." *Daedalus* 106: 87–114.

Degler, C. N. 1980. *At Odds: Women and the Family in America from the Revolution to the Present.* New York: Oxford University Press.

Demos, J. 1965. "Notes on Family Life in Plymouth Colony." *William and Mary Quarterly* 22: 264–286.

_____. 1970. *A Little Commonwealth: Family Life in Plymouth Colony.* New York: Oxford University Press.

_____. 1971. "Developmental Perspectives on the History of Childhood." *Journal of Interdisciplinary History* 2: 123–129.

_____. 1978. "Old Age in Early New England." In J. Demos and S. Boocock, eds., *Turning Points: American Journal of Sociology Supplement* 84: S248–287.

Demos, J., and V. Demos. 1969. "Adolescence in Historical Perspective." *Journal of Marriage and the Family* 31 (4): 632–638.

Dixon, S. 1988. *The Roman Mother*. Norman: University of Oklahoma Press.

Donzelot, J. 1979. *The Policing of Families*. Translated by R. Hurley. New York: Pantheon Books.

Douglas, P. H. 1936. *Social Security in the United States*. New York: McGraw-Hill.

Dowd, J. J., and V. L. Bengtson. 1978. "Aging in Minority Populations: An Examination of the Double-Jeopardy Hypothesis." *Journal of Gerontology* 33: 427–436.

Duben, A. 1985. "Turkish Families and Households in Historical Perspective." *Journal of Family History* 10: 75–97.

Dublin, T. 1979. *Women at Work: The Transformation of Work and Community in Lowell, Massachusetts, 1826–1860*. New York: Columbia University Press.

Dupaquier, J. 1981. "Naming Practices, Godparenthood, and Kinship in the Vexin, 1540–1900." *Journal of Family History* 6: 135–155.

Duval, E. 1957. *Family Development*. Philadelphia: Lippincott.

Dwyer, J. W., and K. Seccombe. 1991. "Elder Care as Family Labor: The Influence of Gender and Family Position." *Journal of Family Issues* 12: 229–247.

Dwyer, J. W., and R. T. Coward. 1991. "A Multivariate Comparison of the Involvement of Adult Sons Versus Daughters in the Care of Impaired Parents." *Journal of Gerontology* 46 (5): S259–269.

Ebrey, P. 1981. "Women in the Kinship System of the Southern Sung Upper Class." *Historical Reflections* 8: 113–128.

_____. 1986. "Concubines in Sung China." *Journal of Family History* 11: 1–24.

Eggebeen, D. J., and D. P. Hogan. 1990. "Giving Between Generations in American Families." *Human Nature* 1: 211–232.

Ehmer, J. 1980. *Familienstruktur und Arbeitsorganization im frühindustriellen Wien*. Vienna: Böhlau Verlag.

Elder, G. H., Jr. 1974. *Children of the Great Depression*. Chicago: Chicago University Press.

_____. 1978. "Family History and the Life Course." In T. K. Hareven, ed., *Transitions: The Family and the Life Course in Historical Perspective*. New York: Academic Press.

_____. 1979. "Historical Changes in Life Patterns and Personality." In P. B. Baltes and O. G. Brim, eds., *Life-Span Development and Behavior*. Vol. 2. New York: Academic Press.

_____. 1981. "History and the Family: The Discovery of Complexity." *Journal of Marriage and the Family* 43: 489–519.

_____. 1982. "Historical Experiences in Later Life." In T. K. Hareven and K. Adams, eds., *Aging and the Life Course in Interdisciplinary and Cross-Cultural Perspective*. New York: Guilford Press.

_____. 1986. "Military Times and Turning Points in Men's Lives." *Developmental Psychology* 22: 233–245.

_____. 1987. "War Moblization and the Life Course: A Cohort of World War II Veterans." *Sociological Forum* 2: 449–472.

_____. 1995. "The Life Course Paradigm: Social Change and Individual Development." In P. Moen, G. Elder, and K. Lüscher, eds., *Examining Lives in Context: Perspectives on the Ecology of Human Development*. APA Science Volumes. Washington, DC: American Psychological Association.

Elder, G. H., and A. Caspi. 1990. "Studying Lives in a Changing Society: Sociological and Personological Explanations." In A. I. Rabin et al., eds., *Studying Persons and Lives*. Henry A. Murray Lecture Series. New York: Springer.

Elder, G. H., Jr., and E. Clipp. 1988. "Wartime Losses and Social Bonding: Influences Across Forty Years in Men's Lives." *Psychiatry* 51: 177–198.

Elder, G. H., Jr., G. Downey, and C. E. Cross. 1986. "Family Ties and Life Chances: Hard Times and Hard Choices in Women's Lives Since the 1930s." In N. Datan, A. L. Greene, and H. W. Reese, eds., *Life-Span Developmental Psychology: Intergenerational Relations*. Hillsdale, NJ: Erlbaum.

Elder, G. H., Jr., and T. K. Hareven. 1993. "Rising Above Life's Disadvantage: From the Great Depression to Global War." In G. H. Elder Jr., J. Modell, and R. Parke, eds., *Children in Time and Place: Developmental and Historical Insights*. Cambridge Studies in Social and Emotional Development. Cambridge, Eng.: Cambridge University Press.

Elder, G. H., L. Rudkin, and R. D. Conger. 1992. "Intergenerational Continuity and Change in Rural America." Paper presented at Conference on Intergenerational Relations and Aging, Pennsylvania State University, University Park.

Engerman, S. 1978. "Economic Perspectives on the Life Course." In T. Hareven, ed., *Transitions: The Family and the Life Course in Historical Perspective. Studies in Social Discontinuity*. New York: Academic Press.

Epstein, A. 1922. *Facing Old Age: A Study of Old Age Dependency in the United States and Old Age Pensions*. New York: Knopf.

Erikson, E. 1964. *Insight and Responsibility*. New York: Norton.

Farber, B. 1973. *Family and Kinship in Modern Society*. Glenview, IL: Scott, Foresman.

Fischer, D. H. 1977. *Growing Old in America*. New York: Oxford University Press.

Flandrin, J. 1976. *Familes in Former Times: Kinship, Household, and Sexuality*. Cambridge, Eng.: Cambridge University Press.

Fortes, M. 1969. *Kinship and the Social Order*. Chicago: Aldine.

Fox, R. 1967. *Kinship and Marriage: An Anthropological Perspective*. London: Penguin.

Fry, C., and J. Keith. 1982. "The Life Course as a Cultural Unit." In M. Riley, R. Abeles, and M. Teitelbaum, eds., *Aging from Birth to Death*. Boulder: Westview.

Furstenberg, F. F. 1981. "Remarriage and Intergenerational Relations." In R. W. Fogel, E. Hatfield, S. B. Kiesler, and E. Shanas, eds., *Aging: Stability and Change in the Family*. New York: Academic Press.

Furstenberg, F. F., and C. W. Nord. 1985. "Parenting Apart: Patterns of Child Rearing after Marital Disruption." *Journal of Marriage and the Family* 47 (4): 893–904.

Furumai, T. 1965. "Nishijin kigyo no daiyoji chosa ni motozuki rodo tokei shiryo [Labor statistics based upon the fourth survey of Nishijin enterprises]." *Keizaigaku Ronso* 14 (8).

Gans, H. 1962. *The Urban Villagers: Group and Class in the Life of Italian-Americans*. New York: Free Press.

Garigue, P. 1956. "French-Canadian Kinship and Urban Life." *American Anthropologist* 58: 1090–1101.

_____. 1967. *La vie familiale des Canadiens Français*. Montréal: Les Presses de l'Université de Montréal.

Gaunt, D. 1987. "Rural Household Organization and Inheritance in Northern Europe." *Journal of Family History* 12: 1–3, 121–141.

Geertz, C. 1973. *The Interpretation of Cultures*. New York: Basic Books.

Gerber, H. 1989. "Anthropology and Family History: The Ottoman and Turkish Families." *Journal of Family History* 14: 409–421.

Gillis, J. 1989. "Proletarian Marriage in England." In D. Levine, ed., *Proletarianization and Family History*. Orlando, FL: Academic Press.

Glasco, L. 1977. "The Life Cycles and Household Structure of American Ethnic Groups: Irish, Germans and Native-Born Whites in Buffalo, New York, 1885." In T. K. Hareven, ed., *Family and Kin in American Urban Communities, 1700–1930*. New York: New Viewpoints.

_____. 1978. "Migration and Adjustment in the Nineteenth-Century City: Occupation, Properties and Household Structure of Native-Born Whites, Buffalo, New York." In T. K. Hareven and M. A. Vinovskis, eds., *Family and Population in Nineteenth-Century America*. Princeton: Princeton University Press.

Glick, P. 1947. "The Family Cycle." *American Sociological Review* 12: 164–174.

_____. 1955. "The Life Cycle of the Family." *Marriage and Family Living* 18: 3–9.

_____. 1977. "Updating the Life Cycle of the Family." *Journal of Marriage and the Family* 31: 5–13.

Goffman, Erving. 1963. *Stigma: Notes on the Management of Spoiled Identity*. Englewood Cliffs, NJ: Prentice-Hall.

Goldin, C. 1981. "Family Strategies and the Family Economy in the Late Nineteenth Century: The Role of Secondary Workers." In T. Hershberg, ed., *Philadelphia: Work, Space, Family, and Group Experience in the Nineteenth Century*. New York: Oxford University Press.

_____. 1986. "The Female Labor Force and American Economic Growth, 1890–1980." In S. L. Engerman and R. E. Gallman, eds., *Long-Term Factors in American Economic Growth*. Chicago: University of Chicago Press.

Goldscheider, F. K., and J. DaVanzo. 1985. "Living Arrangements and the Transition to Adulthood." *Demography* 22: 545–563.

_____. 1986. "Semiautonomy and Leaving Home in Early Adulthood." *Social Forces* 65: 187–201.

Goldscheider, F. K., and L. J. Waite. 1991. *New Families, No Families?* Berkeley: University of California Press.

Goode, W. 1963. *World Revolution and Family Patterns*. New York: Free Press.

_____. 1968. "The Theory and Measurement of Family Change." In E. B. Sheldon and W. Moore, eds., *Indicators of Social Change: Concepts and Measurements*. New York: Sage.

Goody, J. 1972. "Evolution of the Family." In P. Laslett and R. Wall, eds., *Household and Family in Past Time: Comparative Studies in the Size and Structure of the Domestic Group over the Last Three Centuries in England, France, Serbia, Japan, and Colonial North America*. Cambridge, Eng.: Cambridge University Press.

_____, ed. 1971. *The Developmental Cycle in Domestic Groups*. Cambridge, Eng.: Cambridge University Press.

Gordon, L. 1988. *Heroes of Their Own Lives: The Politics and History of Family Violence: Boston, 1880–1960*. New York: Viking.

Goubert, P. 1954. "Une richesse historique en cour d'exploitation: Les registres paroissiaux." *Annales E.S.C.* 9: 83–93.

_____. 1960. *Beauvais et les Beauvaisis de 1600–1730*. Paris: S.E.V.P.E.N.

_____. 1970. "Historical Demography and the Reinterpretation of Early Modern French History: A Research Review." *Journal of Interdisciplinary History* 1: 37–48.

_____. 1977. "Family and Province: A Contribution to the Knowledge of Family Structures in Early Modern France." *Journal of Family History* 2: 223–236.

Greven, P. 1970. *Four Generations: Population, Land, and Family in Colonial Andover, Massachusetts*. Ithaca: Cornell University Press.

Griffen, C., and S. Griffen. 1978. *Natives and Newcomers: The Ordering of Opportunities in Mid-Nineteenth-Century Poughkeepsie*. Cambridge: Harvard University Press.

Gunda, B. 1982. "The Ethno-Sociological Structure of the Hungarian Extended Family." *Journal of Family History* 7: 40–51.

Gutman, H. 1976a. *The Black Family in Slavery and Freedom, 1750–1925*. New York: Pantheon.

_____. 1976b. *Work, Culture, and Society in Industrializing America: Essays in American Working-Class and Social History*. New York: Knopf.

Gutmann, M., and R. Leboutte. 1984. "Rethinking Protoindustrialization and Family." *Journal of Interdisciplinary History* 14: 587–607.

Haak, R. 1975. "The Zesty Structured World of a Weaver." In D. W. Plath, ed., *Adult Episodes in Japan*. Leiden: E. J. Brill.

Haines, M. 1981a. "Industrial Work and the Family Cycle, 1889–1890." In P. Uselding, ed., *Research in Economic History*. Vol. 4. Greenwich, CT: JAI Press.

_____. 1981b. "Poverty, Economic Stress, and the Family in a Late-Nineteenth-Century American City: Whites in Philadelphia, 1880." In T. Hershberg, ed., *Philadelphia*. New York: Oxford University Press.

Hajnal, J. 1965. "European Marriage Patterns in Perspective." In D. V. Glass and D.E.C. Eversley, eds., *Population in History*. London: E. Arnold.

_____. 1983. "Two Kinds of Pre-Industrial Household Formation Systems." In R. Wall, J. Robin, and P. Laslett, eds., *Family Forms in Historic Europe*. Cambridge, Eng.: Cambridge University Press.

Hall, G. S. 1904. *Adolescence: Its Psychology and Its Relations to Physiology, Anthropology, Sociology, Sex, Crime, Religion and Education*. New York: Appleton.

_____. 1922. *Senescence: The Last Half of Life*. New York: Appleton.

Hallett, J. P. 1984. *Fathers and Daughters in Roman Society: Women and the Elite Family*. Princeton: Princeton University Press.

Hammel, E. A. 1972. "The Zadruga as Process." In P. Laslett and R. Wall, eds., *Household and Family in Past Time: Comparative Studies in the Size and Structure of the Domestic Group over the Last Three Centuries in England, France, Serbia, Japan, and Colonial North America*. Cambridge, Eng.: Cambridge University Press.

Handlin, O. 1951. *The Uprooted*. Boston: Little, Brown.

Hanley, S. B., and A. P. Wolf, eds. 1985. *Family and Population in East Asian History*. Stanford: Stanford University Press.

Hareven, T. K. 1971. "The History of the Family as an Interdisciplinary Field." *Journal of Interdisciplinary History* 2: 273–299.

_____. 1974. "The Family as Process: The Historical Study of the Family Cycle." *Journal of Social History* 7: 322–329.

_____. 1975. "Family Time and Industrial Time: Family and Work in a Planned Corporation Town, 1900–1924." *Journal of Urban History* 1: 365–389.

_____. 1976a. "The Last Stage: Historical Adulthood and Old Age." *Daedalus* 105: 13–27.

_____. 1976b. "Modernization and Family History: Reflections on Social Change." *Signs: Journal of Women in Culture and Society* 2: 190–206.

_____. 1977a. "Family Time and Historical Time." *Daedalus* 106: 57–70.

_____. 1977b. "The Historical Study of the Family in Urban Society." In T. K. Hareven, ed., *Family and Kin in American Urban Communities, 1780–1940.* New York: Franklin and Watts.

_____, ed. 1977c. *Family and Kin in American Urban Communities, 1780–1940.* New York: Franklin and Watts.

_____. 1978a. "Cycles, Courses, and Cohorts: Reflections on the Theoretical and Methodological Approaches to the Historical Study of Family Development." *Journal of Social History* 12: 97–109.

_____. 1978b. "The Dynamics of Kin in an Industrial Community." In J. Demos and S. Boocock, eds., *Turning Points: Historical and Sociological Essays on the Family: American Journal of Sociology, 84 Supplement.* Chicago: University of Chicago Press.

_____. 1978c. "Historical Changes in the Life Course and the Family." In J. M. Yinger and S. J. Cutler, eds., *Major Social Issues: A Multidisciplinary View.* New York: Free Press.

_____. 1978d. "The Search for Generational Memory: Tribal Rites in Industrial Society." *Daedalus* 107: 137–150.

_____, ed. 1978e. *Transitions: The Family and the Life Course in Historical Perspective.* New York: Academic Press.

_____. 1981a. "American Families in Transition: Historical Perspectives on Change." In F. Walsh, ed., *Normal Families in Social Cultural Context.* New York: Guilford Press.

_____. 1981b. "Historical Changes in the Timing of Family Transitions: Their Impact on Generational Relations." In R. Fogel, S. B. Kiesler, E. Hatfield, and E. Shanas, eds., *Aging: Stability and Change in the Family.* New York: Academic Press.

_____. 1982. *Family Time and Industrial Time: The Relationship Between the Family and Work in a New England Industrial Community.* New York: Cambridge University Press.

_____. 1985a. "Historical Change in the Family and the Life Course: Implications for Child Development." In A. B. Smuts and J. W. Hagen, eds., *History and Research in Child Development.* Chicago: University of Chicago Press.

_____. 1985b. "The Nishijin Dilemma." Kyoto: *Kyoto Prefecture Labor Institute Publication* (in Japanese). October 24–28.

_____. 1986. "Historical Changes in the Social Construction of the Life Course." *Human Development* 29: 171–180.

_____. 1987a. "Family History at the Crossroads." *Journal of Family History* 12: ix–xiii.

_____. 1987b. "Reflections on Family Research in the People's Republic of China." *Social Research* 54: 663–690.

_____. 1988. "Kazoku—rodo ni oyobosu gijutsu—keizaiteki henka no eikyo. Nishijin no chinbata no baai." [Translated by Sumizawa Toshiko from the English version: "The Impact of Technological and Economic Change on Family and Work: The Case of the Nishijin Silk-Weaving Cottage Industry"] *Shiso* 6 (768): 97–117.

_____. 1990a. "A Complex Relationship: Family Strategies and the Processes of Economic and Social Change." In R. Friedland and A. Robertson, eds., *Beyond the Marketplace: Rethinking Economy and Society. Sociology and Economics.* New York: de Gruyter.

_____. 1990b. "Women's Work and Family Strategies in the Household Industry of Japanese Weavers: A Comparative Perspective." In E. Aerts et al., eds., *Women in the Labor Force: Tenth International Economic History Congress.* Leuven, Belgium: Leuven University Press.

_____. 1991a. "The History of the Family and the Complexity of Social Change." *American Historical Review* 96: 95–124.

_____. 1991b. "Synchronizing Individual Time, Family Time, and Historical Time." In J. Bender and D. Wellbery, eds., *Chronotypes: The Construction of Time.* Stanford: Stanford University Press.

_____. 1992a. "Between Craft and Industry: The Subjective Reconstruction of the Life Course of Kyoto's Traditional Weavers." In S. Formanek and S. Linhart, eds., *Japanese Biographies: Life Histories, Life Cycles, Life Stages. Beiträge zur Kultur und Geistesgeschichte Asiens, no. 11.* Vienna: Österreichische Akademie der Wissenschaften.

_____. 1992b. "Continuity and Change in American Family Life." In L. S. Leudtke, ed., *Making America: The Society and Culture of the United States.* Chapel Hill: University of North Carolina Press.

_____. 1992c. "The Festival's Work as Leisure: The Traditional Craftsmen of the Gion Festival." In J. Calagione, D. Francis, and D. Nugent, eds., *Workers' Expressions.* Albany: State University of New York.

_____. 1992d. "From Amoskeag to Nishijin: Reflections on Life History Interviewing in Two Cultures." In R. Grele, ed., *Subjectivity and Multiculturalism in Oral History: The International Annual of Oral History for 1990.* Westport, CT: Greenwood.

_____. 1993a. "Family Strategies and Economic Change Among Japanese Silk Weavers." In G. Hauch, ed., *Geschlecht, Klasse, Ethnizität: 28. Internationale Tagung der Historikerinnen und Historiker der Arbeiterinnen und Arbeiterbewegung. Geschichte der Arbeiterbewegung, no 29.* Vienna: Europaverlag.

_____. 1993b. *Male Caregivers for Aged Relatives: A Life Course Perspective.* Presented at National Institute for Aging Conference, "Males' Caregiving Roles in an Aging Society," April 19–20, Bethesda, MD.

_____. 1994a. "Aging and Generational Relations: A Historical and Life Course Perspective." In J. Hagan, ed., *Annual Review of Sociology.* Palo Alto, CA: Annual Reviews.

_____. 1994b. "Family Change and Historical Change: An Uneasy Relationship." In M. Riley, R. Kahn, and A. Foner, eds., *Age and Structural Lag: Society's Failure to Provide Meaningful Opportunities in Work, Family, and Leisure*. New York: Wiley.

_____. 1994c. "The Gendered Division of Labor in the Transition from Cottage to Factory." In A. Fauve-Chamoux and S. Sogner, eds., *Socio-Economic Consequences of Sex Ratios in Historical Perspective, 1500–1900: Eleventh International Economic History Congress*. Milan: Université Bocconi.

_____. 1995. "Changing Images of Ageing and the Social Construction of the Life Course." In M. Featherstone and A. Wernick, eds., *Images of Ageing: Cultural Representations of Later Life*. London: Routledge.

_____. 1996."What Difference Does It Make?" *Social Science History* 20: 317–344.

_____. Forthcoming. *The Silk Weavers of Kyoto: Family and Work in a Changing Traditional Industry*.

Hareven, T. K., and K. Adams. 1996. "The Generation in the Middle: Cohort Comparisons in Assistance to Aging Parents in an American Community." In T. K. Hareven, ed., *Aging and Generational Relations over the Life Course: A Historical and Cross-Cultural Perspective*. Berlin: de Gruyter.

Hareven, T. K., and H. P. Chudacoff. 1978. "Familiar Transitions into Old Age." InT. K. Hareven, ed., *Transitions: The Family and the Life Course in Historical Perspective*. New York: Academic Press.

Hareven, T. K., and R. Langenbach. 1978. *Amoskeag: Life and Work in an American Factory City*. New York: Pantheon.

Hareven, T. K., and K. Masaoka. 1988. "Turning Points and Transitions: Perceptions of the Life Course." *Journal of Family History* 13: 271–289.

Hareven, T. K., and J. Modell. 1980. "Family Patterns." In S. Thernstrom, ed., *Harvard Encyclopedia of American Ethnic Groups*. Cambridge: Harvard University Press.

Hareven, T. K., and A. Plakans, eds. 1987. *Family History at the Crossroads: A Journal of Family History Reader*. Princeton: Princeton University Press.

Hareven, T. K., and P. Uhlenberg. 1995. "Transition to Widowhood and Family Support Systems in the Twentieth Century, Northeast U.S." In D. Kertzer and P. Laslett, eds., *Aging in the Past: Demography, Society, and Old Age*. Studies in Demography, no. 7. Berkeley: University of California Press.

Hareven, T. K., and M. Vinovskis. 1975. "Marital Fertility, Ethnicity, and Occupation in Urban Families: An Analysis of South Boston and the South End in 1880." *Journal of Social History* 3: 69–93.

Hareven, T. K., and M. Vinovskis, eds. 1978. *Family and Population in Nineteenth-Century America*. Princeton: Princeton University Press.

Hattori, S. 1948. *Nishijin kigyo ni okeru genseiteki sangyo kakumei no tenkai* [The course of the industrial revolution in Nishijin enterprises]. Kyoto: Takakiri Shoin.

Havighurst, R. J. et al. 1951. *The American Veteran Back Home: A Study of Veteran Readjustment*. New York: Longmans, Green.

Hayami, A. 1973. "Labor Migration in a Preindustrial Society: A Study Tracing the Life Histories of the Inhabitants of a Village." *Keio Economic Studies* 10: 1–17.

_____. 1983. "The Myth of Primogeniture and Impartible Inheritance in Tokugawa Japan." *Journal of Family History* 8: 3–29.

Hayami, A., and N. Uchida. 1972. "Size of Household in a Japanese Country Throughout the Tokugawa Era." In P. Laslett and R. Wall, eds., *Household and Family in Past Time: Comparative Studies in the Size and Structure of the Domestic Group over the Last Three Centuries in England, France, Serbia, Japan, and Colonial North America.* Cambridge, Eng.: Cambridge University Press.

Henrepin, J. 1954. *La population Canadienne au début du XVIII siècle: Nuptialité, fécondité, mortalité infantile.* Paris: Presses Universitaires de France.

Henry, L. 1953. "Une richesse demographique en fiche: Les registres paroissiaux." *Population* 8: 281–290.

_____. 1956. *Anciennes familles Genevoises: Etude demographique: XVI–XX siècle.* Paris: Presses Universitaires de France.

_____. 1968. "Historical Demography." *Daedalus* 97: 385–396.

Herlihy, D. 1985. *Medieval Households.* Cambridge: Harvard University Press.

_____. 1987. "The Family and Religious Ideologies in Medieval Europe." *Journal of Family History* 12: 3–18.

Herlihy, D., and C. Klapisch-Zuber. 1978. *Les Toscans et leurs familles.* Paris: Foundation Nationale des Sciences Politiques.

Hill, R. 1964. "Methodological Issues in the Family Development Research." *Family Process* 3: 186–204.

_____. 1970. *Family Development in Three Generations: A Longitudinal Study of Changing Family Patterns of Planning and Achievement.* Cambridge, MA: Schenkman.

Hill, R., and R. H. Rodgers. 1964. "The Developmental Approach." In J. Christensen, ed., *Handbook of Marriage and the Family.* Chicago: Rand McNally.

Hillery, G. A., J. S. Brown, and G. F. DeJong. 1965. "Migration Systems of the Southern Appalachians: Some Demographic Observations." *Rural Sociology* 30: 33–48.

Hogan, D. 1981. *Transitions and Social Change: The Early Lives of American Men.* New York: Academic Press.

_____. 1989. "Institutional Perspectives on the Life Course: Challenges and Strategies." In D. Kertzer and K. W. Schaie, eds., *Age Structuring in Comparative Perspective.* Hillsdale, NJ: Erlbaum.

_____. 1991. "Reintroducing Culture in Life Course Research." *Contemporary Sociology* 20: 1–6.

Hogan, D. P., D. J. Eggebeen, and C. C. Clogg. 1993. "The Structure of Intergenerational Exchanges in American Families." *American Journal of Sociology* 98: 1428–1459.

Hogan, D. P., D. J. Eggebeen, and S. M. Snaith. 1995. "The Well-Being of Aging Americans with Very Old Parents." In T. K. Hareven, ed., *Aging and Generational Relations over the Life Course: A Historical and Cross-Cultural Perspective.* Berlin: de Gruyter.

Hogan, D. P., and T. Mochizuki. 1988. "Demographic Transitions and the Life Course: Lessons from Japanese and American Comparisons." *Journal of Family History* 13: 291–306.

Honjo, E. 1930. *Nishijin kenkyu* [A study of Nishijin]. Kyoto: Kaizosha.

Hudson, P., and W. Lee. 1990. "Women's Work and the Family Economy in Historical Perspective." In P. Hudson and W. Lee, eds., *Women's Work and the Family Economy in Historical Perspective*. Manchester, Eng.: Manchester University Press.

Hughes, E. 1971a. *The Sociological Eye: Selected Papers*. Chicago: Adline-Atherton.

_____. 1971b. "Cycles, Turning Points, and Careers." In E. Hughes, *The Sociological Eye: Selected Papers*. Chicago: Aldine-Atherton.

Hunecke, V. 1988. *I trovatelli di Milano: Bambini esposti e famiglie espositrici dal XVII al XIX secolo*. Bologna: Il Mulino.

Hunter, V. 1989. "The Athenian Widow and Her Kin." *Journal of Family History* 14: 291–312.

Imhof, A. E. 1976. "Genealogie et demographie historique en Allemagne." *Annales de Demographie Historique*: 77–107.

_____. 1977. "Historical Demography as Social History: Possibilities in Germany." *Journal of Family History* 2: 305–332.

Inkeles, A., and D. Smith. 1974. *Becoming Modern: Individual Change in Six Developing Countries*. Cambridge: Harvard University Press.

Jackson, J. S., P. Newton, A. Ostfield, D. Savage, and E. L. Schneider, eds. 1988. *The Black American Elderly: Research on Physical and Psychosocial Health*. New York: Springer.

Jackson, J. S. et al. 1995. "Exchanges Within Black American Three-Generation Families: The Family Environment Context Model." In T. K. Hareven, ed., *Aging and Generational Relations over the Life Course: A Historical and Cross-Cultural Perspective*. Berlin: de Gruyter.

Jackson, J. S. et al. 1990. "Cultural, Racial and Ethnic Influences on Aging." In J. E. Birren and K. W. Schaie, eds., *Handbook of the Psychology of Aging*. New York: Academic Press.

Jeffrey, K. 1972. *Family History: The Middle-Class American Family in the Urban Context*. Ph.D. diss., Stanford University, Stanford.

Jordan, E. 1989. "The Exclusion of Women from Industry in Nineteenth-Century Britain." *Comparative Studies in Society and History* 31: 273–296.

Journal of Family History. 1992. *Protoindustrialization*. Special issue, vol. 17.

Kaestle, C., and M. Vinovskis. 1980. *Education and Social Change in Nineteenth Century Massachusetts*. Cambridge: Harvard University Press.

Kahk, J., H. Palli, and H. Uibu. 1982. "Peasant Family in Estonia in the Eighteenth and the First Half of the Nineteenth Centuries." *Journal of Family History* 7: 76–89.

Kälvemark, A. 1977. "The Country That Kept Track of Its Population: Methodological Aspects of Swedish Population Records." *Scandinavian Journal of History* 2: 211–230.

Katz, M. B. 1968. *The Irony of Early School Reform: Educational Innovation in Mid-Nineteenth-Century Massachusetts*. Boston: Beacon Press.

_____. 1975. *The People of Hamilton, Canada West: Family and Class in a Mid-Nineteenth-Century City*. Cambridge: Harvard University Press.

_____. 1986. *In the Shadow of the Poorhouse: A Social History of Welfare in America*. New York: Basic Books.

Kaye, L. W., and J. S. Applegate. 1990. *Men as Caregivers to the Elderly*. Lexington, MA: Lexington Books.

Keniston, K. 1971. "Psychological Development and Historical Change." *Journal of Interdisciplinary History* 2 (2): 329–345.

Kertzer, D. I. 1983. "Generation as a Sociological Problem." *Annual Review of Sociology* 9: 130–149.

———. 1984. "Anthropology and Family History." *Journal of Family History* 9: 201–206.

Kertzer, D. I., and C. Brettell. 1987. "Advances in Italian and Iberian Family History." *Journal of Family History* 12: 87–120.

Kertzer, D. I., and D. Hogan. 1989. *Family, Political Economy, and Demographic Change: The Transformation of Life in Casalecchio, Italy, 1861–1921*. Life Course Studies. Madison: University of Wisconsin Press.

Kett, J. 1977. *Rites of Passage: Adolescence in America, 1790 to the Present*. New York: Basic Books.

Kiefer, C. W. 1974. *Changing Culture, Changing Lives: An Ethnographic Study of Three Generations of Japanese Americans*. San Francisco: Jossey-Bass.

Klapish-Zuber, C. 1990. *La maison et le nom: Strategies et rituels dans l'Italie de la Renaissance*. Paris: École des Hautes Études en Sciences Sociales.

Kleinberg, J. 1983. "Where Work and Family Are Almost One: The Lives of Folkcraft Potters." In D. Plath, ed., *Work and Life Course in Japan*. Albany: State University of New York Press.

Kobrin, F. E. 1976. "The Fall of Household Size and the Rise of the Primary Individual in the United States." *Demography* 13: 127–138.

Kohli, M. 1986. "Social Organization and Subjective Construction of the Life Course." In A. B. Sorensen, F. E. Weinert, and L. R. Sherrod, eds., *Human Development and the Life Course: Multidisciplinary Perspectives*. Hillsdale, NJ: Erlbaum.

Kondo, D. K. 1990. *Crafting Selves: Power, Gender, and Discourses of Identity in a Japanese Workplace*. Chicago: University of Chicago Press.

Kumagai, F. 1983. "Changing Divorce in Japan." *Journal of Family History* 8: 85–108.

Kyoto-fu, S. 1983. *Bukka toki no shomin seikatsu ni oyoboseru eikyo chosa* [A survey of the impact of rising prices on the life of the common people]. Kyoto: Kyoto-fu, Shakai-ka.

LeRoy Ladurie, E. 1976. "Family Structures and Inheritance Customs in Sixteenth-Century France." In J. Goody, J. Thirsk, and E. P. Thompson, eds., *Family and Inheritance: Rural Society in Western Europe, 1200–1800*. Cambridge, Eng.: Cambridge University Press.

———. 1978. *Montaillou: The Promised Land of Error*. Translated by B. Bray. New York: Braziller.

Landry, Y., and J. Légaré. 1987. "Seventeenth-Century Immigrants to Canada." *Journal of Family History* 12: 201–212.

Lasch, C. 1977. *Haven in a Heartless World: The Family Besieged*. New York: Basic Books.

Laslett, P. 1965. *The World We Have Lost*. London: Methuen.

———. 1972. "Introduction." In P. Laslett and R. Wall, eds., *Household and Family in Past Time: Comparative Studies in the Size and Structure of the Domestic Group over the Last Three Centuries in England, France, Serbia, Japan, and Colonial North America*. Cambridge, Eng.: Cambridge University Press.

———. 1977a. "Characteristics of the Western Family over Time." In P. Laslett, *Family Life and Illicit Love in Earlier Generations: Essays in Historical Sociology*. Cambridge, Eng.: Cambridge University Press.

———, ed. 1977b. *Family Life and Illicit Love in Earlier Generations: Essays in Historical Sociology*. Cambridge, Eng.: Cambridge University Press.

———. 1983. "Family and Household as Work Group and Kin Group." In R. Wall, J. Robin, and P. Laslett, eds., *Family Forms in Historic Europe*. Cambridge, Eng.: Cambridge University Press.

Laslett, P., and J. Harrison. 1963. "Clayworth and Cogenhoe." In H. Bell and R. Ollard, eds., *Historical Essays, 1600–1750: Presented to David Ogg*. London: Adam and Charles Black.

Laslett, P., and R. Wall, eds. 1972. *Household and Family in Past Time: Comparative Studies in the Size and Structure of the Domestic Group over the Last Three Centuries in England, France, Serbia, Japan, and Colonial North America*. Cambridge, Eng.: Cambridge University Press.

Le Canado-Americain. November 10, 1913. Manchester, NH.

Lee, J., F. Wang, and C. Campbell. 1994. "Infant and Child Mortality Among the Late Chinese Nobility: Implications for Two Kinds of Positive Check." *Population Studies* 48: 395–411.

LePlay, F. 1875. *L'organisation de la famile selon le vrai modèle signalé par l'histoire de toutes les races et de tous les temps*. Tours: Alfred Mame et Fils.

Levine, D. 1977. *Family Formation in an Age of Nascent Captialism*. New York: Academic Press.

———. 1983. "Proto-Industrialization and Demographic Upheaval." In L. Moch and G. Stark, eds., *Essays on the Family and Historical Change. Walter Prescott Webb Memorial Lectures, no. 17*. College Station, Texas: Published for the University of Texas at Arlington by Texas A&M University Press.

———. 1985. "Industrialization and the Proletarian Family in England." *Past and Present* 6: 168–203.

LeVine, R. A. 1978. "Comparative Notes on the Life Course." In T. K. Hareven, ed., *Transitions: The Family and the Life Course in Historical Perspective*. New York: Academic Press.

Levi-Strauss, C. 1969. *The Elementary Structures of Kinship*. Boston: Beacon Press.

Lightfoot, S. L. 1978. *Worlds Apart: Relationships Between Families and Schools*. New York: Basic.

Litwak, E. 1960. "Geographical Mobility and Extended Family Cohesion." *American Sociological Review* 25: 385–394.

———. 1965. "Extended Kin Relations in an Industrial Society." In E. Shanas and G. T. Streib, eds., *Social Structure and the Family: Generational Relations*. Englewood Cliffs, NJ: Prentice-Hall.

———. 1985. *Helping the Elderly: The Complementary Roles of Informal Networks and Formal Systems*. New York: Guilford.

The Lowell Offering. 1840–1845. Repository of Original Articles Written by Factory Operatives, vols. 1–5. Lowell, MA: A. Watson.

MacDonald, J. S., and L. MacDonald. 1964. "Chain Migration, Ethnic Neighborhood Formation and Social Networks." *Milbank Memorial Fund Quarterly* 42: 82–97.

Macfarlane, A. 1978. *The Origins of English Individualism: The Family, Property, and Social Transition*. New York: Cambridge University Press.

Macfarlane, J. W. 1963. "From Infancy to Adulthood." *Childhood Education* 39: 336–342.

———. 1971. "Perspectives on Personality Consistency and Change from the Guidance Study." In M. C. Jones, N. Bayley, J. W. Macfarlane, and M. P. Honzik, eds., *The Course of Human Development*. Waltham, MA: Xerox College Publishing.

Markides, K. S., D. S. Costley, and L. Rodriguez. 1981. "Perceptions of Intergenerational Relations and Psychological Well-Being Among Elderly Mexican Americans: A Causal Model." *International Journal of Aging and Human Development* 13: 43–52.

Markides, K. S., and T. Cole. 1984. "Change and Continuity in Mexican American Religious Behavior: A Three-Generation Study." *Social Science Quarterly* 65: 618-625

Markides, K. S., and N. Krause. 1985. "Intergenerational Solidarity and Psychological Well-Being Among Older Mexican Americans: A Three-Generation Study." *Journal of Gerontology* 40: 390–392.

Mason, K. O., M. A. Vinovskis, and T. K. Hareven. 1978. "Women's Work and the Life Course in Essex County, Massachusetts, 1880." In T. K. Hareven, ed., *Transitions: The Family and the Life Course in Historical Perspective*. New York: Academic Press.

Matthews, S. H. 1987. "Provision of Care to Old Parents: Division of Responsibility Among Adult Children." *Research on Aging* 9: 45–60.

McLanahan, S. 1988. "Family Structure and Dependency: Early Transitions to Female Household Headship." *Demography* 25: 1–16.

Medick, H. 1976. "The Proto-Industrial Family Economy." *Social History* 3: 291–315.

Menard, R. 1981. "Growth of Population in the Chesapeake Colonies." *Explorations in Economic History* 18: 399–410.

Mendels, F. 1972. "Proto-Industrialization: The First Phase of the Industrialization Process." *Journal of Economic History* 32: 241–261.

Miller, D., and G. Swanson. 1969. "The Changing American Parent." In J. N. Edwards, ed., *The Family and Change*. New York: Knopf.

Miner, H. M. 1939. *St. Denis, French-Canadian Parish*. Chicago: Unversity of Chicago Press.

Mitterauer, M. 1986. "Formen ländlicher Wirtschaft: Historische Ökotypen und familiale Arbeitsorganisation im österreichischen Raum." In M. Mitterauer and J. Ehmer, eds., *Familienstruktur und arbeitsorganisation in ländlichen gesellschaften*. Vienna: Böhlau Verlag.

———. 1992. "Peasant and Non-Peasant Family Forms in Relation to the Physical Environment and the Local Economy." *Journal of Family History* 17: 139–159.

Mitterauer, M., and R. Sieder. 1979. "The Developmental Process of Domestic Groups: Problems of Reconstruction and Possibilities of Interpretation." *Journal of Family History* 4: 257–284.

Modell, J. 1978. "Patterns of Consumption, Acculturation, and Family Income Strategies in Late Nineteenth-Century America." In T. K. Hareven and M. Vinovskis, eds., *Family and Population in Nineteenth-Century America.* Princeton: Princeton University Press.

_____. 1989. *Into One's Own: From Youth to Adulthood in the United States, 1920–1975.* Berkeley: University of California Press.

Modell, J., F. Furstenberg, and T. Hershberg. 1976. "Social Change and Transitions to Adulthood in Historical Perspective." *Journal of Family History* 1 (1): 7–32.

Modell, J., and T. K. Hareven. 1973. "Urbanization and the Malleable Household: Boarding and Lodging in American Families." *Journal of Marriage and the Family* 35: 467–479.

_____. 1978. "Transitions: Patterns of Timing." In T. K. Hareven, ed., *Transitions: The Family and the Life Course in Historical Perspective.* New York: Academic Press.

Modell, J., and D. Steffey. 1988. "Waging War and Marriage: Military Service and Family Formation." *Journal of Family History* 13: 195–218.

Moen, P., D. Dempster-McClain, and R. M. Williams. 1992. "Successful Aging: A Life-Course Perspective on Women's Multiple Roles and Health." *American Journal of Sociology* 97: 1612–1638.

Montgomery, D. 1967. *Beyond Equality: Labor and the Radical Republicans, 1862–1872.* New York: Knopf.

Moore, W. E. 1965. *Industrialization and Labor: Social Aspects of Economic Development.* Ithaca: Cornell University Press.

Morioka, K. 1985. *Family and the Life Course of Middle-aged Men.* Tokyo: Family and Life Course Study Group.

_____. 1987. "A Japanese Perspective on the Life Course: Emerging and Diminishing Patterns." *Journal of Family History* 12: 243–262.

Mutran, E. 1986. "Intergenerational Family Support Among Blacks and Whites: Response to Culture or to Socioeconomic Differences." In L. E. Troll, ed., *Family Issues in Current Gerontology.* New York: Springer.

Nascher, I. L. 1914. *Geriatrics.* New York: Arno Press.

Netting, R. 1981. *Balancing on an Alp: Ecological Change and Continuity in a Swiss Mountain Village.* Cambridge, Eng.: Cambridge University Press.

Neugarten, B., and N. Datan. 1973. "Sociological Perspectives on the Life Cycle." In P. Baltes and K. W. Schaie, eds., *Life Span Development Psychology: Personality and Socialization.* New York: Academic Press.

Neugarten, B., and G. Hagestadt. 1976. "Age and the Life Course." In R. Binstock and E. Shanas, eds., *Handbook of Aging and the Social Sciences.* New York: Van Nostrand Reinhold.

Nishijin Ori-Kogyo Kumiai. 1980. *Nishijin orimono-gyo sanchi shinko keikaku* [Plan for the promotion of the weaving district of Nishijin], Nishijin Association of Manufacturers. Kyoto: Nishijin Ori-Kogyo Kumiai.

Ogburn, W. F. 1955. *Technology and the Changing Family*. New York: Houghton Mifflin.

Olson, K. W. 1974. *The G.I. Bill, the Veterans, and the Colleges*. Lexington: University Press of Kentucky.

Ory, M. G. 1985. "The Burden of Care." *Generations* 10: 14–18.

Parke, R., and P. Stearns. 1994. "Fathers and Child Rearing." In G. H. Elder Jr., J. Modell, and R. Parke, eds., *Children in Time and Place: Developmental and Historical Insights*. New York: Cambridge University Press.

Parsons, T. 1943. "The Kinship System of the Contemporary United States." *American Anthropologist* 45: 22–38.

_____. 1955. "The American Family: Its Relation to Personality and to the Social Structure." In R. Parsons and R. Bales, eds., *Family, Socialization, and Interaction Process*. Glencoe, IL: Free Press.

Pasternak, B. 1983. *Guests in the Dragon: Social Demography of a Chinese District, 1895–1946*. New York: Columbia University Press.

_____. 1989. "Age at First Marriage in a Taiwanese Locality, 1916–1945." *Journal of Family History* 14: 91–117.

Peristiany, D. G. 1976. *Mediterranian Family Structures*. Cambridge, Eng.: Cambridge University Press.

Perrot, M., ed. 1990. *A History of Private Life*. Vol. 4, *From the Fires of Revolution to the Great War*. Translated by A. Goldhammer. Cambridge: Belknap Press of Harvard University Press.

Pfister, U. 1989. "Work Roles and Family Structure in Proto-Industrial Zurich." *Journal of Interdisciplinary History* 20: 83–105.

_____. 1992. "The Protoindustrial Household Economy: Toward a Formal Analysis." *Journal of Family History* 17: 201–228.

Philibert, M.A.J. 1965. "The Emergence of Social Gerontology." *Journal of Social Issues* 21: 4–12.

Pirenne, H. 1946. *Medieval Cities: Their Origins and the Revival of Trade*. Translated by F. D. Halsey. Princeton: Princeton University Press.

Pitt-Rivers, J. 1973. "The Kith and the Kin." In J. Goody, ed., *The Character of Kinship*. Cambridge, Eng.: Cambridge University Press.

Plakans, A. 1977. "Identifying Kinfolk Beyond the Household." *Journal of Family History* 2: 3–27.

_____. 1982. "Ties of Kinship and Kinship Roles in an Historical Eastern European Peasant Community: A Synchronic Analysis." *Journal of Family History* 7: 52–75.

_____. 1984. *Kinship in the Past: An Anthropology of European Family Life, 1500–1900*. New York: B. Blackwell.

_____. 1986. "The Emergence of a Field: Twenty Years of European Family History." *Occassional Paper No. 1, West European Program*. Washington, DC: Wilson Center.

_____. 1987. "Interaction Between the Household and the Kin Group in the Eastern European Past: Posing the Problem." *Journal of Family History* 12: 1–3, 163–175.

_____. 1989. "Stepping Down in Former Times: A Comparative Assessment of Retirement in Traditional Europe." In D. I. Kertzer and K. W. Schaie, eds., *Age Structuring in Comparative Perspective*. Hillsdale, NJ: Erlbaum.

Plakans, A., and C. Wetherall. 1995. "Family and Economy in an Early Nineteenth-Century Baltic Serf Estate." In R. Rudolph, ed., *The European Peasant Family and Society: Historical Studies*. Liverpool: Liverpool University Press.

Plath, D. W. 1980. *Long Engagements: Maturity in Modern Japan*. Stanford: Stanford University Press.

_____, ed. 1983. *Work and Life Course in Japan*. Albany: State University of New York.

Pollock, L. 1983. *Forgotten Children: Parent-Child Relations from 1500 to 1900*. New York: Cambridge University Press.

Quataert, J. 1985. "Combining Agrarian and Industrial Livelihood: Rural Households in the Saxon Oberlausitz in the Nineteenth Century." *Journal of Family History* 10: 145–162.

Ransel, D. L. 1988. *Mothers of Misery: Child Abandonment in Russia*. Princeton: Princeton University Press.

Ravitch, D. 1974. *The Great School Wars: New York City, 1805–1973*. New York: Basic Books.

Rawson, B. 1986. *The Family in Ancient Rome: New Perspectives*. Ithaca: Cornell University Press.

Rheubottom, D. B. 1988. "'Sisters First': Betrothal Order and Age at Marriage in Fifteenth-Century Ragusa." *Journal of Family History* 13: 359–376.

Riley, M. W. 1978. "Aging, Social Change, and the Power of Ideas." *Daedalus* 107: 39–52.

_____. 1984. "Women, Men, and the Lengthening Life Course." In A. S. Rossi, ed., *Gender and the Life Course*. New York: Aldine de Gruyter.

Riley, M. W., M. Johnson, and A. Foner. 1972. *Aging and Society*. New York: Sage.

Riley, M. W., R. Kahn, and A. Foner. 1994. "Introduction: The Mismatch Between People and Structures." In *Age and the Structural Lag: Society's Failure to Provide Meaningful Opportunities in Work, Family and Leisure*. New York: Wiley.

Riley, M. W., and J. W. Riley. 1994. "Structural Lag: Past and Future." In M. W. Riley, R. Kahn, and A. Foner, eds., *Age and the Structural Lag: Society's Failure to Provide Meaningful Opportunities in Work, Family, and Leisure*. New York: Wiley.

_____. 1996. "Generational Relations: A Future Perspective." In T. K. Hareven, ed., *Aging and Generational Relations over the Life Course: A Historical and Cross-Cultural Perspective*. Berlin: de Gruyter.

Riley, M. W., J. Waring, and A. Foner. 1988. "The Sociology of Age." In N. Smelser and R. Burt, eds., *The Handbook of Sociology*. Newbury Park, CA: Sage.

Robins, L. N. 1966. *Deviant Children Grown Up: A Sociological and Psychiatric Study of Sociopathic Personality*. Baltimore: Williams and Wilkins.

Rose, S. 1987. "Gender Segregation in the Transition to the Factory: The English Hosiery Industry, 1850–1910." *History Workshop* 21: 114–131.

_____. 1988. "Proto-Industry: Women's Work and the Household Economy in the Transition to Industrial Capitalism." *Journal of Family History* 13: 181–193.

Rosenfelt, R.H. 1965. "The Elderly Mystique." *Journal of Social Issues* 2:37-43.

Rossi, A. 1968. "Transition to Parenthood." *Journal of Marriage and the Family* 30: 26–40.

Rossi, A. S., and P. H. Rossi. 1990. *Of Human Bonding: Parent-Child Relations Across the Life Course*. Hawthorne, NY: de Gruyter.

Rothman, D. 1971. *The Discovery of the Asylum*. Boston: Little, Brown.

Rowntree, B. S. 1901. *Poverty: A Study of Town Life*. London: Longmans, Green.

Ruggles, S. 1987. *Prolonged Connections: The Rise of the Extended Family in Nineteenth-Century England and America*. Madison: University of Wisconsin Press.

_____. 1988. "The Demography of the Unrelated Individual, 1900–1950." *Demography* 25: 521–536.

Ryan, M. 1979. *New Womanhood in America: From Colonial Times to the Present*. New York: New Viewpoints.

_____. 1981. *Cradle of the Middle Class: The Family in Oneida County, New York, 1790–1865*. New York: Cambridge University Press.

Ryder, N. 1965. "The Cohort as a Concept in the Study of Social Change." *American Sociological Review* 30: 843–861.

Saito, O. 1983. "Population and the Peasant Family Economy in Proto-Industrial Japan." *Journal of Family History* 8: 30–54.

Scharlach, A. E. 1987. "Role Strain in Mother-Daughter Relationships in Later Life." *Gerontologist* 27: 627–631.

Schlissel, L. 1989. *Far from Home: Families of the Westward Journey*. New York: Schocken Books.

Schwarzweller, H., J. Brown, and J. Mangalam. 1971. *Mountain Families in Transition: A Case Study of Appalachian Migration*. University Park: Pennsylvania State University Press.

Scott, J. W., and L. A. Tilly. 1975. "Women's Work and Family in Nineteenth-Century Europe." In C. D. Rosenberg, ed., *The Family in History*. Philadelphia: University of Pennsylvania Press.

Segalen, M. 1977. "The Family Cycle and Household Structure: Five Generations in a French Village." *Journal of Family History* 2: 223–236.

_____. 1980. *Mari et femme dans la société payanne*. Paris: Flammarion.

_____. 1983. *Love and Power in the Peasant Family*. Oxford: Blackwell.

_____. 1986. *Historical Anthropology of the Family*. Translated by J. C. Whitehouse and S. Mathews. Cambridge, Eng.: Cambridge University Press.

_____. 1987. "Life-Course Patterns and Peasant Culture in France: A Critical Assessment." *Journal of Family History* 12: 1–3, 213–224.

_____. 1991. *Fifteen Generations of Bretons: Kinship and Society in Lower Brittany, 1720–1980*. Translated by J. S. Underwood. Cambridge, Eng.: Cambridge University Press.

Segalen, M., and P. Richard. 1986. "Marrying Kinsmen in Pays Bigouden Sud, Brittany." *Journal of Family History* 11: 109–130.

Sennett, R. 1970. *Families Against the City: Middle-Class Homes of Industrial Chicago, 1872–1890*. Cambridge: Harvard University Press.

Shanas, E. 1979. "Social Myth as Hypothesis: The Case of the Family Relations of Old People." *Gerontologist* 19: 3–9.

_____. 1986. "The Family as Social Support System in Old Age." In L. E. Troll, ed., *Family Issues in Current Gerontology*. New York: Springer.

Shanas, E., et al. 1968. *Old People in Three Industrial Societies*. New York: Atherton Press.

Shanas, E., and M. B. Sussman. 1981. "The Family in Later Life: Social Structure and Social Policy." In R. W. Fogel et al., eds., *Aging: Stability and Change in the Family*. New York: Academic Press.

Shlakman, V. 1935. *Economic History of a Factory Town: Chicopee, Massachusetts*. New York: Octagon.

Shore, M. F. 1976. "The Child and Historiography." *Journal of Interdisciplinary History* 6: 495–505.

Shorter, E. 1971. "Illegitimacy, Sexual Revolution, and Social Change in Modern Europe." *Journal of Interdisciplinary History* 2: 237–272.

_____. 1976. *The Making of the Modern Family*. New York: Basic Books.

Skocpol, T. 1992. *Protecting Soldiers and Mothers: The Political Origins of Social Policy in the United States*. Cambridge: Belknap Press of Harvard University Press.

Skolnick, A. 1973. "The Limits of Childhood: Conceptions of Child Development and Social Context." *Law and Contemporary Problems* 39 (3): 38–77.

Smelser, N. 1959. *Social Change in the Industrial Revolution: An Application of Theory to the British Cotton Industry*. Chicago: University of Chicago Press.

_____. 1968. "Sociological History: The Industrial Revolution and the British Working-Class Family." In N. Smelser, ed., *Essays on Sociological Explanation*. Englewood Cliffs, NJ: Prentice-Hall.

Smelser, N., and S. Halpern. 1978. "The Historical Triangulation of Family, Economy, and Education." In J. Demos and S. Boocock, eds., *Turning Points: Historical and Sociological Essays on the Family*. (*American Journal of Sociology* 84 [supplement]: S288–315.) Chicago: University of Chicago Press.

Smith, D. B. 1978. "Mortality and Family in the Colonial Chesapeake." *Journal of Interdisciplinary History* 8 (3): 403–427.

_____. 1980. *Inside the Great House: Planter Family Life in Eighteenth-Century Chesapeake Society*. Ithaca: Cornell University Press.

_____. 1982. "The Study of the Family in Early America: Trends, Problems, and Prospects." *William and Mary Quarterly* 39: 3–28.

Smith, D. S. 1973. "Parental Power and Marriage Patterns: An Analysis of Historical Trends in Hingham, Massachusetts." *Journal of Marriage and the Family* 35 (3): 419–429.

_____. 1974. "Family Limitation, Sexual Control, and Domestic Feminism in Victorian America." In M. Hartman and L. Banner, eds., *Clio's Consciousness Raised: New Perspectives on the History of Women*. New York: Harper and Row.

_____. 1979. "Life Course, Norms, and the Family System of Older Americans in 1900." *Journal of Family History* 4: 285–299.

_____. 1981. "Historical Change in the Household Structure of the Elderly in Economically Developed Societies." In J. G. March et al., eds., *Aging: Stability, and Change in the Family*. New York: Academic Press.

_____. 1985. "Child-Naming Practices, Kinship Ties, and Change in Family Attitudes in Hingham, Massachusetts, 1641–1880." *Journal of Social History* 18: 541–566.

Smith, P. C. 1980. "Asian Marriage Patterns in Transition." *Journal of Family History* 5: 58–96.

Smith, R. 1979a. "Kin and Neighbors in a Thirteenth-Century Suffolk Community." *Journal of Family History* 4: 219–256.

_____. 1979b. "Some Issues Concerning Families and Their Property in Rural England, 1250–1800." In R. Smith, ed., *Land, Kinship and the Life Cycle*. Cambridge, Eng.: Cambridge University Press.

Smith, R. J. 1972. "Small Families, Small Households, and Residential Instability: Town and City in 'Pre-Modern' Japan." In P. Laslett and R. Wall, eds., *Household and Family in Past Time: Comparative Studies in the Size and Structure of the Domestic Group over the Last Three Centuries in England, France, Serbia, Japan, and Colonial North America*. Cambridge, Eng.: Cambridge University Press.

_____. 1978. "The Domestic Cycle in Selected Commoner Families in Urban Japan, 1757–1858." *Journal of Family History* 3: 219–235.

_____. 1983. "Making Village Women into 'Good Wives and Wise Mothers' in Prewar Japan." *Journal of Family History* 8: 70–84.

Smith, T. 1977. *Nakahara: Family Farming and Population in a Japanese Village, 1717–1830*. Stanford: Stanford University Press.

Smuts, R. 1971. *Women and Work in America*. New York: Columbia University Press.

Soeda, H. 1973. "Festivity and City: Mobile Stages of Gion Festival." *Concerned Theatre Japan* 2: 190–207.

Sokolovsky, J. 1990. "Bringing Culture Back Home: Aging, Ethnicity, and Family Support." In J. Sokolovsky, ed., *The Cultural Context of Aging: Worldwide Perspectives*. New York: Bergin and Garvey.

Soliday, G., et al., eds. 1980. *History of the Family and Kinship: A Selected International Bibliography*. Millwood, NY: Kraus-International.

Spock, B. 1946. *The Commonsense Book of Baby and Child Care*. New York: Duell, Sloane, and Pearce.

Stack, C. 1974. *All Our Kin: Strategies for Survival in a Black Community*. New York: Harper and Row.

Stearns, C., and P. Stearns, eds. 1988. *Emotion and Social Change: Toward a New Psychohistory*. New York: Holmes and Meier.

Stone, L. 1975. "The Rise of the Nuclear Family in Early Modern England: The Patriarchal Stage." In C. E. Rosenberg, ed., *The Family in History*. Philadelphia: University of Pennsylvania Press.

_____. 1977. *The Family, Sex, and Marriage in England, 1500–1800*. New York: Harper and Row.

_____. 1981. "Family History in the 1980s." *Journal of Interdisciplinary History* 12: 51–57.

Stouffer, S. A., et al. 1949. *The American Soldier: Combat and Its Aftermath*. Vol. 2. Princeton: Princeton University Press.

Struminger, L. S. 1977. "The Artisan Family: Traditions and Transition in Nineteenth-Century Lyon." *Journal of Family History* 2: 211–222.

Sunley, R. 1955. "Early Nineteenth-Century American Literature on Child Rearing." In M. Wolfenstein and M. Mead, eds., *Child Rearing in Contemporary American Culture*. Chicago: University of Chicago Press.

Sussman, M. B. 1959. "The Isolated Nuclear Family: Fact or Fiction?" *Social Problems* 6: 333–347.

Sussman, M. B., and L. Burchinal. 1962. "Kin Family Network: Unheralded Structure in Current Conceptualizations of Family Functioning." *Marriage and Family Living* 24: 231–240.

Taylor, R. J., and L. M. Chatters. 1991. "Extended Family Networks of Older Black Adults." *Journal of Gerontology* 46: S210–217.

Taylor, R. J., L. M. Chatters, and J. S. Jackson. 1993. "A Profile of Familial Relations Among Three-Generation Black Families." *Family Relations* 42: 332–342.

Thelen, D. 1987. "A Round Table: Synthesis in American History." *Journal of American History* 74: 107–130.

Thernstrom, S. 1964. *Poverty and Progress: Social Mobility in a Nineteenth-Century City*. Cambridge: Harvard University Press.

Thernstrom, S., and P. Knights. 1971. "Men in Motion: Some Data and Speculations About Urban Population Mobility in Nineteenth-Century America." In T. K. Hareven, ed., *Anonymous Americans: Explorations in Nineteenth-Century Social History*. Englewood Cliffs, NJ: Prentice-Hall.

Thomas, W., and F. Znaniecki. 1918–1920. *The Polish Peasant in Europe and America*. 3 vols. Chicago: University of Chicago Press.

Thompson, E. P. 1963. *The Making of the English Working Class*. New York: Pantheon Books.

Tibbitts, C. 1960. "Origin, Scope, and Fields of Social Gerontology." In C. Tibbitts, ed., *Handbook of Social Gerontology*. Chicago: University of Chicago Press.

Tilly, C. 1987. "Family, History, Social History, and Social Change." *Journal of Family History* 12: 319–330.

Tilly, C., and C. Brown. 1974. "On Uprooting, Kinship, and the Auspices of Migration." In C. Tilly, ed., *An Urban World*. Boston: Little, Brown.

Tilly, L. 1979. "The Family Wage Economy of French Textile City: Roubaix, 1872–1906." *Journal of Family History* 4: 381–394.

Tilly, L., and J. Scott. 1978. *Women, Work, and Family*. New York: Holt, Rinehart and Winston.

Tilly, L., and M. Cohen. 1982. "Does the Family Have a History?" *Social Science History* 6: 181–199.

Townsend, P. 1968. "The Emergence of the Four-Generation Family in Industrial Society." In B. L. Neugarten, ed., *Middle Age and Aging: A Reader in Social Psychology*. Chicago: University of Chicago Press.

Turner, V. 1967. *The Ritual Process*. Chicago: Aldine.

Uhlenberg, P. 1974. "Cohort Variations in Family Life Cycle Experiences of U.S. Females." *Journal of Marriage and the Family* 34: 284–292.

_____. 1978. "Changing Configurations of the Life Course." In T. K. Hareven, ed., *Transitions: The Family and the Life Course in Historical Perspective*. New York: Academic Press.

_____. 1979. "Demographic Change and Problems of the Aged." In M. W. Riley, ed., *Aging from Birth to Death*. Boulder: Westview.

U.S. Congress. Senate. *Family Protection Act*. 96th Cong., 1st sess., 1979. S. Bill 1808.

_____. Senate. *Family Protection Act*. 97th Cong., 1st sess., 1981. S. Bill 1378.

Vinovskis, M. A. 1972. "Mortality Rates and Trends in Massachusetts Before 1860." *Journal of Economic History* 32: 184–213.

_____. 1977. "From Household Size to the Life Course: Some Observations on Recent Trends in Family History." *American Behavioral Scientist* 21: 263–287.

_____. 1981. *Fertility in Massachusetts from the Revolution to the Civil War*. New York: Academic Press.

_____. 1987. "Family and Schooling in Colonial and Nineteenth-Century America." *Journal of Family History* 12: 3–18.

_____. 1988. "The Historian and the Life Course: Reflections on Recent Approaches to the Study of American Family Life in the Past." In P. B. Baltes, D. L. Featherman, and R. M. Lerner, eds., *Life-Span Development and Behavior*. Hillsdale, NJ: Erlbaum.

_____. 1989a. "Have Social Historians Lost the Civil War? Some Preliminary Demographic Speculations." *Journal of American History* 76: 34–58.

_____. 1989b. "Stepping Down in Former Times: The View from Colonial and Nineteenth-Century America." In D. I. Kertzer and K. W. Schaie, eds., *Age Structuring in Comparative Perspective*. Hillsdale, NJ: Erlbaum.

Vinovskis, M. A., and D. May. 1977. "A Ray of Millennial Light: Early Education and Social Reform in the Infant School Movement in Massachusetts, 1826–1840." In T. K. Hareven, ed., *Family and Kin in American Urban Communities*. New York: Franklin and Watts.

Volkart, E. 1951. *Social Behavior and Personality: Contributions of W. I. Thomas to Theory and Research*. New York: Social Science Research Council.

Waller, W. W. 1940. *War and the Family*. New York: Dryden Press.

Walsh, L. S. 1979. "'Til Death Do Us Part': Marriage and Family in Seventeenth-Century Maryland." In T. W. Tate and D. L. Ammerman, eds., *The Chesapeake in the Seventeenth Century: Essays on Anglo-American Society*. Chapel Hill, NC: Published for the Institute of Early American History and Culture by the University of North Carolina Press.

Ware, C. F. 1942. *The Early New England Cotton Manufacture*. New York: Houghton Mifflin.

Waring, J. 1975. "Social Replenishment and Social Change: The Problem of Disordered Cohort Flow." *American Behavioral Scientist* 19: 237–256.

Weiss, N. P. 1977. "Mother, the Invention of Necessity: Dr. Benjamin Spock's 'Baby and Child Care.'" *American Quarterly* 29 (5): 519–546.

Wells, R. 1971. "Demographic Change and the Life Cycle of American Families." *Journal of Interdisciplinary History* 2 (2): 273–298.

_____. 1982. *Revolutions in Americans' Lives: A Demographic Perspective on the History of Americans, Their Families, and Their Society*. Westport, CT: Greenwood Press.

Welter, B. 1966. "The Cult of True Womanhood, 1820–1860." *American Quarterly* 18: 151–174.

Wheaton, R. 1975. "Family and Kinship in Western Europe: The Problem of the Joint Family Household." *Journal of Interdisciplinary History* 5: 601–628.

_____. 1980. "Introduction: Recent Trends in the Historical Study of the French Family." In R. Wheaton and T. K. Hareven, eds., *Family and Sexuality in French History*. Philadelphia: University of Pennsylvania Press.

_____. 1982. "The Application of Network Theory to the Social Structure of Early Modern European Cities." Paper presented at the annual meeting of the Social Science History Association, November 19, in Bloomington, Indiana.

_____. 1987. "Observations on the Development of Kinship History, 1942–1985." *Journal of Family History* 12: 285–301.

Wheaton, R., and T. K. Hareven, eds. 1980. *Family and Sexuality in French History*. Philadelphia: University of Pennsylvania Press.

Wilensky, H. 1961. "Orderly Careers and Social Participation: The Impact of Work History in the Middle Mass." *American Sociological Review* 26: 521–539.

Wirth, L. 1938. "Urbanism as a Way of Life." *American Journal of Sociology* 44: 1–24.

Wishy, B. 1968. *The Child and the Republic: The Dawn of Modern American Child Nurture*. Philadelphia: University of Pennsylvania Press.

Wolf, A. P., and C. Huang. 1980. *Marriage and Adoption in China, 1845–1945*. Stanford: Stanford University Press.

Wrigley, E. 1966a. "Family Limitation in Pre-Industrial England." *Economic History Review*, 2d ser., 19: 82–109.

_____. 1966b. "Family Reconstitution." In P. Laslett et al., eds., *An Introduction to English Historical Demography*. New York: Basic Books.

_____. 1968. "Mortality in Pre-Industrial England: The Example of Colyton, Devon, over Three Centuries." *Daedalus* 97: 546–580.

_____. 1972. "The Process of Modernization and the Industrial Revolution in England." *Journal of Interdisciplinary History* 3: 225–260.

_____. 1974. "Fertility Strategy for the Individual and the Group." In C. Tilly, ed., *Historical Studies of Changing Fertility*. Princeton: Princeton University Press.

_____. 1977. "Reflections on the History of the Family." *Daedalus* 106: 71–85.

Wrigley, E., and R. S. Schofield. 1981. *The Population History of England, 1541–1871*. Cambridge: Harvard University Press.

Yans-McLaughlin, V. 1971. "Patterns of Work and Family Organization: Buffalo's Italians." *Journal of Interdisciplinary History* 2: 299–314.

_____. 1974. "A Flexible Tradition: South Italian Immigrants Confront a New Work Experience." *Journal of Social History* 7: 429–445.

_____. 1977. *Family and Community: Italian Immigrants in Buffalo, 1880–1930*. Ithaca: Cornell University Press.

Yasuoka, S. 1977. "Edo koki Meiji zenki no Nishijin kigyo no doko [The evolution of Nishijin enterprises during the late Edo and early Meiji periods]." *Shakai Kagaku* 23: 1–23.

Yoneyama, T. 1974. *Gion Matsuri: Toshi jiniurur gaku kythajime* [Gion Matsuri: Urban anthropology in its beginnings]. Tokyo: Chuo Koronsha.

Yoneyama, T., et al. 1986. *Documento Gion Matsuri* [Documenting Gion Matsuri]. Tokyo: NHK Books.

Young, M. D., and P. Willmott. 1957. *Family and Kinship in East London*. Glencoe, IL: Free Press.

Credits

Original Publication Sources
of the Chapters in This Book

1. "The History of the Family and the Complexity of Social Change," *American Historical Review*, (February, 1991).

2. "The Dynamics of Kin in an Industrial Community," *American Journal of Sociology*, (Supplement, 1978) and in *Family Time and Industrial Time*, New York: Cambridge University Press, 1982.

3. "A Complex Relationship: Family Strategies and Processes of Economic and Social Change," in Roger Friedland and A. F. Robertson, (Eds.), *Beyond the Marketplace*, New York: Aldine de Gruyter, 1990.

4. "Historical Changes in Children's Networks in the Family and Community," in Deborah Belle (Ed.), *Children's Social Networks and Social Supports*, New York: John Wiley & Sons, 1988.

5. "Aging and Generational Relations: A Historical and Life Course Perspective," in John Hagan, (Ed.), *Annual Review of Sociology*, Palo Alto, CA: Annual Reviews, 1994.

6. "Synchronizing Individual Time, Family Time, and Historical Time," in John Bender and David E. Wellbery (Eds.), *Chronotypes: The Construction of Time*, Stanford, CA: Stanford University Press, 1991.

7. "The Generation in the Middle: Cohort Comparisons in Assistance to Aging Parents in an American Community" in Tamara K. Hareven (Ed.), *Aging and Generational Relations over the Life Course*, Berlin: Walter de Gruyter, 1996 (with Kathleen Adams).

8. "Rising Above Life's Disadvantage: From the Great Depression to War," in John Modell, Glen Elder, Jr., and Ross Parke (Eds.), *Children in Time and Place*, New York: Cambridge University Press, 1992 (with Glen Elder, Jr.).

9. "Changing Images of Ageing and the Social Construction of the Life Course," in Mike Featherstone and Andrew Wernick (Eds.), *Images of Ageing*, London: Routledge, 1995.

10. "Between Craft and Industry: The Subjective Reconstruction of the Life Course of Kyoto's Traditional Weavers," in Susanne Formanek and Sepp Linhart (Eds.), *Japanese Biographies: Life Cycles and Life Stages*, Vienna: Ästereichische Akademie der Wissenschaften, 1992.

11. "The Festival's Work as Leisure: The Traditional Craftsmen of the Gion Festival," in John Calagione, Doris Francis, and Daniel Nugent (Eds.), *Workers' Expressions: Beyond Accommodation*, Albany, N.Y.: State University of New York Press, 1992.

12. "Divorce, Chinese Style," *Atlantic Monthly*, (April, 1987).

13. "Family Change and Historical Change: An Uneasy Relationship," in M. W. Riley. R. Kahn, and A. Foner (Eds), *Age and the Structural Lag: Society's Failure to Provide Meaningful Opportunities in Work, Family and Leisure*, New York: John Wiley & Sons, 1994.

14. "What Difference Does It Make?" in *Social Science History*, (Autumn, 1996).

Index

Printed in the United States
124295LV00002B/24/A